Internet Success

Internet Success

A Study of Open-Source Software Commons

Charles M. Schweik and Robert C. English

The MIT Press
Cambridge, Massachusetts
London, England

MIT Press books may be purchased at special quantity discounts for business or sales promotional use. For information, please email special_sales@mitpress.mit.edu or write to Special Sales Department, The MIT Press, 55 Hayward Street, Cambridge, MA 02142.

This book was set in Stone Sans and Stone Serif by Toppan Best-set Premedia Limited. Printed and bound in the United States of America.

Library of Congress Cataloging-in-Publication Data

Schweik, Charles M., 1961–
Internet success : a study of open-source software commons / Charles M. Schweik and Robert C. English.
    p.   cm.
Includes bibliographical references and index.
ISBN 978-0-262-01725-1 (hardcover : alk. paper)
1. Open source software. 2. Information commons. I. English, Robert C., 1951– II. Title.
QA76.76.s46s37   2012
005.3—dc23
2011039032

10 9 8 7 6 5 4 3 2 1

In memory of my parents, Robert C. and Joanne L. Schweik, who demonstrated in large and small ways how to take on a project, and life in general, with enthusiasm and verve. I also dedicate this book to the open-source software development community (programmers and their users), which proves the collaborative potential of openness at all geographic scales.

—Charles M. Schweik

To my mother, Catherine P. English, who always wanted me to "finish school." Although it took nearly forty years for her wish to become reality, this book is the result.

—Robert C. English

Contents

Acknowledgments

We deeply appreciate the National Science Foundation (NSF) for funding our research proposal (NSFIIS 0447623). Without that financial help and the ongoing support of two NSF program directors—first Dr. Suzi Iacono, and then later Dr. Bill Bainbridge—this book would not exist. Of course, the findings, recommendations, and opinions expressed here are our ideas alone, and do not necessarily reflect the views of the NSF.

We want to thank our postdoc statisticians, Sandy Haire and Meng Shiou Shieh, who assisted with various analyses performed in part III. Graduate students who contributed to various parts of this research and book include Meelis Kitsing, Quentin Lewis, Qimti Paienjton, Evan Piche, and Brian Rossini. The NSF grant funded some of these students, and UMass Amherst's Center for Public Policy and Administration (CPPA) supported others. We are indebted to the CPPA and its director, Lee Badgett, for appointing these capable research assistants.

In addition, we would like to thank our colleagues at UMass who have provided valuable advice at one time or another. These include Doug Anderton, Kevin McGarigal, Jack Finn, and Brad Compton. Moreover, others at UMass lent their support to this project in a variety of ways; we offer our gratitude here to David Bollier, Doug Downham, Thomas Folz-Donahue, Paul Fisette, Jane Fountain of the National Center for Digital Government, Michele Sagan Goncalves, J. Morgan Grove, Bill Israel, and Brenda McComb.

We are deeply indebted to Megan Squire and Kevin Crowston (and others) at the FLOSSMole project as well as Greg Madey at the University of Notre Dame for the data they supplied for this book. Greg also helped by connecting us to Ross Turk, who at the time was the director of community with SourceForge.net (SF). Ross helped us conduct our survey of SF developers. We are grateful to all involved at SF for their assistance.

Because of the support Elinor Ostrom and the Center for the Study of Institutions, Population, and Environmental Change at Indiana University along with Craig Nicolson at UMass, we were able to solicit editorial help from two extremely capable editors, Joanna Broderick and, Stephen Broyles. We were fortunate to have two other excellent editors affiliated with the MIT Press, Cindy Milstein and Sandra Minkkinen, who also reviewed the manuscript. These editorial efforts greatly improved our book.

Editorial support is only one way that Elinor contributed to this project. She was author Schweik's PhD adviser during the 1990s, and through those years he was lucky enough to work on research projects with her firsthand. Elinor taught Schweik much about how to design and conduct research. We are grateful for her mentoring as well as the ongoing support she provides us to this day.

We much appreciate the efforts of Doug Sery, our editor at the MIT Press, for his time and effort beginning with our first contact more than three years ago, through the review process, and up until publication. Furthermore, we are grateful to the numerous anonymous reviewers of this book who all offered extremely useful reactions to earlier drafts, and others at the MIT Press who assisted in the publication process.

Author Schweik would like to thank Ron and Nancy Bushouse along with Susan Schweik for ongoing support and encouragement throughout this project. Maxwell and Sophia contributed more than they realize through the humor and fun they provide on a daily basis. But most of all, his heartfelt thanks goes to Brenda Bushouse, who each and every day demonstrates what true collaboration really is.

Author English would like to thank friends and family, especially Stephanie Shafran, who provided feedback and support throughout the writing and editing process.

Last and most important, we are grateful to the SF developers who created the projects on SF that we were able to study. In particular, we thank the roughly fifty thousand developers who put up with the annoyance of our emailed survey request and the more than fourteen hundred who gave of their valuable time to take the online survey. We hope that the results we present in this book make the inconveniences to these developers worthwhile.

Preface

In early 2011, we presented some of the findings reported in this book to people interested in natural resource conservation—most of who had little or no knowledge about open-source software (OSS). At the end of our talk, one audience member came up to us and said, "Thank you for presenting something positive about how humans can collectively solve problems. It is a welcome relief from the constant bad news we seem to hear these days, about how human activity is causing problems in the world." The something positive this person referred to is the story of how computer programmers successfully collaborate in innovative ways over the Internet. Some people refer to these collaborations as free/libre software commons, and others call them OSS commons—for reasons we explain in the book. In any case, computer programmers and users of OSS have been quietly working together for many years to create software to solve problems and contribute to the public good.

This book has been a major undertaking, completed by a team of researchers over the course of five years. We might reasonably have studied OSS commons simply because they are positive examples of how people can collaborate over the Internet to create software and contribute to their societies. Yet studying them had even greater importance since there is a connection between OSS collaboration and any situation where collaboration over the Internet can occur. In other words, understanding the OSS collaborative paradigm may help us understand how humans could collaborate regionally, internationally, or globally in the future. Many Internet collaborations (Wikipedia, Twitter, YouTube, and Facebook) have already changed the world, and undoubtedly, others like them will continue to appear. It is this potential for understanding future collaborations that inspired our effort to discover the factors that lead to Internet-based collaborative success.

A number of key books have already been published covering OSS by authors such as Steven Weber, Eric von Hippel, Joseph Feller and colleagues, Yochai Benkler, and Karl Fogel. In addition, a wide variety of journal articles have studied aspects of OSS. No one, however, has produced a large-scale empirical and statistical study that provides a complete view of how Internet-based OSS collaboration works. We hope this book fills that need and will be compelling to a broad audience. We expect that OSS developers, computer scientists, software engineers, and information technology (IT) professionals from business and government will be interested in this book, but we also think that anyone who is drawn to the Internet or social science in general may be interested. Of course, we hope academics from various fields that study OSS, sociology, collective action, commons, political science, and institutions will find in this book at least some contribution toward their areas of concern.

While we have tried to conduct thorough theoretical and empirical work, we also have done our best to make even the quantitative work we report accessible and understandable to readers from many different backgrounds (e.g., academic research-ers, software developers, etc.). For this reason, when needed, we define terms in an effort to make passages meaningful to all audiences.

Some readers who are studying the open-source phenomenon will discover relevant material in each and every chapter. Others may be more interested in the chapters that describe how we as social scientists think about open-source collaboration (e.g., parts I and II), and then move on to the chapters that discuss our findings and reflect on their meanings (e.g., chapters 6, 12, and 13).

A number of extremely capable individuals helped us complete various aspects of the research (see the acknowledgments). The work was often challenging, but also quite enjoyable, thanks in part to the collegiality of our broader research team. We hope our readers will find the topic and our results as intriguing and significant as we do.

I The Power of Openness and Internet-Based Collaboration

1   The Importance of Open-Source Software Commons

The Power of Openness

In fall 2010, O'Reilly Media, Inc., and UBM TechWeb hosted the Government 2.0 Summit in Washington, DC (O'Reilly 2010). What was striking about this conference was the almost-constant underlying theme of the "power of openness" for innovation. The Government 2.0 Summit emphasized the idea that openness and innovation are important for the twenty-first century, but many might sensibly ask, What does openness have to do with innovation?

When we reflect on history, the growth of the World Wide Web (WWW or the Web) from 1996 to 2000 provides one of the best examples of the power of this connection, because openness drove the global explosion of new Web sites in those years. Early Web browsers such as Mosaic, Netscape, and Internet Explorer enabled users, as Tim O'Reilly (2004) explains, to see the hypertext markup language (HTML) software code that the browsers utilized to render the Web pages being viewed. These early browsers as well as those in use today make this HTML source code visible through the built-in "view-source" function. As some readers will recall, in the early days of the Web little material was available on how to develop Web pages using HTML. Many people thus took a search-and-learn approach: they browsed Web site designs that they found innovative and interesting, examined their underlying HTML source code using the view-source browser option, copied the source code they liked to a text editor, manipulated this code, and created their own Web pages from it. In other words, they created new Web sites using source code from existing Web sites. The openness created by the browsers' view-source function fostered an amazing period of global innovation.

Perhaps even more exciting is the notion that similar principles might apply to almost any digital object and produce other powerful innovations similar to the rapid development of the Web. What do we mean by *digital object*, and how might this be the case? A digital object is anything that can be stored in a file on a computer. For example, anything written on a word processor—whether it is an essay, poem, or novel—is a digital object. Since music, images, and even video can be stored on a computer in digital format, musical recordings, photographs, and movies can also be digital objects. We like to refer to freely shared forms of digital content other than software code as "open content."

So how could openness applied to these other digital objects lead to powerful innovations? We have no need to speculate about this, because there are already many examples, such as Wikipedia and YouTube. Wikipedia makes use of an innovative open-source software (OSS) application called MediaWiki that allows anyone to add text or images to a Web page directly from their Web browser, and/or edit text and images already posted to the Web page by others. By simply permitting anyone to add or edit articles, Wikipedia has grown into a global encyclopedia, freely available to all, written in over two hundred languages with over 3.5 million articles in English. YouTube, by facilitating the free uploading, viewing, and sharing of videos, has become everything from a video-based news resource to an educational one that contains videos for learning how to do countless things from using software to fixing your own automobile.

Common to the openness examples that we have described so far is the concept of collaboration. Whether it takes the more passive form of sharing HTML code for Web site designs, or the more active form of several people working together to create a Wikipedia article or YouTube video, people collaborate and innovate. These collaborations can be between two individuals who reside halfway around the world but want to work on a project together remixing music, or efforts by groups of individuals or organizations trying to harness the ideas of openness and open content to move humanity forward in tackling "wicked problems" (Rittel and Webber 1973, 155), such as climate change, that require collaboration across organizational and/or political lines. In the article "High Noon: We Need New Approaches to Global Problem-Solving, Fast," former World Bank vice president Jean-François Rischard (2001, 507) emphasizes that "the current setup for solving global problems doesn't work." Think back to our example of the exponential growth of the early Web as a result of open-source code availability. Could something similar to the open-source idea—whether software code or other forms of open content—when applied in combination with the power of numbers and innovation, solve global problems more quickly?

The idea of openness as a driver for innovation is not new. For instance, openness has provided the bedrock for science since the emergence of technologies for information sharing and communication (Ziman 1969; Kronick 1990; Johns 2001; Spier 2002). Over time, human ingenuity has produced many such technologies, beginning with Johannes Gutenberg's printing press, then the typewriter and carbon paper, followed by photocopying and fax machines, the Internet sharing conventions like file transfer protocol and email, then HTML and the Web, and now, most recently, so-called database-enabled Web 2.0 technologies (what we prefer to call the interactive Web). Each of these technological advances creates new opportunities for promoting and capitalizing on openness (see, for example, Schweik et al. 2005, 2011).

What Is Open-Source Software, and Why Study It?

For those readers unfamiliar with OSS, it refers to computer software code—the readable text of the computer programs that makes the computer do what it does. Similar to our HTML example above, in the case of OSS, the software code is made available in a readable form to anyone who wants it, while in the case of proprietary software the code is kept secret.

The open-source story can be traced back to the mid-1980s and a programmer at the Massachusetts Institute of Technology named Richard Stallman. Stallman (1999, 2002), and others who are now part of the Free Software Foundation (FSF), believed that because of the digital nature of software and low cost of sharing code, users should be given the *freedoms* to use, read, and modify this software as well as distribute it as they deem necessary. This came to be known as free/libre software (Ghosh et al. 2002). The term *free/libre* is fundamentally different from the word *freeware*, which refers to proprietary, unreadable code distributed at no cost.

Stallman's major innovation was the "copyleft" idea. He used copyright law as it applied to software licenses to grant certain liberties to the software's users. These privileges include the right to run the software, read the software source code and modify it, redistribute the original version of the software, and redistribute modified versions of the program (Stallman 1999). A fifth right—access to the source code—is unstated, but required in order to realize the latter three rights. Copyleft also mandates that all future versions of the software be assigned these same principles. The FSF (2009) summarizes its approach this way: "To copyleft a program, we first state that it is copyrighted; then we add distribution terms, which are a legal instrument that gives everyone the rights to use, modify, and redistribute the program's code or any program derived from it but only if the distribution terms are unchanged. Thus, the code and the freedoms become legally inseparable." Copyleft was a brilliant notion given that the accepted convention at the time was proprietary software code, and in most instances, licenses placed strict limitations on software users as to where the software could be installed. Based on the ideas of copyleft, Stallman developed a software license that included free/libre principles, referred to as the GNU General Public License (GPL).

The permission to copy, modify, and distribute readable software source code offers at least two potential advantages over the traditional proprietary, full-copyright approach to software development. First, all OSS packages are provided at no monetized cost to the end user, creating a major incentive for them to be used, especially by people and organizations working with limited budgets (Hahn 2002). Second, by supplying readable source code and permitting new derivative works to be made, OSS licenses have the *potential* to generate a large community of users and developers—larger than any one proprietary organization could create—to develop, test, and debug future versions of the software (Raymond 2001).

We believe that there are several important reasons to study OSS. For one, OSS has not only experienced an explosive growth rate in recent years but has also inserted itself into the very fabric of our technical infrastructure. For example, the number of OSS projects on SourceForge.net (SF), the largest hosting Web site for OSS projects in the world, grew from just over 100,000 projects in 2006 to over 280,000 at the beginning of 2011. Netcraft (2011) reports that an OSS Web server known as Apache hosts over 50 percent of the more than 200 million domain names on the Internet. That means that something like half the Web sites worldwide are displayed to users by a single OSS application.

Furthermore, OSS is one of the earliest examples of the power of openness that uses the Internet as a communication platform, and thus it has a rich history and much data available for study. Given the early explosion of the Web, and other instances of the power of openness like Wikipedia and YouTube, we think most readers will agree that examining the evolution of openness in the Internet era by looking at OSS is worthwhile. By learning how OSS collaborations succeed or in some cases fail, we may be able to learn how to foster OSS collaborations along with other open-content, Internet-based collaborations that have the potential to make powerful contributions to society, including solving global problems like climate change.

There are also crucial economic reasons for studying OSS. Rishab Aiyer Ghosh (2006) predicted that OSS-related economic activity would likely grow to nearly 4 percent of Europe's gross domestic product (GDP) by 2010.[1] In addition, Samuel Bowles, Richard Edwards, and Frank Roosevelt (2005, 539–540) reported that the information technology (IT) sector contributed 9.3 percent of the total GDP of the U.S. economy, and that over two-thirds of labor in the United States was devoted to producing services. They describe this economy as "weightless," because most of the things produced cannot be weighed or easily measured. In their book's conclusion, they explain how the transition from a mostly goods-based economy to a weightless one will likely require significant changes in economic institutions. In chapter 2 of our book, we discuss the OSS "ecosystem," and how more complex governance structures have emerged to govern and provide economic support to some of the large, successful OSS projects. It may be that the evolution of OSS governance and economic institutions could foreshadow more fundamental changes in our national or global economic institutions—yet another reason to study OSS.

Jamie Boyle (2003b, 47), a well-known scholar at Duke University School of Law, reinforces what we have said about the importance of studying OSS when he argues,

The marketplace of ideas, the continuous roiling development in thought and norm that our political culture spawns, is itself an idea that owes much more to the distributed, nonproprietary model than it does to the special case of commodified innovation that we think about in copyright and patent. Not that copyright and patent are unimportant in the process, but they may well be the exception rather than the norm. Commons-based production of ideas is hardly unfamiliar, after all. . . . The importance of open-source software is not that it introduces us to a wholly new idea; it is that it makes us see clearly a very old idea.

Note that Boyle refers to OSS as a form of "commons." As we will discuss further in chapter 2, OSS projects represent a form of commons because the software belongs to everyone who contributes to creating it (Ostrom 1990; Dietz et al. 2003; Benkler 2005). Yet open-source commons differ from the environmental commons familiar to some readers of this book, like public grazing lands, water aquifers, and ocean fisheries (Hardin 1968; Ostrom 1990). In OSS commons, groups act collectively to produce public goods (i.e., software codes or open content) rather than overuse the resource, as often is the case in environmental commons (such as described in Garrett Hardin's *Tragedy of the Commons* [1968]). We treat the phrases "OSS projects" and "OSS commons" as synonyms.

Our Central Research Question

Up to this point, we have shown how powerful the combination of openness and the Internet can be for innovation and the creation of economic value. We used the growth of the Web, Wikipedia, YouTube, and the OSS application Apache as examples. We also discussed how studying OSS projects might produce insights to help us foster new, open collaborations that create similar economic value or solve global problems. In addition, studying OSS is important for understanding essential elements of our global computing infrastructure and how our economic institutions might change now that the U.S. economy is largely weightless. But how do we go about studying OSS?

At the heart of our work is the question of why and how teams of software developers and users, collaborating over the Internet, can build and maintain software as a form of commons. In short, the central research question we ask is:

What factors lead some OSS commons to success and others to abandonment?

By our definitions, described fully in chapter 7, a project achieves success if it produces useful software or else useful software that continues to be developed over time, and abandoned projects, obviously, show no clear signs of activity. If we are able to answer

our central research question in a comprehensive way, we will increase our understanding of OSS—which has taken a critical place in our technology and economy—
and perhaps better know how to encourage other Internet-based commons that
produce value or address pressing concerns.

Answering Our Central Research Question

To begin investigating our key research question, we first decided to identify factors
that might be important for OSS success based not only on past empirical work related
to OSS explicitly but also other relevant academic literature. We studied literature
about software engineering and information systems to find elements critical for producing software in general as well as successfully deploying software systems in businesses and other organizations. In addition, we studied distributed work and virtual
teams, which summarize what is known about how people work together over geographic distances and in the virtual world of the Internet as opposed to the real, face-
to-face world. We also reviewed areas of research that might be less obvious to some
readers, examining literature from political science and economics—including social
movements, collective action, and commons governance and management. We
studied social movement literature because the OSS phenomenon has much in
common with a social movement. Collective action literature encompasses what
scholars have learned over a long time period about factors that help or hinder collaborations between people. Much of the commons governance and management
work focuses on natural resource commons, but some relatively new work centers on
what some scholars call the "new digital commons" (e.g., Hess and Ostrom 2007; van
Laerhoven and Ostrom 2007; Bollier 2008).

Once we reviewed this literature, we developed theories about what might cause
OSS commons to be successful or abandoned. We translated these into hypotheses
that could be tested for correctness by using existing data about OSS projects. For
example, we asked if "OSS commons will be more successful when the projects have
financial support rather than being composed entirely of volunteers," or if "OSS
commons will be more successful when project participants meet face-to-face as
opposed to never meeting in the real world." We developed over forty hypotheses
along with questions based on the existing academic literature about OSS and any
other field we thought might provide insight.

Once we identified the significant components that might affect OSS success, we
needed a way to organize them. We wanted to do a comprehensive study, and thus
chose a framework called Institutional Analysis and Development (IAD), often used
to study environmental commons such as forests, fisheries, and irrigation systems
(e.g., Ostrom et al. 1994; Ostrom 2005; Hess and Ostrom 2007). This framework
allowed us to organize our factors into three categories: the technological character-

istics of the software, the community aspects of the people involved, and the institutional rules and processes that govern OSS projects. IAD helped us consider dynamic change over time, and provided a method to analyze the complex and constantly changing social and technical processes involved in OSS projects.

But theoretical work is not enough to really understand OSS commons; we also needed empirical work based on data and the input of OSS participants. This need presented an entirely different research problem: Will we be able find ways to measure our important factors and identify projects that are successful or abandoned? Although this turned out to be a complex process, in the end we did find ways to measure nearly all our elements for success by using data available for OSS projects hosted on SF, interviewing open-source developers, and conducting one of the few random-sample surveys of OSS developers. We were fortunate to be able to conduct our survey in cooperation with the corporation that owns SF, and develop an automated method for categorizing whether SF projects were successful or abandoned. Having projects categorized in this way allowed us to use statistical techniques on data from over a hundred thousand OSS projects to find which of our factors really helped distinguish between successful and abandoned projects.

After five years of research, we feel that we have answered our central research question and identified the factors we believe are most important for creating successful OSS projects. We found strong evidence in some cases that a particular component "caused" success. In general, our study confirms much of the conventional wisdom about OSS collaboration. Success is community based and uses the Internet to create geographically dispersed cooperative commons structures premised on novel economic arrangements, but it also depends heavily on long-established principles like hard work, good administration, and leadership. Moreover, we found many surprising results. The programming skill of the developers involved in projects, for instance, does not seem to play a strong role in determining success versus abandonment, apparently because a large majority of OSS developers are highly skilled professionals.

What to Expect from the Rest of This Book

This book is about rigorous social science research, which is nearly always complicated because of the many variables involved. We have attempted to simplify our presentation to the degree possible, but have also strived to offer enough information about our variables and hypotheses to provide interested readers with a deep understanding of our research and findings. OSS researchers will probably be interested in reading the entire book, as might computer scientists, software engineers, and scholars who study political science, information science, commons, sociology, economics, and management. Readers who are OSS practitioners or simply have an interest in the evolution of the Internet and our society may be less interested in some of the chapters—those containing detailed descriptions of our data, variables, and statistical methods. Given this, we would like to point out chapters that certain readers may use for reference and still get a good, although perhaps not complete, understanding of our findings and their meaning.

The remainder of the book roughly follows the order of our research process. Part II looks at our literature review—that is, the work of other scholars that helped us better understand OSS, decide on an analytic framework, and identify factors that could influence the success or abandonment of OSS projects, which in turn aided us in formulating our many hypotheses. In part II, we provide a much more detailed portrayal of the OSS phenomenon, including the many reasons why software developers, businesses, governments, and even academic institutions participate in OSS projects. Why would software developers contribute their time and businesses contribute their money to create a product that is simply given away? What about competition among OSS projects? How do OSS participants organize themselves to create extremely complex and valuable software? Do they argue among themselves; is there a lot of conflict among OSS project participants? Part II tackles such questions, and should be of worth to everyone who reads this book.

Part III starts with a case study of Open-Source Geospatial Foundation (OSGeo), a nonprofit foundation that serves as the umbrella organization for a number of important OSS geographic information system (GIS) projects. For those unfamiliar with GIS, it is a technology similar to the global positioning navigation systems found in many of today's automobiles. The OSGeo case study concretizes some of the more abstract theory discussed in part II, and gives the reader a good entry point for the empirical research that is the focus of part III. In part III, we describe the data we used for our study, including a detailed explanation of our "Survey on Free/Libre and Open-Source Success." We illuminate how we made the theoretical factors from part II into measurable variables, and describe exactly how we defined success and abandonment. Our definition is based on the idea of successful collective action rather than producing high-quality or extremely popular software. We also talk about the statistical methods we used to explore which of our forty or so variables were really significant for predicting whether projects would be successful or abandoned. Readers who are less interested in the details of social science research may wish to skim parts of chapters 7, 8, and 11, and then use them for reference.

Part IV ends our five-year research effort. When we began this investigation, we were excited about the possibility that the largely volunteer collaborations that produced complex OSS might be extended to foster scientific or other collaborations to help solve complex technical, social, and political problems. We also wanted to discover some design principles for OSS commons that might assist OSS developers. We believe our work has made progress toward both of these goals. Part IV consists of only chapter 12, which describes our overall conclusions. We include the practical implications of our work, like the design principles for OSS commons, and explain some of the theoretical implications for collective action theory, virtual collaboration, and understanding evolving OSS institutions. Finally, we discuss what our work suggests about creating successful open-content projects and projects that may help solve global problems. We invite readers to take the journey with us.

II What We Know about Open-Source Software Commons: Academic Research and Theory

2 The Ecosystem

In chapter 1, we offered some powerful reasons for studying OSS. Here we provide a broader knowledge of the subject by distilling several years of study, starting with a bit of history that describes how OSS has changed over the last decade or two, and why we use the *ecosystem* metaphor to depict its current state. We then consider *commons* more carefully, because both the framework we use to organize our studies along with many of the factors we explore to understand the success and abandonment of OSS projects originate in commons literature. Our main objective in this chapter is to impart a broad-scale overview of OSS. We focus on the general organizational types—firms, governments, nonprofits, universities, and scientific research organizations—that are interested in using, developing, or promoting OSS technologies as well as the surprising and complex motivations driving their interest.

Why an Ecosystem?

Much of the OSS research in the late 1990s and early 2000s depicted OSS development projects as largely volunteer endeavors without any monetary incentives (Chakravarty, Haruvy, and Wu 2007). OSS development projects often followed a "hacker ethic" (Himanen 2001; von Hippel and von Krogh 2003); individuals freely gave away software they had written so it could be modified and built on, with an expectation of others' returning the favor. More recent studies of OSS (e.g., David, Waterman, and Arora 2003; Ghosh 2005; Lakhani and Wolf 2005) identify both volunteer and paid developers as participants. As Elliot Maxwell (2006, 141) notes, "In an increasing number of cases . . . the production of open source software is a job, not a volunteer activity." And a report by Ghosh (2006, 17) states that OSS "has rapidly shifted from a model driven purely by the developer community and university support to one where a main driver is industry." These firms have developed business models involving OSS, and either financially support projects or pay their own employees to participate (Riehle 2007). As we will describe below, government and nonprofit organizations are also now involved. The OSS development environment, in short, has evolved into

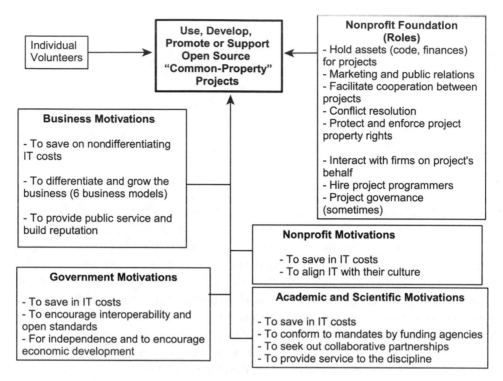

Figure 2.1
A broad-scale view of the open-source ecosystem

a more complicated, interdependent, and changing system of interaction that can be portrayed metaphorically as an ecosystem (Open Source 2005). We present a graphic overview in figure 2.1.

Some More about Commons

Over the last twenty or more years, scholars have produced a significant body of interdisciplinary literature about commons—resources that are somehow collectively shared (for a comprehensive bibliographic database, see Hess 2007). Much of the focus has been on natural resource commons (forests, irrigation systems, fisheries, etc.), but more recently a deep concern has emerged over information and knowledge as a commons (see, e.g., Boyle 2003a, 2003b; Kranich 2004; Hess and Ostrom 2007).

While the term commons is widely used with a variety of meanings (Hess and Ostrom 2003), it is usually associated with public goods or situations where some private property is shared. A public good is something that is hard to keep people from using, and that people do not exclude other people from using or exhaust by their own use of it. The air we breathe is an example of a public good. It would be difficult to prevent people from using air, and by using air, people do not deplete it or keep others from using it. Because air is collectively shared, it is also easily thought of as a commons. Commons where private property is shared are known as common-property regimes (Olson 1965; Bromley 1992; von Hippel and von Krogh 2003). OSS is an instance of a common-property regime because the developers have copyrights to the software they create, thereby making the software private property, even though the developers choose to give the software away and allow it to be collectively shared. Commons—and particularly common-property regimes—usually have established sets of institutional arrangements governing the rights to the access, use, and management of the good (Dietz et al. 2002, 18; Benkler 2003, 6; Benkler 2006, 60).

Yochai Benkler (2003, 2005, 2006) has worked carefully to describe commons in information production situations (see, in particular, Benkler 2006, 61–62). In his seminal work, *The Wealth of Networks*, Benkler (2006, 63) coins the phrase "commons-based peer-production" to depict special circumstances where no centralization exists, no hierarchical assignments occur, and individuals self-select their work tasks.[1] In the best of cases, large numbers of individuals scour their environment in search of the right project and project component to work on (Benkler 2005, 178). Benkler (2006, 63) refers to OSS as the "quintessential instance" of commons-based peer-production:

Open source is an approach to software development that is based on shared effort on a non proprietary model. It depends on many individuals contributing to a common project, with a variety of motivations, and sharing their respective contributions without any single person or entity asserting rights to exclude either from the contributed components or from the resulting whole. In order to avoid having the joint product appropriated by any single party, participants retain copyrights in their contribution, but license them to anyone—participant or stranger—on a model that combines a universal license to use the materials with licensing constraints that make it difficult, if not impossible, for any single contributor or third party to appropriate the project.

As we see it, one can look at Benkler's concept of open-source peer-production commons from two perspectives: the broad-scale perspective of all OSS projects being worked on across the globe, and the fine-scale one of any particular individual project. From the broad, global perspective, the Internet is filled with a large number of potential programmers who might be interested in working on any particular OSS project. Assuming programmers want to devote the time, they might start or join a project that suits their fancy. There is no centralized or hierarchical direction driving their choice of projects.

An individual OSS project, however, is a special type of peer-production commons—what we refer to as "peer-production common property" (Schweik 2005). Some readers may feel this term adds unnecessary jargon to the OSS research conversation. Yet scholars of environmental commons know that there are clear distinctions between different types of commons (see Bromley 1992), and that these distinctions matter. For example, in his famous article "The Tragedy of the Commons," Hardin (1968) referred to a situation where the commons, a pasture, was "open to all." From a property rights perspective, this could be interpreted as "owned by none" or perhaps "owned by all," and Hardin did not clarify precisely what he meant. In OSS commons, explicit property rights exist, and making contributions to the *specific project*'s version of its source code is restricted (not open to all), but the source code is still shared. The emphasis on property rights suggests that there are deeper questions about OSS social relations at the project level as well as the management and governance structure (Ostrom 1990; McKean and Ostrom 1995).

Mapping the Open-Source Software Ecosystem

We explained above why we use *ecosystem* to describe the broad landscape of OSS and discussed its attributes as commons and common property. Armed with this additional knowledge, we can now begin our overview of the OSS ecosystem. During the last five years or so, private firms, governments, and nonprofits clearly have become entrenched in what for a time was considered an all-volunteer OSS ecosystem. In a U.S. free and open-source software (FOSS) survey, the authors report that "only 8.0% of respondents who worked on projects over 10 years ago had some form of external support. The number rose to 15.0% between 6–10 years ago, 35.4% between 3–5 years ago, and within the past 2 years, 53.9% of respondents have had external support" (David, Waterman, and Arora 2003, 23). We believe this change is important, because in addition to other effects, it will likely create institutional complexity within and across open-source projects. Furthermore, these new and evolving OSS institutions may foreshadow shifts in our global economy.

In an effort to fully describe the OSS ecosystem, we need to consider why its composition is moving at least partially away from an all-volunteer situation to one where public and private organizations are interested in and potentially diverting their own resources to open-source projects. We thus will briefly review four general categories of open-source interest groups—businesses, governments, nonprofit organizations, and academic and scientific researchers—and try to explain why they act as consumers, producers, and/or champions of OSS products. These explanations form the basis for our first research question (see table 2.1): *How do open-source projects, supported in some way by businesses, governments, or nonprofits, differ from all-volunteer projects?* The discussion below leads to a number of factors that we investigate later. Readers with particular interests in one or another organizational type may want to skim some of the sections below.

Table 2.1
Open-source ecosystem: Research questions

1. How do open-source projects, supported in some way by businesses, governments, or nonprofits, differ from all-volunteer projects?

2. How does the role of an associated foundation influence the way an open-source project is governed and managed?

Business Motivations

Bruce Perens (2005) uses the phrase "enabling technology" to describe technology that is a required cost to help an organization do business. He argues further that there are two types of enabling technologies: nondifferentiating and differentiating. Perens estimates that as much as 90 percent of the software used in any business is nondifferentiating—meaning that a specific business needs it, but so does every business. A differentiating technology refers to a case in which a company creates a technological innovation that makes its business look more desirable than that of a competitor. Amazon.com's use of "other book" recommendations and Google's underlying Page Rank algorithm are both examples of this kind of technology. Businesses use OSS for differentiating as well as nondifferentiating technologies, and are motivated to do so because they can increase their profits. Businesses also support OSS projects, especially those involving higher education, because they help build a positive reputation for the firm by contributing to the public good.

Business Motivation 1: To Reduce Costs for Nondifferentiating IT

Many nondifferentiating technologies are related to infrastructure (operating systems, Web servers, databases, etc.) and provide the foundation for developing business-differentiating technologies. To make a business more desirable to customers, Perens (2005) argues, firms should be spending more on differentiating software and less on software that does not differentiate their business. OSS helps lower costs by distributing the expense and risk of nondifferentiating software across multiple collaborating firms. "The companies that join OSS collaborations are seeking to use the software in a nondifferentiating cost-center role. *It's not important to these companies that Open Source does not in itself produce a profit*" (ibid.).

Following this logic, firms employ IT professionals to deploy and manage nondifferentiating OSS business-enabling technologies, and in this context, may be encouraging paid employees to participate in OSS projects. For example, a programmer may develop a new function needed for their employer's business for an OSS package and then contribute it to the project as required by the project's license. A recent study by the research firm Gartner supports these contentions and predicts that more than 90 percent of businesses will be utilizing some sort of OSS technology by 2012 (Judge 2008).

Business Motivation 2: To Differentiate and Grow the Business

Businesses also use OSS to differentiate their products and services as well as to grow. Recent studies by Sandeep Krishamurthy (2005), Dirk Riehle (2007), and Fadi Deek and James McHugh (2007, 272–279) explore various business models involving OSS technologies. Each study has its own unique insights and perspectives. In this section, we briefly summarize six open-source-based business strategies described in these readings.

System Integrators

A system integrator contracts with a client to provide an end-to-end integrated product to solve some customer need. This type of business sells a complete product stack containing hardware, software, and support services. On the software end, the product could be entirely OSS, or a combination of proprietary and open-source packages. Riehle (2007, 26) notes that system integrators have the potential to gain the most (compared to other business models) from the use of OSS for two reasons: they increase their profits through direct cost savings by using software that they do not have to pay for, and they can potentially reach a larger number of customers through "improved pricing flexibility." The internal cost savings allows the firm to potentially reduce the price of integrated services to the client, thereby increasing the number of customers who might be willing to contract for these services.

Open-Source Software Service Providers

Two types of providers fall within this business category: first-level support and implementation service providers, and second-level support, training, and development services (Riehle 2007, 29). In some respects, the first-level service providers are similar to the system integrator model above in that they help a client get an OSS product installed and operational. But first-level service providers usually focus on OSS products only and typically do not offer hardware products. Second-level OSS service providers either train clients on OSS technologies so they can implement the technologies themselves or act as a problem solver on technical issues that are beyond the abilities of the technical staff in the client's organization.

Deek and McHugh (2007, 274) offer an example of a firm—GBDirect (2008) in the United Kingdom—that provides both first- and second-tier services. Another example is LimeService, which supplies a hosting site for online surveys based on the OSS LimeSurvey.[2] We use LimeSurvey for our survey research in part III of this book. According to LimeService's Web site, the lead developer of the survey software owns the service firm, and some of the profits from the online survey service help to support further development of the LimeSurvey software. This is an instance of combining a service provider business model with the software development model described in the sixth strategy below. Riehle (2007) observes that one of the keys to a service provider business model is the ability to recruit and retain high-quality people, which in turn relates to discussions in the next chapter regarding OSS developer motivations and "signaling skills."

Distributors

One of the first business models in the "early" days, when firms began entering the OSS ecosystem, was the distributor. Distributors compile and sell packaged distributions of OSS as well as offer support and training services for these distributions. The most widely recognized "field" of distribution is in the area of Linux (the operating system). There are a number of different Linux distribution companies—including Red Hat (Fedora Linux), Novell (SUSE Linux), Canonical Ltd. (Ubuntu Linux), and Mandriva (Mandriva Linux). Many components could go into a distribution, such as the latest stable version of Linux, along with various complementary products like the most recent Web server (e.g., Apache), driver software for input and output, desktop environments (e.g., KDE or GNOME), and other associated OSS packages. A benefit for many end users of a Linux distribution is that they do not need to become highly technical experts to install and set up the system, and some distribution companies offer multiyear contracts where the end user will receive the latest security patches along with any enhanced administration tools (Deek and McHugh 2007).

Hybrid Proprietary/Open Model: Horizontal Development

Horizontal business models describe situations where a business is not directly dependent on an OSS product but rather benefits from its existence and wants to support it. The hybrid proprietary/open component of this label is meant to convey that horizontal approaches can use an all-open-source strategy, or a strategy where proprietary and OSS are utilized together. Deek and McHugh (2007, 277) point to a case where OSS provides low-cost software to run on some companies' equipment, thereby potentially improving the sale of that equipment. Some firms may wish to support an OSS project as part of a strategy to take on a competitor. IBM's support of Linux to compete with Microsoft is one such instance of this strategy. "To the extent that Linux erodes Windows market share, IBM is strengthened because its products run on Linux, while Microsoft is simultaneously weakened" (ibid., 279).

Hybrid Proprietary/Open Model: Vertical Development

Vertical development is meant to convey the process of combining various OSS software packages in new ways and then selling this new product. Deek and McHugh

(2007, 276) use the companies Yahoo! and Google as examples. These companies have created proprietary products and services that are built on an OSS infrastructure. Google, for instance, uses the Linux core operating system (rather than a distribution) to drive its internal servers as well as other OSS products like the programming language Python and database package MySQL. But neither Yahoo! nor Google share their internal code. Instead, they sell these innovations to other customers. According to the author of the PhP programming language, Rasmus Lerdorf, this vertical business model provides the most lucrative opportunities for the future (ibid., 276).

Software Development Firms

This category captures a software producer who either combines the source code from an already-existing OSS product with some other code that they produced to create a new software product; takes an OSS product and bundles it with other existing but stand-alone modules to create some new suite of packages for use by an end user (Krishamurthy 2005, 283); relicenses proprietary code under an OSS license; or dual licenses their software.

In the first two options above—combining code and bundling—Krishamurthy (2005) notes that there are two types of software development business models, and they are distinguished by the general type of OSS license used: the GPL model and the non-GPL one. For readers unfamiliar with these licenses, the GPL is the most widely used OSS license.[3] As we described in chapter 1, by licensing a piece of software under the GPL, the developer ensures that it is kept permanently open and free (as in freedom)—meaning that it can be used without restriction, the source code is accessible, the software can be modified, and it can be redistributed with modifications. The GPL mandates reciprocity (Rosen 2004), whereby the recipient of the GPL code is required, on the redistribution of any new derivative, to pass on the same stipulated freedoms by licensing this new derivative under the GPL as well (Krishnamurthy 2005; Deek and McHugh 2007).

Since the introduction of the GPL by Stallman, many other OSS licenses have been developed (see, e.g., Rosen 2004), some of which have looser requirements or are more permissive than the GPL—what we call, in later chapters, "GPL incompatible." In these incompatible GPL circumstances, firms can derive new works from OSS, but are not obliged to license new derivatives under the GPL. Firms in these instances can develop new derivatives, yet are not obligated to expose the code logic in this new product (Krishamurthy 2005).

This distinction between open-source and incompatible GPL creates two different types of software development business models (Krishamurthy 2005), and the difference is whether the source code of the derived product is open access or not. In the GPL software-development models, the firm is required to make the new derivative code available under the GPL. But in some cases, the development firm still benefits because this model can create tighter bonds between the development firm and customers (ibid.). For example, the client may get the OSS for free (as in cost), but may pay the firm to create a new derivative, which can also create new service opportunities for the firm. In non-GPL software development business models, the software development firm uses OSS code to develop a new derivative that is licensed differently from its parent code, and the firm may have saved development costs by using the parent OSS code as an input.

The third software development option for businesses, in addition to combining code or bundling software, as described above, is what Joel West and Siobhan O'Mahony (2005) call a sponsored "spinout." In this instance, a proprietary software development firm decides to open its code and release it under an OSS license, inviting the external community to join the project in an effort to increase the software's adoption or gain development assistance. This could be undertaken by a firm, government agency, or nonprofit that has developed code can initiate a sponsored spinout, but as far as we can tell, it happens more often in private sector settings. Examples of this are Netscape forming the Mozilla project and IBM releasing code to create the Eclipse project (O'Mahony 2007).

Finally, dual licensing is another option for software development firms. Under the dual-licensing business model, the firm offers two versions of its software: an open-source licensed version and a commercially licensed one. Deek and McHugh (2007) explain two general dual licensing strategies: enhanced functionality, exemplified by the company Sendmail, Inc., and the same functionality approach, exemplified by the firm MySQL AB.

Sendmail, Inc. provides two versions of its Sendmail software, which transfers email from one host server to another. The open-source version essentially offers base functionality. The commercial version supplies enhanced functionality, such as an improved installation component as well as other improved security components, including virus checking. Obviously, Sendmail, Inc. makes money by selling its commercial product, yet at the same time, it manages the continued development of the open-source version of its software.

The company Oracle bought out Sun Microsystems, which owned, developed, and supported the popular MySQL relational database software. But before this buyout, Sun Microsystems had purchased MySQL from a former company, MySQL AB. According to Deek and McHugh, prior to Sun taking it over, MySQL AB did all of its product development in-house. That is, the company accepted enhancements or patches for its open-source version from participants outside the firm, but such contributions were usually reimplemented into the MySQL product by some of the company's three hundred or more full-time employees (Hyatt 2006; referenced in Deek and McHugh 2007, 65). The company made a profit by giving permission, through a commercial license, to other companies or commercial software developers to integrate the MySQL database application into their own proprietary products and sell the resulting product as a closed-source, proprietary package. Karl Fogel (2006, 156) argues that this model works best when a firm provides code libraries rather than stand-alone applications.

Business Motivation 3: To Contribute to the Public Good

As a way to support OSS, firms engage in outreach efforts, such as the relatively high-profile Summer of Code program created by Google. The program began in 2005 and has been growing ever since. Google (2011) says it established this program to inspire young developers to participate in OSS development; provide college students in computer science and related fields with paid opportunities over the summer to do work related to their academic interests; expose these students to the open-source, distributed development approach; get more OSS written; and help OSS projects identify talented new developers. The company claims that since 2005, its program has linked over forty-five hundred student developers with OSS projects, most of which do not compete directly with Google's business interests (ibid.). Little appears to be written on the Summer of Code describing why Google sponsors this program and offers stipends for three months of code, other than the material on the program Web site. But this effort clearly does achieve the objectives listed above, and through this outreach helps to build or maintain a positive reputation for Google within the OSS development community.[4] Other firms have attempted to make similar positive connections with OSS developers, and in some cases, utilize this outreach as a way to promote their business interests. The support of the Eclipse software development environment, by IBM and others, is one such example.

In sum, this section on business motivations emphasizes three reasons for businesses to utilize, support, and/or be a proponent of OSS: to reduce costs in internally used nondifferentiating IT; build and grow their business through differentiating IT; and provide some public service while also building a positive reputation within the OSS development and other communities. Related to the second motivation, we discussed several business models that appear to be dominant. In each type of motivation, there is potential for firms to support OSS projects—through paid employees, direct project financing, or some other kind of assistance. As we will see in chapter 3, some of these business interests motivate programmers directly through pay, or indirectly by encouraging volunteers to build and showcase skills.

Government Motivations

Governments have been showing a gradual interest in open-source-based solutions. While this trend is strongest outside the United States, a growing interest is emerging in the United States as well. In our survey, we asked developers about government involvement in financing OSS projects (see chapter 9) and found that a substantial number of SF projects receive some financial support from governments. There are at least four motivations: cost savings, the public good, independence, and economic development.

Government Motivation 1: To Reduce Costs for IT

Like their business counterparts, governments have nondifferentiating technology needs (Perens 2005). Especially in periods of tight finances, governments look for ways to cut costs, and OSS technologies, with their free (as in cost) licenses, are attractive from this perspective. The total cost of IT ownership is not simply the purchase price, of course. Training, installation, maintenance, technical support, and upgrades add expenses down the road. Moreover, in instances where an organization considers a major shift from one software product to another, there are the price tags of migration along with additional training and support. Nevertheless, given that many governments—especially national and state ones—have sizable IT deployments, avoiding the expense of annual licensing fees can lead to significant cost savings (Muffatto 2006).

Cost sharing offers another potential avenue for savings. OSS provides the opportunity for government agencies to collaborate and share resources (financial or staff) on IT development projects, or to share code. Some examples in the United States of attempts to build government OSS collaboration include the (now-defunct) Government Open Code Consortium (Hamel and Schweik 2009), the annual Government Open Source Conference (goscon.org), and projects like PloneGov.[5] On its Web site, PloneGov (2008) describes itself as a cooperative effort among more than fifty European, North and South American, and African public organizations with an interest in developing e-government applications for local or regional governments.

Government Motivation 2: To Achieve Interoperability and Establish Open Standards

We argue that *the* force driving public sector interest in OSS, at least in the United States, is not its financial benefits but rather its properties as a public good. Since about 2003, the debate in the United States has moved from the topic of open-source versus proprietary technologies to that of interoperability and open standards.

Governments, as public servants, have different information-flow needs and responsibilities from those of the private sector. First, they face situations where they have to exchange information both within and across agencies, and across levels of government. This need can be critical, such as in circumstances involving public safety and emergency response. Consider, for instance, the needs faced by the U.S. government in regard to the Hurricane Katrina crisis and the problems that resulted because of the lack of a coordinated communication system across public safety organizations.

Second, government agencies often need to exchange information with their constituents, in almost any circumstance imaginable, such as taxation, social services, public safety and health, and license renewals. In all these cases, the vehicle for information exchange should not place undue burdens on the citizen. For example, in the United States, when e-government platforms were being built in the mid-to-late 1990s to allow online citizen-to-government transactions, government agencies were required to maintain parallel manual or in-person systems for people lacking Internet access (Fountain 2001).

Third, government agencies frequently collect and store private information about the citizens they interact with (e.g., tax records), and are expected to be careful stewards of these data. Moreover, in some cases related to national security and defense, there is an expectation that government stewards will protect against leaks of sensitive material.

Finally, governments are expected to archive important records, and make sure that such information can be recovered in the future. In the past this was accomplished through paper archives, but now that records are becoming increasingly digital, and software and document storage formats change over time, document retrieval presents a significant challenge (Waters 2006).[6]

It turns out that these needs—for governments to be able to seamlessly communicate and share digital information, maintain their security, and provide the ability to recover archived data—underpinned much of the early debate over IT policy and OSS in the United States. The idea of interoperable systems built on open standards is seen as the basis for solutions to these demands (Simon 2005). Open standards in computing means a generally agreed-on protocol or structure for the sharing or communication of data. TCP/IP, the underlying communication protocol driving Internet transmission, is one well-established open standard for networking. HTML, the foundational language of Web pages, is considered an open standard for Web-based publishing. Determining if a standard is truly open depends on the answers to several questions, including how open and fair the process was in creating the standard, whether the standard is publicly disclosed, whether the standard contains any proprietary technology, and how the standard will be maintained (Maxwell 2006). OSS technologies often comply with established open standards, or can be made to do so because their code is accessible. Grounding software on open-data standards increases the likelihood that interoperability can be achieved, both between current software technologies and across time (the digital archive issue).

A high-profile case concerning the Commonwealth of Massachusetts eventually brought clarity to the issue of OSS as a procurement policy as well as the question of open standards and interoperability (Shah, Kesan, and Kennis 2007). In 2003, the

Massachusetts Department of Administration and Finance initiated a state IT procurement policy giving preference to OSS and products that adhere to open standards, such as the Extensible Markup Language or XML and Secure Sockets Layer (Commonwealth of Massachusetts 2004).[7] It wanted to ensure that all new IT initiatives (and retroactively, legacy systems) would conform to open standards, with the goal of interoperability—allowing various applications to exchange data more readily (Becker 2003)—and that past and present state information could be shared with constituents following open-data standards.

This policy immediately generated significant controversy and some protest, especially regarding the department's efforts to mandate the XML-based OpenDocument Format (ODF) as the storage standard (Oram 2011). ODF, a storage format utilized by the desktop word processor Open Office Writer, was not yet available as an output format in Microsoft Office's Word application. The policy also encountered resistance from disability advocates, because applications that store in ODF were not then compatible with assistive technologies for the disabled (Sliwa 2006). At the same time, the effort by Massachusetts (and others) helped encourage Microsoft to develop an ODF-compatible plug-in for Word. This new technological fix enabled Massachusetts to move toward a vendor-neutral policy without losing its main policy objective while addressing the disability access problem too. It allowed for the continued use of Microsoft Office Word with the ODF-compliant plug-in rather than a complete overhaul of government office desktops to conform to Open Office Writer. This experience shows that the real public good issue has to do with questions about the interoperability of software and not necessarily open-source concerns.

This example also hints at another potential benefit of open standards: the avoidance of vendor lock-in. In circumstances where technology use is built around proprietary communication and/or data formats, the government agency is making a commitment to that vendor alone—a commitment that could potentially extend far into the future (Simon 2005). The adoption of technologies that conform to established open standards helps organizations avoid this situation.

Government Motivations 3 and 4: To Gain Independence and Promote Economic Development

Governments, mostly outside the United States, have implemented open-source-based technologies, or are considering IT procurement policies that either mandate or show preferential treatment toward them (Maxwell 2006). Such efforts began in the early twenty-first century in Singapore, Germany, and Brazil (Hahn 2002), and have expanded globally over the last five years. Since 2004, researchers at the Center for Strategic and International Studies in Washington, DC, have tracked press and other media reports related to government OSS policies, assigning them into four categories: research and development (the support of government research and development attempts related to OSS), mandates (where OSS is required), preferences (where OSS is encouraged but not mandatory), and advisory (where the use of OSS is permitted).

In the center's most recent report, James Lewis (2010) identified 354 national, state, or local OSS policy initiatives worldwide between 2000 and 2009, with 245 of them eventually being approved. Of these approved initiatives, 81 (33 percent) were research and development efforts, 16 (6.5 percent) fell in the mandate category, 78 (31.8 percent) were classified as preferential, and the other 70 (28.6 percent) were advisories. Lewis (ibid., 2–3) summarizes the longitudinal findings to date this way:

Prior to 2001, there was almost no activity in policy related to open-source, which could be the result of a lack of maturity in open-source software development up until this point and/or difficulty in finding documentation of older open-source policies online. The first year in which we see a significant increase in open-source policies is 2002, followed by a sharp jump in 2003. . . . Potential explanations for the marked surge in open-source policies in 2003 could include increased lobbying efforts by large multinational firms invested in open-source, the growth of anti-Americanism and the desire to be less reliant on American brands, and the development of strong viable open-source alternatives. Between 2006 and 2007, we see a second boost in open-source policies, which could be attributed to a reaction to the global release of a major closed-source software package, to avoid vendor lock-in. This reaction was likely driven in part by the desire of governments to avoid costly software renewal as well as unfavorable reception of the closed-source software package. . . . Our results show a greater propensity for the approval of open-source R&D initiatives relative to mandatory, preference, or advisory policies. This is intuitive as R&D initiatives require significantly less investment to implement.

Finally, the Lewis report indicates that policies were split fairly evenly among research and development, preferential, and advisory options in Europe and Asia. Latin American initiatives, however, weighed more heavily toward preferential guidelines for government OSS acquisition efforts. North America, Africa, and the Middle East had fewer approved initiatives (ibid., 3, table 4).

Some of the motivations for these initiatives are the same as we described earlier: financial and interoperability issues (see, e.g., Ghosh 2005). Lower software costs are particularly important in less developed countries, where the government's income is relatively low (Maxwell 2006), but cost savings also have been strongly promoted in some developed countries (see, for example, the exploration of the United Kingdom in Muffatto 2006).

Many countries outside the United States have two other motivations that drive a preference toward OSS technologies: the desire to achieve more independence from foreign software companies (see Aigrain 2005, 452; Maxwell 2006, 170n101), and in some circumstances, an effort to build or support a domestic software development and service industry. The former is similar to our earlier discussion about avoiding vendor lock-in, but in this case there may be some added motivation against doing so with nondomestic firms. And the latter—support for domestically developed OSS technologies and service companies—is seen by some as a way to help level the playing field between smaller domestic software development firms and larger, more entrenched international competition that have advantages due to "network effects" (Evans and Reddy 2003; Simon 2005). For example, several past policy initiatives in China have emphasized the conversion from proprietary operating systems to Linux-based ones in the government sector. The move toward Linux was seen as "China's most important chance to improve its software industry" (Lewis 2010, 9).

Some governments, for some or all of the reasons stated above, have not only used government funds to purchase open-source-based technologies but also have set aside funds to support OSS development efforts or even pay their own government employees to develop code themselves. Brazil is one prominent illustration. The national government has made a major effort to convert to OSS technologies in government offices (Muffatto 2006; Lewis 2010), and has encouraged agencies to develop their OSS technologies to serve their needs and drive domestic industry. One example of this is the TerraLib project, an OSS GIS developed in a partnership between the National Institute for Space Research and the Catholic University of Rio de Janeiro. These two partners have invested more than fifty person-years of programming into TerraLib development, and the Brazilian government continues to support the core development team (Câmara and Fonseca 2007). The effort is helping to build a domestic GIS industry in country (ibid.).

Germany provides another example of a national government funding OSS development (Muffatto 2006). The Ministry of Economics and Labor helped found the Web-based BerliOS "open-source center," intended to serve as a neutral party to mediate between different groups with interests in OSS, such as users, developers, and manufacturers.[8] Germany also has participated in developing OSS for government use. As early as 1999, the ministry joined in financing an open-source encryption project for email systems. More recently, the German national government has aided finance efforts to develop an open-source desktop package for use in public administration settings. This resulted in contributions, for instance, to the KDE desktop package for the Linux operating system (Muffatto 2006, 145).

As this section demonstrates, government organizations, like businesses, have legitimate reasons to use, produce, and/or champion OSS technologies. Yet the actions by governments to push IT policy in their countries toward preferential treatment of OSS have, not surprisingly, received criticism. Robert William Hahn (2002) provides one of the first discussions representing both sides of the debate. The reaction to the ODF policy in Massachusetts is another case in point (Shah, Kesan, and Kennis 2007). David Evans and Bernard Reddy (2003) address many of the motivations we described above, and argue that there is no market-failure condition in the software industry requiring government intervention; there is no reason to believe that government policymakers have the expertise to help "design new and improved software industries"; and there is reason to be skeptical of the network-effect claims.[9] They generally contend that IT technicians, not policymakers, should be deciding on products to use based on standard decision categories such as technical merit and the total cost of ownership. Many governments now seem to be shifting to these criteria (along with an eye toward complying with established open standards). Ghosh (2005) provides arguments on the other side—in favor of government preferential treatment for OSS. This debate will undoubtedly continue, entwined with the issues of interoperability, open standards, and domestic software industry support.

Nonprofit Motivations

Nonprofit organizations are the third broad organizational category active in the OSS ecosystem, and their motivations for adopting, developing, and/or promoting OSS technologies are similar to some of the government ones: potential IT cost savings, and in some instances, an alignment with their public good and collaborative philosophy as well as culture. Nevertheless, with the exception of large nonprofits like international nongovernmental organizations or specialized nonprofit technology organizations, nonprofits may have neither the technical expertise nor the time and resources to participate to the same degree as businesses and governments.

Nonprofit Motivation 1: To Reduce Costs for IT

A survey by the Nonprofit Open Source Institute (NOSI 2008b) reports that the OSS technologies currently in use by nonprofits are primarily Web technologies (e.g., Apache, MySQL databases, and content management systems like Drupal) and desktop applications (e.g., Firefox Web browser, Open Office, and MySQL) running on proprietary operating systems such as Windows (NOSI 2008a). Few organizations appear to be using the Linux operating system on their desktops (NOSI 2008a). The prospect of saving money on IT along with the idea of being able to freely download and install various applications motivate nonprofits to use OSS. In addition, OSS technologies provide opportunities to reuse older computers for firewalls or low-level office computing needs(McQuillan 2003).

Jonathan Peizer (2003), however, warns nonprofit IT decision makers to carefully consider the total cost-of-ownership question. He maintains that nonprofits differ from businesses (or in our view, governments) in that nonprofits cannot as easily recover from a poor choice of technology strategy, and that the total cost of OSS in many instances may be as high as or higher than comparable proprietary applications. Peizer also observes that most nonprofits do not have the technical staff capable of taking on the installation and maintenance of many OSS products, which are often more technically challenging than comparable proprietary products. This appears to still be the case. The NOSI (2008a, 3) study notes that the most significant barriers to OSS adoption are organizational familiarity with proprietary tools and a lack of in-house OSS expertise.

Nonprofits, especially small ones, are constantly facing the challenge of managing technology with little to no technical know-how among the staff. As academics who teach midcareer graduate students working in the nonprofit sector, we have found it common to hear about the "accidental technologist"—the person on staff who seems to know the most about technology because they have experience with it (e.g., the accountant who knows spreadsheets) or who likes technology, but was not hired specifically to be in IT support. For this reason, nonprofit technology service providers have appeared, such as the Nonprofit Technology Network, TechSoup, Npower (a network of locally based nonprofit IT service providers), the Association for Progressive Communications, ItrainOnline, and Geekcorps.[10] These organizations are trying to help close the technology know-how gap in general, regardless of whether the focus is OSS or proprietary technologies. But some of these organizations actively promote OSS. At the time of this writing, for example, the Nonprofit Technology Network had a number of upcoming Web seminars on a variety of OSS technologies, such as community resource management, Linux-based desktop, and blogging tools (NTEN 2008). Some nonprofits also have emerged specifically to promote the use of OSS (see, e.g., NOSI 2008c).

Nonprofit Motivation 2: To Align IT with an Open and Collaborative Culture

McQuillan (2003) talks about the "overlap of values" between nonprofits and OSS communities around the ideals of collaboration and cooperation. The NOSI group identified three specific areas where, philosophically, nonprofits and OSS connect. First, nonprofits frequently rely on collaboration as a foundation for meeting their missions, so the idea of community ownership in software resonates with some people involved in nonprofit work. Second, some nonprofits like the notion that open source is an alternative to the threat that corporate intellectual property or the "enclosure movement" (Boyle 2003b) presents to the intellectual or knowledge commons. Finally, the nonprofit sector is closely associated with or sometimes even referred to as the voluntary sector. Many nonprofits appreciate that a majority of OSS developers are volunteers and have similar values. The recent NOSI (2008a, 3) survey of nonprofits and open source reported that nearly 70 percent of the respondents' agreed that open source was "philosophically or politically in line" with their mission.

Interestingly, most nonprofits have not taken full advantage of the freedom built into open source: the ability to modify the source (Peizer 2003), although there is some awareness of this potential for the future. For example, Pieter Boeder (2002) notes that the open-source licensing innovation creates the opportunity for nonprofit organizations to share their limited software development resources, and for application service providers (like the ones listed above) to emerge and produce open-source applications designed specifically for nonprofits.

Indeed, some development efforts have focused on key application needs in the nonprofit sector. Higher education perhaps leads the way in this area, with an emphasis on course management systems such as the Sakai project or Moodle platform, research e-repositories such as MIT's Dspace, or other related software applications (Pan and Bonk 2007).[11] In addition, other new OSS applications support nonprofit management. CiviCRM (2008), for instance, is an open-source "constituent-relationship management" system that allows a nonprofit to manage fund-raising efforts as well as manage and track volunteers, donors, employees, clients, and vendors. Based on the analysis above, CiviCRM could be classified as a common-property project, coordinated by CiviCRM LLC, with its financing going through the nonprofit Social Source Foundation.

Academic and Scientific Research Organization Motivations

This group of scholars was important in the early days of OSS and can really be considered a combination of the previous three. Academic institutions can be for-profit or nonprofit, and much of the research work they conduct is funded by government grants. Consequently, many of the motivations by preceding groups for using, developing, and/or promoting OSS, such as IT cost savings or cost sharing, or an open and collaborative IT culture, apply to this group as well.

Academic and Scientific Motivation 1: To Reduce Costs for IT

Many people at our own university deploy OSS technologies in a number of areas. They use the open-source Apache Web server to support organization and research Web sites. The Linux operating system is deployed on many of our university Office of Information Technology's computers. Faculty use OSS blogging technologies (such as Wordpress) to share their thoughts to others and communicate with students. The open-source Mailman Listserv software runs various university email lists. Wikis support various forms of academic communication and collaboration—not only at our institution but elsewhere too (Bryant 2006). University IT support staff deploy these technologies because they see them as robust, trustworthy, and a way to help reduce the cost of annual software licenses.[13]

The Campus Computing Project (2007) survey of IT use in higher education in the United States reports that almost three-fifths of campus chief information officers agreed with the statement that "Open Source will play an increasingly important role in our campus IT strategy." Still, with the exception of learning management systems (such as Moodle, which appears to be gaining significant usage), the Campus Computing Project notes that to date, there are few OSS alternatives to support campus administration, such as student information, personnel, or finance systems. At both the chief information officer and provost level, universities have discussed the viability of collaboration across universities on these kinds of applications (see, e.g., Courant and Griffiths 2006).

Academic and Scientific Motivation 2: To Fulfill Funding Organizations' Mandates
Academic research projects, often funded by government agencies, have historically contributed significant efforts to OSS code development (Perens 2005). Peter Wayner (1999) observes, "The United States government long supported OSS before it became known by that name. Most of the research contracts granted by agencies like the National Science Foundation or the Defense Advanced Research Projects Agency require the recipients to publish the final source code." For example, the Berkeley System Distribution project's work, funded by the U.S. Department of Defense and implemented at the University of California at Berkeley, contributed to creating the UNIX operating system (Perens 2005). The U.S. National Science Foundation Office of Cyberinfrastructure (2007) requires that any software products produced as a result of its funding be licensed as open source.

In many instances, graduate students engaged in projects related to their research assistantships or theses undertake the development work supported by these kinds of grants. In the population of OSS projects, college students may have created a relatively large number of OSS applications available on some public OSS hosting sites, such as SF (discussed in detail in chapter 6), as part of their academic programs. We have been unable to find any research investigating how many students are involved in such development work, but the number may be sizable.

Academic and Scientific Motivation 3: To Advance Science or Contribute to the Discipline
As Perens (2005) notes, the community of scientists conducting research in specialized fields may be relatively small. There thus may not be a strong enough profit incentive for firms to create needed analytic software. OSS may be a viable alternative, allowing scholars in specific fields to collaborate on software tools related to their research interests, advancing the software beyond what any one individual can do alone. An example of this is the Open Bioinformatics Foundation, a volunteer nonprofit organization trying to encourage collaborative OSS development in the field of bioinformatics.[14] It is possible that a significant body of more specialized software to support scientific research has been made available under OSS licenses.

Finally, another motivation driving some academics or other scientists to support or participate in OSS is the desire and incentives to contribute or provide service to their discipline or intellectual community. Some software authors may simply donate their innovations to their intellectual community as part of traditional academic discourse and service to their particular field.

The Establishment of Nonprofit Foundations to Support OSS Projects

Until now, our discussions in this chapter have focused on the question of organizational motivations use, produce, or support OSS. But before we move on to other topics we should note that a special type of nonprofit organization—nonprofit foundations—has emerged in recent years to protect, manage, and market OSS projects.

Richard Stallman was key here, creating the nonprofit FSF in the mid-1980s to promote and support free software, as he and others defined it. The FSF (2008) also acts as the organization holding the copyrights to various software applications under GNU GPL, and enforces the GPL's provisions. More than a decade later, Eric Raymond and others formed a comparable group called the Open Source Initiative (OSI 2008) to play a similar role in managing the official definition of open source and maintaining a list of OSI-approved licenses. These two groups can be seen as the overarching nonprofit foundations guiding and promoting free/libre and OSS licenses as well as philosophies.

More important for our purposes in this book, though, nonprofit foundations have emerged at the project level. The work by O'Mahony (2003, 2005) and her colleagues helps to clarify why this occurred. First, foundations formed to protect developers involved in specific projects, especially against potential lawsuits. According to O'Mahony (2005), one of the first examples was the Debian noncommercial Linux distribution project in 1996–1997. There were signs at the time that some companies or developers might sue over potential patent violations in the Linux code (see the discussion of the SCO Group in Fitzgerald 2005). In 1997, the nonprofit foundation Software in the Public Interest (SPI) was created to act as the organizational steward for the Debian project. Other OSS foundations soon emerged to take on similar roles, including the Apache (Web server) Software Foundation, Perl Foundation, and Free BSD Foundation (O'Mahony 2005, 398–399). Since then, the role of foundations has broadened in relationship to projects. As the work of O'Mahony (2005, 409) suggests, in general these foundations:

- Hold assets for the project (e.g., funds, code, and hardware such as servers)
- Protect developers from liability
- Conduct public relations and marketing for the project
- Facilitate communication or collective action between projects
- Help to diffuse potential conflicts between projects

• Help the projects protect their property rights (e.g., enforce the stipulations of the code license)

In addition, foundations quickly became crucial for another reason: helping to establish or coordinate relationships with firms that had adopted one of the business models mentioned earlier. O'Mahony (2005, 396) describes one of the first instances of this, related to the Apache (Web server) project, which occurred before the Apache Foundation was established. A Fortune 500 company executive trying to initiate a more formal relationship with the Apache project complained, "How do I make a deal with a web page?" The nonprofit Apache Foundation was established to provide a broker organization for contractual arrangements and act in the project's interest. Moreover, O'Mahony (2005) notes that the foundation can potentially help firms in the following ways:

• Donate resources to support the project
• Donate software code and assign copyright to the foundation
• Hire or support individual developers associated with the project
• Provide mechanisms (such as formal advisory roles) in some cases for a firm to help guide the future direction of a project

These kinds of foundations initially emerged to support a specific project, and in some cases still do (see, e.g., Drupal Association 2009). A number of them, however, have grown to support not one but rather a whole suite of projects. These projects can have some loose connection to one another, or may have no relationship whatsoever other than being affiliated with the same foundation. For example, the nonprofit SPI (2008), discussed earlier, lists fourteen associated OSS projects, including some well-known ones such as OpenOffice.org (office software suite) and the PostgreSQL (database package). Apache (2011), often considered a model for other foundations to emulate, lists nearly a hundred associated projects (as of April 2011).

Finally, some nonprofits have arisen specifically to help coordinate efforts between firms and other organizations with some interest in the further development of OSS. One of the most prominent cases was the Open Source Development Lab, which in 2007 was merged with the Free Standards Group to form the Linux Foundation (Lohr 2007). This foundation aims to support key developers and foster the growth of Linux (Linux Foundation 2011). Another example is the Open Source Software Institute, a nonprofit organization "comprised of corporate, government and academic representatives whose mission is to promote the development and implementation of open-source software solutions within U.S. federal and state government agencies and academic entities" (OSSI 2008; Hamel and Schweik 2009). We wonder how much the foundations described in this section influence the management and governance of their associated OSS projects, and thus we have added this as a research question in table 2.1.

Conclusion

In this chapter, we began the literature review process in an effort to discover factors that may be influential in the success or abandonment of OSS projects. Based on this review, we present two new research questions in table 2.1.

In addition, this chapter supplied an abundance of information about the context in which OSS developers find themselves. We used the metaphor of an ecosystem to depict how developers exist in a changing environment where businesses, governments, nonprofits, and other organizations are increasingly more involved in OSS projects. We explained that OSS projects are commons, but because individual developers have explicit property rights, OSS projects are a particular type of commons known as common-property regimes. This means that individual developers work in an environment with social and institutional structures that are based to some degree on these property rights. We provided many reasons why organizations are motivated to participate in open source, and how organizations affect projects and developers with their involvement or support. Even if a project has no involvement with an outside organization, though, that project and its developers still exist in an ecosystem composed of organizations such as the FSF or OSI that generally influence the course of OSS.

Although we have offered an overview of the many organizations in the OSS ecosystem, and described the context in which OSS developers work, it is the individual developer who is the focus of our analysis. Since open-source developers write the software, they and the decisions they make are ultimately responsible for whether a project succeeds or is abandoned. Accordingly, in order to take the next step in our research endeavor, we will study the individual developer in chapter 3.

3 The Developer

In the first two or three years of the twenty-first century, economists were puzzled by the volunteer nature of OSS. Why would these developers be willing to give their intellectual property away? Why would they want to spend some of their free time to contribute to such projects? In this chapter, we study these individuals—the individuals who actually create OSS. We describe who they are and where they live, and explore what is known about why they participate in OSS projects. We also explain why the OSS developer is the key element in our research.

To this end, we use several kinds of conceptual tools in our research endeavor, including a framework, theories, and models. We will start by describing these three tools, thereby preparing the way for us to review the framework that guides our research and focus on what makes OSS developers do what they do. Through the process of reviewing the work of other researchers, we uncover many factors that motivate developers, and likely influence the success or abandonment of OSS projects; then we articulate seven hypotheses that incorporate these factors. We will convert many of these factors into measurable variables in part III of this book and then test our hypotheses using data we collect ourselves. All that comes later, however; for now, let us concentrate on our research tools.

Distinguishing Frameworks, Theories, and Models

Frameworks make up the broadest concept, allowing the analyst to specify various clusters of variables and their general relationships to one another. Such a conceptualization helps to structure analytic inquiry around a set of research questions (Schlager 1999). Moreover, conceptual frameworks allow the analyst to focus on particular theories relevant to the research questions at hand (Ostrom 1999).

Theories are more specific than a framework. In science, theories give an explanation for something we witness in the world that is buttressed by evidence gathered over time (National Academy of Sciences and Institute of Medicine 2008). Theories allow analysts to concentrate on subcomponents of their conceptual frameworks—simplifying assumptions, if necessary—in order to understand and explain a phenomenon of interest (Ostrom 2005). And a variety of theories could be applied in a variety of disciplines to study the phenomenon of OSS production. For instance, researchers have used economic and noncooperative game theories to analyze various components of OSS development (Johnson 2002, 2006; Baldwin and Clark 2006). Kevin Crowston and his colleagues provide other examples, such as the use of coordination (Crowston et al. 2005) and behavioral-leadership theories (Heckman, Crowston, and Misiolek 2007) to explain OSS team performance. Our discussion below of Benkler's (2003, 2005, 2006) concept of "commons-based peer-production" is an applicable case here.

Models are more finely grained than theories. They provide precise articulations of phenomena of interest, identifying specific variables and assumptions. Researchers use models to test various hypotheses based on theories, and models can be developed using a wide variety of tools, including mathematics, dynamic systems technologies (such as the software Stella), and statistical techniques. In scientific work, we strive to create or identify parsimonious models that explain much of the variation in the data we collect, but with the fewest number of variables possible.

Now that we have clarified the distinction between frameworks, theories, and models, we can describe the framework we rely on in our research. It will become clear how theories and models fit into the framework as the story of our research continues to unfold in this and the following chapters.

The Institutional Analysis and Development Framework

For more than forty years, social scientists, including one of this book's authors (Schweik, Adhikari, and Pandit 1997; Schweik 1998, 1999), have applied the IAD framework to help analyze a variety of commons situations. Larry Kiser and Elinor Ostrom (1982) published the first articulation of IAD, with the goal of integrating interdisciplinary work, and since then IAD has been applied to a wide variety of situations, many of them natural resource commons settings (see Ostrom 2005, 8–9). More recently, this framework has been used to analyze "knowledge as a commons" settings (Hess and Ostrom 2007). Some of our previous work studying OSS has also utilized this framework (Schweik 2005). Figure 3.1 shows the structure of the IAD framework.

IAD, as a guiding framework, is useful for four primary reasons. First and most important, it focuses attention on an individual developer's decision making, which is crucial for understanding our key research questions. Second, it enables an easier connection to previous theory and field research on commons using this same approach. Third, it helps to conceptually organize much of the large and growing theoretical and field studies on OSS, and track the developers involved in it. Fourth,

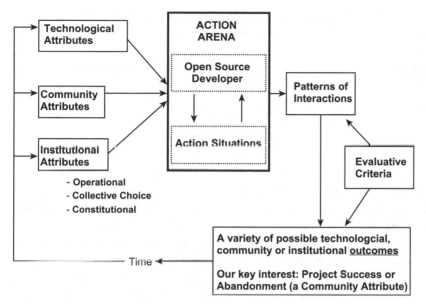

Figure 3.1
The IAD framework (adapted from Ostrom, Gardner, and Walker 1994, 37)

It highlights the governance and institutional design of OSS projects, which to date are recognized as understudied areas (Weber 2004; Crowston 2005; Schweik 2005; O'Mahony 2007; O'Mahony and Ferraro 2007).

Consider the situation where an analyst is trying to understand why a particular OSS project or commons is being actively developed, or why it appears to be losing momentum. Figure 3.1 depicts OSS commons as a dynamic system with feedback. The analyst might begin studying the project by first looking at the elements on the figure's left side: the technological, community, and institutional attributes.

Technological attributes refers to a variety of variables related to the software itself or the infrastructure used to coordinate the team.[1] These include the type(s) of programming language(s) used, the degree to which the software is modular in structure, and the type of communication and content management infrastructure used.

Community attributes refers to a set of variables relating to the people engaged in the OSS project, such as whether they are volunteers or paid to participate, whether they all speak the same language or not, and aspects related to social capital that are more difficult to measure, like how well team members get along and how well they trust each other. This component also includes other nontechnological project attributes, such as its financial situation and funding sources (e.g., a nonprofit foundation).

Institutional attributes refers to the management and governance system used by the project. It also captures the types of rules established to help guide participants' behavior as they engage in their day-to-day activities related to the development and maintenance of the source code, or the use of the software. The specific OSS license used is one important component of an OSS project's rules-in-use. But some projects—especially more mature ones with larger numbers of participants, or hybrid projects with both volunteer and paid participants—may have other sets of formal or informal rules or social norms in place that help to coordinate and manage the project. With the exception of recent work by O'Mahony (2007) and O'Mahony and Fabrizio Ferraro (2007), however, little attention has been given to this element of OSS collaboration. Our book aims to contribute to this crucial area.

The middle section of figure 3.1, the action arena, depicts the key element of analysis (the OSS developer in our case) and their action situation. Depending on the analyst's interests, these components can represent a moment or range of time where the left-side attributes remain relatively constant, and the developers (broadly defined as software developers, testers, and documenters) involved in the software project make decisions and take actions (e.g., programming, reviewing code, and deciding to reduce or stop their participation). Ostrom (2005, 14) describes the action situation as "the social space where participants with diverse preferences interact, exchange goods and services, solve problems, dominate one another, or fight (among the many things that individuals do in action situations)."

The patterns of interactions category in figure 3.1 represents these actors as they make decisions and take actions over the chosen time frame in the action arena. The accumulation of these actions results in one or more outcomes (on the right side at the bottom of figure 3.1). An outcome could be a change in the technological attributes of the OSS commons (such as a new software release), a shift in the community attributes of the project (such as new people joining or people leaving), a change to the existing institutional attributes (like a new set of rules or social norms for resolving conflicts), or any combination thereof. One important outcome measure central to the research presented in this book is the concept of project success or abandonment, which we will describe more fully in this chapter's section on trajectories and in great detail in chapter 7. In figure 3.1, various outcome-related changes are depicted through the feedback system from the outcome to the three sets of attributes on the left side, and a new time period for analysis begins whenever these shifts occur.

Outcomes

Let us now turn to the question of how to evaluate the outcomes component in the IAD framework as it pertains to OSS and our particular research interests. While figure 3.1 reveals a feedback loop to draw attention to the dynamic and evolutionary nature

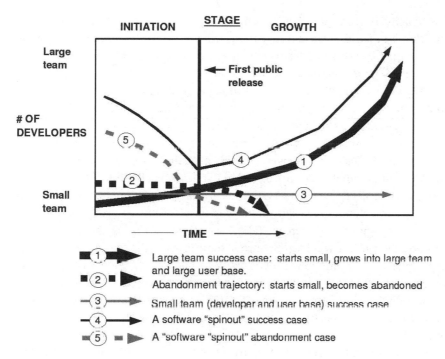

Figure 3.2
Stages and trajectories of OSS commons

of these projects, it does not capture the longitudinal properties very well. For this reason we include figure 3.2.

In figure 3.2, a vertical line bisects the main graph, delineating two main longitudinal stages: initiation (on the left) and growth (on the right). We define the juncture between these two stages as the moment in time when the *first release* of the project source code is made *publicly available* (English and Schweik 2007). Little of the OSS research to date focuses on either this longitudinal dimension or projects in the initiation stage. Yet critical design decisions may be made at this stage, such as the modularity of the code, which might greatly influence how well the software can be developed in an OSS commons setting in the later growth stage. In other words, some of the decisions made in the initiation stage may prove crucial to the outcome of success or abandonment in either the initiation or growth stage; therefore, both stages should be studied.

Given that our central interest in studying OSS commons is the question of how to maintain collective action, one of our focal indicators is the number of active developers in the project over time. We use the term developers quite broadly here. Conceptually, developers could be programmers or other interested people, such as end users, who actively contribute time to testing or writing documentation to support the project. Because of this interest, units along the y-axis in figure 3.2 represent the number of developers, with small teams falling at the bottom and larger teams residing at the top. The x-axis measures calendar time.

As figure 3.2 reveals, an OSS commons can take a number of possible trajectories. We've depicted five types of trajectories using different line textures, shading, and numbering. In the early 2000s, when OSS literature focused often on high-profile projects like Linux and Apache Web server, and OSS proponents like Raymond (2001) were writing about "Linus's law" ("given enough eyeballs, all bugs are shallow"), it was commonly thought that OSS projects took a trajectory like line 1 in figure 3.2. These all-volunteer projects would start out as either single developers or small teams working together, and then release software under an OSS license as soon as they had produced something functional (Perens 2005). Over time, assuming the product was useful to others, the project would grow into a significant collaboration with a large number of participants, adding new functionality as needed. As Eric von Hippel and George von Krogh (2003, 211) put it, "Today, an OSS development project is typically initiated by an individual or a small group with an idea for something interesting they themselves want for an intellectual or personal or business reason."

The hope, at least in some projects, is to gain both a developer and user community. Line 1 in figure 3.2 describes the trajectory that the Linux project took over the last two decades, and it most certainly represents others starting out as small teams, and then gaining larger development and user bases. In this instance, collaboration is sustained over time. Line 1 represents the quintessential successful outcome of OSS projects in the growth stage. But these cases are quite rare.

Line 2 in figure 3.2 captures what is probably the most common OSS commons trajectory. Here, the project also starts with one programmer or a small team working together. The team produces code and offers its first release, only to eventually abandon it. For one or more reasons, the development ceases. Of course, there are issues as to how to measure such a concept. One key question is how much time should pass with no development inactivity before a project is classified as abandoned. We'll discuss this more fully in chapter 7, but for now the noteworthy point is that many projects are eventually abandoned, as measured by developer participation, and line 2 graphically depicts this situation.

Line 3 in figure 3.2 illustrates another successful case that is less well recognized in the literature, but may be a common scenario based on research about OSS development teams (Krishnamurthy 2002; Schweik and English 2007). Like the others, line 3 portrays a project that starts with one developer or a small group of programmers, but remains relatively small in terms of developer team size throughout the growth stage while staying relatively active. Like line 1, we consider line 3 collaboration a success story even though the size of the group is smaller.

Lines 4 and 5 capture the concept we described in the business section of chapter 2: sponsored spinouts (West and O'Mahony 2005), or what Anthony Wasserman refers to as "software dumping."[2] Recall that in these situations, a firm first develops the software under a more traditional, proprietary, closed-source software model. At some point, perhaps after years of work, the decision makers or owners may make a strategic decision not to support the software anymore, and as a consequence make the code available and relicense it as OSS.[3]

Line 4 depicts the successful spinout case, where proprietary code is made open, released under an OSS license, and then gains a vibrant developer community. It illustrates what a firm undertaking this strategy would most likely wish to happen, when it is trying to either gain development assistance or increase adoption of its technology. The Web browser Netscape, which eventually evolved into Mozilla and Firefox, is a high-profile example of the trajectory indicated in line 4. Line 5, on the other hand, shows the alternative scenario, where the code is relicensed from proprietary to OSS, but fails to generate interest and is eventually abandoned. It could describe a case where the initial spinout code is so complex that it is unable to generate much interest from either volunteer developers or other organizations that might pay people to participate.

Other trajectories are not shown on figure 3.2 for readability reasons. For example, all of the abandoned cases here are discarded in the growth stage, after a first public release. But many OSS projects are abandoned before a first release is ever achieved. In cases where a small group initiates the project, this trajectory would start out like it does in line 2, but be abandoned before the first-release "boundary," rather than afterward.

Finally, we should note that conceptually, the measure along the y-axis could just as easily have been "number of users" instead of "number of developers." From this perspective, line 1, the successful growth stage project that is ramping up in terms of a user base, really captures the temporal trajectory of high-profile OSS projects like Linux and Apache Web server. Line 3 captures the successful cases of highly specific software (e.g., bioinformatics analytic tools) that may have a small development base, but also have a relatively small user base because of the highly specific nature of the tool. Yet these projects should be seen as successful even though their developers and user base are probably quite small.

Several main points can be taken from figure 3.2. First, there are at least two important stages in the trajectory of OSS commons: initiation and growth. Over time, OSS commons also will take various success and abandonment trajectories. Third, based on the outcome category (figure 3.1), the measures for success and abandonment will change depending on what stage a project is in at any given time. And as these commons or projects evolve, other outcomes—such as changes to their technological, community, and institutional attributes—will evolve as well (figure 3.1).

Figure 3.2 demonstrates the dynamics of projects captured by the feedback loop in figure 3.1.

Up to this point in the book, we have provided some foundations for our research endeavor, including an overview of OSS, the idea of OSS projects as commons, and the IAD framework as a conceptual guide. Now we begin to generate an abundance of research questions and hypotheses based on factors that academic literature tells us may be significant in the success or abandonment of open-source commons. These research questions and hypotheses follow from our discussion in a rather straightforward way, so rather than complicate the text by posing them one by one, we look at the literature on which they are premised, and then present them at the end of this exploration. In chapter 2, we offered reasons why organizations and individuals might want to use OSS as opposed to proprietary software. We now study the reasons why OSS developers would want to give away their hard work.

The Key Unit of Analysis: The Open-Source Software Developer

The organizational complexity described in chapter 2 leads to a clear conclusion: there are many different OSS development contexts populated with communities of developers with different motivations and characteristics. In other words, there isn't one generic type of OSS developer depicted in the center of figure 3.1 but rather many varieties (see also David and Shapiro 2008).

As we have said, because people create OSS, developing a theory of OSS commons' success or abandonment requires a focus on the participants. Benkler (2006, 107) reminds us that in terms of information production and exchange, we humans face two primary scarcities: creativity-time-attention and computation-communication resources. Computing and the Internet, of course, have greatly reduced the cost of the latter. But this hasn't changed the issue that human creativity-time-attention is still a scarce commodity.

Humans need to make decisions about how they use their time. This point connects to the general theory of bounded rationality and adapted decision making used by many social scientists. In their models of behavior, social scientists assume that individuals base their decisions about what actions to take according to their individual preferences, the constraints they find themselves in, and with incomplete information (Simon 1955). Their decision-making logic, moreover, adapts over time based on previous experience (Mueller 1986). It seems entirely reasonable to assume that all developers engage in some level of internal debate about their ongoing participation in a project, based on their personal situation, organizational context, and the incentives they face. We begin this section by taking a closer look at some characteristics of OSS developers—that is, we get to know them better. The remainder of this section sum-

Table 3.1
Open-source developer demographics

Demographic attributes	WIDI (Robles et al. 2001)	FLOSS-US (David, Waterman, and Arora 2003)[a]	The free/libre and OSS developers survey and study (Ghosh et al. 2002; Ghosh 2005)
Number of respondents	5,593	1,588	2,774
Percent male	98.6%	98.4%	98.8%
Age	27 (mean age)	50% between 23 and 33 years old	> 60% between 16 and 25 years old
Married/ partner	NA	58.5%	58%
Children	NA	21.5%	17% have one or more children

[a] *Source:* http://www.stanford.edu/group/floss-us/report/FLOSS-US-Report.pdf.

marizes the extant literature on the various motivations that contribute to an individual developer's decision to stay with or leave a project.

About Open-Source Software Developers

Between 2001 and 2005, several surveys investigated the characteristics and motivations of OSS developers. The survey results are quite similar. Table 3.1 summarizes some of the demographic attributes from these studies (for a list of more pre-2005 studies, see David and Shapiro 2008, 372). As shown in table 3.1, open-source developers are almost all male, reflecting the significant gender gap in the computer science field (see, e.g., Margolis and Fisher 2002). Developers also are young on average, the majority of them are married, and many have children.

Table 3.1 does not report where developers live; Ghosh (2006), however, studied the geographic distribution of OSS developers. Using two of the large surveys of OSS developers (n = 4,282), Ghosh reports that three-fifths of the developers live in the European Union, one-fifth in North America, and (roughly) the last fifth reside in other countries. Noting that the surveys may be subject to geographic bias, Ghosh's team also analyzed users of the major OSS hosting site SF from year-end 2002 to 2006. The authors found results similar to their survey data: 42 percent of the users are from Europe, 39 percent are from the United States, 7 percent are from Latin America, 4 percent are from Asia, and 8 percent are from other countries. They also observe that because of language issues, SF probably underrepresents OSS activity from China, Japan, and other East Asian countries.

We also know from our discussion in chapter 2 that OSS developers can be either paid staff or volunteers. This fact is important, because the paid/volunteer distinction

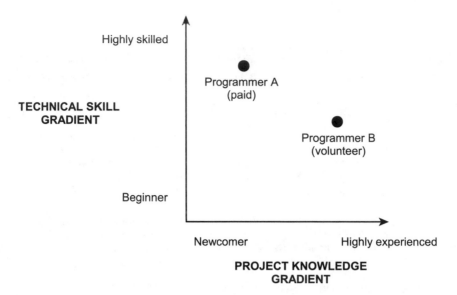

Figure 3.3

Three key developer attributes: Paid/volunteer, project knowledge, and technical skill

likely plays an influential role in whether a programmer continues to contribute to a project or decides to leave it. But the paid/volunteer dichotomy is only one of several attributes related to OSS programmers, and this distinction is only one way to categorize developers and begin to think about their motivations.

There are two other essential ways of thinking about "developer types," either in relation to their experience with the project or technical skill levels (Schweik and English 2007). Unlike the binary choice of volunteer versus paid, project experience and technical skill fall along a spectrum from newcomer to highly experienced in the former, and beginner to highly skilled in the latter (figure 3.3). Theoretically, any given OSS programmer on any project can be placed on a two-dimensional plane based on these attributes. We might, for instance, find a paid project developer who is highly skilled in the use of some relevant programming language (e.g., PhP or C++) or some relevant database package, but is also relatively new to the specific OSS project and thus inexperienced in this case. This describes Programmer A in figure 3.3. Another example in the same figure might be Programmer B, who was one of the initial launchers (David and Rullani 2006) of a project and continues to work on it, but has little formal programming training and possesses less technical skill compared to Programmer A.

It is reasonable to expect that developers who possess both a high technical skill level and considerable experience with the project will be key contributors. Using Linux, one of the most popular and most studied FOSS cases, Bert Dempsey and his colleagues (2002) found that the majority of code came from just over 2 percent of the thousands of people who have made contributions. In their study of Apache and Mozilla development, Audris Mockus, Roy Fielding, and James Herbsleb (2002) discovered that a relatively small, core group of people produced about 80 percent of the new functionality for these products.

In this same vein, scholars often describe OSS projects as meritocracies (O'Mahony and Ferraro 2007, 1082) that formally or informally recognize project leaders and core members (Ye et al. 2005), or "committers," who hold the right to add or change code in the project code repository because of their achievements (Holck and Jørgensen 2005; Riehle 2007). In these meritocracies, developers have had to demonstrate technical competence by providing high-quality contributions for some time before being "promoted" to committer status (Holck and Jørgensen 2005; Mockus, Fielding, and Herbsleb 2002). Most committers on OSS projects consequently will likely fall in the upper-right quadrant of figure 3.3, representing highly skilled, highly experienced developers.

OSS developers, in summary, tend to be mostly male and come from all over the world. From a career standpoint, they are relatively young. They can have some recognized formal position of authority on the project or can contribute infrequently (David and Rullani 2006). They can be volunteer or paid staff, highly skilled programmers or completely new to programming, and knowledgeable about the project or just beginning to familiarize themselves with it. But since the majority of OSS developers are not paid, the question remains, Why do they invest their time and effort?

Motivations and Innovation

The important work by von Hippel and von Krogh (2003) and subsequent work by von Hippel (2005a, 2005b) on user-centered innovation networks provides a good introduction to other motivations developers might have for participating in OSS. In this work, particularly the former one, the authors discuss the two dominant approaches or models used to induce innovation—what they refer to as the private investment and collective action models.

In the private investment model, which is the model of proprietary software, societies encourage innovation through the establishment of intellectual property law (e.g., patents, copyrights, and trade secrets), and the major incentive used to induce innovation is monetary profit. The assumption here is that keeping the innovation secret allows the innovator to make money through the sale of this innovation, with its underlying logic treated as proprietary. On the other hand, the protection of the innovation's logic results in society as a whole losing access to the knowledge as well as innovative ideas.

Alternatively, in the collective action model, the innovation is treated as a public good. The innovator is required to provide the innovation to a "knowledge commons" and relinquish control over it. The obvious example of this is the way most scientific research operates, at least in the academic or public sphere. By making knowledge and innovation freely available, society as a whole benefits because others can easily build on the innovation. But without the private incentives to help motivate innovators, why would people innovate? Some may prefer to wait and see what others produce, and then use that innovation rather than take the initiative to contribute themselves. Economists call this waiting tactic "free riding" (Olson 1965).

As von Hippel and von Krogh (2003) note, a solution to the free rider problem is to create some other incentive to encourage contributions back to the knowledge commons. These incentives could be monetary, reputational, or legal, such as a licensing requirement mandating that new derivatives of the innovation go into the commons, as is done in relation to OSS. Societies provide subsidies like grants to fund basic research for this reason. In academics, universities actively hire and encourage faculty to contribute to their fields, following the norms of reciprocity and knowledge sharing found in science. Faculty members receive promotions in part because of the reputation they gain in their intellectual fields.

But what von Hippel and von Krogh (2003) argue is that neither of the above models captures what is going on in OSS commons. Some projects are comprised of all volunteers who are working on a project that is of specific use to them—that is, they are users of the software they are developing. These developers could follow the private investment model, and claim proprietary rights over their innovation and try to sell it. But instead they decide to freely reveal it (e.g., place it on SF). Von Hippel and von Krogh (2003) introduce a middle ground that provides an explanation for what we are witnessing in OSS: the "private-collective" model of innovation. Essentially, by freely revealing an innovation in a commons, the innovators produce both a public good and private benefits, as explained more in the following paragraphs. In this situation, the private investment and collective action models coexist. Key to this is that several shared assumptions need to be dropped.

First, von Hippel and von Krogh (2003) contend that we should not assume that by freely revealing an innovation, an innovator will forfeit all potential chances for some private profit. In certain conditions, free revealing may "actually result in a net gain in private profit for the innovator" (von Hippel and von Krogh 2003, 216), and this indeed appears to be the case in OSS. Recall the examples in chapter 2 of how businesses are now making a profit by working with OSS technologies.

Second, we should not assume that in the collective action model, free riders and people who create the innovation receive equal benefits. The innovator instead enjoys benefits that the free rider cannot, because the innovator gets software code that is directly relevant to their needs, and the free rider may not. In addition, the innovator may have learned some new skills in the process, while the free rider, who only uses the code, will not gain these skills. The innovator may reap reputation rewards if the innovation is embraced and used by the broader community, which is a private gain. They might also gain new potential work opportunities as a result of this reputation or awareness in the community of their technical expertise; free riders would not achieve the same benefit. Private innovators often will gain significantly by freely revealing their codes. And importantly, the innovator will be able to take advantage of any or all of the other innovations that are developed by others on the project that are of use to them. Why, in short, do programmers contribute to OSS? As von Hippel and von Krogh (2003, 217) succinctly put it, "Programmers contribute freely to the provision of [an OSS commons] because they garner private benefits from doing so."

More Motivations

Turning now to the question of what else motivates developers to contribute, as stated above, we assume that OSS developers are boundedly rational human beings who make the best choices they can about whether to launch or join an OSS project under conditions of incomplete information (Simon 1955; Tversky and Kahneman 1990; Ostrom 1998).

We noted earlier that much of the OSS research in the late 1990s and early 2000s focused on the volunteer nature of OSS collaborations as well as the question of why volunteers devote free time and give up their intellectual property (Ghosh 1998; Lerner and Tirole 2000; Hars and Ou 2001; Kogut and Metiu 2001; Lakhani and von Hippel 2003).[4] A relatively large set of literature addresses this issue, with some excellent and fairly recent work describing or summarizing the reasons for volunteering (e.g., Ghosh 2005; Lakhani and Wolf 2005; David and Shapiro 2008), and by now, these reasons are well understood. Nevertheless, because OSS developers are our key element of analysis, and the central question is why they stay or leave projects, it is necessary to review these motivations.

To best connect to the analytic approach we are using—the IAD framework—we find the work of Steven Weber (2004) (especially chapter 4 on microfoundations), Josh Lerner and Jean Tirole (2005), von Hippel and von Krogh (2003), and Paul David and Joseph Shapiro (2008) particularly useful. Weber (2004) and Lerner and Tirole (2005) utilize a cost-benefit framework for considering the motivations of OSS developers. Consistent with what we suggested earlier related to bounded rationality, these scholars contend that prior to a decision to join or initiate an OSS commons, a developer will undertake some kind of internal calculation to assess the net benefit they will receive in return for their efforts on the project.[5] Lerner and Tirole (2005) argue that internally, this decision-making logic can be explained in this manner: the net benefit a participant receives is equal to the current benefits of participating in the open-source commons, minus the current costs of participating, plus delayed payoffs minus delayed costs. One of the reasons we emphasized the different types of developers (volunteer, paid, skilled at various levels, and experienced) in figure 3.3 is because the cost-benefit logic will vary across these categories.

Current Benefits: Solving a Need

Solving a specific software need or getting a specific need resolved, such as a fix to a bug, is a major motivation for people to participate in OSS projects. This idea captures one of the major concepts thought to drive much of the OSS world: "user-driven innovation" (von Hippel 2005a, 2005b). Von Hippel and von Krogh (2003, 214) note, "In the case of OSS projects, the bulk of all contributions . . . are made by developers that are *users* of that software." Von Hippel (2005b, 271) cites two surveys of OSS developers that lend support to this statement. In the first case, a study done in 2000 on Linux-kernel developers (now reported in Hertel, Niedener, and Hermann 2003), the researchers found that the highest-ranked benefit for participating was "facilitating my work due to better software." In a study done five years later by Karim Lakhani and Robert Wolf (2005, 12; emphasis added), covering more than nine thousand OSS projects, the researchers report that "user needs of the software, both work and nonwork-related, *together* constitute the overwhelming reason for contribution and participation."

David and Shapiro (2008, 376) note that 80 percent of the FLOSS-US survey respondents expected that the software they were contributing to would be personally useful. Viewing this from the vantage point of a paid programmer, Lerner and Tirole (2005, 57) point out that IT staff might reap some job-related rewards if they fix a problem with a particular OSS product they use in their business. Similarly, volunteers would receive some personal satisfaction from fixing broken code they need for their own reasons.

Current Benefits: Enjoyment

One of the immediate benefits often mentioned in studies of OSS is the enjoyment that participants receive from the activity, and while this feeling may apply to both paid and volunteer programmers, it is most likely stronger in the latter. In their survey of OSS developers, Lakhani and Wolf (2005) report that enjoyment or creativity was the strongest motivator for people participating in an OSS project. The first of eight general principles of what OSS developers do, articulated by Weber (2004, 73), captures the enjoyment benefit: "Make it interesting and make sure it happens." Weber argues that there is a natural bias toward choosing programming work that is interesting, significant, and "cool." Some people look for challenges that require them to solve a problem in a unique or elegant way. This element of volunteers' contributing "heavy" intellectual thinking to an OSS project is encompassed in the general concept of "serious leisure," a phrase coined by Robert Stebbins (2001, 54):[6]

"Serious leisure" . . . is the steady pursuit of an amateur, hobbyist, or career volunteer activity that captivates its participants with its complexity and many challenges. It is profound, long-lasting, and invariably based on substantial skill, knowledge, or experience, if not on a combination of these three. It also requires perseverance to a greater or lesser degree. In the course of gaining and expressing these acquisitions as well as searching for the special rewards this leisure can offer, amateurs, hobbyists, and volunteers get the sense that they are pursuing a career, not unlike the ones pursued in the more evolved, high-level occupations. But there is no significant remuneration—in fact, there is usually no remuneration at all.

Stebbins goes on here to remark that volunteers also receive "social rewards" through their participation in projects. Some of these rewards fall under the current benefit category, some under "delayed benefits" (described below), and some fit in both categories. One such social reward is meeting and interacting with people with similar interests as well as participating in a group project with them. A second social reward is a sense of accomplishment when the group achieves something significant. A new software release could fall under this category. A third social benefit received, in both the current and longer time frames, is a sense of being part of a collectivity, having contributed something of value, and being needed. All of these components, we hold, are connected to the emotion of "enjoyment" for contributors to OSS projects.

Current Benefits: Learning and Skill Building

Learning and skill building is an important benefit that relates to both current benefits and delayed benefits. For both volunteers and paid developers, particularly ones with fewer skills, participating in a project of interest will immediately generate some skill-building benefits. In the short term, this might be reading some code and learning a certain technique or specific ways to write in a programming language. This short-term benefit is closely linked to the benefit of getting a need resolved, and the programmer may not even realize the short-term learning. But these types of benefits exist and can be substantial (Von Hippel and Von Krogh 2003).

Current Benefits: Signaling and/or Ego Gratification

As we will describe more thoroughly in the next section, signaling means that developers participate in part to demonstrate to others the skills or experience they possess, or to "prove their worth" (Weber 2004, 142). Signaling provides more delayed than immediate benefits and consists of three components (discussed below). One component, ego gratification, has both immediate and delayed benefits. Ego gratification defines the need some programmers may have for recognition from their peers.

We have witnessed this personally in email dialogues among participants who are subscribed to our local "Linux User Group." These participants take on a particular problem encountered by someone on this list with the partial goal of demonstrating to the group that they are capable of solving the technical problem, or can solve the problem in an elegant way. From this perspective, participation in OSS may be a competitive game that for some, provides ego-boosting benefits both immediately and over the long term.

Current Benefits: Hacker Ethic, Reciprocity and Helping the OS Cause

In Raymond's famous book *The Cathedral and the Bazaar* (2001: 65), he refers to OSS as a "gift culture," where altruism significantly motivates participants. More recently, Lakhani and Wolf (2005) argue that in some circumstances, a sense of obligation or the norm of reciprocity motivates programmers to contribute. They note that in programming circles, the label hacker is like a badge of honor that carries with it certain standards of behavior: having fun, solving challenging programming problems, and sharing software solutions.[7] This hacker ethic (Himanen 2001) motivates some to contribute code.

Related to this is the slightly different concept of reciprocity (one element of the broader notion of social capital discussed more in chapter 4), which can also be a motivating factor in some situations. It's the "pay-it-forward" principle—contribute with a code fix, some new code, or in some other way as a means of giving back to the same community that helped you solve a problem you faced. This norm is what drives some of the hacker ethic, but it is a standard behavior found outside hacker social circles as well.

From a broader perspective and yet connected to the reciprocity idea, some developers believe that software should be treated as a public good, and be open and accessible to anyone. Stallman made this argument in the mid-1980s, leading to the start of libre OSS as a "social movement" (FSF 2008). Because of a desire to further this ideology and compete against dominant proprietary software, many OSS developers felt motivated to create some of the most important OSS, such as the GNU-Linux operating system (Chakravarty, Haruvy, and Wu 2007).

These concepts have real-world support. In a 2001 study of 684 OSS developers, Lakhani and Wolf (2005:15) found that nearly one-third of the participants agreed with the idea that "software should be open," and that this was a motivating factor for why they contribute code. The same study discovered that about the same percentage of respondents felt motivated by a sense of obligation—a desire to give back to the communities that helped them. Finally, Lakhani and Wolf found that a large percentage of their respondents consider themselves to be hackers.

Delayed Benefits: Learning and Skill Building

As suggested above, learning and skill building can also contribute to longer-term benefits that a programmer might consider in contemplating work on an OSS project. In particular, people who fall in the lower or middle ranges in terms of programming skill or experience, as either volunteer or paid participants, may see it as worthwhile to expend the time to learn a project's tools and architecture as long as they think the educational benefits might aid them in the future. The longer-term benefit might be future employment opportunities. In other instances, it might be an opportunity to hone better skills in pursuit of their serious leisure. Yet the delayed benefits here are likely more prominent in the case of volunteer as compared to paid programmers, because volunteers have total freedom in choosing the project they want to work on and thus the skills they seek to hone. This is akin to the idea of college students taking unpaid internships in order to build skills and experience for future jobs in that field.

Delayed Benefits: Signaling

As mentioned above, signaling is another incentive thought to drive some developers to participate in OSS projects (Lerner and Tirole 2005). Signaling has several components, including ego gratification, as noted earlier, but also involves a "career-concern incentive" and a "reputation incentive." The career-concern incentive has to do with people wishing to signal their skills for potential future employment opportunities or possible shares in companies that promote or support OSS products, or to increase the likelihood of securing venture capital. This component applies potentially to both volunteer and paid developers. The reputation incentive was emphasized by Weber (2004, 141) and is seen as closely related to ego gratification, but separable. Weber contends that an interest in what others in a community feel about your work can be important in reinforcing your feelings that your work is of high quality. This can help to strengthen one's own sense that the work being done is useful and crucial.

Current and Delayed Costs: Opportunity Cost of Time

Until now, we've focused on the benefits that an OSS developer might receive from participation in a project. But what about the costs they may incur? In the OSS literature, the main current expense that developers face is the "opportunity cost of time" (Lerner and Tirole 2005, 102). Opportunity cost means that developers lose the benefits they might have received by working on something else, and this "loss" can be viewed as a cost. Weber (2004, 151) puts it this way: "Meaning and value depend on human mind space and the commitment of time and energy by very smart people to a creative enterprise. And the time, energy and brain power of smart, creative people are not abundant."

The current opportunity cost of the use of this valuable time differs between volunteer and paid participants. For volunteer developers, the current expense can be quantified monetarily: they lose the opportunity to use that time to earn compensation in some other endeavor. Lakhani and Wolf (2005) surveyed 684 developers in 287 FOSS projects and reported that volunteer programmers on average worked 11.7

hours per week. For some highly skilled developers, this means they are giving up a sizable amount of money to work on a project.

According to Lerner and Tirole (2005), the current opportunity cost for paid programmers with a firm or some other organization is not the loss of monetary compensation but rather (in some cases) the cost of not focusing on the primary mission. These authors offer the example of a programmer in academia who uses their work time to contribute to an OSS project as opposed to projects that contribute more directly to their core university mission. But this assumption might be changing. As we discussed in chapter 2, firms are more actively contributing human resources to OSS projects, in part because the projects are considered directly related to the organizations' core mission. This is the situation at IBM, for example, when it pays programmers to contribute to Linux or Eclipse (Shah, Wagstrom, and Herbsleb 2008).

Current and Delayed Costs: Emotional Distress

In his explication of serious leisure, Stebbins (2001) points out other costs that detract from the potential enjoyment that a developer might receive. And while Stebbins is describing the emotions of volunteers, these feelings are applicable to paid developers as well. First, some developers may be sharply disappointed if some code they contribute isn't seen by others on the team as worthy of going into the next release. This delayed cost might dilute some of the benefits received (e.g., reputational or ego). Second, conflicts undoubtedly occur in OSS projects, as they do in other collective efforts. These conflicts may arise from some controversial architectural direction or other policies related to project's course. Third, relatively minor dislikes or frustrations may arise during a project, often under circumstances where a team member demonstrates some annoying behavior, or when the team faces some kind of unpleasant discussion or circumstance. Disappointments, conflicts, and other discord that might occur all may reduce the pleasure in participating and add stress to developers' lives.

To wrap up our key unit of analysis section, we provide seven testable hypotheses in table 3.2 based on the various motivations reported above. These hypotheses are related to the community attributes in the IAD framework—hence the labels H-C1 through H-C5, where *H* stands for hypothesis and *C* represents community attribute.

Summary

At this juncture, we are halfway through part II and have become familiar with both individual OSS developers and the environments in which they find themselves. OSS developers are the key element in our research, yet we have shown that there are many different "species" of developers in our ecosystem. Based on this discussion, we con-

Table 3.2

Testable hypotheses (H) about OSS commons community attributes (C)

The hypotheses below are all community attributes in the IAD framework because they are about the people involved in OSS projects

Open-source commons will be more successful when (described in the "Motivations and Innovation" section above)

H-C1: the software product developers are also the users of that product (von Hippel's user-driven innovation hypothesis, described in the "About Open-Source Software Developers" section above)

H-C2: some of the developers are paid participants or make money through products and/or services that depend on the software

H-C3: the project provides substantial enjoyment for the developers (especially volunteers) who participate (the serious leisure hypothesis)

H-C4a: the team's programmers are highly skilled (described in the "More Motivations" section above)

H-C4b: the project offers opportunities for developers to learn new skills

H-C4c: the project affords opportunities for developers to signal their skills to others

H-C5: the project contributes or adds functionality to core OSS technologies related to the open-source movement (the helping the OSS cause hypothesis)

---

structed the two research questions in chapter 2 and seven new hypotheses shown in table 3.2, but because of the complexity of the OSS puzzle, there are many more issues and observations to come.

This chapter began with the IAD framework, which we put to use by describing OSS project trajectories in the context of its outcomes. Surveys taught us more about who developers are and where they live. We also learned that OSS developers have many motivations to work within the private-collective model of innovation as opposed to the private investment model, and we scrutinized OSS developers' motivations for laboring with or without pay.

Despite the fact that OSS developers are the critical element in our analysis, they are not the only one. The technological attributes of the software as well as the attributes of the community created when developers, users, and other participants work together also influence success and abandonment. Are projects with simple software code more likely to succeed? Could developers become leaders, and would it matter? Do software teams ever get together in the real world versus the virtual one of the Internet? Although we have come a long way, we still have more ground to cover before we will be satisfied that we have considered all the factors that might affect the success and abandonment of OSS commons.

4 Technological and Community Attributes

with Meelis Kitsing

During the first two years of our five-year research endeavor we studied literature, uncovering factors that might influence the success or abandonment of OSS commons, and developing hypotheses and research questions. At the same time, we were carefully considering how to define success and abandonment (see chapter 7) We were motivated by a strong desire to understand the quite-amazing OSS phenomena that we were watching evolve, and we continue to illuminate our early steps in that process of discovery in this chapter.

In chapter 3, we used the term technological attributes to refer to a set of variables related to the OSS itself or the technological infrastructure needed to coordinate an OSS team. We used the term community attributes to describe the set of variables linked to the relationships among people who are engaged in developing this software, along with the project's financial and marketing aspects. In this chapter, we elaborate on these concepts. Although most of the attributes discussed below are external to the OSS developer, they all may influence whether a developer chooses to stay with or leave a project. Many of the attributes below also probably influence the quantity and quality of a developer's work. Although there are many factors that can affect the success and abandonment of OSS commons, as we've stressed already, the OSS developer remains the key element in our study.

Technological Attributes of OSS Commons

As we continued to review literature, we identified a number of technological factors that could be important in explaining the success or abandonment of OSS commons. These factors fall into a number of categories, including software requirements, design modularity, granularity, and complexity, product utility, competition, and collaborative infrastructure.

Software Requirements

In the 1980s, author Schweik worked as a programmer for IBM. The software development process at IBM followed the so-called waterfall model and had many phases: requirements, design, implementation, installation, operation, and maintenance (see Hoffer, George, and Valacich 2001). Scholars who studied information systems (IS) discovered long ago that problems in the requirements phase—the early stages where project goals, objectives, and general needs and functions are defined—can be critical in the success or failure of traditional IS projects. Consequently, the classic requirements-gathering process evolved to include eliciting requirements, modeling them formally, analyzing and validating them for completeness, and communicating the results (Kotonya and Sommerville 1998). One study (Cole 1995, cited in Ewusi-Mensah 2003, 51–52) reported that the failure to fully specify project objectives was the most significant factor leading to the abandonment of traditional software projects. The failure to completely lay out objectives can lead to changing requirements during the project's design or implementation phase, and in turn, these changing requirements tend to increase the cost, push back the planned schedule, and frustrate developers because they have to go back and adjust work they often think is complete (Ewusi-Mensah 2003).

An interesting element of the OSS development paradigm is that it does not appear to follow this classic approach. Walt Scacchi (2002) conducted an important ethnographic study looking at the requirements-gathering process in four types of OSS projects: networked gaming, Web/Internet, X-ray astronomy, and academic software design research. He found that in these communities, the functional and nonfunctional requirements were elicited, specified, analyzed, and validated through eight types of mechanisms—"informalisms," as Scacchi (p. 27) calls them—to juxtapose them to the formal methods used in traditional requirements gathering. The eight informalisms include community communications—email lists, bulletin boards, and to a lesser extent Internet Relay Chat (IRC); scenarios shared through screenshot images or Web page mock-ups; online "how-to" guides or "frequently asked questions"; external publications describing the software; open descriptions on the software Web site; bug-tracking systems; traditional documentation for end users; and mechanisms incorporated into the project to allow further extension of the software (such as scripting languages). Related to bug-tracking systems, Jesper Holck and Niels Jørgensen (2005, 8) report that these act as "dynamic requirement specifications," where users frequently record new enhancements rather than errors.

The main point that Scacchi (2002) makes is that OSS projects define and document requirements through these eight informalisms, instead of embracing classic and formal requirements-gathering approaches. But while requirements in an OSS commons can be informal, "successful projects seem to start with a vision and often an artifact (e.g., a prototype) that embodies that vision—at least in spirit. This seems to be the preferred way of communicating top-level requirements to the community" (Weinstock and Hissam 2005, 149). Following the vision or prototype, developers engage in a process of listening to users via communication channels, and making an effort to "release early and often" continues this dynamic, informal, requirements process (Weinstock and Hissam 2005; Scacchi 2003).

In short, the IS field tells us that good requirements gathering with end user involvement is essential to a successful project, and that articulating the project's plan and vision early to developers and users is a critical part of the process. This latter point has also been emphasized in literature about virtual teams (see Hinds and Weisband 2003). OSS teams follow a more informal, iterative process of requirements compared to traditional settings. Our discussion here leads to one theoretically based testable hypothesis—H-P1—listed under software requirements in table 4.1.

Software Design: Modularity, Granularity, and Complexity

Closely related to requirements gathering is the initial OSS product's design, which is thought to be another important factor toward longer-term success (Manley 2000; Hissam et al. 2001). OSS literature commonly refers to the software's modularity as a key design attribute (O'Reilly 1999; Narduzzo and Rossi 2005). From a general systems perspective, Melissa Schilling (2000, 312) defines modularity as "a continuum describing the degree to which a system's components can be separated and recombined." Benkler (2006, 100) emphasizes this separation such that components can be worked on independently before putting them back together again. Charles Weinstock and Scott Hissam (2005, 148) note, "A well-modularized system . . . allows contributors to carve off chunks on which they can work." The original authors of the OSS packages Linux and Perl agree, and have stated that their projects' successes are partly due to modularity early in their design, making it easier for others to contribute (O'Reilly 1999; Deek and McHugh 2007). The concept of modularity applies to many areas, including product design, manufacturing systems, or in this case, OSS. Modularity also pertains to organizations, and task decomposition has been considered a critical organizational principle for fifty years, if not longer (March and Simon 1958). Both product and task modularity apply in the context of OSS commons.

Another attribute of modularity is its granularity, which describes "the size of the modules, in terms of the time and effort that an individual must invest in producing them" (Benkler 2006, 100). Granularity is a crucial concept in peer-production commons because it influences people's decisions on whether to contribute. As Benkler goes on to explain, task granularity "sets the smallest possible individual investment necessary to participate in a project," and "if this investment is sufficiently low, then 'incentives' for producing that component of a modular project can be of trivial magnitude." Benkler uses Wikibooks as an example to highlight the importance of

Table 4.1
Technological (T) attributes of OSS commons: Research questions (RQ) and testable hypotheses
(H) (where possible)

Software requirements

H-T1: OSS commons will be more often successful when the project had a relatively clearly
defined vision and mechanism to communicate this vision early in the project's life, before
moving to the growth stage

Software design: modularity, granularity, and complexity

OSS commons will be more frequently successful when

H-T2a: the initial software design accounts for, up front, a modular design

H-T2b: they provide opportunities for people to contribute in small ways (fine-scale task
granularity)

H-T2c: the software is not initially developed and supported under a closed-source, proprietary
setting, and then relicensed as OSS later

H-T2d: the software complexity is relatively low when initially going public (e.g., moving into
the growth stage in figure 3.2).

Product utility

OSS commons will be more often successful when

H-T3a: the software produced has higher utility as perceived by the end user community

H-T3b: the software produced is a component of what could be considered critical or
foundational infrastructure (e.g., operating systems)

H-T3c: the software being developed is built on hot, "preferred technologies" (e.g., certain
programming languages) that the developer community wants to use and learn

Competition

H-T4: OSS commons will be more frequently successful when there are few alternative
software projects available (limited or no competition)

Collaborative infrastructure

RQ-T1: What collaborative technologies are utilized in successful OSS commons? Is there a
certain suite of technologies or configurations that are more often found in OSS success cases?
Or does the configuration not seem to matter?

---

fine granularity. Contributors have not embraced Wikibooks, a project requiring a
large-grained effort to write a book, as much as they have done so with Wikipedia, a
smaller-grained effort to write encyclopedia articles.

In OSS commons, granularity will probably be coarser in initiation stage projects
than in growth stage ones, because projects in the early stages will need to have more
significant amounts of code written. Or in cases where a project is in an early stage
but is working with formerly proprietary spinout code, the difficulty of reading and
understanding a sizable existing code base also might increase the granularity of tasks.
As Weinstock and Hissam (2005, 148) observe, "Huge, monolithic software does not
lend itself very well to the OSS model. Such software requires too much upfront intellectual investment to learn the software's architecture, which can be daunting to many

potential contributors." In short, the key question regarding granularity is to what degree a project provides a task that matches the time people have available to contribute.

Up until now, we have considered the benefits of modularity. Yet Brian Fitzgerald (2005) notes that modularity can have negative consequences, particularly when it becomes excessive. Fitzgerald stresses the challenge of designing a highly modular product while simultaneously minimizing the number of dependencies between modules. Circumstances where many dependencies exist can result in more difficult maintenance over the longer term, especially when modules contain hard-coded references to the data structures and variables established in other modules. This kind of excessive modularity is one form of complexity in software design. Complexity is an issue found in natural resource commons as well. Situations where participants share a large, complex natural resource make it difficult for people to have a common understanding with regard to resource dynamics (Ostrom et al. 1999). In such settings, the cost and effort to manage the resource is higher. The idea of being excessively modular and complex suggests that similar problems may exist in some OSS settings, making them harder to manage.

Our discussion in this section leads to four hypotheses—H-T2a, H-T2b, H-T2c, and H-T2d—presented under design modularity, granularity, and complexity in table 4.1.

Product Utility

Studies in natural resource commons show that in order for people to participate in commons-related management activities, they must perceive a benefit for doing so (Ostrom et al. 1999). In our study, the "resource" commons is OSS, and "people" refers to the broad community using the software, especially the developers engaged in the maintenance and development of that software. Voicing a similar idea, Weinstock and Hissam (2005, 157) remark that one of the key factors leading to successful OSS projects is that the software "provides a general community service." By this they mean that if the software isn't supplying something that people need, no one will want to use it or be interested in developing it. While this is an obvious statement, it is also true. Nevertheless, these authors raise a utility-related proposition that may not be so apparent. They also argue that more successful projects are ones that are seen as "technically cool" by the developers involved. They stress that there is a higher likelihood of finding an OSS "device driver for a graphics card than an accounting package" (ibid.).[1] The idea of a useful product, it seems, relates to software being both something that people want and need, but also interesting and challenging to a body of potential developers.

Weinstock and Hissam (2005) cite research by Joseph Feller and Fitzgerald reporting that a higher percentage of operational OSS projects fell into several project types: Internet applications (browsers, servers, and clients), system and system development applications (e.g., drivers for devices, code generators, and projected related to operating systems), and game and entertainment software. Given that two of the three items pertain to computing infrastructure, this list suggests that "useful software" in this context might tend to be more technical, "critical infrastructure" projects. Projects that contribute to building functionality in OSS-related platforms (e.g., the Linux operating system, windowing systems such as X-windows, or desktop environments like Gnome or KDE; see Deek and McHugh 2007, 80–118) may be more actively developed than end user applications because of their more critical or foundational need.

Finally, utility has another dimension when taken from a developer's perspective. In chapter 3 we talked about learning as a motivating factor for some developers. The idea that being technically cool (Weinstock and Hissam 2005) is a motivator for developers may have to do with the kind of software under development, but also could relate to the type of technical learning they might gain from participating on that project. From that perspective, a useful project for a developer might be one that is being built using a technology they wish to learn (e.g., a programming language or database software).

The above discussion leads to three testable hypotheses—H-T3a, H-T3b, and H-T3c—listed under product utility in table 4.1.

Competition

The degree to which a project faces competition is another variable we place in the technological attribute category. We've seen lots of examples where a project introduces a new technology or approach, and gains significant use of the software because there is, for the moment, no competition. Even a project with great ideas, however, may be subject to the pressures of abandonment if it faces a seriously competitive environment—meaning lots of other projects creating products with similar functionality. An OSS project will undoubtedly have more difficulty avoiding abandonment if it is met with severe competition from lots of other competing OSS and commercial packages.[2] Our hypothesis is that projects facing stiff competition will more likely become abandoned compared to those that face limited (or no) competition (table 4.1, H-T4).

Collaborative Infrastructure

OSS projects can utilize a variety of technologies for team coordination (Dube and Pare 2001; Kelly and Jones 2001; Serrano and Ciordia 2005). As far as we can tell, no one has examined whether the use of certain technologies over other ones matters in determining project success or abandonment. Part of the reason for this is that many projects use the same platform(s) for coordination, such as SF. The "standard" technologies that may be used include a code repository and version control system; a mechanism for reporting and tracking errors (bugs), and their fixes in the code; informal communication channels (e.g., mailing lists or forums); and a project Web site (Holck and Jørgensen 2005). Fadi Deek and James McHugh (2007, 119–158) provide an excellent history and summary of these technologies. So does Karl Fogel (2006, 28–55). Much of what we write below is based on these authors' work.

Code Repository and Versioning Systems

Anyone who has worked in collaboration with others on a digital product, such as cowriting a document, knows the challenges that can be encountered in keeping track of the latest version and the effort it takes to make sure to include people's most recent work. In team writing, word processing tools such as track changes in Microsoft Word or Open Office Writer are indispensable. Programmers working in OSS commons face similar issues in writing code. Version control systems have been developed to assist in managing the distributed work and ensuring that no one overwrites someone else's code. In other words, these Internet-based systems allow multiple programmers to work on the same software package concurrently, while keeping track of the code modifications.

Historically, the most widely used versioning system is the OSS Concurrent Versions System (CVS), introduced in the late 1980s and still in use today. CVS acts as a repository of the latest code as well as past releases (Asklund and Bendix 2002), and a collaborative management tool in that it guards against programmers working concurrently on the same code and inadvertently overwriting one another's work. CVS provides additional tools to help the programming team analyze and manage collaborative work with commands such as "diff" (compare sets of code for differences), "patch" (introduce a change to some code), and "commit" (store changes into the code library). Fogel and Moshe Bar (2003) as well as Deek and McHugh (2007, 119–158) offer more detail on these and other CVS functions. While CVS is still widely in use (for example, it is available on the large OSS project-hosting site SF), it certainly isn't the only tool employed. Subversion, which could be considered the next-generation CVS, is another tool. Some of the original CVS developers worked on Subversion, with the goals of cleaning up some of the design flaws in CVS and eventually having Subversion replace it (Deek and McHugh 2007). CVS and Subversion are versioning systems that follow the client-server approach, where changes are uploaded to the server from distributed developers. There are also decentralized versioning systems, such as BitKeeper, Monotone, Codeville, and Git.

The details of these systems are unnecessary for our purposes here, but there are two points worth noting. First, every OSS common that involves multiple people will need some form of a versioning system, and this review shows that there are a number of options. Whether the particular one used matters in project success or abandonment is an open question, but we have some evidence that they do matter. In the case of BitKeeper and the Linux project, for instance, Linus Torvalds said that BitKeeper made him "more than twice as productive" in the project's management (cited in Deek and McHugh 2007, 148). This suggests that the type of version control may matter when large teams are being coordinated. Second, rules may be embedded or automated in the versioning system itself, helping to keep the collaboration running smoothly. One clear embedded rule in CVS is that only certain people have authority to commit code into the repository. Because these rules are codified in the versioning system, the security logic in the system influences how teams are managed.[3]

Fogel (2006, 42) describes another example of codified rules related to version control:

Every commit to the repository should generate an email showing who made the change, when they made it, what files and directories changed, and how they changed. The email should go to a special mailing list devoted to commit emails, separate from the mailing lists to which humans post. Developers and other interested parties should be encouraged to subscribe to the commits list, as it is the most effective way to keep up with what's happening in the project at the code level.

This technique helps to protect the project from a problematic commit of code, where code is updated that isn't in sync with other programmers' ideas. Having a versioning system allows an emerging conflict to be diffused early through a rollback to the previous version. One of the projects we discuss in a later chapter has an automated system in place that triggers code quality-assessment procedures (also automated). Some social norms or rules that in the past may have been conducted by humans perhaps are now automated and conducted by computers. We will return to these issues of rules in chapter 5.

Bug Tracking

Bug tracking is the general term for an established system for logging and managing the status of either errors in the code or suggested improvements to the software (for a description of the "classic" bug life cycle, see Fogel 2006, 46–47). These systems typically record information related to each entry, including a description of the bug or enhancement, the current status (e.g., open, assigned, or closed), the severity and/ or priority metric, the originator of the bug, and the person assigned to look into the solution or develop the new enhancement (Holck and Jørgensen 2005). Fogel (2006, 16) emphasizes bug tracking as a signal of project health:

The importance of a bug tracking system lies not only in its usefulness to developers, but in what it signifies for project observers. For many people, an accessible bug database is one of the strongest signs that a project should be taken seriously. Furthermore, the higher the number of bugs in the database, the better the project looks. This might seem counterintuitive, but remember that the number of bugs recorded really depends on three things: the absolute number of bugs present in the software, the number of users using the software, and the convenience with which those users can register new bugs. Of these three factors, the latter two are more significant than the first. Any software of sufficient size and complexity has an essentially arbitrary number of bugs waiting to be discovered. The real question is, how well will the project do at recording and prioritizing those bugs? A project with a large and well-maintained bug database (meaning bugs are responded to promptly, duplicate bugs are unified, etc.) therefore makes a better impression than a project with no bug database, or a nearly empty database.

Bug-tracking systems can be quite sophisticated. For example, the popular Bugzilla allows bugs to be marked as something that needs to be fixed before the next release, and allows the bug entries to be organized in a hierarchical fashion, thereby showing bugs that have some connection or relationship to other bugs. Moreover, depending on how these systems are used, they provide a project management or coordination function. This aspect presents another situation where the technological infrastructure may be connected with informal social norms helping to coordinate the project. There may be an informally understood norm, for instance, shared across project team members that any enhancements must be entered into the bug-tracking system.

Communication Technologies

Not surprisingly, the communication between participants is a key variable for successful cooperation in collective action settings (Ostrom, Gardner, and Walker 1994; Singleton 1998). In addition to version control and bug management, OSS projects use a number of different technologies for communicating with each other. Assuming that the teams are distributed and not colocated, they might communicate and coordinate work using standard email, mailing lists, newsgroups, Web-site-based forums, and IRC.[4]

One of the important functions of these communication tools for many OSS projects is their ability to archive discussions. Archives serve as ways to document decisions that were made and build project documentation for others. A dialogue via a mailing list or forum, for example, might be the first path toward identifying a new bug, and archiving the dialogue serves as a mechanism for others in the future to read about the problem and any solution that might have been written as well (see, for instance, the getting-help process described in Butler and Schmidt 2007), which brings us back to the connection between technologies and project norms. Finally, a standard way of communicating information about the project to others who may be interested is maintaining a Web site (for some of the positives and negatives of hosting sites, see Fogel 2006, 54). How essential is the project's Web site for the success or abandonment of the project?

In summary, OSS commons use a variety of technologies to manage their projects' products and support communication between developers (and software users). We do not know whether any particular technological configuration improves the chances of a successful OSS commons, and we have no a priori expectations to help create testable hypotheses. Consequently, we present research question RQ-T1 under "collaborative infrastructure used" in table 4.1.

Community Attributes of OSS Commons

Let us now examine several concepts thought to be influential in OSS commons success that would be categorized as community attributes in the IAD framework (see figure 3.1, left side). These include, in no particular order, user involvement, leadership, social capital, group heterogeneity, group size, financing, and marketing strategies.

User Involvement

User participation has long been thought to play a key role in ensuring a successful software product (Ives and Olson 1984; Tait and Vessey 1988; Standish Group International 1994; Ewusi-Mensah 2003). In my (Schweik's) own experience with IBM, where I was situated in a programming group supporting an internal procurement organization, I recall our efforts to involve users in every phase of our software development. These users offered critical insights, and without them our design would surely have been off the mark. I also remember the challenges we had getting some of the other users in the organization to accept our new product, given that they were not part of the select few who had assisted in the product's design. That particular circumstance may be unusual, but it hammered home the importance of users in the development and ultimate success of software.

The OSS literature also emphasizes user involvement (Dafermos 2005; Lerner and Tirole 2002). As we discussed in chapter 3, the main idea behind von Hippel's user-driven innovation (von Hippel and von Krogh 2003; von Hippel 2005a, 2005b) is that a proportion, perhaps a large one, of OSS developers are the users of the products they develop. Moreover, Weinstock and Hissam (2005, 157) say that the most important variable in OSS project success is whether the project developers are also users. This lends support to the first community-related hypothesis—H-C1, the User-driven innovation hypothesis—that we presented in table 3.2.

Leadership

In his text on managing public organizations, Hal Rainey (2003, 290) states that the literature on leadership "looms before us as a vast, complex body of human thought and effort . . . that, like other topics in the social sciences and related fields, ultimately plays out as rather confused and inconclusive." Nevertheless, leadership is clearly an influential variable affecting group performance. Kristi Tyran, Craig Tyran, and Morgan Shepherd (2003, 183) claim that "in traditional teams involving face-to-face interaction, leadership has a strong influence on team performance and individual team members' satisfaction." This assertion has also been found to be true in traditional IS development efforts (Ewusi-Mensah 1997). Furthermore, in *Virtual Teams That Work*, Gibson and Cohen (2003, 413) stress that "team leaders often play a key role in ensuring virtual team success."

In their study of thirteen virtual teams, Tyran, Tyran, and Shepherd (2003) discovered that leaders frequently emerge in situations where there are no assigned leaders. Some teams in the study that had high levels of trust among members performed well without a leader, while teams with lower levels of trust seemed to perform better when they had a trusted leader. In other words, the top-performing teams either had high levels of trust between members or a trusted leader. Since trust is quite dependent on regular face-to-face contact, which OSS commons often lack, this particular study suggests that OSS commons where developers don't know each other or meet regularly may perform better when they have a trusted leader. The researchers note that leaders in traditional colocated teams assign tasks effectively, set clear goals, motivate team members, and mediate conflict. In virtual teams, their study found that virtual team leaders exhibited most significantly "the ability to perform tasks effectively" as well as "motivate and inspire others on the team." Since the tool most used in virtual teams is email and other forms of text-based messaging, the study showed that virtual team leaders need excellent writing skills in order to motivate, inspire trust, and mediate conflict among team members.

Not surprisingly, the concept of leadership as a crucial variable for success is also mentioned repeatedly in the OSS literature (Ghosh et al. 2002; Weber 2004). Kieran Healy and Alan Schussman (2003) emphasize a leader's ability to help manage the project and mobilize others, especially in all-volunteer contexts. Respect and admiration for some leaders may be a motivating factor in keeping other participants engaged (Elliot and Scacchi 2002). Weinstock and Hissam (2005, 156–157) note that another important component is the signals of commitment by the leader. This leads to the first leadership-related hypothesis—H-C6a—listed in table 4.2.

A second element of leadership in traditional (nonvirtual) teams relates to how well goals are established and communicated, and the degree to which established timetables are met. According to Rainey (2003, 266), research has confirmed the theory introduced by Edwin Locke stating that "specific, difficult goals lead to higher performance than easy, vague or no goals." Others such as Jon Katzenbach and Douglas Smith (1993) support this contention. The role a leader plays in communicating the goals may be essential for maintaining a successful project. This leads to a second leadership-related hypothesis linked to the communication of goals—H-C6b—presented in table 4.2.

Finally, as we will see in chapter 5, larger OSS commons can have multiple leaders (or committees) in differing project roles. One role may be more of a coordination-type leader, and the other may be more of a technical leader (O'Mahony and Ferraro

Table 4.2
Community (C) attributes of OSS commons: Research questions (RQ) and testable hypotheses (H) (where possible)

User involvement

(see table 3.2, H-C1)

Leadership

OSS commons will be more often successful when

H-C6a: they have one or more leaders who generate excitement and demonstrate "through doing."

H-C6b: they have well-articulated and clear goals established by the leader(s) of the project. (Note: This is closely aligned with H-T1 in Table 4.1.)

Social Capital

OSS commons will be more frequently successful when

H-C7a: participants hold regular face-to-face meetings.

H-C7b: a level of trust exists between team members.

Research questions where no theoretical hypothesis can be yet stated:

RQ-C2: What kind of reciprocity characterizes successful collaboration in OSS commons? Is it specific (I return favors only to people who have done favors for me) or general (I cooperate fully with anyone within the group)?

RQ-C3: Does geographic proximity among participants matter in the success or abandonment of OSS commons?

Group Heterogeneity

RQ-C1: Do various dimensions of developer heterogeneity in open-source commons influence project success or abandonment? More specifically,

RQ-C1a: What, if any, aspects of sociocultural heterogeneity (such as cultural or linguistic heterogeneity) appear to influence whether an open-source commons can succeed or will be abandoned?

RQ-C1b: What, if any, aspects of interest or motivational heterogeneity (such as the paid versus volunteer dichotomy) appear to influence whether an open-source commons can succeed or will be abandoned? Can teams with heterogeneous interests operate satisfactorily?

RQ-C1c: What, if any, aspects of asset heterogeneity (such as technical skill, education, or knowledge) appear to influence whether an open-source commons can succeed or will be abandoned?

Group size

RQ-C4: What, if any, notable direct relationships exist between group size and project success in OSS? Is there any support for Olson and Brooks's law, Linus's law, and the core team theories?

Financing

OSS commons will be more often successful when

H-C8: they have financial backing.

Marketing

RQ-C5: What marketing approaches appear to be most readily used by successful OSS commons? Are different approaches used in successful projects compared to abandoned projects?

2007). We do not know whether this type of leadership structure in any way affects the success or abandonment of an OSS project.

Social Capital

Scholars in the political science and economics fields have stressed the general concept of social capital as a fundamental factor affecting the health and vibrancy of a group or community (Jacobs 1992; Putnam 1993, 2001, 2007; Costa and Kahn 2003). Usually, social capital is understood as "trust" among community members, and has been operationalized by analyzing the strength of ties among them. According to Robert Putnam (1993, 167), social capital "refers to features of social organization, such as trust, norms, and networks, that can improve efficiency of society by facilitating coordinated actions." Even though it is not explicitly clear from Putnam's definition, he emphasizes the geographic community and neighborhood aspects of social capital (Putnam 1993, 2000, 2007). James Coleman (1988), on the other hand, provides a broader description of social capital based purely by its function. He sees social capital as an established social structure that accommodates participant actions within that structure. Social capital resides within the structure of relations, according to Coleman, not within entities and human beings. Scholars have measured social capital by looking at participation in community life, voting turnout, attendance at public meetings, membership in voluntary organizations, the prevalence of group activities such as bowling, and various other indicators of geographic communities (Putnam 1993, 2007; Costa and Kahn 2003).

Given the Internet's reach in the last two decades, researchers have connected the social capital idea to online communities (see, e.g., Blanchard and Horan 1998) and specifically OSS commons (Fischer, Scharff, and Ye 2004). Moreover, Peter Haas (1992) refers to professional peer groups as "epistemic communities," and Kasper Edwards (2001, 26–33) portrays OSS commons as a form of epistemic community. In such groups, community members share normative and principled beliefs, which help to establish trust among them. Trust can be seen as expectation that someone will behave in a particular way in a given situation, and that if they fail to do so, social sanctions will follow. We will return to this idea as well as the general concept of informal norms in chapter 5.

In voluntary and highly informal cooperative arrangements, social capital can be viewed as a substitute for formal contracts and their enforcements. Social capital, in other words, reduces the costs in transacting with others (Putnam 1993, 172; Pretty 2003, 1913). These lowered costs become especially important for OSS commons because more formal arrangements are neither available nor desirable for OSS developers. In OSS commons, the skills of individual software programmers along with the sum of the aggregate human capital or physical resources available to a project would not be sufficient without social capital as a precondition for cooperation. Indeed, scholars have found that establishing identity, trust, and group cohesion through social and cultural structures is essential for creating and sustaining productive virtual work groups (Neus 2001). Lerner and Tirole (2002) take this notion further in the OSS literature, suggesting that trust is established if the leader's objectives are congruent with those of other developers.

More general political science literature on trust observes that in commons settings, trust is often established when participants create "reciprocal cooperation" situations (Putnam 1993, 172–173; Ostrom et al. 1999). Reciprocal cooperation transactions give rise to social capital, but are not the same as market transactions because they are about social intangibles, rather than money and/or material goods (Portes and Sensenbrenner 1998, 130). A key aspect of reciprocity in social capital is that it does not have to be balanced or specific (meaning a quid pro quo situation, where an exchange of equal value occurs between individuals [Koehane 1986, 4]); instead it can be diffuse (ibid.) or generalized (Putnam 1993, 172). In OSS projects with small teams, specific reciprocity may be expected. But as a group gets larger, generalized reciprocity captures the idea that people contribute because they assume that others—perhaps people they do not know at all—would help them in a similar way, and this component of social capital can evolve into a kind of social norm that allows for solving dilemmas within collective action (Putnam 1993, 172). Moreover, looking at the broad OSS community as a whole, where there are large numbers of potential contributors "out there," generalized reciprocity becomes even more applicable. We thus should not always consider social norms as ones that govern behavior in terms of narrow, short-term self-interest. In OSS settings, the establishment of reciprocal cooperation, particularly in the early stages, and based on either balanced and/or generalized reciprocity, is probably crucial for establishing social norms that lead to project success.

Finally, another important element in building social capital is periodic face-to-face meetings among the members of virtual teams. This is a critical ingredient because purely virtual communities may result in low-trust environments (Maznevski and Chudoba 2000, 18; Ostrom and Ahn 2001, 33; Nardi and Wittaker 2002). Researchers have found that virtual communities will increase social capital when they develop around physically based communities (Blanchard and Horan 1998). In comparison with Silicon Valley's physically based IT cluster, which certainly facilitates in-person communication, face-to-face dialogue seems to be less prevalent in OSS development situations.

In some OSS development projects, though, participants make it a point to meet in person for several days of "code sprints," where they work together on design and development issues long into the night (Crowston et al. 2007, 16). Kevin Crowston and his colleagues point out that OSS developers also have face-to-face meetings at conferences and arrange special project meetings, the nature of which depends on the team. Such meetings occur two to three times per year at most, and developers usually meet with other developers after they have already worked several years on the project (ibid., 15). If the face-to-face communication were as key as the literature suggests, we should expect OSS projects where developers meet in person periodically to have higher levels of social capital than groups where this is not the case. We also would expect software development teams that are more geographically proximate (and hence more likely to have face-to-face meetings) to be more successful than those that are geographically dispersed.

These discussions related to the concept and significance of social capital lead to two hypotheses—H-C7a and H-C7b—listed under social capital in table 4.2, and two research questions—RQ-C2 and RQ-C3—also listed in table 4.2.

Group Heterogeneity

For a long time, group heterogeneity has been thought to influence a group's ability to act collectively (Sandler 2004). But for the researcher, one immediate and obvious challenge is that this general concept has multiple dimensions (Agrawal 2002). George Varughese and Elinor Ostrom (2001), building on the work of Jean-Marie Baland and Jean-Philippe Platteau (1996), subdivide the notion into three categories: sociocultural heterogeneity, interest heterogeneity, and asset heterogeneity.

Sociocultural Heterogeneity

Depending on the community of interest, the first dimension, sociocultural heterogeneity, could include attributes such as ethnicity, religion, gender, caste (Agrawal and Gibson 1999), or language. The general presumption is that groups with diverse sociocultural backgrounds will have more difficulties working together because of a lack of understanding and, potentially, trust. For example, Dora Costa and Matthew Kahn (2003) studied the relationship between ethnic diversity and civic engagement in the United States and western Europe, and found that situations with high ethnic diversity are correlated with low levels of civic engagement. Putnam (2007) analyzed forty-one geographic communities in the United States, and discovered that more ethnically diverse areas exhibited lower levels of trust across races and between geographic neighbors. He also found that more heterogeneous areas have less civic and political participation, less volunteering and charitable contributions, and generally lower quality-of-life indicators (ibid., 158–159). Other research related to natural resource commons management suggests that sociocultural differences can lead to challenges in commons governance or developing mutually agreed-on strategies for collaborating on a commons, and could ultimately create internal group conflict (Varughese and Ostrom 2001).

But this inverse relationship between sociocultural heterogeneity and public good provision is not universal. Some field research has identified the opposite relationship from what Costa, Kahn, and Putnam report. For example, in his study of farmers in

South India, Robert Wade (1994) found that heterogeneous groups were able to over come sociocultural differences and successfully work together.

The discussion of OSS demographics above suggests that in some or perhaps many OSS commons, the sociocultural dimension of the group may be fairly homogeneous. Again, as table 3.1 illustrates, most participants are male and fairly young. Given the geographic distribution of developers reported by Ghosh (2006), in some projects there may be some issues related to cultural heterogeneity. Linguistic heterogeneity in an OSS project might create some interesting challenges as well.

Interest Heterogeneity

Varughese and Ostrom (2001) apply the term "participant interests" to a second dimension of heterogeneity in groups. Interests capture people's motivations for wanting to participate in a commons. These authors provide an example of motivational heterogeneities in fishery commons, where subsistence fishers may have strong interests in maintaining the sustainability of local fishing stocks, whereas industrial fishing firms may have less concern because they can fish in locations beyond one particular locality. Differences in interests among participants can be particularly challenging when people are trying to work collectively in self-governing situations (ibid., 749). Furthermore, two or more fundamentally different types of users with different interests will likely have different perceptions of the cost and benefit of participating, which in turn can lead to group conflict.

Many of developer motivations described in chapter 3, along with discussions of business, government, and nonprofit interests in open-source in chapter 2, fall under this dimension of heterogeneity. In the context of OSS, the study by David and Shapiro (2008) directly addresses team interest heterogeneity. It shows that *there is no representative or typical open-source developer*, and developers' motivations change or evolve. Differences also exist between the motivational profiles of developers working on projects with larger developer teams and those working on smaller teams (one to two developers). David and Shapiro conclude their work by suggesting that heterogeneity of interests is a key component of open-source projects.

Asset Heterogeneity

This subcomponent of heterogeneity can also have multiple dimensions. For instance, wealth, property ownership, and political power are three types of assets found in some group settings. Some studies have demonstrated that heterogeneity in assets such as these negatively impact a group's ability to self-organize (Isaac and Walker 1988).

Yet similar other dimensions of heterogeneity, some studies report finding the opposite relationship. The study of community forestry in India by Mark Baker (1998), for example, discovered that villages with slightly unequal distributions in wealth did better in managing forest commons than did those with more equal wealth distributions. Baker suggests that the inequality of wealth creates incentives for some individuals to bear more of the costs in maintaining the commons than others. He also concludes that too much wealth inequality can diminish group interest in the commons and result in a takeover of the commons by the elite. Of course, people possess other assets beyond money and property, such as knowledge or skill (recall figure 3.3), which in fact could be considered another dimension of power. In another case, Ronald Johnson and Gary Libecap (1982) have argued that differences in the knowledge and abilities of different fishers often get in the way of their ability to arrive at an agreement over fish-harvesting quotas.

This kind of asset heterogeneity—differences in knowledge or skill—could potentially affect the way that OSS commons operate. IS literature views adequate expertise, experience, and "domain knowledge" as important factors contributing to the success or failure of traditional software projects (Ewusi-Mensah 2003, 52). As we have noted, "promotion" (for lack of a better word) in open-source is frequently based on knowledge and skill as well as contribution—the idea that OSS projects are run as meritocracies. Like the environmental commons situations, some heterogeneity along this asset dimension could be a good thing for open-source collaboration. Less skilled, educated, or knowledgeable programmers learn by working with more skilled or knowledgeable ones with similar technological interests. Yet in open-source settings, it is not well understood whether diversity in skill, education, and/or knowledge between group participants (particularly between core team members), similar to what was reported by Baker (1998; wealth assets) and Molinas (1998; land assets), causes problems within open-source teams.

Summary of Heterogeneity

As research in natural resource commons settings shows, there are a number of dimensions to group heterogeneity, and the relationship between these various components and successful group cohesion is complex. The investigation by Varughese and Ostrom (2001) into the influence of these dimensions of heterogeneity in eighteen forest-user groups in Nepal, however, found that they were not strong predictors of the ability of the groups to work together. These researchers conclude that heterogeneity in groups can present an additional challenge to collective action, but it can be overcome through good institutional designs (e.g., rule systems) that govern group activities. Other work in forestry settings has arrived at similar conclusions (Poteete and Ostrom 2004). Despite the complexity along with the possibility that heterogeneity may not be a major factor in the success or abandonment of OSS commons, we have nonetheless included this factor in our research because it has not been widely studied. We present three research questions on heterogeneity—RQ-C1, RQ-C1a and RQ-C1b—in table 4.2.

Group Size

Group size has been identified as an important factor in understanding cooperation and coordination in the general literature on collective action as well as in the IS and OSS literature. But as we will show, the relationship between group size and the success or abandonment of a commons is complex. There are a number of theoretical and field studies on group size that relate to OSS commons settings, which we describe below.

Brooks's Law

In traditional software development situations, where employees within firms write the software, the main concerns with adding programmers to a project are cost and schedule overruns. Frederick Brooks, in his oft-cited *The Mythical Man Month* ([1975] 1995, 25), argues that "adding manpower to a late project makes it later." Factors that contribute to the lateness, in what is now known as "Brooks's law," include communication complexities and coordination costs with new team members as well as the training needed to familiarize them with a project.

Some researchers have contended that Brooks's law does not directly translate to OSS because there are no set project completion dates (Abdel-Hamid and Madnick 1990; Jones 2000), while others have made direct comparisons (e.g., Raymond 2001). Srdjan Rusonvan and his colleagues (2005) analyzed the code of one OSS Linux module in detail, and found it to be poorly documented, complex, and in general, poorly written compared to that of a similar module developed using strictly controlled source code and conventional methods. While they (rightfully) note that the analysis of one module is insufficient to draw general conclusions, they also say, "What we did find in this case is exactly what Fred Brooks' more than three decades-old observations would lead us to expect. The attraction of [OSS] development is its ability to get lots of people to work on a project, but that is also a weakness" (ibid., 120). They suggest that larger group size may contribute to the absence of design and documentation standards, and the ability to enforce those standards, and as a result, code quality suffers.

Olson's Group Size Paradox

As we have observed elsewhere (Schweik et al. 2008), Brooks's assertions are closely aligned with a famous theory related to the effect of group size in collective action situations. Political economist Mancur Olson (1965, 35) argued in his groundbreaking work *The Logic of Collective Action* that "the larger the group, the less likely it will further its common interests"—what is sometimes referred to as Olson's group size paradox. Quite similar to Brooks, Olson (ibid., 48) emphasizes that large groups face significantly higher organizing costs than do small groups. These expenses include, among others, costs in communication, bargaining, and creating and maintaining formal organization. Collective action problems in large groups lead to the existence of free riders and the reduction of incentives to contribute to the collective good (Olson 1965; Isaac and Walker 1988, 196–197).

Findings since Brooks and Olson

Since Brooks and Olson offered these theoretical notions, researchers have reported findings that run counter to the Brooks-Olsonian logic. For example, using game theory related to the provision of public goods, Paul Pecorino (1999) concluded that cooperation does not necessarily break down in large group settings, as Olson suggests. Moreover, other studies relevant to Olson's theory have reported a positive relationship between group size and successful cooperation (Marwell and Oliver 1993; Isaac, Walker, and Williams 1994; Esteban and Ray 2001). Specifically addressing programming group size and the complexity it brings, Tarek Abdel-Hamid and Stuart Madnick (1990) maintain that whether Brooks's law is true or false depends, in some cases, on other project attributes. Bringing on exceptionally skilled developers might result in the project moving forward, not behind.

Linus's Law in OSS

In his frequently cited book *The Cathedral and the Bazaar*, Raymond (2001) introduces another famous theory related to project group size known as Linus's law, which applies specifically to the OSS domain. This "law," named after Linus Torvalds, the lead developer of the Linux operating system, states, as noted earlier, "Given enough eyeballs, all bugs are shallow." In other words, in OSS settings with a relatively large testing and developer community, code problems will be identified quickly and solutions will be rapidly produced. Raymond specifically mentions Brooks's law in this work, and contends that it assumes that "everyone talks to everyone else." He argues that in OSS projects, because of separate subtasks (modularity), the communication and coordination costs that Brooks worried about should be greatly reduced.

Following up on the Linus's law idea, other scholars have claimed that gaining a "critical mass" is important for OSS projects (Weinstock and Hissam 2005; Benkler 2006). Benkler (2006, 111) argues that the widely distributed, large-scale, peer-production OSS model of information production will help to identify the best programmers to deliver a necessary component, while taking into account programmer ability and availability to work within a given time frame.

The Core Team Hypothesis

In our view, field research on OSS suggests that Linus's law does not apply often. According to a number of studies, as we noted in chapter 2, a majority of OSS projects have small teams (Jones 2000; Dempsey et al. 2002; Ghosh et al. 2002; Krishnamurthy 2002; Healy and Schussman 2003) or a high percentage of the contributions come from only a few participants. If a small group of core developers does the majority of the work, the size of the "official" group (the core developers and others who are connected to the project but do little) shouldn't matter. This idea is what we have referred to in an earlier work as the core team hypothesis related to group size (Schweik et al. 2008).

Summary of Group Size

The above discussion on group size indicates contrary relationships between group size and OSS project success: smaller development teams will be more successful than larger groups, larger groups will be more successful than smaller groups, group size won't matter because most of the work is done by a core team anyway. Still, these theories—Brooks's law, Linus's law, and the core team, respectively—do not necessarily have to contradict each other because they focus on somewhat different aspects of OSS collaboration. As we stated above, some researchers have maintained that Brooks's law doesn't readily apply because it is addressing the idea of a late project, which is usually not relevant in an OSS context. Linus's law is about fixing bugs and making the end result of the project better. At the same time, in certain circumstances, a core team may do most of the work that leads to project success, but they may benefit from the additional help of people who point out bugs and other small problems. These theories, in short, may be entirely compatible despite the way we have presented them here. Nevertheless, our discussion serves to highlight some of the literature that results in our research question—RQ-C4—under group size in table 4.2.

Financing

We pose the question here of whether financial support—in the form of direct donations or through an organization's paying its own employees to participate—makes a difference in an OSS project's success or abandonment. In 2003, I (Schweik) participated in the International Symposium on Open Access and Public Domain in Digital Data and Information for Science hosted by the United Nations Educational, Scientific, and Cultural Organization (Schweik, Grove, and Evans 2003). One participant at the event who was a developer on a government-funded OSS project emphasized in his talk that the *only way* OSS projects will be successful is with government financial support. While I questioned the "only way" aspect of his statement in general, I think he was trying to highlight the importance of having some kind of financial support, specifically in regard to larger-scale OSS projects. James Dalziel (2003, 5) supports this point, noting that "most open-source e-learning projects have not arisen spontaneously from the goodwill of freelance developers. They are typically the result of government or foundation funding, where developers are paid for their contributions to the project."

Weinstock and Hissam (2005, 145) describe a situation where an OSS project progressed only when it had a sponsor that provided employee time and other resources. Fogel (2006, 64–76) also suggests the importance of money in ensuring project success:

Financial backing is, in general, welcomed by OSS development communities. It can reduce a project's vulnerability to the Forces of Chaos, which sweep away so many projects before they really get off the ground, and therefore it can make people more willing to give the software a chance—they feel they're investing their time into something that will still be around six months from now. After all, credibility is contagious, to a point. When, say, IBM backs an OSS project, people pretty much assume the project won't be allowed to fail, and their resultant willingness to devote effort to it can make that a self-fulfilling prophecy.

In short, financial support might be the key difference between whether a project succeeds or is abandoned. Moreover, funding, at least in some areas of OSS, is indeed being supplied. O'Mahony (2007, 144) reports that between 2004 and 2005, over three hundred million U.S. dollars went to thirty-three OSS firms—the largest such investment since 2000.

Yet it is not clear from a donor perspective whether providing financial support will necessarily lead to a desirable outcome for the donor organization. Riehle (2007, 30) argues that there is real value for a firm that relies on a certain OSS project in its business model to have an employee who has higher-level project commit status. According to Riehle, the firm gains several advantages this way:

• Problems in the code may be fixed both faster and with higher quality
• The company's strategy can be better aligned with the OSS project's strategy
• The company may be seen as a more attractive employer by OSS project participants
• There are marketing benefits, as we described in chapter 2

But Fogel (2006) warns organizations considering such donations to be careful. He says that in many OSS projects, the entrance of a paid employee will not (or should not) automatically lead to that person's having write (commit) access to the source-code repository. He contends that the employee will need to prove their worth in a meritocracy-like fashion. Fogel also advises firms that may pay multiple people to participate to "appear as many, not as one." In short, Fogel suggests that volunteers or other project participants may look with a critical eye at the donations and participation by a firm, and that the tensions they could generate related to project direction could lead, in some situations, to collaboration problems and possibly project abandonment. In our judgment, though, projects that have paid employees or financial support will have a higher likelihood of success than ones without it. Consequently, we present one hypothesis—H-C8—under financing in table 4.2 and remind the reader of another hypothesis—H-C2—that we presented in chapter 3, which indicates that OSS commons will be more successful if some of the developers are paid partici-pants, or make an income through products and/or services that depend on the software.

Marketing Strategies

Marketing is our last topic in this chapter. The question is, To what degree does a marketing strategy influence the success or abandonment of an OSS project? Surpris-ingly, there appears to be little scholarly literature on this issue. Scattered information is available on blog sites and in more popular press magazines about high-profile cases. For example, David Freedman (2007) describes the Mozilla Corporation's efforts in the early days of the Firefox Web browser release. The company had made progress on the product under an OSS development paradigm and wondered if it could use its nontechnical user base to create a kind of open-source marketing campaign. Mozilla hired one of its most active volunteer bug reporters to help undertake such a strategy. Shortly thereafter, the company created a "spread-the-word" Web site and worked to recruit the nontechnical community (e.g., bug reporters and documentation writers) to help get the word out on the new release. It asked this group of Mozilla "faithful" to identify blogs that might embrace the new Firefox browser initiative. Within four days, one million downloads of Firefox occurred, and a few thousand people joined the marketing campaign. Later, as their numbers grew, these people asked for contri-butions to do ads in newspapers like the *New York Times*, which ran twice, and then during the next year over a hundred thousand people joined the marketing effort.

The Mozilla experience is probably somewhat of an anomaly. This is a high-profile OSS company with a high-profile product at a time when there were serious security concerns over the dominant browser—Microsoft Internet Explorer. That situation provided a great marketing advantage on its own, given that many end users were concerned about their personal exposure to security problems. But what this case illustrates is the idea of "viral marketing" at work. This kind of marketing relies on the interested parties or "customers" to promote the product via network-based online mechanisms (Richardson and Domingos 2002). Because this method couples word-of-mouth recommendations with online communication, it is sometimes referred to "word-of-mouse" marketing (Helm 2000) and can foster dramatically faster speeds in communication (Godin 2000).

Our sense is that viral marketing might work, but for most open-source projects it will most likely be gradual or contained within smaller communities than in the Mozilla Firefox case. Fogel (2006, 98) describes some "distribution channels" that open-source projects tend to use for marketing and promotion: the home page on a project Web site, news or press releases on that Web site, Really Simple Syndication (RSS) feeds, announcements on open-source hosting sites like Freshmeat.net, and an email to a project announcement mailing list. The first two in Fogel's list are self-explanatory. But for the benefit of those readers who may not be familiar with them, let us explain the other three. RSS feeds are mechanisms to transmit data and corresponding metadata (data about data) to others who have subscribed to receive these feeds. This technology, for example, allows one Web site to automatically list news that is posted on another Web site's RSS feed. Freshmeat.net and others, such as Berlios.net and SF, are Web sites devoted to communicating about OSS technologies and usually have sections where announcements can be posted. Finally, Fogel discusses "project announcement" mailing lists, which he notes are different from other mailing lists that a project may have.

Nonprofit foundations may also play a role in marketing. In her discussion on the role of foundations in OSS, O'Mahony (2005) mentions the marketing of affiliated projects as one of the activities they may undertake. Indeed, the foundation we look at in the case study in chapter 6 sees marketing as one of its roles.

Little academic research, in general, appears to have been conducted on the marketing or publicity side of OSS commons, especially exploring its influence on the success or abandonment of a project. We therefore have no a priori hypotheses or expectations related to marketing, but it is a research question worth investigating (RQ-C5 under marketing in table 4.2).

Conclusion

In this chapter, we have described two important sets of attributes thought to influence the success or abandonment of open-source commons: technological and community attributes. We uncovered yet more factors that might affect OSS commons, and we posed twenty-three additional testable hypotheses and research questions, which are shown in tables 4.1 and 4.2. We are not yet finished; the review in this chapter demonstrates how OSS commons are Internet-based social-technical systems that need to be studied as such. There is one missing ingredient for such an analysis, however. As the IAD framework shows (see figure 3.1), we need to turn our attention to a final set of important attributes: institutions. These are to date perhaps the least-studied components of OSS commons, but they could be considered the glue that holds together the technical and community components. We take up OSS institutions in chapter 5, and when that is accomplished, we will bring our literature review to a close.

5 Institutional Attributes

We have nearly reached the end of part II, where we have reviewed academic literature to find factors critical to the success or abandonment of OSS commons. Part II represents the beginning stage of our research endeavor, and many steps remain. In part III, following this chapter, we will find ways to define success and abandonment so we can classify existing OSS projects into those two categories; then we will find or generate data that provide measures for the factors we have presented as important. Finally, we will select statistical techniques that allow us to discover which factors are associated with success or abandonment in a significant number of real-world OSS projects. At this point in our work, about two years after we had begun, we did not know whether we would be able to find measures for many of our factors or would be able to analyze all of them in a coherent way. In the end, we were able to meet all these challenges, building in part on the previous work of other academics and then complementing it with our own substantial work. We invite readers to continue to watch the story unfold in the ensuing chapters.

For now, though, we will describe OSS institutions—the glue that binds the technological and community attributes of OSS projects into a functioning whole. We start by presenting what some other OSS researchers have said about the importance of OSS institutions and then delve deeper by defining institutions more carefully. Next, we study Lynn Markus's thoughts about OSS institutions, and move toward analyzing both informal and formal institutions in the context of the IAD framework.

The main purpose of this chapter, similar to other chapters in part II, is to find institutional factors that may be key in the success or abandonment of OSS commons, and generate research questions and hypotheses based on these factors. Yet much of this chapter introduces and describes an analytic approach that supports systematic comparison of OSS institutions *across cases* as well as promotes analysis of OSS institutional evolution over time. We offer this methodology because we think it will fill a critical need in the OSS research community, and help the community to move beyond descriptive case studies on how these projects grow and evolve. The methodology we propose provides a syntax, or structure, to systematically analyze the institutional design of a particular OSS project, or how this structure develops over time. Moreover, it will supply a method for the comparison of institutional designs across OSS cases. We close the chapter by applying our analytic approach to the Debian Linux project, and discussing some institutional considerations regarding organizations that sponsor and support OSS projects.

The Current State of Knowledge about Open-Source Software Institutions

A number of OSS researchers recognize that OSS institutions exist and are important. Ben Collins-Sussman, Brian Fitzpatrick, and C. Michael Pilato (2005, xv) say that "most OSS projects" are "governed by a loose, transparent set of rules that encourage meritocracy." Weber (2004, 189) depicts OSS as an "imperfect mix of leadership, informal coordination mechanisms, implicit and explicit norms, along with some formal governance structures." Ron Goldman and Richard Gabriel (2005, 232) argue that "every OSS project has some sort of governance because decisions must be made all the time," and suggest that "institutional structures get more complicated when firms become involved." They also recognize the dynamic, evolutionary nature of governance and institutions in OSS commons (ibid., 233). Crowston (2005) hints at the need for institutional analysis of OSS projects when he asserts that the future research agenda should hone in on how work is coordinated and how "shared understandings" (informal norms) affect the development process. Most recently, O'Mahony and Ferraro (2007)—the two researchers who have done the most work to try to understand OSS institutional design—describe the institutional structure and evolution of the Debian Linux project. Serious discussions of OSS institutions, however, have taken place only in the last seven years or so (e.g., Schweik and Semenov 2003; Schweik 2005; de Laat 2007; Jørgensen 2007; O'Mahony and Ferraro 2007).

In our initial exploration of the IAD framework in chapter 3, we referred to institutions as "the management and governance system used by the project," and "the types of rules established to help guide participants' behavior as they engage in their day-to-day activities related to development and maintenance of the source code." These were adequate definitions for the purposes of that chapter. Given that one of our goals is to fill in the knowledge gap related to OSS institutions, we will now look at the concept more thoroughly.

Institutions is one of those terms that can mean different things to different people. People often equate institutions with organizations. Nobel Laureate in Economic Sciences Douglass North (1990, 3) disagrees, and defines institutions as "the rules of the game in society or, more fundamentally, . . . humanly devised constraints that shape human interaction." For North, these "rules of the game" interact with or help define organizations, and are "a function of the shared mental models and ideologies of the actors" (Denzau and North 1994, 15).

Ostrom's *Understanding Institutional Diversity* is arguably the definitive work on how to analyze institutions in commons settings. In his book, Ostrom (2005, 3) offers a definition in line with North's: "Institutions are the prescriptions that humans use to organize all forms of repetitive and structured interactions."[1] Ostrom (ibid., 3) further notes that "the opportunities and constraints individuals face in any particular situa tion, the information they obtain, the benefits they obtain or are excluded from, and how they reason about the situation, are all affected by the rules or absence of rules that structure that situation." Institutions, for North, Ostrom, and many others, set the stage and guide the interactions among participants in collective action situations. Moreover, institutions can be informal (habits, social norms, etc.) or formal (laws, constitutions, etc.) (North 1990), or in some instances, consist of partially or fully embedded rules within the software logic of technologies used for collaboration (Lessig 2006; Markus 2007). Those individuals with the authority to devise such rules are also the ones who craft OSS institutions (O'Mahony and Ferraro 2007; O'Neil 2009). From this perspective, when we use the phrase *OSS institutions*, it includes the concept of governance in OSS commons.

M. Lynne Markus (2007) asks three questions about OSS governance: How is OSS governance defined? Is OSS governance monolithic or multidimensional? And what is the purpose of OSS governance? Regarding the first question, Markus concluded that there really was no accepted definition. Consequently, she adapts a definition of public sector governance by Laurence Lynn Jr., Carolyn Heinrich, and Carolyn Hill (2002): "[OSS software] governance can be defined *as the means of achieving the direction, control, and coordination of wholly or partially autonomous individuals and organizations on behalf of an [OSS] development project to which they jointly contribute*" (Markus 2007, 152; emphasis in original). This depiction is entirely consistent with Ostrom's general definition of institutions above. Institutions—social norms and formalized rules along with established mechanisms for rule creation, maintenance, monitoring, and enforcement—are the means through which direction, control, and coordination can occur.

By asking her second question, Markus is asking how much diversity exists in OSS institutions. Her review of OSS literature leads her to conclude that there are two camps on this issue. The monolithic camp suggests that OSS institutional form is quite similar across projects, grounded on the idea that developers choose for themselves the work to be done. What variation exists can to a large extent be found within the sometimes-subtle differences between OSS licenses utilized. Conversely, Markus's other camp, the multidimensionalists, maintains that there is wide diversity in OSS institutional designs. In addition to license variation, OSS institutions' legal organizations, relationships with firms or other organizations, participant role structures, and under-lying work processes (e.g., the way requirements are gathered or release management) can vary. Markus clearly falls in the multidimensionalist camp, and given our own emphasis on the complexity in OSS, at both the ecosystem and developer levels, we do too.

It could be that these two camps are entirely compatible, however, and their dif-ference has to do with the evolution of institutions. In other parts of this book we have noted that field research on OSS shows that within the overall population of projects, a large number of projects consist of small teams (one to two people). It could be that the majority of OSS projects are monolithic in structure with few or no formal institutions, but the minority of larger development team projects—with more diverse interests—evolve toward more formal institutional design and become multidimen-sional. This is a question that has yet to be addressed in the literature, and we hope to shed some light on it later in this book.

Markus then presents three answers to her third question. The first response is intended to solve collective action dilemmas. Proper institutional designs can help to encourage collaboration. The second purpose of OSS governance is to assist in the coordination of the software development process. Development teams need some system to coordinate work, and they put institutions in place to guide team processes. The third reason for OSS governance is to create a "(better?) developer climate" (Markus 2007, 156). Markus suggests that a project having a democratic approach—that is, where the individual developers have a greater say in the project's direction—may attract and motivate developers more than a project that is more autocratic. This idea is consistent with the argument put forth by Mathieu O'Neil (2009, 75) that rules in OSS exist to define who members of the commons are and to support democratic systems in OSS. The idea is also in line with theoretical and field research found in the management of natural resource commons, where evidence demonstrates that rule systems developed with participant input will lead to more sustainable commons set-tings (Ostrom 1990; Agrawal 2002). "Is a democratic governance structure more moti-vational to OSS developers than more autocratic systems of governance? This is an important question that is still unanswered in OSS research" (Markus 2007, 157).

Analyzing Open-Source Software Institutions

Let us briefly return to the IAD framework presented in figure 3.1.[2] Recall that our primary unit of analysis is the OSS developer, at any point in time, making choices about what actions they should take. Actions could include some programming on project modules, helping another member with a challenging bug fix, or in some instances, leaving the project. In their day-to-day activities, developers face "action situations." For Ostrom (2008, 52; emphasis in original), action situations are "composed of *participants* in *positions* choosing among *actions* at particular stages of a decision process in light of their *control* over a choice node, the *information* they have, the *outcomes* that are likely, and the *benefits and costs* they perceive for these outcomes." In OSS commons, developers self-select or else can be voted or promoted into a position that may have particular actions associated with it (testing, developing, or committing code to a code repository). Some developers may have more control over the project than others, and make choices at a particular juncture (Ostrom's "choice node") based on the available information and the outcomes they expect to occur from various actions. Consistent with what we observed in chapter 3, there may be some cost-benefit calculations undertaken in making such decisions.

Institutional analysis is about the study of rules that influence individuals' cost-benefit calculations. In general, rules are defined as instructions that describe what actions or outcomes are permitted, required, or prohibited. They also need to be understood by group participants and enforced (Ganz 1971). Furthermore, the study of institutions involves the study of formally documented rules (such as which OSS license is attached to the software, or a formal project constitution), and perhaps more significant in the OSS context, rules that can be informally established "modes of standard behavior" or social norms. In another important book, *Governing the Commons*, Ostrom (1990) describes cases where local natural resource users have created their own self-governing systems that overcome free rider problems and overharvesting, which are the result of self-interested behavior. Ostrom has emphasized in her work over the years that this collective development of institutions to govern natural resource commons is by no means easy. Institutional design can be hard, challenging work, to the point where the people who craft and maintain them could be considered "artisans" (Ostrom 1992). While the institutional designs across cases certainly vary, many evolve from initial interactions that establish trust and social capital, to the establishment of acceptable norms of behavior, to the establishment of more formalized rules coupled with monitoring and sanctioning mechanisms for rule breakers (Ostrom et al. 1999). How might all of this work in an OSS setting?

Examples of Informal Rules: Social Norms

First, let us present a hypothetical, but perhaps typical, example of how informal norms can be developed initially by adapting a passage written by Victor Nee and Paul Ingram (1998, 25), and placing it in an OSS context. Suppose Dana, a software developer, decides to kick off a new OSS project, places it on SF, and invites others to participate. Eventually, on her own, Dana produces a first, early release of code. John, someone who has a need for Dana's software but also someone with programming skills, locates Dana's project by searching the Internet, and after reading some of the project metadata, John realizes this project meets his needs and wants. He decides to download and use the software. Sooner or later, John sends an email to Dana about particular problems that he encounters and how he might contribute to the project. Dana answers these questions, perhaps in a standard communication medium such as a project forum, using time that could have been spent on other work. John reciprocates by bestowing on Dana a higher level of social approval. Both parties are rewarded by this exchange. John is learning, and Dana is (perhaps) hoping that John might help advance the software or at least promote it. Their exchange builds on mutual understanding and expectations that may be initially unspoken.

Dana may expect John to eventually reciprocate by at least following her lead related to informal norms of conduct, and providing some new code or enhancements to old code. She may also expect John to consider her as a kind of "leader," in that she has more technical knowledge of the project and controls the code repository. Nee and Ingram (1998, 25) note that "such an implicit contract, an informal norm, may sooner or later be expressed in some communication in statements of expected behavior. Violation of the norm leads to such forms of punishment as anger or refusal to continue the interaction." For example, a common norm that can be violated is the often-used email shorthand RTM (read the manual) (O'Neil 2009, 82). If John repeatedly ignores this norm and asks questions without reading the existing documentation first, this could lead Dana to terminate their relationship. At this juncture, a small team consisting of Dana and John is emerging, along with the establishment of some behavior norms, such as coding and documentation conventions.

Howard Butler and Chris Schmidt (2007) provide a second example of social norms in OSS through their normative analysis of the getting-help process. They outline recommended steps that developers and users alike should take to resolve an error they've encountered with an OSS application. First, they suggest, the software user should investigate the frequently asked questions and other error-related documentation on the project's Web site. If there is nothing there, the next step would be to enter the error message encountered, along with the name of the software, using an online search engine to see if there is a discussion list where this error and its solution is listed. If this doesn't work, they suggest that the user write a detailed description of the error, along with what they have done so far to solve the problem, and send it to the project's mailing list. If as a result of this documented process, the problem appears to be a bug in the software or corresponding documentation, they recommend that a "bug report" be posted on the project's bug-tracking system. If the problem eventually gets fixed, Butler and Schmidt recommend that the original user who found the problem should make a final post to the mailing list, so that the solution is archived. Finally, these authors also urge that this user thank, publicly, the developer who helped solve the problem.

The getting-help process that Butler and Schmidt describe is a set of social norms that likely exist in many OSS commons. Moreover, there are undoubtedly a variety of areas in OSS collaboration where similar norms of behavior are established.[3] Through abiding by these norms through iterative interactions, participants create important project social capital (Coleman 1988; Putnam 1993; recall also chapter 4), such as the development and maintenance of trusted relationships, the norm of reciprocity, and informal contracts. In other words, through the establishment of these kinds of norms, participants make informal commitments to one another and, over time, knit a kind of social fabric for the project. In some instances participants may attach a sense of belonging to the project, which contributes to some of their motivations to further contribute (Smith 2007). These kinds of informal norms are crucial because they reduce uncertainty in human interactions and help solve coordination problems, especially when specialization and division of labor emerge within a project (Nee and Ingram 1998).

Examples of Formal Rules: OSS Licenses

In some situations—particularly in larger groups—social norms may not be enough. Formal rules are often needed to back up norm-based systems (Ostrom 2005). In cases where OSS projects grow in terms of the number of participants, or when firms or government agencies contribute resources to the effort, we expect that these sets of informal norms will develop or evolve into more formalized systems of rules. As the size of the development team increases, for example, coordination norms, conventions, or even decrees might evolve to help the team coordinate its activities (Ullmann-Margalit 1977).

Perhaps the most well-known formal rules are those specified by a product's OSS license. We have discussed the FSF's GPL, authored by Stallman, which is a widely used license for free/libre software and OSS, but there are many others.[4] Lawrence Rosen (2004) groups them into four categories: academic, reciprocal, standards, and content. According to Rosen, academic licenses were created by academic institutions and allow the software to be used with no obligation on the licensee's part to later provide the source for derivative work. In essence the user is not obligated, as GPL users are, to give back under the same license. Reciprocal licenses, such as the GPL, have this "give back" requirement—any new, derivative work must take the licensing of its parent product. This difference makes the two licenses incompatible.

A relatively large literature now exists regarding the legal distinctions between various licenses. Andrew St. Laurent (2004) and Lawrence Rosen (2004) devote whole books to the topic. Deek and McHugh (2007) provide a helpful overview as well. For our purposes, the main points are that the stipulations in a project's license are one set of what we call "constitutional-level rules" (described more fully below), and we wonder whether the *kind* of license influences the success or abandonment of an OSS project. A starting point for the study of OSS licenses would be to investigate—and we do this in later parts of this book—whether either GPL-compatible or GPL-incompatible licenses are associated with OSS project success or abandonment.

Institutions as "Friction"

In a moment we will present a finer-scale categorization scheme for documenting OSS norms or rules. But before we move on, we want to underscore a potential problem that tends to arise as OSS institutions evolve from simple norms to more complex, formally described systems of rules. Raymond, a famous proponent of OSS, raises this issue in a statement regarding the economic concept of free riders in OSS and the role that institutions play. He states,

The real free-rider problems in OSS software are more a function of *friction costs* in submitting patches than anything else. A potential contributor with little stake in the cultural reputation game . . . may, in the absence of money compensation, think "It's not worth submitting this fix because I'll have to clean up the patch, write a ChangeLog entry, and sign the FSF assignment papers. . . ." It's for this reason that the number of contributors (and, at second order, the success of) projects is strongly and inversely correlated with *the number of hoops* each project makes a contributing user go through. (Raymond 2001, 127; emphasis added)

Raymond's statement brings us back to our discussion in figure 3.3 about developer attributes. Recall that we classified OSS developers based on three general attributes: volunteer/paid, project experience, and technical skill. For developers who are volunteers and relatively inexperienced programmers, skill building and signaling are strong motivators. For paid programmers of all types, the primary motivation to participate is obvious: they are doing what they are asked by their employer, who pays them. But the category of developers that Raymond refers to in the above quote—people with "little stake in the cultural reputation game" and "in the absence of money compensation"—are highly skilled technically or have significant project experience (or both), volunteer their time, and have little need or desire to further build their skills or signal their abilities to others.

Consequently, Raymond argues that the key free-rider problem in OSS settings is how to get volunteer programmers who are highly skilled and/or knowledgeable about the project to contribute their time and resources. The references to friction costs and the number of hoops in Raymond's quote suggests that the existence of too many established rules and procedures (formal or informal) related to a project's operation might be a factor in driving away these key volunteer developers. Indeed, these claims are supported by the work of O'Mahony (2003), which shows that OSS developers resist centralized governance and formal methods for organizing. Holck and Jørgensen (2005, 2) summarize this nicely in relation to OSS projects: "Developers would prefer loosely controlled projects with a flat hierarchy, relying on individual autonomy, tacit norms, and self-organization rather than commands, control, and explicit rules." Yet Raymond's point was written before paid professionals entered OSS commons in significant numbers. The question now is whether formal rules, in these new OSS settings where firms, foundations, or other organizations are involved, are still seen as friction or now viewed as necessary tools to keep coordination going. This is an open question, which at this juncture is unanswered.

Three Levels and Seven Classes of Rules

Moving toward our goal of a structure for the analysis of OSS institutions, let us now take a moment to elaborate on the three nested levels of rules we introduced in the IAD discussion in chapter 3 and depicted in figure 3.1.

The first level, the *operational level*, is a general name for rules that influence the everyday decisions and actions of project participants. In an OSS setting, these are the norms or more formal rules that specify how the further development and support of the software may proceed. Examples of operational rules might be the procedures for adding a new module to the next-release library or the procedure followed to make a new release of the project's software.

The second institutional level, *collective choice*, can be thought of as two general sets of rules that oversee operational-level rules and structures (Ostrom, Gardner, and Walker 1994). The first set defines who is eligible to undertake certain operational-level activities. For example, in OSS, most projects will probably have a norm or rule specifying who has the authority to promote or commit code changes to the next-release library (Fogel and Bar 2003). In some projects there may be only one or two people on the team, and as a consequence, one or both might have this authority. In other, larger projects, this authority might be highly centralized, or alternatively, the authority could be distributed, allowing each developer to promote their code when it is ready. The second set of collective choice rules specifies who can change operational-level rules and the procedure to make such a change. For instance, using the same example as above, as more developers join a project, there may be a need to change the operational-level rule describing how code is committed. Collective choice rules would determine how to change an existing operational procedure.

Finally, the top or highest level in these nested institutions is referred to as *constitutional-level* rules. Most readers will probably interpret this as the constitutional provisions that govern an OSS commons, such as the particular software license used. But constitutional-level rules also specify who is allowed to change collective choice rules and the procedures for making such changes. An example in an OSS setting might arise when the recognized leader of a project decides to move on to a new opportunity; constitutional-level rules would specify who takes over this person's position. In the Debian Linux case, which we'll discuss below, this situation ignited some major institutional design changes.

These three levels of rules are well established, and have been used by Ostrom and her colleagues, including author Schweik, for many years. Nevertheless, one of the advances that Ostrom (2005) made in *Understanding Institutional Diversity* was adding a framework for classifying or organizing rules found in commons settings at any or all of these levels. Ostrom presented seven rule categories, described in table 5.1 and summarized here:

• *Position rules* articulate what roles people play in the project.
• *Boundary rules* define who is eligible for a position, the process of how they are assigned to that position, and rules related to how the person leaves that position.
• *Choice rules* define actions that can, cannot, or must be done. Some of these rules, driven by the authority given to various participants' user IDs, may be built directly into the version control system that the project is using. These types of rules focus on actions.
• *Aggregation rules* articulate the process for how conflict should be resolved. Within this category, Ostrom presents three subcategories: nonsymmetrical, symmetrical, and lack-of-agreement rules. A nonsymmetrical aggregation rule describes the situation where a designated leader of an OSS project is given the authority to self-select the right course of action when a conflict occurs between others on the team. In this context, the leader has more power than the developers. A symmetrical aggregation rule allocates the decision-making power equally across all participants, such as employing a voting rule to solve a dispute. Ostrom also notes that in either of these circumstances, a "no agreement" condition should specify what happens when no agreement can be reached either through a nonsymmetrical or symmetrical process.
• *Information rules* specify how and what kind of information flows between project members and other interested parties as well as how information is archived throughout the project's life cycle.
• *Payoff rules* assign some kind of reward or sanction to specific actions or outcomes.
• *Scope rules* specify which outcomes may, must, or must not be affected or produced in a given situation. They focus on outcomes.

Default Open-Source Software Institutions

To begin utilizing these rule categories, we follow the lead of Ostrom (2005, 210) and ask this question: What happens if no rules exist in an OSS commons? In other words, what are the default institutional conditions in cases where there are only one or possibly two developers on a team? Table 5.2 summarizes such default conditions, most of which apply primarily to the operational level of the IAD framework.

We suspect that even in small-team OSS projects, though, these default conditions probably would not hold. As our earlier discussions show, at the very least, there will be some established social norms. For example, if the project moved from a simple situation of two developers collaborating to even a group as small as three or four, we doubt that the default-choice rule condition at the operational level—that anyone can

Table 5.1

Ostrom's seven general rule categories

Rule category	Definition (can apply to any or all of the three nested levels: operational, collective choice, or constitutional)
Position	Define the positions that participants hold
Boundary	Define • who is eligible to take a position (succession rules) • the process that determines which participants may enter (entry rules), such as by invitation, through some sort of competition, or compulsory • how an individual can leave a position (exit rules) Rules also may exist regarding the relationship between multiple positions, such as a mandate that no one person can hold multiple positions at the same time
Choice	Specify what participants must, must not, or may do in their positions and particular circumstances Choice rules focus on *actions*
Aggregation	Determine whether a decision by a single or multiple participants is needed prior to an action at a decision point in a process Aggregation rules are needed whenever choice rules provide partial control to multiple positions over the same sorts of actions Aggregation rules can be symmetrical (e.g., unanimous) or nonsymmetrical (e.g., a leader can make a decision for a group), and each of these rules must also include a nonagreement rule
Information	Specify the channels used to communicate information among participants as well as what kinds of information can be transmitted by what positions Rules also may specify required frequency of interaction or an official language
Payoff	Assign external rewards and sanctions for particular actions or outcomes (for example, some kind of payment for completion of a task)
Scope	Specify which outcomes may, must, or must not be affected or produced within a situation Scope rules focus on *outcomes* (compared to choice rules, which focus on *actions*)

Source: Adapted from Ostrom 2005, 193–210.

Table 5.2
The default rule conditions in OSS commons, primarily applied to the operational level of analysis

Default rule	Conditions
Position	Only one position exists—"the developer"—operating at all decision-making levels (operational, collective choice, and constitutional)
Boundary (entry/exit)	Anyone can hold this position, and anyone can leave at any time
Choice	Each developer on the project can take any physically possible action (e.g., change any code or create new versions) as long as that action complies with the OSS license (constitutional-level rules)
Aggregation	Developers act independently
Information	Developers can communicate any information using any channel they desire
Payoff	Developers can retain any outcome they can obtain and defend
Scope	Developers can affect (e.g., edit) any component of the project that is physically accessible to them

Source: Adapted from Ostrom 2005, 211, table 7.2.

change the code or create new versions of the software—will remain in place. Without some minimal set of norms guiding who can do what to what components of the project, one programmer could potentially overwrite the work of another programmer.[5] The default-choice rule condition thus might be replaced with one that says "Developer 1 is the only one who can upload or commit work (to the versioning system) related to Component A; Developer 2 is the only one who can commit work on Component B." Or similarly, a social norm might be established that creates a new position rule—the position of project leader or maintainer. Our earlier description of the norms in the getting-help process provides excellent examples of information rules, such as "always respond to a bug through the bug-tracker mechanism so a history of the problem is recorded." But it is an open question to what degree these kinds of rules exist or are important in OSS commons. We investigate this in chapter 6.

Applying Ostrom's Rule Classification Scheme to Debian Linux

Just as we were fortunate to have Markus's and Ostrom's rule classifications to build on, we are also fortunate to have a documented case on OSS governance that we can use to demonstrate the utility of Ostrom's rule classification system. O'Mahony and Ferrarro (2007) provide a fairly detailed description of OSS rules in their case study of the governance of a large development team in the Debian Linux project.

As we will see, the O'Mahony and Ferrarro study is important for another reason: it highlights the dynamic nature of OSS institutions. Recall that the IAD framework in figure 3.1 represents a range of time, with feedback. We didn't articulate it in this way earlier, but the outcome variable we are most interested in is a change to the community attributes on the left side of figure 3.1, where people either join or stay with the project (success), or decide to leave it (abandonment). But looking at the outcome feedback loop in figure 3.1, another possible change over a chosen time range could be a shift in the project's institutional attributes. What O'Mahony and Ferraro's study explains are four phases in the evolution of the Debian Linux project's institutions and governance. Using their terminology, these are de facto governance (1993–1997), designing governance (1997–1999), implementing governance (1999–2003), and stabilizing governance (2003–2006). We provide a summary of the phases, defining events, and important details of the case in table 5.3.

In phase 1 of the Debian Linux case, de facto governance, O'Mahony and Ferrarro describe the first five-year period where the Debian developers worked under a set of informal norms at two levels (operational and collective choice). The details about these informal norms are sketchy, except for references to an established and recognized project leader—an operational-level position rule—who "provides contributing members with representation or to resolve disputes" (O'Mahony and Ferrarro 2007, 1087). This situation suggests there was some accepted set of norms related to developer dispute resolution (an operational-level aggregation rule). The authors mention other participants, referred to as "trusted lieutenants" (ibid., 1088). This label is used in much of the OSS literature to refer to developers who have more authority than other developers in terms of making technical changes to the next source code release. The reference to trusted lieutenants indicates the existence of other position rules, boundary rules (how people become trusted lieutenants), and choice rules (what actions trusted lieutenants can take, such as code commits, that are different from other Debian participants). So in the first phase of the Debian Linux project, there were minimally position, aggregation, choice, and boundary rules in place, operating at the operational and collective choice levels. Moreover, the OSS license specified constitutional-level rules, and thus all these types of rules existed as norms before there were any formal or written rules. In table 5.4, we provide a summary of the rules in the Debian case study (for two phases) and their associated rule categories (based on Ostrom 2005).

In phase 2 of the Debian Linux case, a formal constitution for the project was "designed, revised and ratified by 357 developers" (O'Mahony and Ferrarro, 2007, 1087). Therefore in this phase, rules at the constitutional, collective choice, and operational levels were formally defined, and sets of boundary, choice, and aggregation rules within these levels became apparent (column 2 in table 5.4).

Table 5.3
Summary of the institutional evolution of the Debian Linux OSS commons

Institutional evolutionary phase	Defining events	Important details
Phase 1: De facto governance (1993–1997)	Autocratic leadership emerges and is challenged by participating developers	Tensions with new leader (appointed by founder) because of being perceived as taking too much control of project led to want to instead formalize roles, rights, and responsibilities
Phase 2: Designing governance (1997–1999)	Formal positions of authority developed; formal authority is limited through democratic means	Drafted constitution formalizes roles, rights, and responsibilities, and 350 developers ratify it Key provisions: • requires developers with positional power to defer to collective wishes • project leader is subject to same rules as any member • any members can propose a general resolution to counter leader's actions • technical committee established with authority over technical debates and decisions
Phase 3: Implementing governance (1999–2003)	Various conceptions of type of leader needed are debated; community leaders are elected through democratic means	Annual elections Various leadership types: • "hands-off" leadership • technical manager • visionary • organizational building Visionary and organizational types elected during these four years
Phase 4: Stabilizing governance	Shared conception of project leader type emerges	General trend appears to be organizational-building type, probably partly reflecting that a technical committee also exists

Source: Adapted from O'Mahony and Ferraro 2007, 1085, table 2.

At the constitutional level, project participants created a constitution that formally defined the positions of members/developers, project leader, and technical committee members, and established rules at the collective choice and operational levels describing the duties of these positions. Moreover, boundary rules specified a one-year tenure for the project leader, a process for electing new leaders that included a self-nomination process, a period in which leadership platforms were to be vetted, and a three-week polling period to ensure all members would have time to weigh in. Choice rules placed parameters around technical committee actions and provided rights to general members so they could counter, if needed, a disputed action by a project

Table 5.4

Rules identified in phases 1 and 2 of the Debian Linux case

Phase 1 (de facto governance)	Phase 2 (defining governance)
Boundary rules (norms)	**Boundary rules (formal)**
None mentioned in case write-up	Constitutional level
	• project leaders are limited to one year
	• annual elections, with self-nominations allowed; three-week polling period
	Collective choice level
	• clear distinction between project leader's role and the technical committee's role
Position rules (norms)	**Position rules (formal)**
Constitutional and collective choice levels	Constitutional and collective choice levels
• project leader and trusted lieutenants	• Member/developer, project leader, and technical committee members
Choice rules (norms)	**Choice rules (formal)**
Operational level	Constitutional level
• trusted lieutenants' actions (e.g., code commits)	• technical committee cannot introduce new proposals, but has the authority to resolve disputes
• actions permitted/ prohibited to users or developers by the OSS license	• any member has the right to propose a general resolution that can counter a leader's actions
	Collective choice level
	• technical committee can decide any technical matter where developer jurisdictions overlap
	Operational level
	• the technical committee and project leader must make decisions that are consistent with the consensus of the opinions of the developers
Information rules	**Information rules**
None mentioned in case write-up	None mentioned in case write-up
Aggregation rules (norms)	**Aggregation rules**
Operational-level	Constitutional level
• project leader responsible for dispute resolution	• in order to overrule a developer, a supermajority (three-fourths) of the [technical] committee must agree
	• the case study suggests that there is a process for dealing with a general resolution in response to a leader's actions, but it is not described in any more detail
Payoff and scope rules	**Payoff and scope rules**
None mentioned in case write-up	None mentioned in case write-up

Source: Adapted from descriptions in O'Mahony and Ferraro, 2007, 1088–1092.

leader. Aggregation rules described how the technical committee overrules a developer. For example, the case states, "In order to overrule a developer, a supermajority (three-fourths) of the [technical] committee must agree" (O'Mahony and Ferarro 2007, 1089).

At the collective choice level, boundary rules distinguished the project leader and technical committee's jurisdictions, and a choice rule provided the technical committee with the authority to decide technical matters where developer jurisdictions overlap (O'Mahony and Ferarro 2007, 1089).

At the operational level, a scope rule required the technical committee and project leaders to make decisions consistent with a consensus of opinions of the developers. And while the constitution did not describe specific operational-level choice rules related to the Debian project leader, there were hints that some indeed exist, as this quote by one Debian Linux developer suggests: "We had this DPL [Debian project leader] . . . but we never really said what he could or could not do. He had been doing things, so it [the constitution] kind of codified what he had been doing or what we wanted [him] to be doing and what we did not want him to be doing" (O'Mahony and Ferarro 2007, 1089).

The descriptions of the final two governance phases in O'Mahony and Ferrarro's Debian Linux case—implementing governance and stabilizing governance—focus more on the types of people who were nominated or took on the project leader position, and how a shared understanding eventually developed of what kind of leader was needed in that position. In other words, it took several years to develop a common understanding about the role of the leader position, which was refined through the process of annual elections. The authors point out that in the first four years after the constitution was ratified, four different leadership types appeared: hands-off, technical manager, visionary, and organization builder. Gradually, and into the last phase of stabilizing governance (2003–2006), the project leader's scope and role became more refined (indicating changes in operational-level rules through collective choice processes), and people of the organization-builder type were elected. These people were more concerned about the functioning of established institutions, leaving technical decision making to the developers and technical committee.

As we noted earlier, this case study offers some deeper insight into the evolution of OSS institutions. The Debian Linux case moved over time from a system of informal norms to a formal constitution that articulated position, boundary, choice, and aggregation rules. O'Mahony and Ferrarro did not intend to document every rule in the case; consequently, it's likely that they did not report some operational, collective choice, and constitutional rules that existed. Nevertheless, using a case study, their work demonstrates that many informal and formal OSS institutions do exist. Even more important, we were able to use their work to show that the three IAD levels (operational, collective choice, and constitutional) and seven rule types noted by

Ostrom (2005) provide a standard structure or framework that is useful for articulating the informal and formal rules established in OSS commons.

Sponsors, Nonprofit Foundations, and Open-Source Software Institutions

In chapter 4, we mentioned organizational sponsorship through financial donations or by directing employees to contribute to OSS projects. We also noted that in these kinds of situations, a project may or may not permit the sponsoring organization any extra input into decision-making processes because of their sponsorship. It could be that even with this external support, the project's governance structure remains the same. In other cases, however, it could be that sponsorship somehow results in a change in the governance structure, and either breathes new life into the project or leads it closer to abandonment because the governance (and culture) has shifted so radically.

Related to organizational sponsorship, one major change in OSS in general is the emergence of nonprofit foundations that provide shelter and support for one or more OSS projects. O'Mahony (2007, 140) puts it this way: "Most successful, mature OSS projects producing commercial grade code have well developed approaches to not only software development, but to their overall governance. Often this includes a formal leadership role, a representative body of decision-makers and a non-profit foundation to protect the community's interests." We described this situation in some depth in chapter 2, and pointed toward a variety of roles for the nonprofit, including holding assets (hardware and code) for the project, protecting developers from liability, conducting public relations and marketing, facilitating communication between related but separate projects, conflict mediation, and property rights enforcement.

O'Mahony (2007, 145) lists five general principles that characterize several large OSS commons (Debian, Apache GNOME, and Linux Standards Base) that have nonprofit umbrella organizations like those we described above. These principles are:

Independence: The project makes decisions and acts independently of any particular sponsor

Pluralism The project embraces multiple points of view, even when they sometimes are in conflict with one another

Representation Members of the contributing team have representation in decision-making situations

Decentralized decision making Members of the contributing team participate directly in decision-making situations

Autonomous participation The community embraces new participation, and new members contribute on "their own terms"

Table 5.5

The institutional (I) design of OSS commons: Research questions (RQ) and testable hypotheses (H) (where possible)

Understanding OSS Institutions

RQ-I1: How are OSS projects governed?

H-I1 (large team hypothesis): OSS commons with larger teams will have more formalized and complicated institutional designs compared to ones with smaller teams

H-I2 (hybrid team hypothesis): All-volunteer OSS commons will have less formalized institutional designs compared to hybrid (e.g., volunteer and paid) OSS commons

RQ-I2: What kinds of rules (e.g., position, boundary, and choice) are commonly found in OSS commons?

RQ-I3: Does sponsorship or foundation involvement appear to influence the institutional design of OSS projects?

RQ-I4: Is there an evolutionary pattern to OSS institutions?

H-I3 (institutional evolution hypothesis): OSS commons will move from informal norms to more formalized rules and governance structures as more developers join the project, or as firms or other organizations become involved

Investigating the role institutions play in project success and abandonment

RQ-I5: Does the choice of OSS license effect the success or abandonment of a project? For instance, do GPL-compatible licensed projects outperform GPL-incompatible projects, or vice versa?

RQ-I6: Are certain governance structures associated with the success or abandonment of OSS commons?

H-I4 (friction hypothesis): The more formalized that institutions become, the more likely the project will be abandoned

H-I5 (Debian hypothesis): As OSS projects evolve and grow (in terms of developer numbers), formal institutions become a necessary condition in order to avoid abandonment

RQ-I7: Are OSS projects that exhibit more democratic, collective choice mechanisms more successful than ones appearing more autocratic?

H-I6 (aggregation rule hypothesis): OSS commons with aggregation rules where the developers have a say in the design of those rules will be more successful than ones where developers have little or no say

---

Like rule categories offered by Markus (2007), these concepts easily map or overlay with the ideas of operational, collective choice, and constitutional rules as well as the seven rule types put forth by Ostrom (2005), and they may serve as a platform for us here as we work toward design principles for OSS commons.

To summarize, the emergence of the more complex OSS ecosystem, with organizations involved in OSS projects, raises new questions about what this means for OSS self-governance and institutional design. The effort by Mahony (2005, 2007) to establish baseline principles for foundation-managed situations is a significant step forward. But there still is much we do not understand about how institutions are structured in various situations. More generally, does a formal connection with a nonprofit foundation help ensure OSS success? Or do the added institutional frictions mandated by an overarching foundation create additional tensions that move a project toward abandonment? These are questions not well understood, and ones we hope to shed light on in the later portions of this book.

Conclusion

This brings us to the completion of part II of this book; we now have a theoretical foundation, solidly grounded in decades of past research from a variety of relevant disciplines. But we have much more to do. We achieved our goal in this chapter of uncovering some institutional factors that bind the software and the community involved in OSS projects into a productive enterprise, and we have generated seven research questions and six testable hypotheses about these institutions (shown in table 5.5). Across chapters 2–5, we have generated more than forty research questions and testable hypotheses as part of our ambitious attempt to take a comprehensive approach to understanding what makes OSS projects successful or causes them to be abandoned.

Also, we have explained concepts contained within our guiding analytic IAD framework. We have described the central actor (the open-source developer) along with his or her motivations within the context of a complex ecosystem of organizations and people. We covered two sets of factors—technological and community attributes—thought to drive the actor's ongoing decision to stay and keep working, or alternatively, leave a project. Finally, we have discussed OSS institutions and presented a methodology, taken from natural resource commons research, for studying these institutions going forward. Scholars like O'Mahony, Ferraro, Markus, and O'Neil have lifted the lid of the black box we call OSS institutions, and helped us create hypotheses that we will examine in following chapters in the hope of shedding even more light on this understudied area of OSS research.

We have now reached an exciting juncture: we leave the theoretical study behind and, in part III, turn to our own empirical investigation (research based in real world observation). We are ready to begin answering the research questions and hypotheses in chapters 2 through5 we have worked hard to identify.

III Our Empirical Studies of Open-Source Software Commons

Part II examined our two years of theoretical research and thinking about the OSS phenomenon, but theory and thought are not enough. For our research to be convincing, we must test our theories and ideas against observations. This part of the book describes several empirical studies we undertook over a three-year period in order to do that.

In chapter 6, we begin by interviewing people working on OSS projects in the real world. Based on these interviews, we present a case study of OSGeo, a federation composed of OSS projects associated with an overarching nonprofit support organization. We hope that chapter 6 will help to make real some of the more abstract ideas we presented in part II as well as prepare the way for the statistical work that answers many of the research questions and hypotheses that we have articulated to this point in the discovery process.

In chapter 7, we explain how we carefully defined the success and abandonment of OSS projects, and classified nearly all the projects hosted on SF into those categories. Having accomplished that, we studied the voluminous data already available about SF projects to get a preliminary idea about some of our hypotheses, and what factors differ between successful and abandoned projects, as explored in chapter 8. As documented in chapter 9, taking those findings into account, we constructed a questionnaire and surveyed SF developers to create measures for factors that were not in the existing SF data. All that work taken together ultimately led to answers, presented in chapter 10, for nearly every one of our testable hypotheses. In chapter 11, we describe the final step in our empirical research: a multivariate model of OSS success and abandonment that takes all the factors we uncovered and measured into consideration. Once again, we caution readers that we are presenting ambitious, rigorous, complex social science research. Some readers may wish to skim detailed discussions of our variables and statistical methodology; other readers, however, may want to refer to this book's Web site (http://www.umass.edu/opensource/schweik/supplementary.html) to find even more detailed information, which we removed from the book to make it more concise and readable. Whatever your preference, we inivte you to continue with us in our journey of discovery in part III.

6 The OSGeo Case: An Example of the Evolving OSS Ecosystem

with Meelis Kitsing

OSGeo is a nonprofit foundation that provides support to a number of OSS projects creating software in the GIS domain. GIS software can be generally described as mapping software that links information to its position on the earth's surface. For instance, we know one person who used GIS software to pinpoint the locations of nests of the national bird of the Caribbean nation of Saint Lucia in an effort to create a rich visual representation that would help the government preserve that species' habitat. Open-source GIS software makes a major public goods contribution by giving average people, especially those in developing countries, access to free GIS software. In addition, author Schweik is leading an OSGeo-based global effort to encourage educators at all levels to develop and share educational material related to open-source GIS technologies.

We placed this chapter on OSGeo at the beginning of part III because it provides a break from the theoretical work of part II, and focuses on a real organization and the people involved in it. Nevertheless, this chapter still contributes to our theoretical research by systematically studying the community and institutional settings of projects that reside in a more complex open-source ecosystem—one where firms and nonprofits as well as volunteers are working together. From this study, we gained insight, coming from developers in the field, about community and institutional variables they think lead to the collaborative success of their projects, and we made sure to include these factors in our quantitative research in later chapters. The work done here also helped us create questions for our "Survey on Free/Libre and Open Source Success," described in chapter 9.

We start this chapter by discussing why we chose OSGeo for our case study. Next, we look at the history of OSGeo, including quite interesting information about its finances and assets. This history helps to concretize the open-source ecosystem we portrayed in chapter 2. Then we examine the methods we used to conduct our interviews. Finally, we report what interviewees said about their projects, and analyze what their responses mean in the context of the technological, community, and institutional attributes of OSS projects that we looked at in part II and that enable case comparisons.

Why OSGeo?

We selected OSGeo as a case study for two main reasons. First and most important, it exhibits the kind of complexity we described in chapter 2; a number of individual open-source projects that involve firms or government support as well as volunteer contributors, and are loosely connected with one another through affiliation with an overarching nonprofit foundation. Second, and in the interest of full disclosure, author Schweik has been working with this foundation as its education and curriculum committee chair.[1] This affiliation provided easier access to respondents because of the trust built already, but because Schweik did not conduct the interviews personally, the connection should not bias what we do here.

Before we go further, we need to point out several key considerations related to our selection of OSGeo as a case to study. On the one hand, using OSGeo complicates our analysis because many governance variables are not dependent on the individual projects but instead stem from the bargaining between the foundation and specific projects. On the other hand, our selection strategy simplifies our research because the requirements of OSGeo reduce institutional variation and thus the number of variables we need to study. Since all projects in this study also fall in the category of geospatial OSS, we further minimize the variation that would be caused by the many different software categories that exist in the vast domain of OSS development. Even though the variation of some variables is limited, our approach allows us to be somewhat representative of the broader open-source community because we have different institutional evolutions, different roles of firms, different communities, and different interactions between informal and formal institutions across the cases. Hence, the cases represent sufficient variation in many independent variables to produce meaningful results.

About the OSGeo Foundation

OSGeo (2009c) succinctly describes its purpose on its Web site: "To support the development of open-source geospatial software, and promote its widespread use." In November 2005, in Delaware, a diverse group of individuals and organizations involved with open-source geospatial software created the foundation as a nonprofit corporation under section 501(c)(3) of the United States Internal Revenue Code. The founders initially named the organization the Mapserver Foundation after one of the major associated projects, but later changed the name to OSGeo in February 2006.

History

We can best understand OSGeo and its structure as a federation of OSS projects by looking at the history of geospatial software in the United States. Although some proprietary geospatial software was available at the time, some U.S. government agencies decided to develop geospatial software for their own use. Specifically, the U.S. Army Corps of Engineers developed the Geographic Resources Analysis Support System (GRASS), which it used extensively during the 1980s (OGC 2008). When these agencies decided to stop developing GRASS and other geospatial software in 1992, a group of interested users, software developers, academic organizations, and business organizations formed the Open GRASS Foundation (OGF). OGF, structured as a nonprofit, made decisions in a consensus-based, cooperative manner. By 1994, OGF had transformed itself into the Open Geospatial Consortium, Inc. (OGC), and changed its focus from creating software to creating interoperability standards for the geospatial software industry (Mitasova and Neteler 2004).

A great deal of crucial open-source GIS software has been developed since 1994, and this fact, together with the vacuum left by the OGC's transformation, created a need that has been filled by the establishment of the OSGeo (2011) in 2006. Like OGF, OSGeo uses consensus and democratic structures to make decisions cooperatively in a federation that has gathered over a dozen open-source geospatial software projects under its wing.

Finances

The finances of OSGeo are transparent and readily available on the organization's Web site. From 2006 to 2007, income grew from about $63,000 to almost $623,000—a nearly tenfold increase. Expenses went from $22,000 to $488,000 over the same period. In 2007, approximately 30 percent of revenues consisted of donations from sponsors (mostly businesses), with the remaining revenues coming from conference fees. About 68 percent of the expenses went to running an annual conference on free and open-source geospatial software, with the remaining expenditures going to other operating costs.[2] Clearly OSGeo has grown since its creation.

According to Tyler Mitchell (2009), OSGeo's executive director, the software projects gathered under the foundation's umbrella required approximately 2,114 person-years of programming. Using U.S. Bureau of Labor Statistics information for the average cost of computer programmers, Mitchell estimates that this would mean that the foundation manages programming assets of at least US$116 million.

Institutional Structure

OSGeo and the projects under its umbrella have a rich institutional structure that includes all the rule categories described in chapter 5 and shown in table 6.1. Rather than specifying detailed and specific rules, however, as we did in table 5.4

Table 6.1

Ostrom's seven general rule categories in OSGeo's institutional design

Ostrom's rule category	Ostrom's definition	Examples in OSGeo's institutional design
Position rules	Define the positions that participants hold	Board of directors (BOD) President and CEO Vice president Committee chair Corporate officer Member Participant
Boundary rules	Define: • who is eligible to take a position (succession rules) • the process that determines which participants may enter (entry rules), such as by invitation, through some sort of competition, or compulsory • how an individual can leave a position (exit rules) Other rules may exist regarding the relationship between multiple positions, such as a mandate that one person cannot hold multiple positions at the same time	BOD election BOD member leaving Committee chair Charter versus other members
Choice rules	Specify what participants in positions must, must not, or may do in their positions, and in particular circumstances Choice rules focus on *actions*	Bylaws for BOD Bylaws for officers Committee rules/policies Incubation process
Aggregation rules	Determine whether a decision by a single or multiple participants is needed prior to an action at a decision point in a process Aggregation rules are needed whenever choice rules provide multiple positions or partial control over the same sorts of actions Aggregation rules can be symmetrical (e.g., unanimity) or nonsymmetrical (where a leader can make a decision for a group), and each also must include a nonagreement rule	Symmetrical: Consensus in committees Nonsymmetrical: BOD creates committees

Table 6.1

(continued)

Ostrom's rule category	Ostrom's definition	Examples in OSGeo's institutional design
Information rules	Specify the channels used to communicate information among participants as well as what kinds of information can be transmitted by what positions Other rules may exist to specify required frequency of interaction or an official language	Meeting minutes required Meeting notification required Annual meetings required Financial statements required
Pay-off rules	Assign external rewards or sanctions for particular actions or outcomes (e.g., a payment for completion of a task)	Executive director and others can be paid BOD cannot be paid
Scope rules	Specify which outcomes may, must, or must not be affected within a situation Scope rules focus on *outcomes* (compared to choice rules, which focus on *actions*)	Organizational mission Committee mission

Source: Adapted from Ostrom 2005, 193–210.

for the Debian Linux case, we will provide broad examples of what we have discovered.

As mentioned above, OSGeo is a state of Delaware corporation having detailed bylaws at the constitutional and collective choice levels. Position rules define and place ultimate power with the charter members, who elect the board of directors (BOD) and vote to admit other charter members. In addition to charter members, OSGeo recognizes *members* and *participants*. Members are people who can participate in foundation-related activities (e.g., write code to specific projects, participate in the committees, or follow and contribute to mailing list dialogue) and have formally self-registered on the foundation's Web site. Participants can do the same things as members, but have not self-registered (OSGeo 2009b). Choice rules specify that both members and participants can contribute to projects and join foundation committees, but cannot vote for the BOD or to appoint new charter members.

The choice rules specified in the OSGeo constitution give the BOD exclusive rights to create committees and appoint the committee chairs as well as take any lawful actions not specified in the bylaws. A position rule requires that a committee chair must either hold a seat on the BOD or be an officer of the corporation. Currently there are eight committees: Web site, finance, incubation, marketing, public geospatial data, education and curriculum, system administration, and conference. Operational-level choice rules describe how OSS projects that are not yet formally affiliated become official OSGeo projects. These rules lay out a detailed and well-documented incubation process presided over by the incubation committee. Each official OSGeo project has a representative on the incubation committee (another specified position rule), and each project in incubation is assigned a mentor, who is also a member of the committee. Thus, someone who is familiar with or previously went through the process guides each project during incubation.

In order to become an official OSGeo project, the project in incubation must form a project steering committee that is also a legal committee of OSGeo. As required by a constitutional boundary rule, the committee chair either must be a member of the OSGeo BOD or an OSGeo corporate officer. The requirement of being corporate officer is met when the BOD appoints the person whom the project selects to be chair as a designated vice president (see OSGeo 2009a). Although this process technically puts each project officially under the control of the OSGeo BOD, in practice the projects maintain freedom and autonomy. Official OSGeo projects, for example, are encouraged to use OSGeo-provided hosting services (Web sites, version control, mailing lists, etc.), but are not required to do so.

The OSGeo corporate officers include the BOD chair, a president, secretary, and treasurer, plus other officers that the BOD may appoint as necessary. The president automatically becomes the CEO, unless the board votes otherwise, and along with the secretary and treasurer, is responsible for the day-to-day foundation operations. As of this writing, there are sixteen vice presidents tasked with specific projects and functional areas (OSGeo 2009a).

In sum, at multiple IAD levels (constitutional, collective choice, and operational) OSGeo has established position rules that define the positions participants hold (board members, committee chairs, corporate officers, and incubation project mentors). Boundary rules specify processes for how people enter these positions as well as how successors take over. Choice rules regarding what participants in positions may, must, or must not do are outlined in organizational bylaws as well as committee rules and policies. Aggregation rules guide committees and the board at decision-making junctures. Other rules specify information flow, payoff, and general organization and committee mission statements, which qualify, to some degree, as a scope rule.

Our Research Methods

In their book *Case Studies and Theory Development in the Social Sciences*, Alexander George and Andrew Bennett (2005, 75) describe six different approaches to case research. The study we undertake here comes under their "disciplined configurative" category, which implies the use of established institutionalist theories to explain the case. In addition to offering a systematic way for conducting empirical research, this approach can help create a new theory or point out the need for adjusting existing theory (ibid.).

Based on our chosen approach, we start our case research with institutionalist theories that allow us to make predictions about what kinds of relationships we expect to see between our independent variables and the success or abandonment of OSGeo projects. If on the basis of our interviews we found out that the predicted relationship exists, then we can entertain the possibility that there is a causal relationship. For instance, if our theory tells us that high levels of social capital allow for the solving of collective active dilemmas in OSS commons, and we observe high levels of social capital across the successful cases we study, then we can conclude that a causal relationship might exist between the level of social capital and a project's success. We must be careful, of course, not to make a case for causality on the presence of mere consistency. Similar logic applies here as in statistical analysis, where correlation does not necessarily imply causality.

To further clarify the discussion of causality, we need to underscore that six of the seven projects we study are collaborative success stories using our definition of success (see chapter 7). The other project was discontinued or abandoned a few days before the interview was conducted with the project leader. There is consequently little variation in the dependent variable. Yet from the methodological point of view, having the one abandoned case is a positive development as it allows us to see whether some important variables that were present in the successful cases are missing in the failed one. The lack or weak presence of these variables may explain why the failed case was abandoned. In addition, the lack of variation in success and abandonment is not as severe as it may seem, because we asked developers about their involvement with OSS projects outside OSGeo, and factors that might have led to the success or abandonment of those projects. Because many of these developers have worked on other projects that could have been abandoned, we also collected variation based on their previous experiences. Nevertheless, we do recognize that having only one abandoned case is not sufficient to make a substantive conclusion. Our method therefore is closest to what John Stuart Mill identified in his 1843 *A System of Logic* as the "method of agreement," which is also known as a positive comparative method (George and Bennett 2005, 153). This method reveals similarities in the independent variables related to a common outcome in several cases, but is mainly capable of discovering "necessary" but not "sufficient" conditions for the success of OSS projects.

Interview Methodology

In fall 2008, we studied the Web sites of individual projects and OSGeo, and then conducted individual, semistructured elite interviews with project participants. Semistructured interviews offer a sufficient amount of structure for making comparisons across the cases, but provide deeper insights than supplied by rigidly structured interviews. By "elite" interviews, we mean that we interviewed people in important positions. We conducted our interviews with two representatives from each project (except in one project, which was abandoned and for which we were able to conduct only one interview). We usually interviewed the formal or informal project leader along with a core developer. We chose this approach because our interview questions were complex and required a good knowledge of institutional history.

We contacted only full-member OSGeo projects, as opposed to up-and-coming ones, which are not yet deemed full foundation members and thus are in the incubation phase. Initially, we contacted all ten (at the time) full-member OSGeo projects; however, only seven representatives of the ten OSGeo-affiliated projects were willing to be interviewed. We chose only full-member projects because we needed to have projects with sufficient institutional history to see the change of their governance structures over time. In other words, we wanted to study how an overarching foundation with formally affiliated projects as well as the involvement of both volunteer and paid developers affects the institutional and community evolution of such projects.

We used Skype or the telephone to conduct interviews. The interviewees were located in the United States (Alaska, Arizona, and Massachusetts), Canada (British Columbia and Ontario), Europe (Poland, Switzerland, Italy, Germany, and France), and Australia. We are keeping the project names anonymous, identifying them here as A, B, C, D, E, F, and G.

The Interviews

We start this section by looking at what our interviewees said about the histories of their projects, then report what these OSS developers said about their communities, and finally turn to the institutional structures that guide their projects and make them successful.

What Interviewees Said about Their Project Histories

All seven OSGeo projects that we studied have diverse historical characteristics, as shown in table 6.2. One of them traces its history back to the early 1980s, when the U.S. Army Corps of Engineers initiated it. Three projects began in the 1990s (one in the early 1990s, and two in the late 1990s). The other three are relatively young, starting in this century.

Two projects (B and D; see table 6.2) follow a development trajectory in which a company realized that it had insufficient resources for developing needed software on its own and decided to make its development process open-source (such as the examples of software spinouts mentioned in chapter 3). In comparison with the other projects, these two exhibit a more limited, narrow technical solution and/or geographic focus, implying that their reach is more local than global.

Table 6.2
Some general historical characteristics of OSGeo-affiliated projects

Project's historical and institutional characteristics	Project A	Project B	Project C	Project D	Project E	Project F	Project G
Year started	Early 1980s; in its current form since 1999	1997 initial idea; 2003 in open-source environment	2003	2005	2002	1998	Early 1990s; in its current form since 2004
Began initially as closed-source code (e.g., spinout project)	Government spinout	Corporate spinout	No	Corporate spinout	No	No	No
Dominant governance form prior to joining the OSGeo	Decentralized	Dominant firm and person in charge	Dominant person in charge	Dominant firm in charge	Dominant person in charge	Dominant person in charge	Dominant person in charge
Abandoned?	No	No	Yes	No	No	No	No
Open-source license used	GPL	GPL	Lesser GPL	BSD-style license	GPL	X/MIT	Lesser GPL

The other five projects, from their inception, have been more significantly shaped by the developers' community and have not necessarily followed a linear development path (meaning the more traditional development processes found in firms). The degree of uncertainty in these projects' futures has been greater because they have not received the same financial or human resources as the other two projects. In other words, in the spinout projects, the firms have given them more support because they tend to use the projects as an open-source substitute for in-house proprietary software development. The nonspinout projects nevertheless tend to evolve, and their outcomes are a result of interactions of multiple key players, whose interests may not be as consistent, and whose strategies and vision may not be as focused. This does not mean that the other projects are better; they just follow different development courses. In the case of these five noncorporate projects, the initial organization of software development went through several changes before settling in its current form.

In six out of seven projects we studied, we can identify a dominant person and/or firm in charge before the project joined OSGeo and adopted its project management guidelines. The implications of this dominance should not imply that other project developers have little say. Quite to the contrary, interviews revealed that one of the rationales for why the project founders turned to the open-source model of software development is to cultivate a diversity of ideas and input. Yet the developers' community either implicitly or explicitly accepted the basic direction given by the authority of the dominant firm or person.

This dominance takes many different forms ranging from dictatorship, to a being a leader by default when collective action dilemmas require someone to be in charge and make a final decision. In other words, we found cases of a strong leader model, where one person always makes key project decisions and other cases where the leadership is slightly looser, but in all instances, it becomes necessary for someone to step up and give the project a clear direction at critical decision-making junctures. Some of the project leadership arrangements that existed before OSGeo membership, however, had to change as a condition of formal OSGeo affiliation. For example, the founder and dominant person of project F noted that in order to become an OSGeo partner, the project needed to replace a benevolent dictatorship type of leadership system with a steering committee model within two years.

All projects have some established hierarchy, and some asymmetries exist among different participants. Moreover, even if the size of the development team affiliated with the project varies significantly, the core team in each project studied is relatively small. The projects have embedded property rights, and six of seven projects have a dominant person in charge, which gives them implicit ownership of the project (recall our discussions of open-source projects as common property in chapter 2).

What Interviewees Said about Community

Despite the differences in history, all the projects have highly similar community characteristics, and interviewees assign importance to these factors in explaining their projects' successes. Tables 6.3 and 6.4 summarize these attributes. This discussion relates back to chapter 4 (see table 4.2), where we described heterogeneity and other community attributes.

Heterogeneity

In chapter 4, we noted that the concept of team heterogeneity or homogeneity has, potentially, many components. We highlighted three: interest or motivational, socio-cultural, and asset or skill. Table 6.3 illustrates our findings for OSGeo projects for each of these three concepts.

Regarding interest or motivational heterogeneity, the first three rows in table 6.3 show firm, nongovernmental organization (NGO), or government involvement in the seven projects we studied. Beginning with the row labeled "involvement of firms," we see that direct involvement varies across these projects. Two projects (A and E) have no direct firm involvement: business interests do not play a significant role in project management, and the majority of the project's core developers are not on the firm's payroll. Both projects have support from public sector organizations, though. In two other cases (projects B and D), we can identify a dominant firm that was instrumental in initiating the project and managing its development process, and continues to do so. In these two cases the firms were involved because they needed the software to support their businesses, but did not have sufficient development resources to do this completely in-house. Three other projects (C, F, and G) have several firms directly involved and paying the salary of the core development team. In these situations, the firms contribute resources because they either consult using the software or need the software to support internal business processes.

Moving to the "involvement of NGOs" row in table 6.3, NGOs are directly involved in the development of two projects (D and G). In project G, about 50 percent of the core development team is paid by this NGO. The third data row in table 6.3, labeled "involvement of public sector," shows that five of the seven projects have some degree of direct, public sector involvement. Yet public support in all these cases is less compared to the involvement and support by firms. Most core developers are paid and also receive significant work-related benefits for advancing the projects. Firms, government agencies, or NGOs pay some programmers to participate because those organizations use the software. Firms use the software in their service offerings to clients, and the advancement of the software leads to direct benefits to the firm. To a certain extent, the same can be said of the cases with public sector support. The bottom line is that the benefits take multiple forms, but the main benefit is the use of software by the organization itself or some of its employees.

Table 6.3
Community heterogeneity characteristics of OSGeo-affiliated projects, 2008

General concept (chapter 3)	Project characteristic	Project A	Project B	Project C	Project D	Project E	Project F	Project G
Interest/ motivation heterogeneity/ homogeneity	Involvement of firms	No	Yes; dominant firm	Yes; several firms	Yes; dominant firm	No	Yes; several firms	Yes; several firms
	Involvement of NGOs	No	No	No	Yes	No	No	One dominant NGO; pays 50% of core team
	Involvement of public sector	Yes	Yes; one programmer paid by government	No	Yes	Yes	No	Yes
	Core developers: paid or volunteer	Volunteer	Paid	Paid	Paid	Volunteer	Paid	Paid
Sociocultural heterogeneity/ homogeneity	Geographic location of developers	All continents covered except Africa and South America	Core team is from one location in Germany; others are from India, United States, Greece, and Finland	All around the world	United States, Mexico, Netherlands, France, Spain, and Austria	United States, Australia, New Zealand, Switzerland, South Africa, Sweden, and Czech Republic	United States, Canada, Czech Republic, Poland, and Russia	United States, Canada, Australia, Europe, and Asia
Asset (skill) heterogeneity/ homogeneity	Skill levels of developers (similar/ diverse)	Diverse	Diverse	Diverse	Diverse	Diverse	Diverse	Diverse

Table 6.4
Community attributes of OSGeo-affiliated projects, 2008

General concept (chapter 4)	Project characteristic (chapter 4)	Project A	Project B	Project C	Project D	Project E	Project F	Project G
Group size	Size of the core development team	5–10 developers	4 developers	6–7 developers	10–12 developers	4–5 developers	7 developers	10 developers
	Approximate size of developer community	40 developers; 10 are active	15 developers; about 10 are active	20 developers; 10 are active	377 on the list; 50–100 are active	13–14 developers	37 developers; 15 are active	50 developers; 35 are active
Social capital	Regular face-to-face meetings	No	Regular meetings	No more than once per year	Regular meetings	No more than once per year	No more than once per year	No
	Relationship among the team members	Professional but friendly	Friends	Friends	Friends	Professional but friendly	Core team members are friends	Professional but friendly
	Degree of trust	High	High	High	High	High	High	High
	Sense of community	Yes	Yes	Yes	Yes	Yes	Yes	Yes
	Reciprocity (general or specific)	General	Specific	General	General	General	General	General and specific

As shown in the fourth row in table 6.3, two projects (A and E) are primarily volunteer, meaning that a significant percentage of paid programmers have been involved in these projects' development. But this does not mean that the programmers' key interest or motivation is to provide a public good. Rather, in these cases, the contributors are also users of software, and they are interested in improving the quality of it, at least in part, for their own reasons. Project A core team members, for instance, are affiliated with universities, and use the software in their research and teaching. This offers evidence in support of the user-driven innovation hypothesis (table 3.1, H-C1): projects will be more successful when developers of the software product are also the software users.

As David and Shapiro (2008) point out, developer incentives and motivations change over time. The majority of these projects have generated commercial interest that led to the hiring of previously volunteer developers. In the case of several projects (E, F, and G), the current state of relying primarily on paid programmers was preceded by a phase in which most of the development team was volunteer. As success breeds more success, the projects attract new developers, who may start as volunteers but soon find an opportunity to get paid for their development efforts. As the leader of project B emphasized in our interview, "Good programmers do not volunteer for a long time because firms quickly hire them."

Regarding sociocultural heterogeneity, individual OSGeo-affiliated projects give the impression that they are all generally diverse. The row labeled "geographic location of developers" in table 6.3 shows that with the possible exception of project B, each project has developers contributing from a number of different countries. While there is some geographic variation, which provides some sociocultural heterogeneity, at the same time all the developers we interviewed were male, and primarily from Western, economically well-developed countries. In other words, geographically these projects are moderately diverse, but other aspects suggest relatively homogeneous sociocultural attributes.

In terms of asset heterogeneity, most project development teams exhibit a fairly diverse skill level, which for our interviewees is considered an advantage rather than a weakness. The bottom line, according to the respondents, is that projects need people with different skill levels. People with less sophisticated skills still find plenty of ways to contribute to the project, such as editing manuals and/or testing software.

Group Size

Now let's turn to the other community characteristics described in chapter 4 and summarized in table 6.4. The first is the role of group or development team size. Within our OSGeo-affiliated projects, all teams have a clearly definable core group of programmers, which seems to take care of most of the work. The size of the core developer group (first row, table 6.4) varies across the projects, with the smallest being four developers (project B), and the largest being ten to twelve developers (project D). All of these projects have teams larger than the mean group project size we found in our quantitative work that follows in later chapters. All projects report a larger development community beyond this core team, some of which are sizable (for example, project D reports fifty to a hundred contributors).

In a follow-up discussion, we asked OSGeo director Mitchell to explain this finding. He responded that we'd "hit on one of the core strengths of OSGeo. The incubation process does not allow or encourage projects that are not already mature. It's part of being an OSGeo project. You must have a diverse development team—not one person in a single company—and the incubation committee must be convinced you have a real community. It can be young, but not just you and your brothers in an organization."[3]

Social Capital

In chapter 4 (table 4.2), we listed several attributes and hypotheses related to the general concept of social capital, including the potential importance of geographic proximity and ability to hold regular face-to-face meetings; the establishment of friendly relationships, trust, and sense of community among developers; and the existence of general and/or specific reciprocity. Table 6.4 summarizes the other social capital attributes for OSGeo-affiliated projects.

Looking at table 6.4, we see that all projects exhibit high levels of trust among the developers, and the concept of trust was noted repeatedly in our interviews as an important factor in explaining the success of the projects. Relationships among team members were perceived as more than purely professional, but the emphasis varied. In four projects, developers consider themselves to be friends. In three projects, the relationship was characterized as being professional but friendly. These characterizations correlate with the geographic locations of the project members and frequency of face-to-face meetings—the greater the distances between programmers involved, the less likely they meet regularly or at all. This aspect, in turn, minimizes the chances that team members see each other as friends. In two cases (projects D and F, table 6.4), interviewees stressed that regular, face-to-face meetings among core developers was a crucial success factor. One firm dominates each of these two projects, and many core developers are located in the same city. In the other five cases, in-person meetings were not considered critical. In projects C, D, and F, some core developers meet face-to-face at most once a year, and in Projects A and G they do not meet face-to-face at all (table 6.4). Project A respondents told us that most key people have never met in person.

As a whole, the social capital rows in table 6.4 reveal that in most cases, the projects have established a sense of team community. They have attained high levels of trust, and core developers cooperate on the basis of general rather than specific reciprocity (see the reciprocity discussion in chapter 4). They do not meet regularly in person but instead rely on the use of communication technologies. Some groups depend more heavily on real-time synchronous IRC communication, and others rely more on asynchronous email, but the particular communication tools used do not seem to be an important variable. Only in the case of one project (B) did interviewees emphasize specific reciprocity as opposed to general. Yet this team is relatively small and dominated by one firm, with the majority of the core team in the same company and city.

What Interviewees Said about Institutions

Recall from chapters 3 and 5 that there are three primary rule levels that may govern open-source commons—operational, collective choice, and constitutional. As all the projects have joined OSGeo, the variation in the levels of rules across them is reduced. In the following analysis, the emphasis is on the "rules in use" resulting from the combination of established formal and informal rules. Our focus, in other words, is on the actual or de facto rules that make the projects work, rather than describing de jure, formal rule categories without considering how these rules are applied and interact with informal rules in reality.

Operational Rules

Our interviews documented the limited role of the formal operational-level rules (e.g., written rules on how the day-to-day coordination of work should be conducted or how decisions are to be made) required by OSGeo membership. In general, most of the core developers we interviewed were not sure of or familiar with the formal rules that govern their projects. Usually the project leader and/or head of the project steering committee was more familiar with the rules, but in many cases when we asked them about formalized (written) rules at any level (operational, collective choice, or constitutional), they had to look them up and/or did not remember what the rules said exactly. This implies, as was underscored throughout many interviews, that projects are often run on the basis of social norms versus any established formalized rules. In many cases, the evolution from informal to a more formal rule set was correlated with joining OSGeo, but in some instances, just the prospect of joining OSGeo triggered rule formalization. The formalization of rules in other projects occurred before OSGeo membership and did not stem from the process of OSGeo incorporation. Most important, these fairly similar sets of formal rules are not fully put into practice across all projects.

Interviewees also stressed the role of operational rules instead of constitutional and/ or collective choice ones in smoothing out the day-to-day management of projects. Collaborative technology helps to reduce transaction costs for implementing and maintaining operational rules. For example, the embedded logic contained in the versioning systems codify operational rule systems and replace the need for humans to manage them. Many functions of daily project management are also automated by using version control and bug-tracking systems. Interviewees reported that version control is important for operational coordination, and all projects now use the Subversion system, which replaced the CVS they used in the past. Hence, in these cases there is no variation in the versioning system. Yet no one claimed that only this particular version control system would serve their needs. One interviewee criticized Subversion for being too centralized and suggested that Mercurial, a distributed source code management system used by some other major open-source projects, might serve their needs better. In short, interviews confirmed that the rules embedded in the versioning technology play a critical part in which operational rules exist in these projects. We'll return to more specifics on a comparative analysis of established norms and rules in the next section.

Collective Choice Rules

Collective choice rules (rules and procedures about changing operational rules) did not seem to be important. Because all projects are under the OSGeo umbrella, they have similar collective choice rules where the project steering committee makes any operational change decisions by voting. In reality, however, the social norm seems to be to discuss everything and reach a consensus informally instead of formal voting. The process of choosing members for the project steering committee is not contested either. There is variation in the evolution of the collective choice rules because some projects were "dictatorships" before joining OSGeo and others followed a more collegial decision-making model (even though a dominant leader was usually in charge). Nevertheless, all projects have fairly clear developer hierarchies established, and not all programmers have exactly the same responsibilities.

Constitutional Rules

The developers we interviewed had some difficulty distinguishing between constitutional and operational rules. In some cases, answers to the question of whether the project had a formal constitution were affirmative, but then immediately followed with references to the developer's guide, which is more of a operational guide rather than a set of rules determining how decisions about community and operational rules are made. In other cases, the answer was "no," and the developer's guide was seen as operational rules. In still other ones, the response to the question of a formal constitution was affirmative, but the developers pointed out that the constitution is relatively short. Project A's leader, for instance, said the project's formal constitution is only about a half page of written text. This confusion across all projects over the idea of a formal project constitution generally implies that it is not a significant factor in a project's day-to-day governance. This does not mean that some formal constitutional components do not exist—certainly they do, such as the open-source license used (table 6.2) and the rules related to the project steering committee—but these issues are clearly not foremost in the developers' minds.

Ostrom's Rule Categories

Although the OSGeo projects do not depend greatly on formal rules, we wanted to tease out interactions between the formal rules that do exist *and* the social norms or informal rules that guide the day-to-day functioning of these projects. To do this, we applied Ostrom's rule categories to study in more detail the similarities and differences between the institutional structures of the OSGeo projects.

Table 6.5 summarizes institutional comparisons across our seven cases. Starting with the position rules (positions that people hold), all of them have a project steering or management committee (these labels generally mean the same thing) and an informal group of core developers that frequently overlaps with the formal management committee. Two projects do not have formal leaders (C and G), though. As we noted earlier, project C was abandoned in summer 2008. Project G is successful by our growth stage definition, but in interviews it was revealed that the project was dealing with some more extensive challenges in its daily management and addressing team conflict over potential direction compared to the others we studied. So the projects that were missing the informal position of a project leader seem to be at a disadvantage when compared with the other projects.

As far as boundary rules (eligibility for along with entering and leaving positions) are concerned, all projects studied have formal rules, but often they are not followed and instead replaced by a set of social norms. Similarly, in the case of choice rules (actions that people can take in various positions), projects rely primarily on social norms for guidance. Our comparisons of aggregation rules (specifying how key decisions are made) across these cases revealed that all projects have a steering or management committee that relies on voting as its decision-making method. Usually only committee member votes count. Yet most decisions are made on the basis of consensus (which is not required by OSGeo rules), settled by discussion, and in one case all developers vote, but only the committee vote matters. The project thus is primarily managed on social norms versus strictly following the formal rules. As one project leader pointed out, having too many formal rules can dampen developers' motivation. Managing the project on the basis of formal rules, in other words, can make it difficult to keep current developers and gain new ones, reflecting the idea of formal rules as friction that we raised in chapter 5.

Similarly, information rules (what and how information is communicated, by whom, and how frequently) rely on social norms as opposed to strict formal rules that stipulate which channels will be used. Projects depend on both email and IRC. Some projects have weekly IRC meetings. But what really seems to matter is not the norm for communication itself but instead how much effort is put into using the communication channels to make vital information easily available. For instance, projects C and D essentially provide the same functionality, and could be considered competitors, but project D appears to have used IRC communication more effectively. One of project D's core developers was available on the IRC almost all the time and is known for quickly answering questions posed by other developers.

Payoff rules (external rewards or sanctions) work in an indirect way and are relatively complex. Crucially, they are disconnected from the project management—that is, project management does not decide who gets paid and does not reward completion of particular tasks. Hence, no rules are related to compensation and rewards. All that project participants can expect to receive stems from social norms and is of a nonmaterial nature (except perhaps a T-shirt). Successful completion of a task, for instance, may increase a developer's reputation, and can be rewarded by receiving a nice email praising their work (a reputational or signaling-related reward, as discussed in chapter 3). Similarly, according to interviewees, when a developer's actions have caused problems, an inflow of angry emails serves as a penalty, motivating them to be more careful in the future. Rewards and sanctions are well understood in the OSS literature, and our interviews confirm this behavior in the OSGeo context.

We do not intend to imply that monetary compensation is unimportant. As we have said, in five of the seven projects almost all core group members receive compensation for their contributions. In these projects, firms, public sector organizations, and/or NGOs pay programmers directly for their development work on projects. Only projects A and E are primarily based on volunteer contributions. Developers may have a concrete contract with an employer, which asks them to dedicate a particular percentage of their time to the project. For example, project D's leader is required to dedicate 20 percent of their time. Or the arrangement may be more flexible. Interviewees, however, emphasized many times that compensation is not the only motivator and that monetary compensation is not directly linked to performance. No respondents knew of any penalties or rewards that developers might receive for a particular outcome. Many projects also started as volunteer efforts, and success brought opportunities for paid work. Similarly, volunteers who join the existing projects and demonstrate their skills, perform well, and so on, usually end up as paid contributors. All of this lends support to the incentives as well as current and delayed benefits described in chapter 3.

Recall from table 6.1 and chapter 5 that scope rules specify which outcomes may, must, or must not be affected within a situation. Scope rules focus on outcomes as compared to choice rules, which concentrate on actions. Interviewees responded to our queries about scope rules by saying that specific, required outcomes depend on

Table 6.5
Ostrom's rule categories applied to OSGeo project cases

Ostrom's rule category	Project A	Project B	Project C	Project D	Project E	Project F	Project G
Position rules	Project leader Project steering committee member Core developer (informal; often overlaps with the committee member) Developer	Project leader Project steering committee member Core developer (informal; often overlaps with the committee member) Developer	No formal project leader Informal lead team of three people Project steering committee member Committers	Project leader Project steering committee member Core developer (informal; often overlaps with the committee member) Developer	Project leader Project steering committee member Core developer (informal; often overlaps with the committee member) Developer	Project leader Project steering committee member Core developer (informal; often overlaps with the committee member) Developer	No formal project leader Informal lead team of four people Project management committee member Core developer (informal; often overlaps with the committee member) Developer
Boundary rules	Formal rules Community members elect to project steering committee No term limits	Formal rules	Formal rules copied from another project	Formal rules copied from another project Almost never consulted	Formal rules	Formal rules exist, but primarily depend on social norms	Formal rules, but not necessarily followed

Choice rules	Some formalized Program steering committee makes some major rules Primarily social norms Open exchange in the list Mutual expectations	Some formalized; available in the wiki Primarily social norms	Some formalized; available in the wiki Primarily social norms	Social norms	Social norms	Social norms	Formalized rules written down Program management acts, if necessary Social norms important
Aggregation rules	Informal-symmetrical: consensus in program steering committee and discussion, including developers who are not on the committee Formal voting: rarely occurs, even though formal rules stipulate it Only project steering committee members can vote	Steering committee: almost all developers are on the committee Voting: if veto, vote is used and discussion follows	Informal-symmetrical: consensus in program steering committee Formal voting rarely occurs even though formal rules stipulate it Only project steering committee members can vote	Steering committee makes decision by consensus or voting All developers can vote as well, but their votes do not count	Informal-symmetrical: consensus in program steering committee Formal voting: rarely occurs even though formal rules stipulate it Only project steering committee members can vote	Informal-symmetrical: consensus in program steering committee and discussion, but often back channels used before the decision is reached Voting is a last resort	Program management committee votes

Table 6.5
(continued)

Ostrom's rule category	Project A	Project B	Project C	Project D	Project E	Project F	Project G
Information rules	Social norm: open exchange of information Unwritten rule that email list is the main communication tool	Limited formal rules Most decisions are made via IRC, and mailing list is used as well	Social norms Talking over email and weekly IRC meetings	Social norms Project leaders available on IRC almost all the time	Social norms	Social norms All communication is based on writing	Social norms Weekly IRC meetings; otherwise no clear rules
Payoff rules	No rules	No rules	No rules	No rules	No rules	No rules	No rules
Scope rules	Design rules	Design rules	Design rules	Design rules	Design rules	Design rules	Design rules

the technical design of the project. Yet there were no formal rules related to technical design outcomes. The social norms or outcome specifications that do exist are usually specified in project communication channels (e.g., IRC, forum posts, or email discussions) or the bug-tracker system.

In short, table 6.5 illustrates the formal rules and informal norms we identified in these cases. Even though these cases are under the OSGeo umbrella, variation exists within most, if not all, rule categories. Position rules exist, and in particular, the existence or lack of a designated leader appears to make a difference. The two projects without a designated lead appear to be facing more challenges (one is now abandoned) compared to the others, all with established leadership positions. Formal boundary rules exist, but in some instances are not consulted or are overridden by informal rules. Variation exists between formal and informal or social norms across projects in the choice, aggregation, and information rule categories. None of the projects had established payoff rules. Scope rules exist and exhibit little variability, are articulated primarily through informal norms related to software functionality outcomes, and are written in standard communication channels.

Our Analysis

The interviews section above described the results of our interviews and summarized them in tables 6.2–6.5. This section discusses our analysis of those results.

Technological Attributes

Although we did not set out to study the technological attributes of the OSGeo projects, it turned out that the one abandoned project became abandoned for technological reasons. According to personal conversations with the associated developers, part of the explanation for project C's abandonment had to do with increased competition from other software providing similar functionality. As we noted earlier, one such competitor is another OSGeo-affiliated project. In a public document describing the demise of project C, the former developers note that project D is "simpler to use, has attracted an incredibly strong developer community, has good quality control and development processes, and has developed most of the functionality previously only offered by [project C]. Basically [project D] is attracting the majority of the users and developers that previously would have used [project C]." Moreover, in a conversation with one developer familiar with these projects, a related driver was that there were fewer technologies (e.g., programming languages) for developers to learn to contribute to project D compared to project C. Serious competition with other software offering essentially the same functionality—one of the technological attributes described in chapter 4—is thus the primary driver for this project's abandonment.

Community Attributes

Five of the seven projects have core teams of paid programmers, providing a clear incentive to contribute. This does not imply that pay is the only incentive because, as in any work, there are additional rewards. Since several projects began as all volunteer and have evolved into ones in which many of these same people are now paid to do their work, it is hard to argue that their founders followed a purely economic-rationalistic model and were able to foresee these future benefits. Rather, their motivations can be explained by bounded rationality where the changing context has adjusted their incentive structure. Only two projects follow the all-volunteer model where the key incentives for programmers are found in the benefits of using the software that they develop.

Our analysis shows that all these projects have been able to establish a sense of community, high levels of trust, and friendly relations among their programmers, whatever the projects' size, institutional history, location of programmers, and functionality. Heterogeneities of motivation, culture, and assets do not appear to have hindered this sense of community, and in the case of the "skill," asset, heterogeneity seems to help projects succeed. Projects exhibit reciprocity, and this reciprocity among the team members can be categorized as general in six out of the seven projects. Overall, we think that these community variables are important for explaining success.

Institutional Attributes

All projects can be characterized as common-property regimes where asymmetries among project members exist. Projects exhibit relatively flat governance structures, although clear hierarchies exist (e.g., recognized team leadership). OSGeo supplies an explicit framework for protecting the intellectual property of projects, although some variation in software licensing exists (see fable 6.2). Implicitly, projects are owned through their dominant leaders or groups in charge. All projects have core teams that conduct most of the work, regardless of the actual size of their contributor communities.

All projects also have simple and straightforward operational rules, which are usually implemented by the use of technological solutions, such as a version control and bug-tracking system. As a result of their institutional evolution and joining OSGeo, projects have formalized many of their rules and have established a management system based on a steering committee. The daily management of projects, however, rely more on social norms than formal rules.

We should note that while it was difficult in our interviews with OSGeo participants to clarify in some situations the meanings of various rule types, or the differences between operational, collective choice, and constitutional rules, our findings suggest that there *is* variation in these types of rules across projects. The fact that institutional variation exists—even in a set of projects that are associated with the same overarching nonprofit foundation—indicates that a wide variation of informal rules may exist too in OSS commons. How these rules or norms influence success or abandonment is not clear, given our small sample and lack of variation in the dependent variable. The two rule-related findings that were consistent across OSGeo cases were that many operational rules are driven or removed from the duties of humans, and managed by the technical infrastructure of the collaboration; and as Raymond (2001) has suggested, many participants see formal rules as frictions hindering the work they want to accomplish.

Analysis Summary

While we cannot generalize from this set of cases, this analysis provides some evidence of what factors may be important toward the success or abandonment of OSS collaborations.

• *Competition* As our one abandoned case shows, competition can be critical, at least in some cases.

• *Financial backing* Most of these projects have paid developers or other financial backing from one or more organizations, and this backing is probably associated with the projects' continued success.

• *Social capital* We also found that these projects had built high levels of social capital; the software developers had high degrees of trust, were friends, and had diverse skill sets. Contrary to what is reported in virtual team literature (see chapter 4), interviewees did not say that geographic proximity and regular face-to-face interaction were critical factors that explain how these projects build social capital, but they did note that social capital was crucial for success.

• *Institutions* Social norms stand out more than formalized rules in these projects, and there is a great deal of variation in these institutions. Even though all projects had adopted fairly similar formal institutional structure as a result of OSGeo affiliation, developers emphasized that it is the internally developed sets of social norms rather than formal rules that are key to solving their collective action dilemmas. What is particularly interesting here is that these projects have larger development teams than the average project hosted on SF. This size difference suggests that established social norms continue to be the dominant institutional form even as core developer teams grow to groups as large as ten participants. In addition, collaborative technology, such as version control systems, often automate the management of operational rules, freeing up project leadership from having to monitor or worry about the enforcement of such rules. This is a significant distinction from natural resource commons, where rule enforcement is a primary element in governing such commons (Ostrom 1990, 2005).

Conclusion

We have taken the first step in our empirical research by speaking with some OSS developers involved in an organizationally complex setting. We hope that this chapter helped readers to come down to earth from the theoretical clouds we presented in part II, and get a better feeling for OSS development as it really exists in the world. Since community and institutional attributes are poorly represented in the SF data we use in the following chapters for our quantitative analysis, speaking with these developers helped us devise survey questions that filled these gaps. Nevertheless, we kept in mind that the projects in OSGeo are not typical of OSS software projects. A majority of non-OSGeo projects have only one or two developers, and a small or nonexistent community associated with them, so we tempered our survey questions accordingly.

Now that we have questioned OSGeo developers about community, institutions, and the factors they think make for successful projects, we take up the crucial task of defining success as well as classifying all the projects on SF as successful or abandoned. We saw in this chapter the importance of a having a large, varied sample of successful and abandoned projects, if we are to really determine the critical factors that lead to those outcomes. In the next chapter, we once again consult developers by interviewing them about what success or abandonment means to them. Based on those interviews and some thoughts of our own, we define success and abandonment, and show how we accurately classified all the projects on SF according to our definitions. The results of our research would have been much less gratifying if we had not been able to accomplish the task we describe next in chapter 7.

7 Defining Open-Source Software Success and Abandonment

We now turn to an important topic that we only touched on in chapter 1: How *do* we define and measure success and abandonment in OSS commons?[1] Does success mean that a project has developed high-quality software or that the software is widely used? How might valuable software that is used by only a few people, such as software for charting parts of the human genome, fit into this definition? We wanted to discover what factors affect success or abandonment, but first we needed define and actually measure these two outcomes. This chapter tells the story of how we reached that milestone. Statisticians and other scientists often call the subject you are trying to explain the dependent variable. In our study, the success or abandonment of OSS projects is our dependent variable.

We begin this chapter by describing the hosting site SF in more detail because we use data from SF to classify projects as successful or abandoned as well as for our work in all the empirical studies in the following chapters. We also take the time to discuss how representative SF is of the "universe" of OSS projects so readers can evaluate what our empirical results mean in terms of OSS in general. After that, we interview eight OSS developers to collect feedback about our initial ideas on how to define OSS project success, and taking those interviewees' thoughts together with ours, we construct a theoretical classification system for OSS commons. As we said before, though, theory is not enough; we needed to be able to measure success and abandonment in the real world. We end the chapter by looking at how we classified nearly all the projects existing on SF (in 2006) and then checked that classification for accuracy. Our result is—as far as we can tell—the first comprehensive success and abandonment classification of SF OSS projects.

The purpose of this chapter is to introduce our dependent variable and, from there, answer simple yet previously unanswered questions like, How many projects hosted on SF continue to be worked on collaboratively? How many are abandoned? Are projects using particular programming languages or in certain topic areas of software development more likely to achieve collaborative success? Or are projects targeted at particular audiences or being developed for open-source operating systems more likely to succeed? The data stored on SF (and other hosting sites) on OSS projects are critical because they hold the answers to these and similar questions.

About SourceForge

While there are rivals, SF has traditionally been thought of as the largest open-source project-hosting Web site (Deek and McHugh 2007, 152). As of this writing (February 2011), SF reports over 2.7 million registered developers, and provides free-of-charge Web hosting services and collaborative tools for over 260,000 OSS projects (Source-Forge 2011). It offers Web-based tools such as software code repositories (with version control), bug-tracking utilities, online forums, email mailing lists, a wiki, links to a separate project Web site in addition to the project's presence on the SF Web site, file downloading services for the project's software, and a Web-based administrative interface for project administrators. In short, SF supplies the tools that most projects require to develop OSS. The oldest projects in our data set (described below) were registered in 1999, when the service started.

Data Available for Projects Hosted on SourceForge

SF makes publicly available much of the information generated by a project's administrator when the project is created as well as any information generated over time by the tools that the project uses. For example, the project's pages on SF provide the project's registration date and number of developers working on the project as well as the number of times the project's code repository has been accessed, historical records of the number of bug posts and feature requests, searchable archives of forum posts and emails, the number of project software releases, and the total number of times the software has been downloaded. And this only depicts a portion of the information available for a given project. We will explore these data in more detail later in this chapter.

Early on, researchers associated with two academic projects—one at the University of Notre Dame called the Sourceforge Research Data Archive (Van Antwerp and Madey 2008) and the other, the FLOSSmole project (Howison, Conklin and Crowston 2006), based at Syracuse University—understood the significance of capturing and keeping historical SF data.[2] They have been backing up "snapshots" of the SF database for years now at different points in time. For researchers like us who are trying to learn about and explain the open-source development phenomenon, the availability of these historical repositories is critical. We view these projects as "remote sensors" of OSS project activity. Through their efforts to collect temporal "slices" of the SF database, these projects are actively building a historical repository of OSS projects similar to the way NASA's Landsat satellite system and the EROS Space Center have collected and archived historical data about changing conditions of the earth's surface. There are great analytic opportunities in these data sets. Although we only look at one period of the SF database in the empirical analysis of its projects that we present here and in chapter 8, we believe our analysis captures a time-series element because the data set is a snapshot of approximately 107,000 projects all at different points in their project life cycle.

Is SourceForge Representative of All Open-Source Projects?

Because our classification of SF projects and analysis in the chapters to follow exclusively using data gathered from SF, it is important to ask, To what degree is SF representative of the population of open-source projects "out there"? To what extent would any findings based on SF apply to or be representative of the population of open-source projects out there? In our view, the representativeness of SF can be defined along at least two dimensions: whether or not the projects on SF are representative of the broader universe of open-source projects, and whether or not developers on SF are representative of the broader universe of open-source developers.

While SF historically has hosted the greatest number of open-source projects, there are many other open-source project hosting sites, including BerliOS, Freepository, GitHub, Savannah, ShareSource, Google code, and others (see Open Directory Project 2011). In addition, many open-source projects maintain their own Web sites and other project infrastructure on their own servers. Based on an Internet search and literature review, it appears that no one has a firm estimate of how many free/libre and OSS projects exist, or how many people are working on them.[3] Indeed, Ghosh (2005) made this point in 2005; at that time, there was no census of the universal population of open-source developers, and this still seems to be the case today.

Given that the full population of open-source projects and developers is unknown, it is not surprising that we were not able to find any empirical analysis to assess how representative SF is of this unknown population. But some researchers have considered this or closely related questions. In one of the earliest references to the representativeness of SF, Gregory Madey, Vincent Freeh, and Renee Tynan (2002, 1812) mention that they assumed SF was representative because of its popularity and the number of projects hosted there, although they note that this "needs to be confirmed." Such a task will prove difficult because it requires determining the extent of the open-source universe—which as mentioned above, has not yet been accomplished.

Additionally, there does not appear to be any estimate of the total number of OSS projects, although Carlo Daffara (2007) helped to create an estimate of the number of "active and stable" projects for the FLOSSMetrics (2006) project. Daffara defined active projects as those with an 80 to 100 percent activity index (SF and some other hosting sites generate an "activity" index) and a release within the last six months. He examined 100 projects each from SF, BerliOS, Savannah, Gna!, and other hosting sites that showed that *active* projects comprise about 8 to 10 percent of their total ones. By using various techniques and information from other sources, Daffara arrived at a *lower-bound* figure of 195,000 projects in the open-source universe, with about 13,000 active projects, and around 5,000 active, mature, and stable projects. He did not, however, try to estimate an *upper-bound* figure for the population of OSS projects.

With regard to the second representative dimension—developers—Ghosh (2005) states that the FLOSS survey was random and thus the survey results are applicable to the entire universe of OSS developers. One way to help establish whether SF is representative would be to duplicate Ghosh's FLOSS survey on a random sample drawn from SF developers. If the results were statistically similar, then this would support the hypothesis that SF developers are representative of the universe of OSS developers. To our knowledge, no one has conducted such a study. Yet Raymond (2004) did a Web search on the use of the terminology open-source versus the terminology free software on both SF and the Internet as a whole.[4] Raymond found that about 3 percent of the developers on SF use the term free software, and about 4.5 percent of the developers on the Web in general use the term free software, while some 99 percent of the developers on Savannah.gnu.org (a hosting site set up by free software advocates) used the term free software. Although this does not make a strong case—it represents only one (philosophical) attribute of software developers—it suggests that the developers in SF use philosophical terminology roughly similar to the more broad population of open-source developers found across the Internet.

Sebastian Spaeth and his colleagues (2007) argue that sampling the Debian GNU/ Linux Distribution is more representative for some purposes than sampling SF. They cite two reasons: because "a distribution . . . represents the population of projects in use," and because Debian includes projects hosted on several open-source hosting sites in addition to projects that host their own projects on their own hardware. A "distribution" is a release of an operating system, often Linux, combined with a large number of commonly used software programs, and thus, Spaeth and his colleagues refer to a distribution as being representative of OSS projects that are actually used by a large number of people. Because Debian selects projects from a number of hosting sites as well as projects that are hosted privately, Spaeth and his colleagues feel that this diversity may be more representative than a single hosting site like SF.

Nevertheless, Spaeth and his colleagues (2007) also point out that projects associated with Debian must have a free license. In addition, all associated Debian free software projects will be successful by our definition (see below) in order to be included in the Debian package. And software that runs on Windows is not included in the Debian Distribution. From this we conclude that Debian is not representative of the entire population of OSS projects, because projects with nonfree licenses, failed projects, and projects that run on operating systems other than Linux are not included.

Many reasons exist for believing that the projects hosted on SF are more representative of the open-source universe than any other repository. First, at the time we wrote this (initially in 2006), SF hosted more projects and users than any other repository.[5] Second, Daffara (2007) shows that the rate of active projects on SF is nearly the same as other hosting sites, thus providing a piece of evidence that SF is representative of other hosting sites. Third, the Web search done by Raymond (2004) provides evidence that the developers on SF are roughly representative of those on the entire Internet, at least in terms of their use of certain terminology. Finally, using the data we have for around the time Daffara's study was done (FLOSSmole 2006), SF had over 1,000 projects having 100,000 downloads or more, and over 147 projects having over 1 million downloads. If Daffara (2007) is correct that only about 5,000 stable mature and active projects exist in the entire population of open-source projects, then it is likely that many of them are represented on SF.

An anonymous reviewer of an earlier version of this book said: "There is often an unstated assumption [in OSS research] that there is such an animal as 'The Open-Source Developer' and that he/she lives in SF—and neither is true. There are dozens of radically different development contexts, many highlighted in the previous chapter, and each context is populated with communities of developers with very different motivations and characteristics." We agree. Chapter 4 emphasized the heterogeneity in developer types, and we recognize that there are a variety of contexts (project hosting sites or self-hosted collaboration platforms) where open-source developers work. Moreover, SF is "noisy," housing some projects that were set up, for example, by college students posting software for a college homework assignment and nothing more. Many other projects also may have an entry on SF, but are fully hosted on their own site by a firm or foundation.

But that said, as of this writing, there is evidence indicating that SF is representative of other hosting sites, and has more projects, more failed projects, and a significant number of active, mature, and stable projects (Daffara 2007; English and Schweik 2007). While this is an area that is changing rapidly, at the time of this writing (and when we collected our data), we felt that SF was the best single source of data representative of the entire open-source population, and consequently, provided a good place for investigating the research questions and hypotheses posed in chapters 2–5.

What Developers Say about Success and Abandonment

We conducted eight interviews (Schweik and English 2007) with OSS developers between January and May 2006 to get opinions about definitions of success, and at that time, we were using the term failure rather than abandonment.[6] We stratified our sampling by categories of projects with less than five, five to ten, eleven to twenty-five, and greater than twenty-five developers, and interviewed developers from two projects in each category. Interviews were conducted over the phone, digitally recorded, transcribed, and analyzed. We asked interviewees how they would define success in an OSS project. Interviewees responded with five distinct views. One defined success in terms of the vibrancy of the project's developer community. Three defined OSS success as widely used software. Two others defined it as creating value for users. One developer cited achieving personal goals, and the last interviewee felt his project was successful because it created technology that percolated through other projects even though his project never produced a useful stand-alone product.

Immediately after asking interviewees about success, we asked how they would define failure in an OSS project. Interestingly, all eight developers said that failure had to do with a lack of users, and two indicated that a lack of users leads to project abandonment. In a probing question that followed, we asked if defining a failed project as one that was abandoned before producing a release seemed reasonable. Four interviewees agreed outright, three agreed with reservations, and one disagreed. Two of those with reservations raised concerns about the quality of the release. One project might not make its first release until it had a stable, well-functioning application, for example, while another project might release something that was nearly useless. Another interviewee had concerns about how much time could pass before a project was declared a failure or abandoned. One developer argued that a project that was abandoned before producing a release could be successful from the developer's point of view if they had improved their programming skills by participating. The dissenting developer felt that project source code would often be incorporated into other open-source projects and would not be a failure even if no release had been made. These discussions prompted us to the use the term abandonment rather than the term failure because many projects that had ceased collaborating still would not be seen as failed projects.

So how do these responses inform working definitions of project success and abandonment? Because we view OSS projects as a commons driven by collective action with the goal of producing software, defining success in terms of producing "useful software" makes sense. Six of the eight interviewees suggested that success involves producing something useful for users. Since the real "tragedy of the commons" for an open-source project (see Schweik and English 2007) involves a failure to sustain collective action to produce, maintain, or improve the software, defining failure in terms of project abandonment makes sense, and generally our interviewees agreed. Treating the first release as a milestone or transition point between what we refer to as the initiation stage and the project's growth stage (recall chapter 3, figure 3.2) emerges logically from this line of thinking.

Our Success/Abandonment Classification System

In recent years, scholars have investigated different approaches to measuring the success and failure of OSS projects. Studies by, for instance, Katherine Stewart and

Anthony Ammeter (2002), Andrea Capiluppi, Patricia Lago, and Maurizio Moriso (2003), and Kevin Crowston, Hala Annabi, and James Howison (2003) and Robles-Martinez and colleagues (2003) measured open-source project "life" or "death" by monitoring project activity measures such as: the release trajectory (e.g., the movement from alpha to beta to stable release); changes in version number; changes in lines of code; the number of "commits" or check-ins to a central software code repository, and activity or vitality scores measured on collaborative platforms such as SF and Freshmeat.net. Dawid Weiss (2005) assessed project popularity using web search engines. Crowston, Howison, and Annabi (2006) reviewed the traditional models used to measure information systems success, and then adapted them to open source. They collected data from SF, measuring community size, bug-fixing time, and the popularity of projects.

After conducting our interviews, reviewing the ideas and work of the other researchers mentioned above, and carefully considering those inputs along with our own thinking from a commons and collective action perspective, we developed a six-class system for describing success and abandonment of open-source projects across our two longitudinal stages of initiation and growth (see table 7.1). Recall that in chapter 3 (figure 3.2), we defined initiation as inclusion of the start of the project to its first public release, and growth as the period after this release.

We classify a project as *successful in the initiation stage* (SI) when it has produced "a first public release." This can be easily measured because SF lists all of a project's releases. A project that is SI automatically becomes an indeterminate project in the growth phase.

Projects are classified as *abandoned in the initiation stage* (AI) when the project exhibits little or no signs of development activity before producing a first public release. We define abandonment as few forum posts, few emails to email lists, no code commits, or few other signs of project activity over a one-year period. The preliminary data we analyzed from SF indicates that projects in initiation that have not had a release for a year are generally abandoned (see the discussion of the test sample below).

A project is classified as a *success in the growth stage* (SG) when it exhibits three releases of a software product that performs a useful computing task for at least a few users (it has to be downloaded and used). We decided that the time between the first release and the last one must be at least six months because it needs to capture some relatively significant effort. (In some SF cases, we found that multiple releases were posted over a single day, which would in relative terms not be a meaningful new release.) As noted above, we can easily measure the number of releases and time between them, since SF tracks this information. Measuring "a useful computing task" is harder and more subjective, though. Acquiring the number of downloads recorded on project Web sites is probably the easiest measure, with the assumption that many downloads captures the concept of utility.

Table 7.1

Our dependent variable: Six OSS project success and abandonment classes, and their methods of operationalization

Class/abbreviation	Definition (D)/Operationalization (O)/SF variables used (SFV)
Success, initiation (SI)	**D**: Developers have produced a first release **O**: At least 1 release (note: all projects in the growth stage are SI) **SFV**: Number of releases
Abandonment, initiation (AI)	**D**: Developers have not produced a first release, and the project is abandoned **O**: 0 releases *and* > = 1 year since SF project registration **SFV**: Number of releases and project life span
Success, growth (SG)	**D**: Project has achieved three meaningful releases of the software, and the software is deemed useful for at least a few users **O**: 3 releases, *and* > = 6 months between releases, *and* has > 10 downloads. **SFV**: Number of releases, first release date, last release date, downloads, and data collection date
Abandonment, growth (AG)	**D**: Project appears to be abandoned before producing 3 releases of a useful product, or has produced three or more releases in less than 6 months and is abandoned **O**: 1 or 2 releases and > = 1 year since the last release at the time of data collection, *or* 3 or more releases and < 11 downloads during a time period greater than 6 months starting from the date of the first release and ending at the data collection date, *or* 3 or more releases in less than 6 months and > = 1 year since the last release **SFV**: Number of releases, first release date, last release date, data collection date, downloads, and project life span
Indeterminate initiation (II)	**D**: Project has yet to reveal a first public release but shows significant developer activity **O**: 0 releases and < 1 year since project registration **SFV**: Number of releases and project life span
Indeterminate growth (IG)	**D**: Project has not yet produced three releases but shows development activity, or has produced 3 releases or more in less than 6 months and shows development activity **O**: 1 or 2 releases and < 1 year since the last release, *or* 3 releases and < 6 months between releases and < 1 year since the last release **SFV**: Number of releases, first release date, last release date, and data collection date

A project is considered *abandoned in the growth stage* (AG) when it appears to be abandoned without having produced three releases or when it produced three releases but failed to produce a useful software product. We classify a project as *indeterminate in the initiation stage* (II) when it has yet to reveal a first public release but shows significant developer activity. Finally, projects are assigned *indeterminate in the growth stage* (IG) when they have not produced three releases but show development activity, or when they have produced three releases over less than six months and show development activity.

Making Our Classification Work in the Real World

For those who do not know, "operationalizing" something in research work generally means finding ways to measure it. Another definition might be to find a way to put a theoretical concept into practice so it can be used in empirical research. As a first step in operationalizing our definitions for OSS success and abandonment using the definitions (denoted as D) in table 7.1, we took a random test sample of sixty projects hosted on SF using the FLOSSmole (2006) project data. The FLOSSmole data are collected by the automated "spidering" of SF and other OSS hosting sites, and made publicly available.[7] We decided to conduct this test sample from the FLOSSmole database to look for problems with our classification scheme and get some idea about the number of projects likely to fall within each of the classes.

Following the logic used in our OSS developer interviews and knowing that we wanted to study projects with larger numbers of developers because of their more interesting collective action issues, we stratified by number of developers into categories of less than ten, ten to twenty-five, and more than twenty-five developers. We randomly sampled twenty projects from each category for a total of sixty projects. We chose twenty projects because it was a reasonable undertaking given our time constraints. For these sixty sampled projects, we *manually* compiled data on project registration, last release date, number of downloads, project Web site URL, and forum/ email/ postings among other data. From these data, similar to the coding often done in qualitative case study methods, we made a judgment about whether the software was useful and whether the project was abandoned. We classified the projects as SI, AI, SG, or AG based on this information. No indeterminate cases were found in this sample.

Perhaps the most important information we acquired from this test sample effort is that the vast majority of projects that have not had a release for a year are abandoned. All twenty-five projects in the sample that had not provided a release in over a year and had less than three releases were abandoned. This finding suggested that we could produce a relatively simple but approximately accurate classification by using a project's failure to release within a year as a proxy for abandonment. This test sample process and qualitative analysis gave us confidence that our conceptual ideas for these definitions were accurate. Our next step was to implement these concepts using SF data in our data set.

Getting the Data

We needed a number of variables to operationalize our classification system, including the project life span, number of releases, first release date, last release date, data collection date, and downloads. We used FLOSSmole data from August 2006 because this was the most recent available at the time that we developed this classification and provided most, but not all, of the variables we needed. We then spidered the SF Web site ourselves between September 24, 2006 and October 16, 2006 to gather the variables that FLOSSmole lacked: the number of releases, first release date, and last release date. We call the data that we spidered ourselves the "UMass data."

The FLOSSmole data had complete information for 119,355 projects, but 8,422 of these either had missing data, or were purged from SF between the time the FLOSSmole data were collected and the time the UMass data were collected, thus leaving 110,933 projects. We eliminated another 3,186 projects from our classification because they had zero releases and downloads listed on SF, but also had project Web sites not hosted on SF that may have been used to distribute files.[8] In the end, we classified 107,747 projects. Our data set also includes other numerical and categorical independent variables for these projects. Independent variables (and the associated approach to analysis) will be discussed in chapter 8. The variables used to create our dependent variable are explained more precisely below, and table 7.2 shows descriptive statistics for these variables.

Project Life Span

The project life span is the time between the date the project was registered on SF and the time our data were collected. Since the UMass data were collected after the FLOSS-

Table 7.2
Descriptive statistics for dependent variable components: FLOSSmole (2006) and UMass, September–October 2006 spidered data

Variable name	Min	First quad	Median	Mean	Third quad	Max
Project life span (yrs)	0.003	1.08	2.39	2.54	3.70	6.74
Number of releases	0	0	1.00	2.77	2.00	537
Downloads	0	0	23	12,835	494	228,643,712

mole data, the data collection dates for the UMass data were used in some of our calculations of the project life span.

Number of Releases

SF OSS projects can release one or more packages that can each contain one or more releases. At the time we collected this data, SF provided release totals at the bottom of each project's download page. In our data set, the number of releases variable is the total of all releases in all packages.

First Release Date

This variable is the date of the first release.

Last Release Date

This variable is the date of the last release.

Data Collection Date

The spidering software records this variable when the Web page is downloaded from SF.

Downloads

Our downloads variable is the total number of downloads over the project's lifetime for each project.

Classification Results

Table 7.3 provides the number of SF OSS projects classified in each of our two longitudinal stages: initiation and growth using the FLOSSmole (2006) and UMass spidered data. In these 107,747 SF projects, about half were in the initiation stage and the rest were in the growth stage. Table 7.3 also reports projects that could not be classified.

Table 7.3
SourceForge.net OSS projects organized by longitudinal stage (as of August 2006)

Stage	Number of projects (% of total classified)
Initiation stage	50,662 (47)
Growth stage	57,085 (53)
Not classified	3,186*
Total classified	107,747

* These are valid projects, yet they could not be classified because they have zero releases and downloads on SF, but have other Web sites that may be used for these functions.

Table 7.4

Classification of all OSS projects on SourceForge.net (as of August 2006)

Class	Number of projects (% of total)	Possible classification errors (other than errors in the SF data)
AI	37,320 (35)	The project is not abandoned but > 1 year old
II	13,342 (12)	No classification errors (by definition)
IG	10,711 (10)	No classification errors (by definition)
AG	30,592 (28)	The project is not abandoned, *or* it produced useful software even though it met the download criteria for abandonment
SG	15,782 (15)	The software is not used in spite of not meeting the download criteria for abandonment
Total	107,747	

Note: SI is not listed because these successes are now growth stage projects; including SI would double the count. AI = Abandoned in Initiation; II = Indeterminate in Initiation; IG = Indeterminate in Growth; AG = Abandoned in Growth; SG = Successful Growth.

Table 7.5

OSS project classification validation results

Original class (number of cases)	Correct	Incorrect	Deleted or missing data	Error rate percent
AI (106)	77	10	19	11.5
AG (101)	93	8	0	7.9
SG (93)	92	0	1	0
Totals (300)	262	18	20	6.4

Table 7.4 summarizes our results from the success and abandonment classification of all OSS projects on SF as of August 2006. As table 7.4 column 3 shows, potential classification errors stem primarily from two sources: source 1 error—using one year without a release as a proxy for abandonment; and source 2 error—using the number of downloads per month as a proxy for the software being useful.

Checking Our Results for Accuracy

To test the validity of the results in table 7.4, we took a random sample of 300 classified projects and checked each OSS project's classification results by manually reviewing its SF pages. Table 7.5 lists our validation results. Of the 106 projects originally classified as AI, 77 were correctly classified, 10 were incorrectly classified, 18 were deleted from SF and 1 had missing information and could not be validated (19 were missing or deleted in total), resulting in our highest classification error rate of 11.5

percent. The 10 misclassifications did not list a release for a year after they were registered, but did show some developer activity in the year before our data were collected (source 1 error). Regarding the 18 deleted projects, it is highly likely that most, if not all, were classified correctly, given that SF regularly purges inactive projects. Yet it is also possible that some were active and were moved to other hosting platforms by the project developers. Consequently, we keep 11.5 percent as the error rate for AI, but the true error rate is probably lower.

Of the 101 cases that were originally assigned to the AG class, eight were active and incorrectly classified for an error rate of 7.9 percent. Finally, of the 93 cases that were classified as SG, 92 were classified correctly and 1 could not be validated because of missing data on SF. In other words, our SG classification had an error rate of close to 0. These validation results show that the classification varies from what we would consider "reasonably accurate" (AI) to "extremely accurate" (SG). More important, this classification was independently replicated by Andrea Wiggins and Crowston (2010). This gives us a high level of confidence that we have a robust dependent variable for the analysis we present in the chapters that follow.

In the spirit of openness and transparency that is exemplified in OSS, all our data used in our classification along with more detailed working notes on our process have been given back to the FLOSSmole project and are available on our project Web site.[9] We hope that other researchers will consider using this classification definition—and also in the spirit of open source, build and improve on it— to classify projects at various points in time other than August 2006. In fact, Wiggins and Crowston (2010) make some useful recommendations for how this classification could be improved. They also provide us with independent validation that this key foundational measure for the rest of the empirical work in this book is sound.

Conclusion

In chapter 6, we broke from the theoretical work in part II and began our part III empirical work with a study of OSGeo. In this chapter, we continued the empirical work by creating our dependent variable. With this robust dependent variable in hand, we have reached an exciting new juncture in our endeavor: we can now quantitatively study how various technological, community, and institutional factors influence OSS project success and abandonment.

These quantitative studies, described in following chapters, will use a variety of SF data, which is one of the reasons we started this chapter by discussing SF data and how representative they are of the universe of OSS projects. Although we cannot know for sure whether SF is truly representative of the open-source phenomenon as a whole, we believe it is the most representative single source of data currently available. Our dependent variable also comes from SF data, and since the credibility of our ultimate findings about OSS software will be strongly linked to the strength of our dependent variable, we went to great lengths to make it as sound and robust as possible. First, we interviewed SF developers because we wanted their valuable insight, and then based on those interview results, we designed our classification system, operational-ized it, and checked it for accuracy.

We now reach the zenith of our investigation, and are positioned to use our brand-new dependent variable to answer the research questions and hypotheses developed earlier. We accomplish this in two stages. In the first stage, described in chapter 8, we ask, What can SF data *alone* tell us about what makes open-source projects a successful collaboration? We explore the second stage across chapters 9, 10, and 11. In chapter 9—with the assistance of the SF organization itself—we conduct a major survey of SF developers to gather data for theoretical concepts (mostly community and institu-tional ones) not found in SF project metadata. One by one, in chapter 10, we take the research questions and hypotheses that we generated in part II, and supply answers based on the factual results of our empirical work. In chapter 11, we address the central research question of this book by presenting statistical models of success and abandon-ment using both SF data and our survey results. This is the icing on the cake for readers interested in what makes OSS projects succeed as well as for readers interested in the factors that make Internet-based collaborations in general succeed.

8   What Can SourceForge.net Data Alone Tell Us about Open-Source Software Commons?

with Sandra Haire

In this chapter, we are ready to use statistical methods to identify factors that influence OSS project success. We again turn to the 2006 data set of 107,747 SF projects that we used to construct our dependent variable in chapter 7, asking two important questions:

1. Does this SF data set capture any of the technological, community, and institutional factors we described in chapters 2–5?
2. If so, are any of these factors more often associated with successful or abandoned OSS projects?

You may recall from chapter 7 that we see SF as a kind of remote sensor of OSS projects, analogous to satellites like Landsat that monitor the earth. Given that SF and other similar hosting sites will likely be around for some time, we want to learn what we can about OSS collaboration from the data they provide, without the help of other external, non-SF data. In the chapters that follow, we will augment the SF data with survey data we have collected ourselves to fill in missing theoretical concepts. Nevertheless, the use of SF data alone provides an excellent starting point for us to discover some of the underlying factors that help differentiate successful from abandoned projects, and may help to develop a relatively easy and accessible set of metrics for people wishing to monitor OSS projects in the future.

This chapter begins by looking at how the SF data is generated and how we created fifty-nine different variables using 2006 SF data. Since many of these variables play a role in the research we discuss later, most readers should take the time to become familiar with them. Following a short description of some limitations of the data, we succinctly explain the statistical methods we use to make sense of this vast data set. Again, since these statistical methods are critical in our later analyses, most readers will want to review this section to get some idea of how they work. We then summarize what we learned from this initial statistical analysis. The results here supply the foundation for our later research. Since we perform a similar analysis on a more complete data set in chapter 11, we have condensed this chapter as much as possible.

Making Independent Variables from 2006 SF Data

In chapter 7, we talked about the origins of our 2006 SF data, and how we used it to create our success and abandonment dependent variable for the two OSS commons longitudinal stages—initiation and growth. In this section, we describe the SF data that captures some of the theoretical concepts of chapters 2–5 that we think affect success or abandonment. These are *independent variables*, in other words, that might be able to predict which projects will be successful or abandoned. Our independent variables using SF data consist of five numerical variables and seven groups of categorical ones. The *numerical variables* are made up of continuous numbers, and in our case they represent the counts of various things related to OSS projects. *Categorical variables* depict the characteristics of OSS projects or the categories that they fall into. The five numerical variables are: developers, tracker reports, page visits, forums posts, and projection information index (PII). The seven groups of categorical variables are: intended audience, operating system, programming language, user interface, database environment, project topic, and project license.

How Does SF Generate This Data?

Before we explore these variables in more detail, we want to provide information about how the SF data are generated. With the exception of the PII, the numerical variables are created or updated in three situations: when an OSS project administrator first creates the project in SF, when the project administrator modifies the project through the SF administrative Web interface (e.g., adds a new developer to the team), and when members of the project's community submit bug reports, create forum posts, or visit the project's Web site. In 2006, the SF Web site automatically calculated the values for the numerical variables in response to these activities. The only numerical variable not calculated by the Web site is the PII, which we derived ourselves using the categorical independent variables described below. The categorical variables differ from the numerical ones because they are specific answers supplied by the OSS project administrator in response to questions about their project. These questions along with a group of possible answers to each one are displayed to the project administrator via the SF administrative Web interface, and are answered either at the time the administrator created the project on SF or some later date. For each group of answers, the project's administrator has the choice of selecting no answer, or one or more responses associated with that question.

An example will help to clarify this. Consider the programming language question and group of answers, which we call the programming language group of categorical variables. When initially creating a project on SF, the project's administrator is asked which programming languages the project uses. They might answer C++, a single selection from all the possibilities that SF lists (for a condensed list of possible programming languages, see table 8.1). If the project uses more than one programming language, the administrator would select all that apply, such as C++, Perl, and Python. If the project is just starting and the language has not been chosen, the administrator would leave all the programming language answers unselected. Each answer chosen by the project administrator becomes a separate categorical variable for that project within the programming language categorical variable group.

At the time of our data collection, project administrators could select from a total of over five hundred answers within the seven groups of categorical variables listed above. From an analysis standpoint, using that many variables is impractical. We thus consolidated the five hundred options into fifty-four aggregated subcategories or separate, independent variables in our analysis. The consolidation process is described in more detail below. The important point to understand here is that we consolidated data where we thought it made sense, in order to reduce the total number of variables used in the statistical analysis. When the five numerical variables are added to the categorical variables, our analysis data set becomes a more manageable fifty-nine independent variables.

Below, we briefly examine each of these variables or groups of variables, and their connections to the theories and concepts discussed in previous chapters. We also present some descriptive statistics for these variables in tables 8.2 and 8.3.

Our Numerical Independent Variables

Developers

The developers variable is the total number of developers listed for each project. All 107,747 projects have developer data, although 263 projects list 0 developers. The largest project lists 340 developers (for more statistical details, see table 8.2). This variable is particularly important because the developer is our key unit of analysis within the IAD framework (see figure 3.1), and because group size, a community attribute in the IAD framework, is a central concept in the theory of collective action (see table 4.2, group size, RQ-C4).

Tracker Reports

The tracker reports variable represents the total number of bug reports, feature requests, patches, and support requests added together for each project. The Alexandria project has the largest number of tracker reports for a project in our 2006 data set—86,242 (see table 8.2). Alexandria was originally the project that developed the OSS code on which the SF Web site is based, but in this 2006 data set, the Alexandria project

Table 8.1
Dependent and Independent variable dictionary

Numerical variable or categorical variable group	Abbreviations for variables	Numerical or Categorical	Description/definition	IAD category/hypotheses (in tables 3.2, 4.1, 4.2, and 5.5)
Project class	AI, II, SI, IG, AG, and SG,	C	Dependent variable	None
Developers	None	N	Number of developers participating	Community/group size: RQ-C4
Tracker reports	None	N	Number of reports: Bugs, feature requests, patches, and support requests	Technological/collaborative infrastructure and product utility: RQ-T1, H-T3a
Page visits	None	N	Number of page visits for the project Web site	Technological/product utility and community/group size: H-T3a, RQ-C4
Forum posts	None	N	Posts to project online forums	Technological/collaborative infrastructure, and product utility: RQ-T1, H-T3a
PII	None	N	Number of subcategories chosen for all categorical variables	Technological/clear vision, product utility and community/leadership: H-T1, H-T3a, H-C6a, H-C6b

		Who will use the software	Community/user involvement and financing
Intended audience	C		
ia1		End users	H-C1, H-C8
ia2		Computer professionals	
ia3		Business	
ia4		Other	
ia5		Government/nonprofit	
		Operating system the software runs on	**Technological/product utility: H-T3a**
Operating system	C		
os1		POSIX	
os2		Independent	
os3		Linux	H-C5, H-T3b, H-T3c
os4		MS Windows	
os5		Mac	
os6		BSD	H-C5, H-T3b, H-T3c
os7		UNIX like	
os8		Other	
		Programming languages used	**Technological/product utility and preferred technologies: H-T3a, H-T3c**
Programming language	C		
pl1		Java	
pl2		C	
pl3		PHP	
pl4		Perl	
pl5		Python	
pl6		Microsoft	
pl7		Other	
pl8		Assembly	

Table 8.1
(continued)

Numerical variable or categorical variable group	Abbreviations for variables	Numerical or Categorical	Description/definition	IAD category/hypotheses (in tables 3.2, 4.1, 4.2, and 5.5)
User Interface		C	**How users interact with the program**	**Community/helping the cause and technological/product utility and preferred technologies: H-C5, H-T3a**
	ui1		Web based	
	ui2		MS Windows	
	ui3		X Windows	
	ui4		Noninteractive	
	ui5		Console	
	ui6		Java	
	ui7		Gnome	H-C5
	ui8		Other	
	ui9		KDE	H-C5
Database environment		C	**Database application used in the software**	**Technological, community/utility, and developer motivations/ preferred technology: H-T3c, H-C5**
	de1		Open-source database	H-C5
	de2		Proprietary database	H-C5
	de3		Other	
Project topic		C	**Subject or theme of the software**	**Technological/product utility and community/helping the cause: H-T3a, H-C5**
	t1		Communications	H-C5
	t2		Database	H-C5
	t3		Desktop environment	
	t4		Education	
	t5		Formats and protocols	H-C5

t6	Games/entertainment	
t7	Internet	
t8	Multimedia	
t9	Office/business	
t10	Other/nonlisted	
t11	Printing	
t12	Religion and philosophy	
t13	Scientific/engineering	
t14	Security	
t15	Sociology	
t16	Software development	
t17	Systems	H-C5, H-T3b
t18	Terminals	
t19	Text editors	
Project license	**Software licenses the project uses**	**Community/helping the cause and institutional/license choice: RQ-15, H-C5**
gpl_compatible		H-C5
gpl_incompatible		

Table 8.2
Descriptive statistics for numerical independent variables (all 107,747 projects)

Variable name	Minimum	First Quad	Median	Mean	Third Quad	Maximum	Number of projects with a value of zero	Total number of projects with data
Developers	0	1	1	1.977	2	340	263	107,747
Tracker reports	0	0	0	19.6	0	86,240	83,554	107,742
Page visits	0	313	979	59,870	4051	673,800,000	107	107,742
Forum posts	0	0	0	3.65	0	17,770	99,385	107,740
PII	0	0	6	5.373	8	25	30,276	107,747

contains the tracker reports for the SF Web site itself and does not develop any software. Conceptually, tracker reports represent use of a project's collaborative infrastructure (a technological attribute of the IAD framework), and can also be considered a measure of community activity and interest in the project—in other words, *project utility* (see table 4.1, collaborative infrastructure used, RQ-T1, and product utility, H-T3a).

Page Visits

SF provides hosting services for project Web sites free of charge. Most SF projects take advantage of this service and create SF-based Web sites, although some SF projects have Web sites that are hosted elsewhere. Page visits represents the total number of requests to view any page of the project's Web site, but only if that Web site is hosted by SF. We have eliminated all projects from our data set that list Web site addresses different from SF addresses. We were, however, unable to eliminate projects that use code to redirect users from an SF-hosted Web page to a Web site hosted elsewhere. Therefore, the value of the page visits variable for projects that redirect users to other Web sites may be understated. Based on an analysis of a random sample of one hundred projects performed by Stefano Comino, Fabio Maneti, and Maria Laura Parisi (2007), we estimate that only about 5 percent of the projects in our data set redirect users.

As noted in chapters 3 and 4, page visits and downloads can be interpreted as a measure of software *product utility* as well as the *size* of the project's user community (see table 4.1, product utility, H-T3a), but only if we take into account the successful projects that for a variety of reasons have an inherently low number (Howison and Crowston 2004), such as specialized software with small populations of potential users.

Forum Posts

In our data set, forum posts represents the total number of postings made to the project's public forums on SF over the eleven-month period from October 6, 2005, through August 2, 2006. Forum posts before that time were not available in the FLOSS-mole data set. Only 8,355 projects in our data set have a value greater than zero for the number of forum posts (see table 8.2). Some forums and email lists can be reserved for the project's developers, and hidden from public view, so these forum posts are also missing from our data.

Like tracker reports, forum posts represent use of a project's collaborative infrastructure (a technological attribute; see table 4.1, collaborative infrastructure used, RQ-T1). This variable is also a measure of the *activity* of the group and its *interest* in the project (e.g., utility; see table 4.1, product utility, H-T3a).). A limitation of this variable is that the project may use other communication technologies that don't go through the SF system (e.g., a separate email Listserv, or an IRC or IRC channel).

Project Information Index

As we studied our SF data set, we noticed that the more subcategories to the categorical variable questions that a project's administrator had chosen, the greater the chance that the project would be successful. In order to further examine this observation we created the PII variable, which totals the number of subcategories of the categorical variable groups that a project's administrator has chosen to describe the project. Below we explain how we condensed the categorical group answers into subcategories, so the PII's composition will become clearer. We also explain how our theories and hypotheses relate to each categorical variable group that the PII is built on.

Interestingly, 30,276 projects in our data set have selected no categorical data and thus have a value of zero for the PII.[1] The highest value for the PII is twenty-five, meaning that the most subcategories selected for any project was twenty-five of the fifty-four possible categorical independent variables (see table 8.2).

Our Categorical Independent Variables

Intended Audience

The variables in this group were created on SF when project administrators chose from nineteen different answers that portrayed the type of user community that might use their software. The administrators could select from multiple answers, one answer, or no answers to depict their intended audience. Administrators for 72,212 projects chose at least one answer for the intended audience group, and administrators for 35,535 projects chose no answers, meaning they did not assign an intended audience to their project (for more statistical information, see table 8.3).

This variable group is the first example of where we needed to consolidate answers for categorical variable groups into subcategories in order to reduce the number of variables and make analysis of such a large data set feasible. We consolidated the nineteen original SF intended audience answers down to five subcategories (or independent variables) based on similar characteristics. For instance, we grouped the intended audience answers—customer service, financial and insurance, health care industry, legal industry, manufacturing, telecommunications industry, quality engineers, and aerospace—into a new subcategory called business. We grouped end users/ desktop and advanced end users into a new aggregated subcategory named end users. Under the new subcategory computer professionals, we grouped developers, IT, and system administrators together. We consolidated government and nonprofit organizations into one subcategory, government/nonprofit, and grouped education, religion, science/research, and other audience under the new subcategory other. In general, we left answers chosen by a large number of projects as individual subcategories.

Table 8.4 shows the original SF answers, our new aggregated subcategories, and the number of projects that chose each answer for the SF intended audience question.

Table 8.3
Descriptive statistics for categorical groups (each group has data for 107,747 projects)

Categorical variable group	Number of projects listing no subcategories	Number of projects listing at least one subcategory	Number of SF subcategories (original answers)	Number of "new" subcategories (our subcategories)
Intended audience	35,535	72,212	19	5
Operating system	37,412	70,335	59	8
Programming language	33,787	73,960	73	8
User interface	36,719	71,028	48	9
Database environment	97,826	9,921	33	3
Project topic	33,532	74,215	243	19*
Project license	33,172	74,575	60	2
Total			535	54

* The SF hosting site has a detailed categorization (having 243 subcategories) and less detailed categorization (having 19 subcategories) for the project topic; we simply consolidated the 243 subcategories into SF's 19 broader categories.

Because of space limitations, we cannot include similar tables for all our categorical variable groups. We instead have made all the data referred to in this analysis, including tables of our aggregations, available on this book's supplementary material Web page.[2]

One of the reasons we chose to use intended audience as an independent variable is because we think it captures aspects of the idea of user-driven innovation put forth by von Hippel (2005a, 2005b; see table 3.2, H-C1). Based on this idea, we could hypothesize that projects listing our intended audience subcategory computer professionals might have a higher success rate than those with other intended audiences, since computer professionals may be more likely to contribute to the software project because they need and use the code being developed.

Operating System

The operating system group of variables describes the operating system or systems that the project's software has been developed to run on. The original SF data contains fifty-nine answers for this group of variables, and we consolidated them to eight new subcategories. For example, we grouped the answers "All 32-bit MS Windows (95/98/ NT/2000/XP)," "32-bit MS Windows (NT/2000/XP)," "WinXP, 32-bit MS Windows

Table 8.4
Consolidation table for the intended audience group of categorical aariables

New code	New subcategory	SF code	SF answer	Number of projects
1	End users	536	Advanced end users	5417
1	End users	2	End users/desktop	32248
2	Computer professionals	4	System administrators	14402
2	Computer professionals	3	Developers	37931
2	Computer professionals	363	IT	6864
3	Business	365	Manufacturing	664
3	Business	362	Health care industry	684
3	Business	368	Telecommunications industry	1674
3	Business	359	Customer service	1458
3	Business	361	Financial and insurance industry	877
3	Business	364	Legal industry	258
3	Business	537	Quality engineers	615
3	Business	599	Aerospace	122
4	Other	360	Education	5757
4	Other	366	Religion	304
4	Other	367	Science/research	6004
4	Other	5	Other audience	6019
5	Government/nonprofit	569	Government	299
5	Government/nonprofit	618	Nonprofit organizations	503

(95/98)," "Win2K," "Microsoft Windows Server 2003," "WinNT," "WinME," "Win98," and "Microsoft Windows 3.x" into the new subcategory called windows. Answers chosen by large numbers of projects were generally kept as individual subcategories. We consolidated those answers picked by small numbers of projects into the new subcategory other (for descriptive statistics, see table 8.3).

The operating system variable captures one aspect of the technological attributes in the IAD framework (figure 3.1). We see this variable as associated with the hypothesis "Helping the open-source cause" (table 3.2, H-C5). One might expect projects designed to run on Linux operating systems to have a higher likelihood of collaborative success than ones written for other platforms, because of the close relationship between Linux (as an OSS project) and other OSS projects. In other words, programmers would be working to push the "open-source social movement" forward. This category also relates to the hypotheses discussed in chapter 4 that asks if certain preferred technologies attract more developer interest, thereby producing more successful projects (see table 4.1, H-T3c). Finally, this variable could capture another aspect of product utility: the influence of contributing to critical or foundational infrastructure (table 4.1, H-T3b).

Programming Language

This group of independent variables in SF captures the programming language or languages that the project uses to write its software. It originally contained seventy-three subcategories (or seventy-three different programming languages), which we consolidated down to eight new subcategories. For example, we grouped C#, Visual Basic, Visual Basic .NET, ASP, ASP.NET, VBScript, and Visual FoxPro together under the new subcategory MS, since they are all Microsoft programming languages. Programming languages used by only a few projects were placed in the new subcategory other (for descriptive statistics, see table 8.3).

Analyzing the programming language variable might answer the question whether projects written in certain programming languages tend to be more successful. Like the operating system category above, this question relates to the preferred technologies hypothesis (see table 4.1, H-T3c). Which programming languages (e.g., Java, C, or Perl) might be the preferred technologies is an open question.

User Interface

The user interface group of categorical variables represents the way in which the project's software interacts with the user. For instance, the software may use a console interface that requires the user to type commands on a command line, or it may use one of various systems that produce a windowed graphic user interface, such as Microsoft Windows, X Windows, KDE, or Gnome. Some readers will be familiar with the proprietary Microsoft Windows desktop interface, but perhaps not as familiar with similar open-source versions like KDE and Gnome. (For a list of the user interface categories, see table 8.1; for descriptive statistics, see table 8.3).

This variable is another one associated with a project's technological attributes (figure 3.1, IAD framework). Like the operating system variable above, following the "Helping the Open-Source Cause" hypothesis (table 3.2, H-C5), it could be that projects associated with open-source operating system user interfaces such as KDE or Gnome might be more successful than ones not associated with these operating systems. In addition, this variable captures potential aspects of product utility. A project that runs on more user interfaces will be of more utility to more users (table 4.1, H-T3a).

Database Environment

The database environment group of variables describes the type of database that is incorporated into a project's software. Of course, many types of software don't use or are not involved with databases, so quite predictably fewer projects list a database environment than list other categorical independent variables (see table 8.3). This categorical group provides a good example of where a developer may not have chosen any subcategories because the categorical group did not apply to the project's software. As seen in table 8.3, we consolidated the original thirty-three SF answers into just three new subcategories: open-source database, proprietary database, and other. We assigned open-source databases, such as MySQL and PostgreSQL, to the open-source database subcategory, and proprietary databases, such as Oracle and Microsoft Access, to the proprietary database subcategory. The other subcategory includes flat file databases as well as projects that were themselves databases or database related, such as the original SF answers "Project is a network-based DBMS" or "Project is a database conversion tool."

We designed our new subcategories for the database environment variable to test another aspect of the "Helping the Open-Source Cause" hypothesis (table 3.2, H-C5)—whether or not projects using open-source databases were more often successful than those using proprietary databases.

Project Topic

The project topic group of categorical variables consists of the topics or subjects that SF uses to classify the projects hosted on the SF Web site. These topics help SF users find the kind of software they are searching for. Project administrators generate the project topic data by selecting from the list of topics that the SF administrative interface provides. Nineteen major project topic groupings are listed that, in turn, contain 243 more detailed topics (see table 8.1). The FLOSSmole data set that we used supplied all 243 topics. We consolidated these 243 back into the 19 major SF project topic headings.

One of the project topic variables listed in table 8.1 can help in accepting or rejecting a hypothesis we presented in chapter 4. Recall our suggestion that projects that are a component of what could be considered critical or foundational infrastructure may be more likely to succeed than other project topics (see table 4.1, H-T3b). The project topic variable titled "systems" includes subcategories like systems administration, networking, logging, installation/setup, Linux operating system kernels, and other key infrastructure. If H-T3b is correct, this variable should stand out in terms of discriminating between success and abandonment.

Project License

This group of variables refers to the type of OSS license or licenses that a project uses. At the time of this writing (April 2011), the SF Web site provided project administrators with sixty licenses to choose from. We consolidated these types into two main subcategories: GPL compatible or GPL incompatible (table 8.1). We based our consolidation on a list of GPL-compatible and GPL-incompatible licenses compiled by the FSF, the organization responsible for enforcing the GPL's terms.[3]

The FSF list divides OSS into two categories depending on whether or not it can be incorporated into GPL software programs. If it can, the license that the software uses is GPL compatible; if it cannot, then the license is GPL incompatible. With the exception of the MIT license and two others that are not widely used, the FSF list of GPL-compatible licenses is a good proxy for so-called restrictive or business-unfriendly licenses. To some, restrictive licenses are considered business unfriendly because software using them cannot be converted or utilized in proprietary software. The GPL-incompatible licenses are considered less restrictive and more business friendly, on the other hand, because many do allow incorporating the source code into a proprietary commercial product.

The project license variable based on the FSF list therefore may help us understand whether the choice of license affects success or abandonment (see table 5.5, RQ-I5). In addition, one could argue that the more restrictive projects following the GPL might be more successful because they attract more of the free/libre software purists who support the open-source cause (see table 3.2, H-C5). Alternatively, one could contend that OSS projects with licenses permitting proprietary commercial use of the code might be more successful than projects with more restrictive licenses because the former encourage more participation and support by firms (see table 4.2, financing, H-C8). Which is correct? An examination of these variables will help inform this question.

Summing Up Our SF Variables

Table 8.1 summarizes our SF-generated variables. The project class row of table 8.1 shows the abbreviations for the different dependent variable classes (e.g., AI, II, and

SI) as explained in chapter 7. Table 8.1 also includes the abbreviations we have assigned to the subcategories of each categorical variable group. The abbreviation starts with the group's name (*ia* for intended audience, *os* for operating system, and so on) and then assigns a number for each subcategory of that group. In addition, table 8.1 shows the description for each subcategory, which is needed for interpreting the statistical output discussed below. The last column of table 8.1 associates our independent variables with the IAD attributes, hypotheses, and research questions that we presented in chapters 2–5 as well as the discussions below about individual independent variables. All the data for these independent variables, both numerical and categorical, came from the FLOSSmole (2006) data set and are the same 107,747 projects described in chapter 7.

Conceptually, the project license group of categorical variables fits within the collection of institutional attributes variables in the IAD framework (see figure 3.1). The developers variable and intended audience group fit in the collection of community attributes variables in the framework, but the majority of SF data fall under the technological attributes component of IAD. Some of the independent variables (for example, tracker reports and forum posts) fit in both the community and technological attribute components, because they reflect both community activity and the use of collaborative technologies.

Some Data Limitations

We noted earlier that some projects have Web sites hosted on the SF Web site, and that forum posts cover only a limited time span. We also need to acknowledge other data limitations. For instance, all the categorical data and some of the numerical data are generated by the project's developers through the SF project administration Web pages, and thus are open to individual project leader's interpretation. Different project administrators, for example, might categorize the same project's topic differently. Other variables, like operating system or programming language, are relatively unambiguous.

It is also important to remember that SF data change over time. SF purges abandoned projects regularly, and the SF site administrators occasionally revise the number of answers for some of our categorical groups. For example, before 2002, the intended audience group had seven answers, and after 2002 it had ten answers (Comino, Maneti, and Parisi 2007). At the time that our 2006 data were collected, the intended audience group contained nineteen answers. As another example, at the time of this writing, SF requires that a project administrator choose answers for at least five categorical groups in order to register a new project, even though at least some of these answers can be deleted at a later date. Many projects registered as late as June 2006 in our data (our data were collected on July 31, 2006) have no answers selected, so it appears that a project's administrator could ignore all the categorical data groups and not select any answers when registering a new project. These anomalies could become significant if readers were to compare our analysis of SF data with analyses done by others (such as Comino, Maneti, and Parisi 2007), either in the past or future. Finally, we excluded a financing-related variable that listed donations to projects because only a small number of projects (n = 1368) had received donations. We also excluded an activity ranking variable, because the available data were quite limited.

How Do We Make Sense of All This Data?

Explaining Classification Trees

Now that we have laid out our variables and data limitations, we will explain how we analyzed all this data to identify factors that help to distinguish between successful and abandoned OSS projects. In general, we could use a variety of statistical classification techniques, including cluster analysis, discriminate analysis, logistic regression, and classification and regression trees (De'ath and Fabricius 2000). The purpose of all these approaches is to efficiently divide the sample data into groups based on one or more independent variables. For example, logistic regression, a commonly used statistical approach, accomplishes classification by determining combinations of the independent variables that correlate with (or predict) dependent variable groupings (Hosmer and Lemeshow 2000).

After examining the data we had from SF, we decided to use classification trees because they are a unique, nonparametric approach that offers several analytic advantages, including accommodation of both categorical and numerical variables along with the ability to model complex interactions (Breiman et al. 1984; De'ath and Fabricius 2000). In the research summarized here, and again later in chapter 11, we use this technique to test the ability of the SF independent variable data to discriminate between projects that were successful and those that were abandoned in the initiation and growth stages (figure 3.2). Recall as discussed in chapter 3 that we expect important factors to be different between these two stages.

Classification trees are constructed through three steps. First, the entire data set is divided into two subsets that maximize correct classification of the dependent variable on the basis of values for a selected independent variable. Second, a large, highly accurate tree is built through repeated dividing (i.e., recursive partitioning) that can be based on any of the independent variables. The resultant tree is then pruned to a size that maximizes classification accuracy while minimizing complexity. The partitioning process is governed by evaluation of an index that maximizes correct classification in the subsets and also identifies the independent variables that maximize correct classification overall.

In the work we present here, we use the Gini index to maximize correct classification in the dividing process. The number of leaves in the final, pruned tree is based on a cost-complexity statistic that prevents overfitting the data. Overfitting would produce a complicated tree that might not characterize OSS project success and abandonment in a useful, interpretable way. We cross-validated the trees with a subset of the sample to ensure the result was robust to small variations in the data, similar to procedures used by Glen De'ath and Katharina Fabricius (2000). In short, we utilize classification tree analysis to discover which independent variables best distinguish among projects that were successful and those that were abandoned in the initiation and growth stages.

An Example of How to Interpret a Classification Tree

Among the advantages of classification trees is that they are relatively easy to interpret and are intuitive. To help readers unfamiliar with classification trees, we present a simple example in figure 8.1. This tree was constructed using a random selection ($n =$ 1,000) from all the projects we classified as successful in the initiation stage (SI) or abandoned in the initiation stage (AI), including all independent variables (see table 8.5, sampling strategy 1). We will describe the reasons for these sampling strategies shortly.

The primary splitting variable is at the top of the tree—in this case, the total number of downloads, with its split value of one (downloads < 1). Projects present in the left node (where $n = 399$ in the tree) were classified as AI and had zero downloads. A

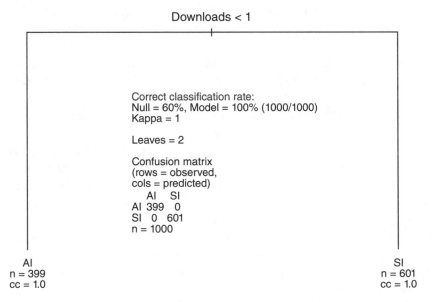

Figure 8.1
A classification tree for the initiation stage using sampling strategy 1 (see table 8.5)

Table 8.5
Sampling strategies used to construct classification trees and variable importance plots for the initiation and growth stages (A = abandoned and S = success)

Sampling strategy number	Stage	Independent variables	n	Random	Categorical variable values*	Variable importance plots	Notes
1	Initiation (A/S)	All variables	1,000	Yes	0, 1, 2	No	Example of tree graphics
2	Initiation (A/S)	All variables minus downloads and page views	2,000	Yes	0, 1, 2	Yes	Main focus for analysis (controls for dependent variable definition problem)
3	Initiation (A/S)	All variables minus downloads and page views	5,037	No	0,1	Yes	Complete observations only (controls for missing data)
4	Growth (A/S)	All variables	1,000	Yes	0, 1, 2	Yes	Main focus for growth stage analysis (sample size based on random samples from all growth [A/S])
5	Growth (A/S)	All variables	2,052	No	0, 1	Yes (but not shown)	Complete observations only (controls for missing data)
6	Growth (A/S)	Minus downloads and page views	1,000	Yes	0, 1, 2	Yes	Mitigates concerns about dependent variable definition and facilitates comparison to initiation stage

* Code definitions: 0 means the specific categorical variable not selected; 1 means the specific categorical variable was selected; and 2 means that no categorical variables from this group were selected at all.

standard convention in classification tree output (not just figure 8.1) is that cases satisfying the true side of the expression (such as downloads < 1 in this case) always sort into the left node, for all levels or branches in the tree.

The right node in figure 8.1 is classified as SI, and contains projects with one or more downloads. The ratio of correctly classified (cc) observations in each node was added to the graphic to provide information on the classification's accuracy within the tree. This simple model with only one split and two leaves had an overall accuracy of 1.0 (100 percent) on both sides. That means that the 399 projects in the left node and 601 projects in the right node were all classified correctly. The model also has a kappa statistic equal to 1. Kappa represents the improvement that the model made in accuracy over a classification done by random selection. A classification done by random selection has no explanatory power and is often called a *null* model (Czaplewski 1994). The accuracy percentage of the null model (60 percent) is shown along with the model's accuracy (100 percent) in figure 8.1. When a kappa statistic was 1, the model improved the classification accuracy by 100 percent over a random classification. This unusual result was produced because projects with downloads must have releases and thus are SI by definition (see chapter 7). Since we have eliminated indeterminate projects from the data used for this tree, projects without releases (and thus zero downloads) are abandoned by definition (also described in chapter 7). We intentionally selected this 100 percent accurate tree as an example because of its interesting, clearly interpreted properties.

Finally, we should mention the so-called confusion matrix (figure 8.1). This is important because it shows the number of projects classified correctly and incorrectly. Adding across the AI row of the confusion matrix gives the total number of projects in the AI class in the sample (i.e., 399 + 0 = 399 AI projects). For the AI row, the AI column shows how many AI projects the model classified correctly as AI (in this case, 399), and the SI column shows how many AI projects the model classified incorrectly as SI (in this instance, 0). The same is true for the SI row, which shows that the original sample had 601 SI projects that were all classified correctly.

Why Use Samples Instead of All the Data?

In the section above, we promised to explain why we used a variety of sampling strategies in our analysis. This decision was not our first choice. Initially, we tried to run a classification tree analysis on the entire data set ($n = 107,747$), but we ran into an unusual and surprising problem: the computational requirements for running a classification tree analysis of the entire 107,747 case data set were too high, even when we divided the data set into two stages (initiation and growth) and ran the software on a high-performance computer. To circumvent this problem, we devised the strategy of taking multiple random data samples to develop trees for each stage (see table 8.5).

In implementing this strategy, our goal was to determine a representative sample size that would produce useful results for the purpose of exploring the data, while still keeping below the computational threshold we were up against. We therefore developed test trees using all independent variables for the growth stage for twenty different random samples at each of fourteen sample sizes (n = 100, 200, . . . 1,000, 2,000, 3,000, 4,000, 5,000), and looked for stability of results. Small sample sizes either could not produce a solution or had only two leaves, with an occasional tree having greater than two leaves. As the sample size increased, more trees had greater than two leaves. At n = 1,000 or greater, the sample apparently included enough variability and enough replicates to produce interpretable as well as fairly accurate results in most cases. For the initiation stage, we excluded the page visits and downloads variables, and instead looked at trees having a sample size of 1,000 (ten trees), 2,000 (three trees), and 5,000 (one tree). This analysis determined that a sample size of 1,000 also produced quite consistent results for the initiation stage.

Random Forests and Variable Importance Plots (VIP)

During the process of determining an appropriate random sample size, we observed that some variables always appeared in the trees, while others only infrequently came into play. In trees with more than two leaves, other variables were used to produce additional splits and improve classification accuracy, but the variables were sometimes inconsistent across trees. This is a common phenomenon in classification tree analysis when different variables provide good surrogates for each other (De'ath and Fabricius 2000). Another possibility was that the appearance of different variables could have been due to high variability in our random data sets.

Because of this uncertainty, we wanted to develop a robust representation of the relative importance of the independent variables. We thus turned to the "random forests" classification method, which fits many classification trees to a data set and then combines the predictions from them all (Breiman 2001). The random forests procedure outputs a variable importance plot (VIP), which shows the relative importance of variables having the most effect, and we used it for various sampling strategies (table 8.5).[4] Examples of VIP output are shown below in figures 8.3 and 8.5. These VIPs present the most crucial variables, in descending order, for predicting the success and abandonment of projects in our data set.

For those interested in the details of how random forests works, the algorithm proceeds as follows (Cutler et al. 2007). First, fit a classification tree to random samples taken from a given data set (approximately 63 percent of the observations in the original data occur at least once), using only a small number of randomly selected independent variables for the partitioning in each node. Then grow each tree fully and use them to predict observations in the remaining data (called "out-of-bag" observations) that were not included in the random sample used to create the tree. Next, calculate the misclassification rate for the predicted out-of-bag observations versus the original observations. Fourth, for each tree in the forest, calculate a misclassification rate for a modified data set, where values of a particular variable have been randomly permuted among projects. Then compare the average misclassification rates for the original data sets and the ones (which include the permuted variables). The larger the difference in the misclassification rate for a variable, the more important that variable is. Similarly, changes in the Gini index, used to maximize homogeneity in the dividing process, indicate relative variable importance. Variables whose values have been permuted with little effect on misclassification rates and Gini index are less significant.

What We Discovered from Our Analysis of SF Data Alone

Three members of our research team spent almost a year preparing the data, undertaking a classification tree and VIP analysis to look at success and abandonment in, respectively, the initiation and growth stage, and then writing this chapter and the online appendixes 8.1–8.3 that explain the data along with the results. Our analysis used only the data found on SF in 2006 and the variables derived from that data as described above. We show examples of the classification tree and VIP output from the initiation stage analyses in figures 8.2 and 8.3 (respectively, classification tree and VIP),

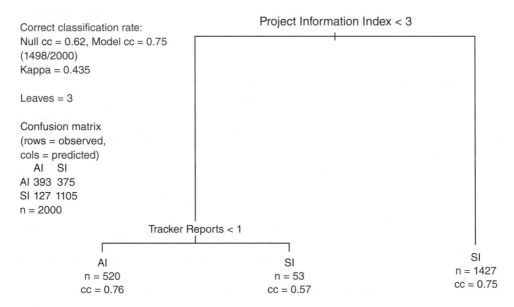

Figure 8.2
An example of an initiation stage classification tree using sampling strategy 2 (see table 8.5)

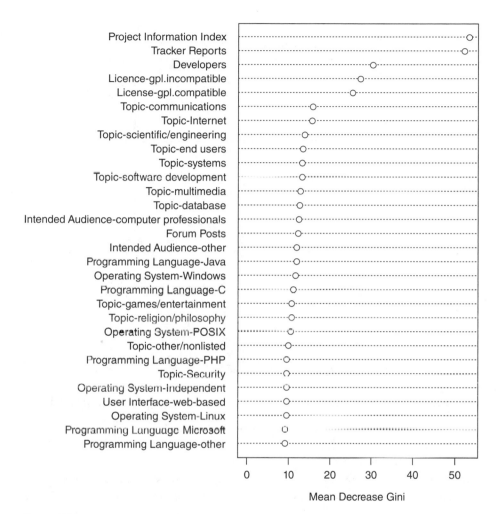

Figure 8.3

An initiation stage variable importance plot using sampling strategy 2 (*n* = 2,000, based on five hundred classification trees, see table 8.5)

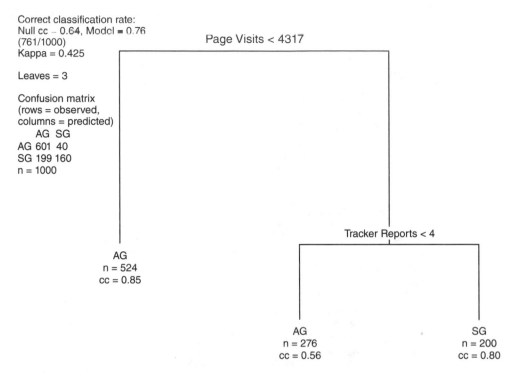

Correct classification rate:
Null cc – 0.64, Model = 0.76
(761/1000)
Kappa = 0.425

Leaves = 3

Confusion matrix
(rows = observed,
columns = predicted)
   AG SG
AG 601 40
SG 199 160
n = 1000

Page Visits < 4317

AG
n = 524
cc = 0.85

Tracker Reports < 4

AG
n = 276
cc = 0.56

SG
n = 200
cc = 0.80

Figure 8.4
An example of a growth stage classification tree using sampling strategy 4 (see table 8.5)

and show examples of growth stage analysis output in figures 8.4 and 8.5 (again, respectively, classification tree and VIP).

As we explained at the beginning of this chapter, we will conduct a similar classification tree analysis of a more complete data set in chapter 11, so we will not discuss the details of these examples of statistical output here. Rather, we have condensed our presentation to focus on the results of this early statistical work rather than a detailed explanation of the statistical output. Those interested in the methodological details may read appendixes 8.1–8.3 on our Web site.[5] Appendix 8.1 provides additional information about data operationalization and some data challenges that we encountered. Appendix 8.2 describes fully the classification tree results for SF projects in the initiation stage. Appendix 8.3 undertakes a similar analysis for SF projects in the growth stage. In each, we supply details about the classification tree output (such as figures 8.2 and 8.4) and VIPs along with complete discussions of the results.

Which Variables Are Important?

In the initiation stage analysis, we found that the PII (figures 8.2 and 8.3) was the most critical variable for discriminating between success and abandonment. At first

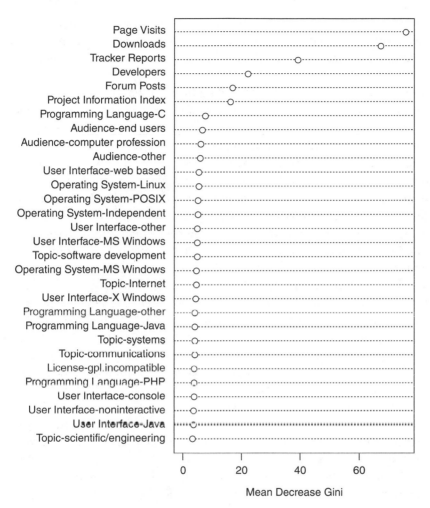

Figure 8.5

A growth stage variable importance plot with page visits and downloads included, sampling strategy 4 (*n* = 1,000, see table 8.5)

glance, figures 8.2 and 8.3 seem to show that tracker reports are also significant, but further investigation revealed that tracker reports increase greatly in number only *after* a project becomes SI. Tracker reports thus are not an important factor for becoming SI.

After extensive analysis to validate the PII finding in the initiation stage, we think that the reason this variable is so crucial is because it captures aspects of three hypotheses proposed in chapter 4. First, when projects in the initiation stage have higher levels of completed SF categorical data, this suggests a more clearly defined vision in the project's early stages (H-T1). Second, more categorical data about the project reflects a more useful project. Projects intended for multiple audiences or to run on multiple operating systems, for instance, are likely to have greater utility to more people than more specialized ones (H-T3a). Third, projects where the categorical variables on SF are more fully completed reflect a more diligent or committed leadership (H-C6a and H-C6b), or in other words, better project management. This finding indicates that having a vision for producing software that is useful to a substantial number of people as well as providing good leadership and management to achieve that vision may be major factors for achieving successful collaboration up until the time a project has its first release. One or another of these factors may turn out to be more important, so we investigate this finding further in our survey, in chapter 9.

In the growth stage analysis (figures 8.4 and 8.5), the PII helped to distinguish between success and abandonment, but with a reduced level of influence when compared to the initiation stage. The two most important variables for distinguishing between success and abandonment in the growth stage are the SF variables page visits and downloads, which capture the importance of product utility. In short, the larger the number of people interested in the software, the more likely the project will continue to be worked on. Our page visits and downloads variable findings support this hypothesis for the growth stage. Tracker reports and developers also appear among the most significant variables in figure 8.5, and we look at these variables further in the discussion of the group size research question below.

What about Our Hypotheses and Research Questions?
A few variables rose to the top in our analysis by being more often associated with successful projects than they were with abandoned ones. But do we have any insight from this preliminary statistical analysis about our hypotheses and research questions? As it turns out, we do.

Supported Hypotheses
The hypotheses below were highlighted in the discussion about important variables above, so we simply list them here. To differing degrees, these hypotheses are supported for both the initiation and growth stage.

OSS commons will be more successful when:

• The project had a relatively clearly defined vision and a mechanism to communicate the vision early in the project's life, before getting to the growth stage (H-T1, chapter 4).
• The software produced has higher utility as perceived by the end user community (H-T3a, chapter 4).
• They have one or more leaders who generate excitement and demonstrate "through doing" (H-C6a, chapter 4).
• They have well-articulated and clear goals established by the project leader(s) (H-C6b, chapter 4).

Unsupported Hypotheses

In many of the variable descriptions above, we highlighted hypotheses that the variable might be related to, and we were able to test some of them in our analysis. We were quite surprised initially to find that none of our categorical variables was strongly associated with success or abandonment. In other words, successful projects do not more frequently use a particular programming language, operating system, or user interface, and success is not associated with any particular intended audience or type of software. To put it positively, success and abandonment are evenly divided across all these different categories. We therefore found no support in our data for any of the hypotheses listed below, in either stage. The specifics related to these three non-findings are discussed more fully online in appendixes 8.1 and 8.2.

OSS commons will be more successful when:

• The project contributes or adds functionality to core OSS technologies related to the open-source movement (H-C5, chapter 3).
• The software produced is a component of what could be considered critical or foundational infrastructure (e.g., operating systems) (H-T3b, chapter 4).
• The software being developed is built on hot, "preferred technologies" (e.g., certain programming languages) that the developer community wants to use or learn (H-T3c, chapter 4).

Research Questions

Through our statistical analysis of SF data, we also gained insight about the following research questions:

What collaborative technologies are utilized in successful OSS commons? Is there a certain suite of technologies or configurations that are more often found in OSS success cases? Or does the configuration not seem to matter? (RQ-T1, chapter 4)

We discovered that the use of bug tracker and forum posts, two SF-based collaborative infrastructure components, are not important success and abandonment discriminators in the initiation stage, but *are* significant in the growth stage. In the initiation stage, the presence or absence of these collaborative infrastructures had little discriminating capability between success and abandonment. This is not surprising, since at this stage there is no release to debug, and with no release, there is probably no user community to discuss the project. Nevertheless, we included these variables in our analysis because the teams could conceivably use these communication tools to maintain or explore feature requests for the upcoming release. While this type of dialogue exists in some projects, it does not appear to be a key factor in distinguishing between SI and AI.

The opposite result was found in the growth stage analysis. The use of these tools is the second most important success factor after the utility finding (page visits and downloads). This provides evidence to support Fogel (2006, 16) and Paul Ramsey (2007), who have noted that these tools supply metrics for gauging the health of these projects.

What, if any, notable direct relationships exist between group size and project success in OSS? Is there any support for Brooks's law and Olson's theory, Linus's law, or the core team theories? (RQ-C4, chapter 4)

In chapter 4, we thoroughly examined the theoretical and empirical work on the question of group size as well as collective action, and presented three alternative hypotheses:

1. Smaller development teams will be more successful than larger groups (the Brooks and Olson hypothesis).
2. Larger groups will be more successful than smaller ones (the Linus's law hypothesis).
3. Group size won't matter because a core team does most of the work anyway (our core team hypothesis).

Two major findings came out of our analyses. First, we discovered that development team size does not help distinguish between successful and abandoned projects in the initiation stage, but it does help to distinguish successful growth stage projects. In the initiation stage (online appendix 8.2), we found that on average, developer team size was small (one to two people), and that the group's size did not help distinguish between success and abandonment.[6] The core team hypothesis was supported here. On the other hand, in the growth stage (online appendix 8.3), we have strong evidence that successful projects are associated with slightly larger (and statistically significant) developer communities compared to abandoned growth stage projects (see, for example, table 8.6). Moreover, our more detailed analysis in online appendix 8.3 provides strong empirical proof that *adding more developers causes success as we have operationalized it*. We think this is one of our most important empirical findings in

Table 8.6
Mean number of developers

Project class	Mean number of developers	Number of projects
Abandoned in initiation	1.70	37,320
Indeterminate in initiation	1.40	13,342
Projects with exactly one release	1.62	20,347
Indeterminate in growth	1.76	10,711
Abandoned in growth	1.78	30,592
Projects with exactly two releases	1.86	10,248
Projects with exactly three releases	2.06	5,917
Successful in growth	3.66	15,782

this analysis, with the caveat that the majority (but not all) of successful growth stage projects still consist of two to three developers. In short, we found some limited support for Linus's law in the growth stage analysis.

Linus's law, however, refers not only to the project development team but the larger user community as well. This leads us to our second key group size finding: a substantial community of users and developers is associated with success in the growth stage. In online appendix 8.3, we report that the majority of successful growth stage projects have fairly large numbers of visits to their Web sites, and substantial numbers of downloads, tracker reports, and forum posts. We argue that these variables capture not only the software's utility but also reflect a larger community of people interested in these projects. At this juncture we should note that we might have found the opposite to be true: that the majority of SG projects are projects with small, specialized software and communities (e.g., bioinformatics software). But this is not the case. This is not unexpected, though, and suggests that projects with a greater potential for a large user community have a higher likelihood of success.

Taken together, these two findings indicate that in addition to building software that is useful to a substantial number of people, building a community of users and developers is a crucial factor for growth stage success. This provides empirical support to the conventional wisdom about OSS. In turn, building this community probably involves good management, leadership, communication skills, and attention to incentives for participation. We explore these factors further in the survey analysis in the forthcoming chapters.

Does the choice in OSS license effect a project's success or abandonment? For instance, do GPL-compatible projects outperform GPL-incompatible ones, or vice versa? (RQ-I5, chapter 5)

In our classification tree analysis, we discovered that the general choice of OSS license, either in the category of a more restrictive GPL-like license or a less restrictive non-GPL license, appears to have little relationship to success and abandonment in the initiation as well as growth stage. Like our findings with the other categorical variables, success and abandonment are well distributed across different license types in both stages.

What Does All This Mean?

Our analysis and findings of SF data, summarized in table 8.7 and described in more detail in online appendixes 8.2 and 8.3 (initiation and growth stage, respectively), lead us to a number of insights about OSS projects. First, a comparison of initiation and growth stage classification tree results suggests that the collaborative processes are different in each case. Our analyses find different sets of important discriminators of success and abandonment for the two stages, as shown in table 8.7. This is an important finding, for it strongly indicates that these two stages require different elements to achieve collaborative success.

Second, effective leadership is important in both the initiation and growth stages, but especially in the initiation (prior to the first release) stage. Projects that articulate clear visions and goals in this stage are more often associated with ongoing development success than ones that do not. We inferred these ideas about leadership from the PII, which we believe captures these concepts.

Third, in both stages, projects with clear utility for a substantial number of end users are more frequently successful than those that are useful to fewer people. By a substantial number of end users, we mean at least several hundred users in the growth stage. Choosing to develop software that has a large body of potential users is probably more likely to result in success than developing software with an inherently small audience.

Fourth, slightly larger teams are associated with successful growth stage projects, even though they remain small (two to three people on average). Strong statistical evidence supports this conclusion. This means that projects in this stage will have a higher likelihood of continued development if they are able to find an additional developer to join the team. Hosting sites like SF probably play a significant friend-finding or matchmaking role, providing a platform where developers looking for projects to contribute to can find one that matches their critical need or passion. In other words, making a project visible to a large number of developers globally may lead to finding additional development team members and increasing the chances for success. The developer survey in chapter 9 investigates this further.

Fifth, in the growth stage (after the first release), projects with higher numbers of SF Web page visits, downloads, tracker reports, and forum posts—measures of project interest—were associated with continued development activity—our measure of success. Successful growth stage projects are associated with larger user communities. We interpret this to mean that if the project has a user base, developers are more apt to join or continue working on the project, and it is likely that the projects will be more vibrant with user input and potential contributions. In short, projects with members who have leadership skills that build community along with management skills that make good use of collaborative infrastructure will be more likely to succeed in the growth stage.

Sixth, all our other nonfindings described fully in online appendixes 8.2 and 8.3 suggest that OSS is maturing. Our findings show that successful collaborations are not associated with particular kinds or categories of software (e.g., ones that are built for specific operating systems such as Linux, or particular user interfaces, database engines, or GPL versus non-GPL type licenses). These nonfindings indicate that developers can start OSS projects in any software category and use any popular technology, with roughly equal chances of success.

Conclusion

In this chapter, we have begun the process of discovering which of the independent variables or factors we proposed in earlier chapters are important in distinguishing between the success and abandonment of OSS projects. Many of these factors, however, are not represented by the 2006 SF data set that we used here. In the order that we presented them in earlier chapters (tables 3.2, 4.1, 4.2, and 5.5), these missing factors include:

- Project financing (table 2.1; table 4.2, H-C8)
- Paid versus volunteer participants (table 3.2, H-C2; table 4.2, H-C8)
- Developer motivations (serious leisure, skill building, and signaling; table 3.2, H-C3, H-C4b, and H-C4c)
- The homogeneity/heterogeneity of participants (table 4.2, RQ-C1)
- The skill/knowledge continuum of developers (no hypothesis presented)
- Software modularity, granularity, and complexity (table 4.1, H-T2a–H-T2d)
- Competition (table 4.1, H-T4)
- Approaches to requirements gathering (table 4.1, H-T1)
- Some elements of leadership (table 4.2, H-C6a–H-C6b)
- Social capital (table 4.2, H-C7a, H-C7b, RQ-C2–RQ-C3)
- Marketing (table 4.2, RQ-C5)
- Institutional structure and design (the majority of table 5.5)

Clearly, the list above shows that we have much left to do.

Table 8.7
Summary of hypotheses/research questions supported by analysis of SF data*

Hypothesis or research question	Table	Description	Associated variables	Support initiation stage	Support growth stage	Notes
H-T1	4.1	Projects with a **clearly defined vision** will be more successful	PII	Yes	Yes	Supported more in the initiation than the growth stage
H-T3a	4.2	**Utility** is an important factor in project success	PII Page visits, downloads, tracker reports, and forum posts	Yes	Yes	Initiation stage—PII only, but most important distinguishing variable Growth stage—page visits, downloads, tracker reports, forum posts and PII; PII much less important in growth stage
H-C6a	4.2	**Leadership:** Projects will be more successful when "they have one or more leaders who generate excitement and demonstrate 'through doing'"	PII	Yes	Yes, but less important than in initiation	PII distinguishing influence between success and abandonment much more in initiation than the growth stage
H-C6b	4.2	**Leadership:** Projects will be more successful when "they have well-articulated and clear goals established and articulated by the leader(s)"	PII	Yes	Yes, but less important than initiation	PII distinguishing influence between success and abandonment much more in initiation than the growth stage

RQ-T1	4.1	What **collaborative infrastructures** are utilized in successful OSS commons?	Tracker reports and forum posts	No	Yes	The use of tracker reports and forums are not important in the initiation stage, but are important in the growth stage
RQ-C4	4.2	Is there any support for Brooks's law and Olson's theory, Linus's law, or core team theories? Is **group size** an important factor in project success?	Developers	Core team theory supported. No, group size is not important in this stage	Some support for Linus's law. Yes, group size is important	Group size does not help to distinguish between successful and abandoned projects in the initiation stage. Successful growth stage projects are associated with larger communities (users and developers). Larger development teams are associated with growth stage success, although most successful growth stage projects are still comprised of small groups (e.g., 1–3 developers); some limited support is provided for Linus's law
H-C5	3.2	Project will be more successful if it **helps the cause**, and contributes or adds functionality to core open-source technologies	Operating system, user interface, database environment, and project license	No	No	
H-T3b	4.1	Projects that are part of **critical infrastructure** will be more successful	Operating system and project topic systems	No	No	No evidence that being in the systems category makes projects more successful

Table 8.7
(continued)

Hypothesis or research question	Table	Description	Associated variables	Support initiation stage	Support growth stage	Notes
H-T3c	4.1	OSS commons will be more successful when the software being developed is built on hot **preferred technologies**	Operating system, programming language, user interface, and database environment	No	No	We do not see evidence that projects using particular technologies are more successful
RQ-I5	5.5	Does the choice in **OSS license** effect the success or abandonment of a project? For instance, do GPL-based projects outperform non-GPL licenses, or vice versa?	Project license (GPL or non-GPL)	No	No	
Other unexpected findings		Collaborative success and abandonment are widely distributed across SF categories	No categorical variables being important	Yes	Yes	Suggests that OSS has matured or expanded into a broader array of topic areas, and not just in traditional OSS ones

* Gray cells highlight where there are different findings between initiation and growth stage analyses.

Nevertheless, we have succeeded in our two goals for this chapter, because we identified SF data that measure some of the concepts presented in chapters 2–5, and discovered that leadership, development team size, and user community size are more often associated with successful projects. We also learned that some elements we thought might help distinguish between success and abandonment did not aid in making this distinction.

We have created a foundation here for the next steps in our research, but could some of the factors we were unable to investigate in this chapter be even more important than the ones we discovered? Also, will the findings reported here be validated as we examine data sets representing later years? In forthcoming chapter 9, we start to answer these questions by working with a new 2009 SF data set made available by the University of Notre Dame. We create the same success and abandonment dependent variable as we did in chapter 7 but representing SF for the year 2009. We then describe a major online survey that we conducted in the fall of 2009 to collect additional data (e.g., community and institutional) not available in the SF data set, survey results, and the new variables we created using this newly acquired data. When we reach the end of chapter 9, we have measures for all the factors that we think are key for the success or abandonment of OSS commons, and we will be ready to take the final steps toward the ultimate goal of answering our central research question.

9   Filling Gaps in Our Data with the Survey on Free/Libre and Open-Source Success

We were fortunate to be able to conduct *The Survey on Free/Libre and Open-Source Success*, with the cooperation and active support of SourceForge Inc., the corporation that owns SF. This assistance made it possible for us to survey a random sample of all active SF developers, resulting in one of the few representative and potentially generalizable surveys existing in the OSS research field. We conducted the survey in fall 2009, after we had done our OSCeo case study (chapter 6), created our dependent variable (chapter 7), and completed our analysis of 2006 SF data (chapter 8). The work from all these chapters contributed to the nearly yearlong effort to create and conduct our survey.

We start this chapter by describing the survey's goals. We needed the survey to generate measures for all the factors that we developed in earlier chapters, but that were missing from SF data alone, and we wanted our results to be as representative as possible of the universe of existing OSS projects. We also wanted to test the findings we revealed in chapter 8. To accomplish those goals, we had first to update our dependent variable to make it contemporaneous with the survey, but we wondered if our technique for classifying SF projects would still work in 2009, as it had in 2006. Would our classification technique still produce an accurate result three years later? Next, we had to create our survey questions, test them for clarity, decide exactly who we would ask to take the survey (our sample), and administer the survey and gather the results. Finally, we had to transform these results into variables we could use to create a model of OSS success and abandonment in order to reach the ultimate aspiration of answering our central research question. Needless to say, this was a lot of work, as this chapter will explain in more detail.

Survey Goals

Often, OSS researchers focus their research on large, well-known OSS projects, such as Debian Linux (Gonzalez-Barahona et al. 2005; O'Mahony and Ferraro 2007) and Mozilla (Mockus, Fielding, and Herbsleb 2002; Holck and Jørgensen 2005). These larger projects usually have many developers on the team, have a larger user base, and are generally success stories from which much may be learned. It is therefore easy to see why researchers focus attention on projects of this kind. Yet the SF project data for May 2009 (n = 174,333) that we acquired from the University of Notre Dame repository (Madey 2010), described more in the next section, reveal that about 70 percent of the hosted projects list only one developer as a project member. About 84 percent of the projects have fewer than three developers. Furthermore, 64 percent of successful projects in the initiation stage and 47 percent of successful projects in the growth stage (following our definitions of success) list only one developer as a project member (the term that SF uses).

Recall our contemplations in chapter 7 about the representativeness of SF to the unknown population of OSS projects in the world today. We argued that while SF isn't a perfect approximation, it may be the closest approximation we could find to this "grand universe" (in 2009 when we conducted this research). If we take that statement to be true, it may be that the majority of OSS projects in the entire population of open source are made up of teams with fewer than three developers (but varying sizes of end user communities), and perhaps substantially more than half of these small projects produce useful software.

In assessing the our survey goals, we asked ourselves whether we should follow the lead of other researchers and focus on larger OSS projects. If so, we would stratify our sample to choose proportionately greater numbers of large projects than a random sample of the SF population would produce. This strategy would have the added advantage of surveying more large projects with a potentially richer institutional structure—one area of focus in our research. On the other hand, we considered whether to take a random sample of all SF projects, and have our survey be directly representative of the SF population and potentially provide more insight into the universe of OSS projects. If we did that, 70 percent of our survey invitations would go to projects with only one developer. But do projects with one developer represent collaboration?

In the end, since the main focus of our research is to discover the principles of successful OSS collaboration in general, we found little justification for stratifying our sample. If we truly wanted to understand success and abandonment in the entire population of OSS projects, it seemed best to include a representative number of single developer projects in our sample. We therefore chose to take a random sample of all projects hosted on SF. As for the question of what constitutes collaboration, we know that the interaction between developers and users is an important element in OSS software development. Many developers also can contribute to a project without being listed as members (end user contributors, for example). For these two reasons, we believe that projects with only one developer can still be meaningful collaborations.

In summary, the goals for our survey are as follows:

• Generate data to construct variables that will allow us to test hypotheses we were unable to test with SF data alone (e.g., community and institutional variables).
• Generate data to build a more complete model of OSS success that would be more representative of the entire open-source population.
• Verify our chapter 8 findings about vision, leadership, and utility in the initiation stage, and building community in the growth stage.

Our hypotheses and statistical results to this point all depend on our definition of success. As we discussed fully in chapter 7, there are a variety of ways to conceptualize and quantify success. In the work that follows, we utilize the same success/abandonment measure from chapter 7 and put it to use in chapter 8—a conservative measure that captures both use or popularity measures, and also projects life and death metrics (for details, see table 7.1). We ultimately define growth stage success as producing several releases of useful software over at least a six-month period. To us, this is a successful collaboration, whether among many software developers or between a single developer and the user community, however large or small it may be.

Updating Our Dependent Variable

We designed our survey instrument, described later in this chapter, to collect responses from developers who worked on either successful or abandoned projects in either the initiation or growth stage. Given that our survey was administered in fall 2009, we needed to update our dependent variable, which we had created using 2006 data, so that we could accurately choose successful and abandoned projects to survey. Fortunately, as mentioned above, we were able to obtain the data we needed from the repository at the University of Notre Dame (Madey 2010), which receives data directly from SF monthly. The data it receives, with the exception of sensitive personal data, also is a nearly complete copy of the SF database. We used the May 2009 Notre Dame data because that was the most recent data set available at the time we began our survey, and followed exactly the same methodology described in chapter 7 to classify all projects existing on SF as of May 15, 2009.

Does Our Classification Technique Still Work in 2009?
We were not sure whether our process for classifying projects would still work in 2009 because SF had experienced many changes since 2006.[1] For example, our 2006 SF database contained 107,747 projects, but by 2009 SF had grown, and our 2009 Notre Dame database contained 174,333 projects. Were these new projects similar to the old, or had the substantial growth and evolution of OSS over the previous three years changed the characteristics of projects so much that our classification system had

become obsolete? To answer this question, and also to double check our results, we performed a validation of the 2009 classification using the methodology described in chapter 7, with the difference that we validated only 100 projects from the 2009 classification rather than 300, as in the previous (2006 data set) validation (see table 7.5). Due to financial and time constraints, we reduced the number to be tested. The results are displayed in table 9.1 below.

The results shown for our 2009 data set (table 9.1) correspond well to those found for the 2006 data set (table 7.5), with the exception that in our previous validation the error rate for the SG class was 0 percent, whereas in the classification of 2009 data, the error rate is 15.1 percent. We believe that the SG error rate is actually less than depicted in table 9.1. The validation methodology for the SG class requires that we find evidence that the software is indeed useful to at least a few people. In the classification procedure, we use downloads as a measure for usefulness. But in our validation work, we need to find alternative evidence of utility. Suitable evidence would include, say, postings on the Internet by those who have used the software. Most of the incorrect cases for the SG class in table 9.1 were classified as incorrect because we had found insufficient proof to support software utility; due to our time constraints, however, we had been unable to do as thorough an Internet search as we had done in the first validation, and we believe this largely explains the discrepancy for the SG class. In short, this validation exercise provided relatively strong evidence that our 2009 Notre Dame classification remained reasonably accurate and produced a useful dependent variable for our survey. This also suggests that our success/abandonment measure could be used in future studies to look at longitudinal questions related to OSS—a point made by Wiggins and Crowston (2010).

How Much Has SourceForge Really Changed?

Table 9.2 compares the percent of projects in each of our classes for the 2006 SF data set and the 2009 Notre Dame data set. Table 9.2 shows that the percent of total projects in each class (comparison of columns 3 and 5) has remained quite stable over the

Table 9.1
2009 Notre Dame classification validation results

Original class (number of cases)	Correct	Incorrect	Deleted or missing data	Error rate %
AI (36)	32	4	0	11.1%
AG (31)	28	3	0	9.7%
SG (33)	28	5	0	15.1%
Totals	88	12	0	12.0%

Table 9.2

Comparison of 2006 SourceForge.net and 2009 Notre Dame classifications

Class	2006 SF data (107,747 projects)		2009 Notre Dame data (174,333 projects)	
	Number of projects	Percent of total projects	Number of projects	Percent of total projects
AI	37,320	34.6	67,126	38.5
II	13,342	12.4	16,806	9.6
IG	10,711	9.9	12,052	6.9
AG	30,592	28.4	53,450	30.7
SG	15,782	14.6	24,899	14.3
Total	107,747	100	174,333	100

period August 2006 to May 2009. This result encourages us because it suggests that there is some constancy in the characteristics of OSS development, and therefore the chance of finding factors for success that remain constant over time seems more probable.

Table 9.2 also reveals that as the number of total projects hosted on SF has increased from 107,747 to 174,333, the number of successful (SG) projects hosted on SF has increased from 15,782 to 24,899. This means that the number of successful OSS projects has increased by 9,117, or about 58 percent, over three years—a stunning increase. Clearly OSS has broadened, at least in the total number of projects and the number of successful projects hosted on SF. But have successful projects expanded into more categories or types of software, thus broadening the range of OSS available? Has the increase in paid development over this period, discussed in chapter 2, contributed to this increase in the range of software available? Does this broadening over the three dimensions—the number of successful projects, range of applications available, and financial involvement of organizations—provide evidence of an extension of von Hippel's ideas from user-driven innovation outside the firm to an "organizational-driven innovation" that includes firms? It seems likely that the answer to all of these questions is yes, and we hope that our survey will shed light on these questions by generating more empirical evidence.

Our Survey Methods

Creating the Survey

We chose to use an Internet survey, rather than a mail or phone survey, for several reasons. For one, our respondents are software developers who regularly use computers, and we know they use the Internet because they use SF. Second, Internet surveys are relatively low cost. And we had data to access the entire population of SF developers through email, but we had no comparable mailing addresses or telephone numbers.

Although Internet surveys have advantages, contacting respondents via email is not without problems. First, sending unsolicited email (that is, spam) would be considered by many potential respondents unethical and irritating. There also is the practical problem of spam filtering. The email addresses we had for SF developers were all within the SF domain (user_name@sourceforge.net), and we considered it likely that SF would quickly filter out as spam any bulk mailing about our survey. Last, a goal all along in this research was to produce information of interest to developers and potentially the SF organization itself. For these reasons, we contacted the SF organization with the help of Madey (2010), the director of the Notre Dame SF repository data project. SF became interested in what we were doing, and agreed to email our solicitations to respondents using its mass emailing system and with its official endorsement as well as support.

We designed our survey based on Internet survey recommendations by Don Dillman, Jolene Smyth, and Leah Christian (2009). Like our efforts in chapter 8, and because of our interest in identifying similarities and differences between pre- and postrelease projects, we implemented two separate surveys, one for the initiation stage and another for the growth stage. At this point in the survey development, we used an OSS survey package called LimeSurvey on a Web server we controlled. We developed questions designed to achieve the goals mentioned above, and then pretested them using two methods. First, we asked several professional developers and computer science students at UMass Amherst to take the survey online in an interviewer's presence. The purpose of these sessions was to get respondents to talk about their thought processes as they answered the survey questions. The interviewer recorded the results, which identified questions that were confusing or incomplete. We then asked other developers and students at our university to take the online surveys on their own and respond in writing about their perceptions, including any problems they had. After completing the pretesting, we made adjustments to the questions plus changed instructions and formatting as necessary.[2] Finally, we implemented the production versions of the initiation and growth online surveys using a LimeSurvey hosting site to make sure that the server could handle the potential volume once we sent out our invitation email.[3] Only one thing remained to be completed: the list of who we would invite to take our survey.

Choosing Who Would Take the Survey

As we mentioned in chapter 7, we took random samples of all projects hosted on SF in order to maximize our chances of generalizing our results, not only to the entire SF population, but also to the broader universe of OSS projects. While this sampling process seemed relatively straightforward conceptually, we encountered practical problems.

To begin with, using the May 2009 Notre Dame data set (Madey 2010), we started with a database of 174,333 projects, but we immediately found that 1,551 of these projects did not have a contact person, so we eliminated these projects, leaving 172,782 in our sample. Second and more important, we needed to address the potential problem of emailing a respondent more than once if they were actively working on more than one project. To explain this in more detail, all projects have at least one person in the role of project administrator as opposed to a developer or some other role. The administrator is often the person who initiated the project, and thus we decided to survey only project administrators. Yet it turns out that many SF project administrators are listed on more than one project. When we sampled randomly from the entire list of our 172,782 SF 2009 projects, many administrators appeared more than once in the results. We (and the SF organizational staff members who were working with us) did not want to annoy SF users by sending them multiple survey invitations. We needed to eliminate this duplication and at the same time remain true to the idea of a random sample from which legitimate generalizations can be drawn.

In our first step, we noticed that many of the duplicate administrators belonged to multiple projects having only one member. We reasoned that we were unlikely to get different information by surveying a single administrator several times about single-member projects. Consequently, we eliminated these duplicates and left only a single, one-member project for each administrator in the SF population we sampled. This process weeded out 23,176 projects.

In addition, we did not use the Indeterminate Initiation (II) stage projects in our analysis, because by definition we did not know whether they would become successful or be abandoned. This eliminated another 16,715 II projects from our pool, leaving 132,891 projects from which to sample.

Practical hurdles continued when we realized that there were challenges with trying to sample abandoned projects in both the initiation and growth stage. Because these projects appear to be abandoned (no development activity), it is much less likely that an administrator will respond. They may not monitor the project anymore, for example. Furthermore, an examination of table 9.1 above shows that about 10 to 12 percent of the projects we classified as abandoned using our automated classification process are not really abandoned at all; they are simply misclassified. We reasoned that we were much more likely to receive responses from these misclassified projects than from projects that had actually been abandoned. To avoid this bias, we estimated response rates for the classes we intended to sample and adjusted the number of projects sampled accordingly in an attempt to get a representative response.

For the initiation stage, we intended to sample Abandoned Initiation (AI) and SI projects. By our definitions, any project that has a public release *is* an SI project, so SI projects include Indeterminate Growth (IG), Abandoned Growth (AG), and Successful Growth (SG) stage projects. For the growth stage survey, we wanted to sample AG and SG projects. We estimated that we would get a 20 percent response rate (typical for Internet surveys; see Dillman, Smyth, and Christian 2009) from samples of the IG and SG classes, and we guessed we might get a 5 percent response rate from the AI and AG classes. We wanted to get about one thousand responses for each of the four classes, based on the idea that this would give us ±3 percent accuracy with regard to the entire SF project population.

Table 9.3 shows the number sampled from our pool of 132,891 projects versus the number of survey invitations actually sent out for each class. As a reminder, successful projects in the initiation stage are ones that have made it to the growth stage (IG, AG, and SG classes), and this is why we have sampled from those classes for the initiation survey. More generally, the number of projects sampled and invitations actually sent in both surveys differ because some projects having at least two members had the same administrators. Similar to our process with single-member projects described earlier, duplicates were eliminated so that each administrator received only one invitation. This resulted in 390 (30,000 – 29,610) fewer initiation stage surveys being sent and 164 (19,000 – 18,836) fewer growth stage surveys being sent.

The data in table 9.3 highlight our efforts to sample abandoned projects more heavily than successful ones in order to elicit a similar number of responses for each class (AI, SI, AG, and SG). Overall, we sampled 49,000 project administrators, and sent surveys to 48,446 of them.

How We Administered the Survey

With the samples created, we were ready to launch the surveys. We uploaded needed information from our sample to our LimeSurvey installation and generated *tokens*

Table 9.3
Sample size versus the number of survey invitations actually sent

| Class | Initiation stage survey | | Growth stage survey | |
	Sample	Number of invitations sent	Sample	Number of invitations sent
AI	20,000	19,740	0	0
II	0	0	0	0
IG	1,000	987	0	0
AG	8000	7,896	15,000	14,871
SG	1000	987	4,000	3,965
Total	30,000	29,610	19,000	18,836

that allowed us to associate a project name with a survey response. We sent these tokens as part of invitations to take the survey in the form of a clickable link that brought the respondent to either the initiation or growth survey, as necessary. Also, we customized the emails so the specific project name was referenced in the text of each email.

In order to make sure that our system worked properly, in cooperation with SF we sent out a test of 1,000 invitations to each survey on September 2, 2009. On September 10, 2009, after verifying that the system worked properly, we sent the first wave of 23,500 invitations. Our intention was to monitor the results of the first wave and send as few additional invitations as needed to obtain an acceptable response rate. We were already concerned about the number of survey requests we were sending out, and along with SF, were concerned about disturbing members more than necessary to accomplish the survey goals. For this reason we did not send reminder emails. As it turned out, the response rate to the first wave was low, and we needed to send out another round of invitations to a second group of about 24,500. This second and final batch of invitations was sent out on November 5, 2009, and we closed the surveys to participation on November 22, 2009.

Did We Get a Representative Response?

With all the practical problems we encountered in our sampling process, we were anxious about whether the survey responses would be representative of the greater SF population. Table 9.4 below presents information about the response. Both the

Table 9.4

Number of survey responses and response rates

Initiation survey

Class	Number of invitations sent	Number of useful responses (%)	Percent of questions answered
AI	19,740	237 (1.2)	84%
SI	9,843	446 (4.5)	87%
Total	29,610	683 (2.3)	85%

Growth survey

Class	Number of invitations sent	Number of useful responses (%)	Percent of questions answered
AG	14,871	350 (2.3)	84%
SG	3,965	370 (9.3)	87%
Total	18,836	720 (3.8)	85%

initiation and growth stage surveys contained questions to verify whether a project
was abandoned or not, according to our dependent variable definitions. We eliminated
surveys where respondents indicated that our automated classification was incorrect.
We also eliminated surveys where respondents did not answer enough questions to
provide meaningful information toward achieving our survey goals. The useful
responses column (and the corresponding response rate in parentheses) does not
include surveys where our automated classification was incorrect or cases in which
respondents answered an insufficient number of questions. As table 9.4 demonstrates,
response rates were generally low, and we did not achieve our goal of getting one
thousand responses in each of the four classes.

Despite these low rates, we found that our responses were quite representative
of the population of SF projects across multiple dimensions. We compared the composition of survey responses to the SF population with respect to project class, license
type, developer count, number of downloads, life span, and number of releases
for both the initiation and the growth survey. With the exception of a disproportionately higher response from the SG class in the growth survey, the distributions of
all these variables were remarkably similar in both our survey responses and the SF
population. We present only three examples here due to space limitations. Detailed,
color-coded graphs for all the variables are available on this book's accompanying
Web site.[4]

Figure 9.1 below compares the distribution of the proportions of project classes for
our survey responses and the SF population for both surveys. The distributions for
the four classes represented in the initiation survey (classes AI, IG, AG, and SG) are
close. They are close enough in fact that we decided not to weight them to achieve a
more representative balance. On the other hand, the distributions of the two classes
in the growth stage (AG and SG) are quite different. The number of survey responses
from AG and SG projects is roughly equal, while the proportion is about 70 percent
AG and only about 30 percent SG in the SF population. In the analysis of our results,
we weight our survey responses to correct for this imbalance, as further described in
chapter 11.

Table 9.5 below contrasts the distribution of project developer counts (the number
of developers who are formal project members) for our growth stage survey responses
and the SF population. As mentioned above, we received a disproportionate survey
response for the SG class (370 responses, or 51 percent of our 720 AG and SG survey
responses) in contrast with the SF population, which has only 32 percent SG projects
(24,815 projects) in the total of 77,761 AG plus SG projects. We can see from table
9.5, on the other hand, that we received responses from projects with a wide range
of different developer counts, and that for each developer count in our survey
responses, the proportion of projects compares reasonably well with the distribution

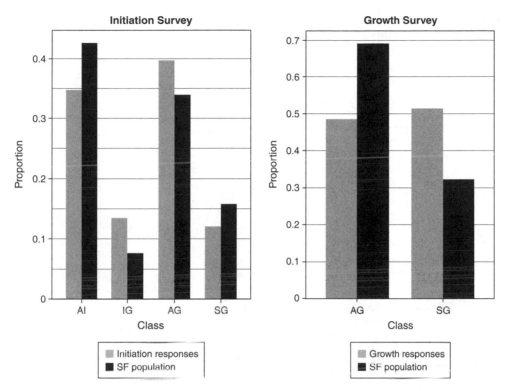

Figure 9.1
Comparison of the proportion of project classes in our survey responses and the May 2009 SourceForge population

of proportions in the SF population. We received fewer responses from one-person AG projects (36 percent) than exist in the SF population (48 percent), but at the same time, we received more responses from one-person SG projects (22 percent) than exist in the SF population (15 percent). The proportions for the remaining developer counts are within a few percentage points of each other.

Figure 9.2 compares the number of downloads for our growth survey responses along with the SF population for the AG and SG classes. We can see that some of the extreme outliers from the SF population are missing from our responses, but the medians and ranges of the quartiles are quite similar. This graph shows that projects in our growth survey responses have a similar distribution of numbers of downloads as do projects in the SF population in general. Overall, the evaluation findings described in this section gave us confidence that our response was reasonably representative, and hence we proceeded with our data analysis.

Table 9.5
Developer counts for the growth stage survey responses versus the May 2009 SourceForge population (percent of total in parentheses)

Developer count	Survey: Class AG	SF population: Class AG	Survey: Class SG	SF population: class SG
1	257 (36)	37,259 (48)	161 (22)	11,765 (15)
2	49 (7)	8,329 (11)	66 (9)	4,420 (6)
3	26 (4)	3,236 (4)	35 (5)	2,380 (3)
4	8 (1)	1,573 (2)	27 (4)	1,515 (2)
5	4 (1)	921 (1)	19 (3)	1,076 (1)
6	3 (0)	525 (1)	13 (2)	731 (1)
7	1 (0)	316 (0)	6 (1)	514 (1)
8	1 (0)	198 (0)	7 (1)	424 (0)
9	0 (0)	141 (0)	4 (1)	309 (0)
10	0 (0)	90 (0)	2 (0)	234 (0)
11–20	1 (0)	305 (0)	19 (3)	990 (1)
> 20	0 (0)	53 (0)	11 (2)	457 (0)
Totals	350 (49)	52,946 (68)	370 (51)	24,815 (32)

Note: The total equals AG + SG for the survey (720 responses) and AG+SG for the SF population (77,761 projects). The totals for the "SF population: Class AG" and "SF population: Class SG" columns differ slightly from totals found elsewhere in this chapter, because some projects in the AG and SG classes have a "0" developer count.

How We Constructed Our New Variables and Indexes

Table 9.6 depicts the new variables that we created from the initiation and growth survey results. By *new*, we mean variables or indexes that capture various theoretical concepts built on one or more survey questions. Table 9.6 also includes the old SF project metadata variables that we found to be most important in our chapter 8 results (i.e., downloads, developers, tracker reports, forum posts, and the PII). We will incorporate these old variables into the more complete model of OSS success explained in chapter 11 in order to verify our chapter 8 results.

We updated our database for these old variables with May 2009 data taken from the Notre Dame repository mentioned above, so that the data for these variables would be from the same period as the survey results. The Notre Dame repository does not have page visits statistics, so that variable is missing. Since page visits is highly correlated with Downloads, however, we do not feel that this is an important omission. The Notre Dame repository does have the data necessary to construct the PII, and table 9.6 shows that we created two variables, PII consolidated and PII unconsolidated, using that data. In chapter 8, we discussed how it was necessary to consolidate some

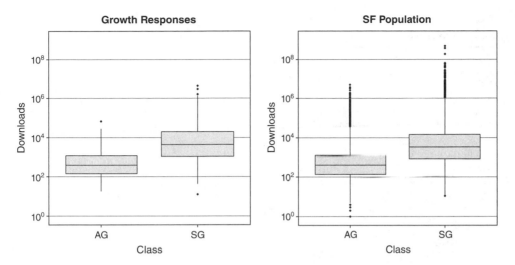

Figure 9.2
Comparison of the proportion of downloads in our growth survey responses and the May 2009 SourceForge population

of the variables that comprise the PII in order to reduce the number of variables for our earlier analysis, so PII_consolidated was constructed in the same way as the PII described in chapter 8. For comparison, we have included an unconsolidated PII that uses the Notre Dame data with the SF categories unaltered.

Table 9.6 includes the five old variables plus the thirty-nine new ones for a total of forty-four variables. The initiation survey did not include the conflict variable, so there are only thirty-eight new initiation variables. The variables numbered 1A, 18A, and 19A are alternative measures of the variables directly above each of them in the table, and are used in our initiation stage analysis for reasons explained in chapter 11. Because there are so many variables, it is not possible to look at each in detail here. Many readers will undoubtedly not need precise definitions of every variable, and the variables that turn out to be most significant are more carefully described in chapters 10 and 11. For those who do want a better definition, a more complete portrait can be found in the "new variable" documents found on our book's Web site.[5] The precise description of these variables resides in the "R" statistical software code used to construct the variables, also located on our Web site. For those who are interested, the next three paragraphs focus on how to use table 9.6 to get a fairly good idea of what each variable represents.

The variable construction column in this table brief lays out the variable that may be used along with the question(s) and values columns as well as the survey form to get a reasonable idea of what the variable represents. For example, the continuity

Table 9.6
New variables based on survey questions and important variables from chapter 8

| ID | Variables* | Type | Variable construction | Initiation stage | | | |
				Percent missing	Values	Question(s)	P-value
1	Community	Continuous	Sum (each scaled to 1)	6.0	0–1.8	Q28, Q29	9.620E-12
1A	Community_Q29_only (community29)	Continuous	Number of nonmember contributions	7.0	0–100	Q29	8.387E-1
2	Competition	Ordinal	None to more than a few (0–2)	20.5	0–2	Q22	3.980E-01
3	Complexity	Ordinal	Not complex to very complex (1–5)	14.1	0–4	Q19	1.490E-01
4	Conflict	Ordinal	Poor to excellent (0–4)	Not used	Not used	Not used	Not used
5	Continuity	Binary	No/yes (0, 1)	1.5	0, 1	Q7, Q7b	1.371E-05
6	Developers	Continuous	Notre Dame 05/15/09	0.0	1–21	None	2.510E-01
7	Downloads	Continuous	Notre Dame 05/15/09	Not used	Not used	Not used	Not used
8	Education	Ordinal	Low to high (0–3)	9.7	1–3	Q43, Q48	9.640E-01
9	Financial_index (f_index)	Ordinal	Number of answers	7.5	0–11	Q39	1.661E-01
10	Financial_motive (fin_motive)	Ordinal	Number of yes answers	29.0	0–2	Q40_6, Q45_6	4.140E-02
11	Finance	Binary	No/yes (0, 1)	12.7	0, 1	Q38	2.038E-01
12	Forum posts	Continuous	Notre Dame 05/15/09	Not used	Not used	Not used	Not used
13	Governance_evolution (gov_evolution)	Categorical	None to firm (0–3)	15.8	0–3	Q34, Q34A	3.210E-01
14	Governance (govern)	Ordinal	None to formal (0–3)	10.5	0–3	Q33	3.420E-01
15	Homogeneity_education (homo_ed)	Binary	Low/high (0, 1)	15.8	0, 1	Q48	3.028E-01
16	Homogeneity_geographic (homo_geog)	Binary	Low/high (0, 1)	5.1	0, 1	Q14 (Q23)	3.186E-01

| ID | Variables* | Type | Variable construction | Growth stage | | | |
				Percent missing	Values	Question(s)	P-value
1	Community	Continuous	Sum (each scaled to 1)	1.0	0–1.8	Q16, Q17, Q26, Q27	0.0000
1A	Community_ Q29 only (community29)	Continuous	Number of nonmember contributions	Not used	Not used	Not used	Not used
2	Competition	Ordinal	None to more than a few (0–2)	27.8	0–2	Q22	0.3550
3	Complexity	Ordinal	Not complex to very complex (1–5)	10.8	0–4	Q12	0.0000
4	Conflict	Ordinal	Poor to excellent (0–4)	15.5	0–4	Q31	3.160 E-14
5	Continuity	Binary	No/yes (0, 1)	1.3	0, 1	Q6, Q6b	2.947 E-01
6	Developers	Continuous	Notre Dame 05/15/09	0.0	1–51	None	3.870 E-12
7	Downloads	Continuous	Notre Dame 05/15/09	0.0	0– 4,417,126	None	1.450 E-12
8	Education	Ordinal	Low to high (0–3)	9.1	1–3	Q48, Q53	6.280 E-01
9	Financial_index (f_index)	Ordinal	Number of answers	6.7	0–10	Q44	4.090 E-05
10	Financial_ motive (fin_motive)	Ordinal	Number of yes answers	6.9	0–2	Q45_6, Q50_6	1.090 E-03
11	Finance	Binary	No/yes (0, 1)	6.7	0, 1	Q43	8.562 E-10
12	Forum posts	Continuous	Notre Dame 05/15/09	0.0	0–37,931	None	2.690 E-04
13	Governance_ evolution (gov_evolution)	Categorical	None to firm (0–3)	14.9	0–2	Q38, Q38A	5.336 E-02
14	Governance (govern)	Ordinal	None to formal (0–3)	8.8	0–3	Q37	3.723 E-15
15	Homogeneity_ education (homo_ed)	Binary	Low/high (0, 1)	21.8	0, 1	Q53	1.350 E-03
16	Homogeneity_ geographic (homo_geog)	Binary	Low/high (0, 1)	5.6	0, 1	Q18 (Q28)	9.861 E-03

Table 9.6

(continued)

				Initiation stage			
ID	Variables*	Type	Variable construction	Percent missing	Values	Question(s)	P-value
17	Homogeneity_ motives (homo_motive)	Ordinal	Number of yes answers	12.0	0–9	Q45	2.429E-01
18	Hours	Continuous	Sum questions	Not used	Not used	Not used	Not used
18A	Hours_Q16_ only	Continuous	Number of hours worked by administrator	5.9	0.05–11	Q16	7.85 E-15
19	Leadership_ with_hours (leadership_ hours)	Continuous	Low to high (0–7.6)	Not used	Not used	Not used	Not used
19A	Leadership_ without_hours (leadership_ nohrs)	Continuous	Low to high (0–6.6)	0.3	0–6.6	Q9, Q11, Q13, Q18, Q20, Q24, Q35	1.57E-08
20	Leisure	Ordinal	Number of yes answers	18.4	0–2	Q40_4, Q45_4	7.300E-01
21	Marketing	Continuous	Sum (each scaled to 1)	1.5	0–2.66	Q21, Q35, Q11a	9.750E-06
22	Found_ member_on_ Internet (memb_inet)	Binary	No/yes (0, 1)	8.8	0, 1	Q15	6.830E-04
23	Modularity	Binary	No/yes (0, 1)	5.0	0–2	Q10	7.948E-01
24	Motivation	Ordinal	Number of answers	8.9	0–19	Q40, Q45	1.610E-02
25	Need	Ordinal	Number of yes answers	14.5	0–4	Q40_7, Q40_9, Q44_7, Q45_9	2.660E-02
26	OS_experience	Continuous	Sum (each scaled to 1)	1.3	0–1.34	Q2, Q3	2.670E-01
27	Paid_or_ volunteer (paid_ volunteer)	Binary	No/yes (0, 1)	13.0	0, 1	Q38	2.075E-01
28	PII_ consolidated (pii_cons)	Continuous	Notre Dame 05/15/09	0.0	0–18	None	3.000E-01

| ID | Variables* | Type | Variable construction | Growth stage | | | |
				Percent missing	Values	Question(s)	P-value
17	Homogeneity_ motives (homo_motive)	Ordinal	Number of yes answers	4.4	0–10	Q50	1.470 E-13
18	Hours	Continuous	Sum questions	0.0	46	Q14, Q15	1.060 E-07
18A	Hours_Q16_ only	Continuous	Number of hours worked by administrator	Not used	Not used	Not used	Not used
19	Leadership_ with_hours (leadership_ hours)	Continuous	Low to high (0–7.6)	0.0	0–7.32	Q8, Q9, Q7, Q13, Q14, Q20, Q39, Q29	< 2E-16
19A	Leadership_ without_hours (leadership_ nohrs)	Continuous	Low to high (0–6.6)	Not used	Not used	Not used	Not used
20	Leisure	Ordinal	Number of yes answers	6.9	0–2	Q45_4, Q50_4	9.740 E-05
21	Marketing	Continuous	Sum (each scaled to 1)	1.2	0–2.43	Q21, Q39, Q9a	< 2E-16
22	Found_ member_on_ Internet (memb_inet)	Binary	No/yes (0, 1)	12.2	0, 1	Q19	< 2E-16
23	Modularity	Binary	No/yes (0, 1)	2.8	0–2	Q10	8.390 E-02
24	Motivation	Ordinal	Number of answers	6.9	0–20	Q45, Q50	1.120 E-09
25	Need	Ordinal	Number of yes answers	6.9	0–4	Q45_7, Q45_9, Q50_7, Q50_9	1.060 E-09
26	OS_experience	Continuous	Sum (each scaled to 1)	0.0	0–1.714	Q1, Q2	8.380 E-01
27	Paid_or_ volunteer (paid_ volunteer)	Binary	No/yes (0, 1)	6.7	0, 1	Q43	1.717 E-04
28	PII_ consolidated (pii_cons)	Continuous	Notre Dame 05/15/09	0.0	0–24	None	1.610 E-06

Table 9.6

(continued)

ID	Variables*	Type	Variable construction	Initiation stage			
				Percent missing	Values	Question(s)	P-value
29	PII_ unconsolidated (pii_uncons)	Continuous	Notre Dame 05/15/09	0.0	0–32	None	3.750E-01
30	Professional_ skill (prof_skill)	Ordinal	None to more (0–3)	12.4	0–3	Q23, Q41, Q42, Q46, Q47	3.330E-01
31	Proprietary	Binary	No/yes (0, 1)	1.3	0, 1	Q8	8.371E-01
32	Reciprocity_ general (recip_general)	Ordinal	Disagree to agree (1–5)	72.8	0–4	Q27	4.203E-02
33	Reciprocity_ specific (recip_specific)	Ordinal	Disagree to agree (1–5)	72.0	0–4	Q26	4.842E-02
34	Requirements_ index (require_ index)	Continuous	Low to high (0–2.714)	1.3	0–2.71	Q11,Q11A,Q12	4.740E-03
35	Project_ decision_maker (rule_decision)	Ordinal	Dictator to consensus (1–4)	15.8	1–4	Q31	2.420E-02
36	Rule_to_ replace_leader (rule_leader)	Ordinal	None to democratic (0–3)	17.0	0–3	Q32	4.430E-01
37	Operational_ level_rules (rule_ops)	Ordinal	Informal to formal (0–6)	34.1	0–6	Q30	9.000E-01
38	Social_capital (soci_capital)	Continuous	Sum (each scaled to 1)	6.1	0–3	Q25, Q50, Q51	7.904E-01
39	Tracker_reports	Continuous	Notre Dame 05/15/09	Not used	Not used	Not used	Not used
40	Utility	Ordinal	Sum low to high (1–6)	16.0	1–6	Q36, Q37	1.300E-01
41	Writing_quality (writing)	Ordinal	Poor to excellent (1–5)	8.6	1–5	Q44, Q49	2.680E-01

* The variable names in parentheses are the names we used in early portions of our research. We include them to permit cross-referencing with documents we wrote in earlier stages of analysis that are stored on the book's accompanying Web site.

| ID | Variables* | Type | Variable construction | Growth stage | | | |
				Percent missing	Values	Question(s)	P-value
29	PII_ unconsolidated (pii_uncons)	Continuous	Notre Dame 05/15/09	0.0	0–35	None	2.510 E-06
30	Professional_ skill (prof_skill)	Ordinal	None to more (0–3)	12.9	0–3	Q28, Q46, Q47, Q51, Q52	4.380 E-01
31	Proprietary	Binary	No/yes (0, 1)	2.8	0, 1	Q11	3.576 E-01
32	Reciprocity_ general (recip_general)	Ordinal	Disagree to agree (1–5)	73.8	0–4	Q33	4.052 E-01
33	Reciprocity_ specific (recip_specific)	Ordinal	Disagree to agree (1–5)	74.5	0–4	Q32	1.346 E-01
34	Requirements_ index (require_ index)	Continuous	Low to high (0–2.714)	2.0	0–2.714	Q9,Q9A,Q25	< 2E-16
35	Project_ decision_maker (rule_decision)	Ordinal	Dictator to consensus (1–4)	20.1	1–4	Q35	3.050 E-03
36	Rule_to_ replace_leader (rule_leader)	Ordinal	None to democratic (0–3)	18.6	0–3	Q36	9.580 E-02
37	Operational_ level_rules (rule_ops)	Ordinal	Informal to formal (0–6)	37.6	0–6	Q34	4.030 E-04
38	Social_capital (soci_capital)	Continuous	Sum (each scaled to 1)	7.0	0–3	Q30, Q55, Q56	6.900 E-12
39	Tracker_reports	Continuous	Notre Dame 05/15/09	0.0	0–4368	None	3.730 E-12
40	Utility	Ordinal	Sum low to high (1–6)	16.5	1–6	Q40, Q41	< 2E-16
41	Writing_quality (writing)	Ordinal	Poor to excellent (1–5)	8.1	1–5	Q49, Q54	1.770 E-04

variable has a value of 0 (no) if the answers to the initiation stage survey questions Q7 and Q7B indicate that none of the current members have been with the project since it was registered on SF, or a value of 1 (yes) if someone has been with the project since its registration. The type column indicates that the continuity variable is binary. The percent missing column shows that only 1.5 percent of the respondents did not answer this question. The p-value column gives the result of the appropriate statistical test for the variable versus our dependent variable, and illustrates whether the survey responses for that variable differ significantly between success and abandonment. For variables based on survey questions, the p-value incorporated a finite population correction and weighting for the growth stage, as described above. We found the p-value using a chi-square test (corrected for large "n" in the growth stage) for binary variables as well as variables with a large amount of missing data, and a logistic regression in all other cases. The p-value of 0.00001371 for the continuity variable for the initiation stage survey reveals that there is a highly significant difference between responses from AI and SI projects.

We created the other variables of the binary type in the same way that we created the continuity variable, but we need to provide examples of the other types of variables (continuous, ordinal, and categorical) to help clarify how we constructed them. For instance, examining the community variable for the initiation stage in table 9.6, we took the number of answers selected for initiation Q28 (1–5 possible answers) and divided by 5 to scale the result to a 0–1 scale. Thus a value of 0 indicates that the project received no nonfinancial contributions, and a value of 1 indicates that it received five different types of contributions. We then scaled the answers to initiation Q29 to a 0–1 scale by dividing the number of nonmembers who made nonfinancial contributions to the project by the maximum value of all answers to that question (100 contributing nonmembers). The word sum in the variable construction column for the community variable indicates that we added the two values together, producing a value ranging from 0 to 1.8. We constructed other continuous variables in a similar manner as the community variable, with the exception that the old variables are continuous and simply use the data retrieved from the Notre Dame repository.

For the ordinal variable we call complexity, we simply assigned the value 1 to the Initiation Q19 answer "Not complex at all," the value 2 to the answer "Less complex," and so on, ending with the value 5 for "Much more complex." In cases where an ordinal variable is based on more than one question, we often summed the number of yes answers to binary questions. The single categorical variable (governance evolution), for example, simply assigns a value of 1–4 to the unordered answers. Finally, some variables like leadership are based on many questions, and their construction can be quite complex. The variable construction column in these cases provides an indication of the meaning of their values. The details of their construction can be found in the variable construction document on the book's accompanying Web site.[6]

Conclusion

We did not receive as high a response rate from our survey as we had planned, partly because we attempted to accomplish the difficult task of eliciting responses from abandoned projects, and partly because we were unable to send reminder emails. Nonetheless, we elicited a substantial number of responses that appear to be generally quite representative of the SF population. In addition, as the analysis in chapters 10 and 11 will demonstrate, we succeeded in achieving the survey goals.

The survey produced statistically significant responses that allowed us to construct variables to test all our untested hypotheses, which we do in chapter 10. Also, we will use these same variables in chapter 11 to build a more complete multivariate model of OSS success, and examine our chapter 8 findings about vision, leadership, and utility for the initiation stage as well as building community in the growth stage. Now we have everything we need to uncover the answers we have worked so hard to find.

10 Answering the Questions Raised in Part II

with Meng-Shiou Shieh

This chapter and the next one mark the pinnacle of our five-year effort to understand OSS commons. We closed *The Survey on Free/Libre and Open-Source Success* at the end of 2009, and did the analytic work described in this chapter and the next during the fifth and final year of our research endeavor. This chapter is exciting because it provides information and insight about every hypothesis and research question that we posed in part II. In chapter 11, we will present statistical models that take all our variables into consideration at the same time—in order to find those that rise to the top in importance—but here we look at our hypotheses and research questions one by one to gain detailed knowledge.

In the following sections, we examine both the initiation and growth stage side by side. We systematically reintroduce the hypotheses or research questions raised earlier, and then we analyze most of them using contingency tables built by tabulating the responses to our survey questions. Consequently, this chapter starts with an explanation of contingency tables, and then looks at the technological, community, and institutional hypotheses and research questions organized according to those categories. Although the results are exciting, we caution readers that this chapter is lengthy, and many will wish to focus on topics or hypotheses of particular interest. After reading the section below explaining contingency tables, we suggest that readers look over the tables found in the chapter, concentrating on tables 10.2, 10.3, 10.6, and 10.14, and then read the sections on the specific topics, hypotheses, or research questions that interest them. The tables in the chapter follow the same order that the subjects appear in the text below.

What Are Contingency Tables?

For readers unfamiliar with contingency tables, let us start with a description of how they work. Many of our survey questions asked for a simple yes or no. For example, initiation stage survey question 11 asks, "Was there a clear plan established for the software's functionality in the time period before [the project name's] first release?"

Table 10.1

Example of a contingency table, initiation survey, question 11

I-Q11 initiation survey	Yes	No	Total	Chi-square p-value	Response rate	Odds/ odds ratio
AI	101	117	218		0.94	0.86
SI	247	178	425	0.005***		1.39
Total	348	295	643			0.62

Statistical confidence level: *** 0.01 (99 percent); ** 0.05 (95 percent); * 0.10 (90 percent).

The contingency table shown in table 10.1 contains the counts of responses to this question. The table depicts how many respondents from abandoned (AI) and successful (SI) initiation stage projects answered yes or no to the question. For example, 101 respondents from AI projects answered yes, they had a clear plan for their software's functionality, and 348 respondents from both AI and SI projects in total answered yes.

Table 10.1 also shows that we use a chi-square test to produce a corresponding p-value that signifies whether the response counts are statistically significant. The chi-square test determines statistical significance by testing whether the distribution between counts of yes and no answers really differ between AI and SI projects. A highly statistically significant p-value (less than 0.1) suggests that there is a real difference between abandoned projects and successful ones for that particular question, meaning that we would get the same net result if we asked the same question of a different random sample of SF developers. A nonsignificant p-value (greater than 0.1) signifies that the difference could be the result of sampling errors and might not be a real difference. In other words, a nonsignificant p-value indicates that if we asked the same question again of a different randomly sampled group, we might get the opposite result.

Also, when appropriate, we use the odds ratio to get a sense of the relationship between the answers. In the case of table 10.1, odds are a ratio of positives to negatives. The odds for yes in AI is calculated by 101/117 to produce 0.86. Similarly, the odds for yes in SI is calculated by 247/178 or 1.39. The odds ratio, then, provides a ratio of the odds of being in the yes category in AI, to the odds of being in the yes category of SI, and is calculated by the odds of yes in AI (0.86) divided by the odds of yes in SI (1.39) or 0.62. The odds ratio in this case tells us that AI projects only have functionality plans 62 percent as often (in terms of odds) as SI projects, and this finding is statistically significant with greater than 99 percent confidence. (We'll return to the actual analysis of this question's results later.)

The data in table 10.1 represent the responses to a question in our survey that was included to test the clear vision/goals hypothesis (H-T1) presented in chapter 4. Similarly in this chapter, we present contingency table chi-square p-values for responses to various survey questions that test hypotheses and research questions we posed in chapters 2–5. We also present odds ratios for the items that have statistically significant findings. Following our earlier approach, these items are organized by technological, community, and institutional attributes for *both* the initiation and growth stage survey. Unfortunately, space limitations make it impossible for us to include the complete contingency tables for all questions. We do, however, provide these fully in appendix 10.A, available on our book's accompanying Web site.[1] For easy reference to the results described below, we summarize them in tables 10.1–10.14. Let's now turn to our findings.

Technological Attributes

Chapter 4 presented most of the discussion related to the technological attributes of OSS commons. Here we return to the hypotheses and research questions listed in table 4.1 in the order we presented them earlier. For the reader's convenience, we repeat the hypothesis or research question again along with a summary of whether our results support the hypothesis in our two stages. The results in this section are organized in table 10.2 for easy reference.

Software Requirements

H-T1: OSS commons will be more often successful when the project has a clearly defined vision and a mechanism to communicate this vision early in the project's life, before the growth stage.
Initiation and growth: *Supported*

In our surveys, we used several questions to test this hypothesis. While the hypothesis is specifically targeting the initiation stage, we included questions related to this in both the initiation and growth surveys.

First, in both surveys, we asked, "Was there a well-defined architectural design established for the software in the time period (before or after) [project name's] first release?"[2] The variable architecture captures a yes, no, or don't know response to this question. While architecture can be interpreted in multiple ways, to software engineers it generally captures the structural elements, components, or modules that make up the software and their properties as well as how they relate to one another (for an extensive discussion of this, see Bass, Clements, and Kazman 2003).

The chi-square statistics comparing Abandoned in Initiation (AI) to Successful in Initiation (SI,) and, alternatively, Abandoned in Growth (AG) to Successful in Growth (SG) in table 10.2 (row H-T1) are highly significant for both stages. The odds ratio suggests that AI projects are only 64 percent as likely to have architectural plans as SI

Table 10.2
Contingency table tesults: Technological attributes (refer back to table 4.1)

Concept/hypothesis/ research question (supported/not suported)	Survey concept and question number (I: initiation survey; G: growth survey)	Initiation stage results		Growth stage results	
		Chi-square p-value[1]	Odds ratio[2]	Chi-square p-value[3]	Odds ratio[c]
Software requirements					
H-T1: Clear vision/ goals (Initiation and growth: Supported)	Architecture: I-Q9; G-Q8	0.008***	0.64	0.000***	0.55
	Functionality plan: I-Q11; G-Q9	0.005***	0.62	0.000***	0.45
	Goals: I-Q18; G-Q7	0.000***	0.49	0.000***	0.36
Modularity, granularity, and complexity					
H-T2a: Modularity (Initiation and growth: Not supported)	Modularity: I-Q10; G-Q10	0.567	Not calculated	0.272	Not calculated
H-T2b: Granularity (Initiation: Not tested; growth: Supported)	Granularity: No question asked in initiation stage survey; G-Q24	Not calculated	Not calculated	0.003***	0.53
H-T2c: Initially closed source (complexity) (Initiation and growth: Not supported)	Proprietary: I-Q8; G-Q11	0.837	Not calculated	0.358	Not calculated

H-T2d: Complexity of code (Initiation and growth: Not supported)	Code complexity: I-Q19; G-Q12	0.362	Not calculated	0.000***	0.42
Product utility, foundational infrastructure, and preferred technologies					
H-T3a: Utility (Initiation: Not supported; Growth: Supported)	Functionality: I-Q36; G-Q40	0.411	Not calculated	0.000***	0.14
	Quality: I-Q37; G-Q41	0.347	Not calculated	0.000***	0.15
H-T3b: Critical or foundational infrastructure (Initiation and growth: Not tested)	Not implemented; chapter 8 addressed this adequately	Not calculated	Not calculated	Not calculated	Not calculated
H-T3c: Preferred technologies (Initiation and growth: Not tested)	Not implemented; chapter 8 addressed this adequately	Not calculated	Not calculated	Not calculated	Not calculated
Competition					
H-T4: Limited competition (Initiation: Not supported; Growth: Supported)	Competition: I-Q22; G-Q22	0.697	Not calculated	0.001***	0.64

Table 10.2
(continued)

Concept/hypothesis/research question (supported/not suported)	Survey concept and question number (I: initiation survey; G: growth survey)	Initiation stage results		Growth stage results	
		Chi-square p-value[1]	Odds ratio[2]	Chi-square p-value[3]	Odds ratio[4]
Collaborative infrastructure used					
RQ-T1 (this also relates to H-T1 above)	Plan communication; I-Q11A; G-Q9A				
	1. SF page	0.399	Not calculated	0.003***	0.39
	2. Web site	0.226	Not calculated	0.003***	0.45
	3. Developer email lists	0.943	Not calculated	0.005***	0.38
	4. Community email lists	0.717	Not calculated	0.005***	0.31
	5. Other, developers	0.806	Not calculated	0.039**	0.56
	6. Other, users	0.895	Not calculated	0.004***	0.42
	7. Code documentation	0.291	Not calculated	0.659	Not calculated
	Advertising; I-Q21; G-Q21	0.007***	0.60	0.000***	0.48
	Web site quality; I-Q35; G-Q39	0.000***	0.57[3]	0.000***	0.41[3]

1. Chi-square test with finite population factor. Statistical confidence levels: *** 0.01 (99 percent); ** 0.05 (95 percent); * 0.10 (90 percent).

2. We present odds ratios only when useful. There are two situations where we do not present them: when the result of the chi-squared test is not statistically significant; and when the contingency table involves more than two responses. In both of these circumstances, we note this with the phrase "not calculated."

3. Chi-square test with Rao-Scott second-order correction. Statistical confidence levels: *** 0.01 (99 percent); ** 0.05 (95 percent); * 0.10 (90 percent).

4. In some instances where there were more than two answers, we added categories together to get an appropriate odds and odds ratio. Full calculations are provided in appendix 10.A, available at http://www.umass.edu/opensource/schweik/supplementary.html.

projects. Similarly, having a well-defined architectural design in the growth stage doubles (55 percent) the odds of success. Architectural design captures one component of a vision or goal for the project, and it appears to be associated with success both early on and later in the project's life cycle.

The functionality plan is a closely related question—which we used for our contingency table explanation above—where we asked, "Was there was a clear plan established for the software's functionality in the time period (before [initiation] or after [growth]) the first release?" Like architecture, the chi-square statistics in table 10.2 (row HT-1) are highly statistically significant for both stages, and the odds ratio suggests that AI projects have some kind of plan related to future functionality only 62 percent as frequently as SI projects, and even less often (45 percent) in the growth stage. This finding also lends support to H-T1 for both stages.

We also asked respondents in each survey, Were "clear goals established for the development of the software in the time period (before or after) the [project's] 'first release' (yes, no, or don't know)?" As shown for goals in table 10.2 (row H-T1), both chi-square test p-values reveal a highly statistically significant difference between AI and SI projects as well as AG and SG projects. In the initiation stage, the odds ratio of 0.49 suggests that SI projects are almost twice as likely to have established goals prior to the project's first release as AI projects. The growth stage odds ratio (0.36) indicates SG projects are about three times as likely to have stated goals after the first release compared to AG projects.

The second part of H-T1, mechanisms to communicate the plan, is tested in the collaborative infrastructure section below.

Modularity

H-T2a: OSS commons will be more often successful when the initial software design accounts for, up front, a modular design.
Initiation and growth: *Not supported*

In each survey, we asked the respondent, "Did you design the software to be modular so that it would be easier for other contributors (i.e., 'members,' volunteers, or users) to work on [the project]?" The survey respondent could answer either yes, somewhat, or no. We tested for these three categories as well as the combination of yes and somewhat into one yes category.

The responses for both the initiation and growth surveys reveal no significant difference between modularity in AI and SI projects (table 10.2, row H-T2a). This does not mean, though, that modularity is unimportant in OSS; indeed, across the whole survey respondents said projects were modular at a rate of more than three to one. What our finding shows is that both AI and SI projects are highly modular, but that the idea that modularity contributes more to success, in either stage, is not supported.

Granularity

H-T2b: OSS commons will be more often successful when they provide opportunities for people to contribute in small ways (fine-scale task granularity).
Initiation: *Not tested*
Growth: Supported

Because of survey length limitations, we decided not to ask a question about granularity in the initiation stage survey, but we did ask the following question related to this concept in the growth stage survey: "On any given day in the time after [your project's] 'first release,' were there some easy-to-accomplish tasks available for contributors (e.g., volunteers or users) to do?" Possible answers were more than a few, a few, and none. The contingency data for this question (table 10.2, row H-T2b) reveal differences between AG and SG, with SG projects answering significantly higher proportions of the "a few" option. The chi-square p-value is highly significant. SG projects report higher levels of fine-scale task granularity compared to AG projects, and the odds ratio (calculated by adding counts for more than a few and a few, and dividing this by the number of surveys answering none) suggests that SG projects are about twice as likely to have fine-scale granular tasks available for people compared to AG projects.

Complexity

H-T2c: OSS commons will be more often successful when the software is not initially developed and supported under a closed-source, proprietary setting and relicensed as OSS later.
Initiation and growth: *Not supported*

To get at this concept we asked, "Prior to becoming open-source software, was [project name's] code proprietary/closed source (yes, no, or don't know)?" We thought that previously closed-source software would be more complex from the beginning and therefore less successful. Ninety-three of 674 initiation stage projects surveyed answered yes to this question, but chi-square results suggest that the distributions of yes and no answers between SI and AI projects are not statistically different. Eighty-nine of 701 growth stage projects answered yes to this question, but like the initiation stage, the chi-square test (0.358, table 10.2, row H-T2c) indicates there is no relationship between OSS that was previously closed source and abandonment of these projects.

Yet from this survey data, we did learn that a fairly large number of OSS projects are opened after being initially proprietary. In our data, 14 percent of initiation projects (SE 0.0134; 95 percent confidence interval 0.10—0.15) and 13 percent of growth projects (SE 0.0123; 95 percent confidence interval 0.11—0.16) were previously closed source.

H-T2d: OSS commons will be more often successful when the software complexity is relatively low when initially going public.

Initiation: Not supported

Growth: *Not supported* and the opposite relationship was identified

In addition to the closed-source question above that indirectly gets at the issue of potentially complex code at a project's beginning, we investigated the software complexity hypothesis directly. Specifically we asked, "How would you rate the complexity of [project name's] code as it was developed prior to the 'first release' in comparison to the complexity of the code of an average [open-source] project (much more complex, more complex, the same, less complex, and not complex at all)?" We developed a contingency table for the five options, but also combined the top two categories as complex and bottom two categories as not complex to investigate the sensitivity of this question to the categories we presented. In table 10.2 (row H-T2d), we present the p-value for the five-category question for both stages. For the initiation survey, no matter how the responses are combined, there is no apparent difference between the distributions of AI and SI responses. The hypothesis is not supported.

While this hypothesis was originally proposed only for the initiation stage, we decided to ask the same question of respondents working on projects classified in the growth stage. The result is highly statistically significant (99 percent level of confidence; table 10.2, row H-T2d), but we find the opposite relationship than what might have been expected. A larger proportion of respondents for SG projects say that their project is more complicated than average while a larger percent of AG projects tend to say they are less complicated than the average OSS project. Further investigation in our response data shows 3 percent (10 out of 321) of our SG projects surveyed report code much more complex than average and another 17 percent (54 out of 321) answering "more complex," compared to 1 percent (4 out of 325) and 8 percent (27 out of 325) of our AG projects, respectively. We can only speculate the reasons for these proportional differences, but it could be that SG projects are more complex than an average project simply because they are successful and have several releases.

Product Utility

H-T3a: OSS commons will be more often successful when the software produced has higher utility as perceived by the end user community.

Initiation: *Not supported*

Growth: *Supported*

We asked two questions that captured elements of software utility. First, in both surveys we inquired, "How would you rate your software's *functionality* (or 'planned functionality' if your project has not had its 'first release') in comparison to other similar proprietary or open-source software products (high, average, low, or don't know)?" We assumed that more functionality would translate to higher utility. As shown in the H-T3a row (survey concept functionality) in table 10.2, according to chi-square test results, there appears to be no difference between the distribution of answers comparing AI and SI projects. The answers in the growth stage survey, however, show highly statistically significant differences (99 percent level of confidence) between AG and SG projects. Nearly half of the SG projects in the growth stage survey (147 out of 305) report high functionality in comparison to other similar software products, whereas only 56 of 279 AG projects say the same. Note that the hypothesis mentions a higher utility for end users, and project developers report this question. We assume that the developer's opinions on functionality can be used as a proxy for end user opinions.

Second, we asked, "How would you rate your software's *quality* (or 'planned quality' if your project has not had its 'first release') in comparison to other similar proprietary or open-source software products (high, average, low, or don't know)?" Once again, we infer that higher quality translates to higher utility. As shown in table 10.2 (row H-T3a), chi-square tests for differences in quality between SI and AI in the initiation stage are not statistically significant. Yet chi-square tests for differences between SG and AG are highly statistically significant (99 percent confidence), and display a similar distribution as our findings for functionality (see paragraph above). Forty-five percent (141 out of 309) of SG projects report higher than average quality, compared to only 20 percent (58 out of 279) supposedly high-quality AG projects. Likewise, 26 percent of AG projects rated their project as low quality compared to only 8 percent of SG projects.

In short, both of these questions suggest that utility to the end user community is associated with success in the growth stage, but isn't a factor that distinguishes between success and abandonment in the initiation stage.

H-T3b: OSS commons will be more often successful when the software produced is a component of what could be considered critical or foundational infrastructure (e.g., operating systems).
Initiation and growth: *Not tested*
H-T3c: OSS commons will be more often successful when the software being developed is built on hot, preferred technologies (e.g., certain programming languages) that the developer community wants to use and learn.
Initiation and growth: *Not tested*

In chapter 8, we described several categorical variables—operating system, project topic, programming language, and database environment—that captured these concepts, and tested these associate hypotheses using these variables. We found no support for either of these hypotheses, suggesting that successful and abandoned projects are found across the spectrum of these categories. Because the evidence was so strong, and because we needed to keep our survey reasonably short to get acceptable response rates, we decided against investigating this any further.

Competition

H-T4: OSS commons will be more often successful when there are few alternative software projects available (limited or no competition).
Initiation: Not supported
Growth: *Not supported* and strong evidence that the opposite relationship exists

In both surveys, we inquired, "How many free/open-source projects were in competition with [your project] (more than a few, a few, none, or don't know)?" As shown in table 10.2 (H-T4 row), we discovered no apparent distributional differences between successful and abandoned projects in the initiation stage survey. Less (or more) competition does not distinguish successful from abandoned projects in the initiation stage.

In our growth stage survey results, with 99 percent confidence, the opposite of what we hypothesized in H-T4 is supported: success is correlated with having, rather than not having, at least a few competitors. We investigated this further by aggregating the number of responses for projects answering "more than a few" and "a few" versus ones that answered "none" (no competition), and testing for differences in the answer distributions between AG and SG. Chi-square tests (not shown in table 10.2) still identified a difference, with SG being associated with more competition, but at the 95 percent confidence level. This suggests perhaps that having at least some limited competition in the growth stage motivates the team to continue to work on the project.

Collaborative Infrastructure

RQ-T1: What collaborative technologies are utilized in successful OSS commons? Is there a certain suite of technologies or configurations that are more often found in OSS success cases? Or does the configuration not seem to matter?

Initiation: Advertising outside SF is associated with SI projects

Growth: Communication of plans, advertising outside SF, and Web site quality all distinguish SG from AG projects

In our analysis of SF data in chapter 8, we found that the use of SF collaborative technologies such as the project forum or bug tracking did not help to distinguish between success and abandonment in the initiation stage, but they *did* help to distinguish between success and abandonment in the growth stage. Consequently, in our developer surveys, we focused on other technologies potentially used to move the project forward. We asked three questions in both surveys related to collaborative infrastructure

First, to the projects that reported having a functionality plan, we asked a follow-up question about how they communicated this plan to others. Possible answers included listing the information on the SF project page, posting the information on the project's (own) Web site, communicating the plan via developer email lists, communicating the plan via user community lists, using other methods for communication of this plan to developers, using other methods for communicating the plan to users, and communicating the plan only through code documentation.

In the initiation survey, we compared the answers across all these options for AI and SI, and found no evidence to suggest that any of these methods differentiated between success and abandoned projects (table 10.2, row RQ-T1). But in all cases except the seventh option (code documentation), answers received for the growth survey question revealed differences in the yes/no distributions for SG versus AG. SG cases had a higher percent of yes answers in all the communication options except the last (code documentation) compared to their AG project counterparts, and in most instances these SG and AG differences measured by the chi-square statistic were statistically significant at the 99 percent confidence level. In addition to indicating what kinds of infrastructure are used, this hints at to how SG projects build a user community: through better outreach and communication.

Second, in each survey we asked whether the project "advertised itself in places other than the SF project pages or SF project Web site (yes or no)." Here we found strong statistical evidence in both surveys suggesting that advertising in places outside the SF Web site approximately doubles the odds of success (table 10.2 row RQ-T1; odds ratio 0.60 for initiation and 0.48 for growth). For the growth stage, the importance of advertising and letting others know about the project is obvious, and we discovered that nearly 50 percent (178 out of 350) of the SG projects did this kind of promotion, compared to approximately 33 percent (107 out of 323) of the AG projects. Moreover, the lower odds ratio for the growth stage (0.48 for growth versus 0.6 for initiation) means that more SG projects advertise in comparison to AG projects than SI projects in comparison to AI projects. The larger odds ratio in the initiation stage means a smaller advantage to advertising than in the growth Stage.

Third, we asked the respondent to "rate the quality of their project Web site (this could be on or outside SF) compared to other projects' Web sites" (excellent, above average, average, below average, poor, or no Web site). A glance at the raw distribution data (contingency table I-Q35 in online appendix 10.A) reveals higher proportions of average or above average Web sites in the SI compared to AI responses with a highly statistically significant chi-square test. Given that so many of these projects have reported average, poor, or no Web site in the SI cases, however, quality Web sites are probably no more than a minor factor for success in the initiation stage. Web site quality appears to be slightly more important in the growth stage. SG projects reported better than average Web sites about 20 percent of the time (63 out of 328 SG projects), whereas AG projects report better than average Web sites only 5 percent of the time (17 out of 315 AG projects). Furthermore, 58 percent of the AG projects (183 out of 315) report that they have poor or no Web sites established compared to 20 percent of the SG projects reporting. This chi-square test is statistically significant at the 99 percent level of confidence. This indicates that a high-quality Web site is associated with success in the growth stage—which is not surprising. A professional Web presence would certainly help impress potential users and potential future new developers.

Community Attributes

In chapters 3 and 4, we discussed a variety of community attributes that are thought to have some influence on the success or abandonment of OSS commons. Along with institutional attributes (explored below), this group of variables was a key component of our surveys, given that many of these concepts could not be operationalized using SI project data in chapter 8. As above, we present our original stated hypotheses and contingency table results for the two stages examined in our surveys, summarizing the results in table 10.3.

Developer Attributes and Motivations

Use of Software

H-C1: OSS commons will be more successful when the developers of the software product are also the users of that product (von Hippel's user-driven innovation hypothesis).

Initiation and growth: *Not supported* for respondent or team personal need; *supported* for employer need

To get at this (and several other hypotheses below) we asked (I-Q40; G-Q45), "Why do you [the respondent] participate in [project name]?" We provided a number of different options, and the user could select all that were relevant. Two options were salient to von Hippel's concept of user innovators: Option 7 (I need the software for my personal use), and option 9 (the organization I work for needed the software).

Our survey data show that user innovation is something that underlies OSS projects. In the initiation survey, 71 percent (133 out of 187) of the AI respondents and 77 percent (280 out of 365) SI projects answered yes to the personal use question (online appendix 10.A). Even higher yes answer percentages were found in the growth survey (75 percent in initiation and 78 percent in growth). This is strong evidence that user innovation is an important driver of OSS. Still, the chi-square tests (table

Table 10.3

Contingency table results: Community attributes (refer to table 3.2)

Concept/hypothesis/ research question	Survey concept and question number (I: Initiation survey; G: Growth survey)	Initiation stage results		Growth stage results	
		Chi-square p-value[1]	Odds ratio[2]	Chi-square p-value[3]	Odds ratio[4]
Developer attributes and motivations					
H-C1: Developers are users (Initiation and growth: Not supported for respondent or team personal need; supported for employer need)	Respondent personal use; I-Q40 option 7; G-Q45 option 7	0.152	Not calculated	0.247	Not calculated
	Team personal use; I-Q45 option 7; G-Q50 option 7	0.079*	0.50	0.117	Not calculated
	Respondent's employer as user; I-Q40 option 9; G-Q45 option 9	0.095*	0.70	0.097*	0.74
	Team's employer as user; I-Q45 option 9; G-Q50 option 9	0.519	Not calculated	0.001**	0.39
H-C2: Participants are paid or make money through products/services dependent on project (Initiation: Not supported; Growth: Supported)	Respondent motivated to participate because they benefit financially; I-Q40 option 6; G-Q45 option 6	0.388	Not calculated	0.293	Not calculated
	Team members motivated to participate because they benefit financially; I-Q45 option 6; G-Q50 option 6	0.031**	0.26	0.29	Not calculated
	One or more members were paid; I-Q38 and G-Q43	0.425	Not calculated	0.000***	0.46
	To make money through the use of software; I-Q38 option 5; G-Q43 option 5	0.400	Not calculated	0.02*	0.44

H-C3: Serious leisure (Initiation and growth: Not supported)	Respondent participates for leisure; I-Q40 option 4; G-Q45 option 4	0.995	Not calculated	0.55	Not calculated
	Other members on project participate for leisure; I-Q45 option 4; G-Q50 option 4	0.110	2.13	0.463	Not calculated
H-C4a: Highly skilled (Initiation: Partially supported; Growth: Partially supported [see text])	Professional skill measures				
	Respondent's highest educational degree; I-Q43; G-Q48	0.92	Not calculated	0.081*	Not calculated
	Respondent and professional developer; I-Q41; G-Q46	C.290	Not calculated	0.435	Not calculated
	Respondent self-reported programming skill rating; I-Q42; G-47	0.064*	0.69	0.964	Not calculated
	Other members' are professional developers; I-C46; G-Q51	0.898	Not calculated	0.760	Not calculated
	Overall skill of members compared to average professional developers; I-Q7; G-Q52	0.718	Not calculated	0.510	Not calculated
	Respondent self-reported writing skills; I-Q44; G-Q49	0.217	Not calculated	0.509	Not calculated
	Team writing skills; I-Q49; G-Q54	0.833	Not calculated	0.772	Not calculated
	Knowledge continuity; I-Q7; I-Q7b; G-Q6; G-6b	0.000***	0.30	0.556	0.79

Table 10.3
(continued)

Concept/hypothesis/research question	Survey concept and question number (I: Initiation survey; G: Growth survey)	Initiation stage results		Growth stage results	
		Chi-square p-value[1]	Odds ratio[2]	Chi-square p-value[3]	Odds ratio[4]
Developer attributes and motivations					
H-C4b: Learning (Initiation and growth: Not supported)	Respondent participates to learn and improve skills; I-Q40 option 1; G-Q45 option 1	0.975	Not calculated	0.682	Not calculated
	Team members participate to learn and improve skills; I-Q45 option 1; G-Q50 option 1	0.208	Not calculated	0.576	Not calculated
H-C4c: Skill signaling (Initiation and growth: Not supported)	Respondent participates to demonstrate programming skills; I-Q40 option 5; G-Q45 option 5	0.220	Not calculated	0.55	Not calculated
	Team members participate to demonstrate programming skills; I-Q45 option 5; G-Q50 option 5	0.267	Not calculated	0.983	Not calculated
H-C5: Helping the OSS cause (Initiation and growth: Not supported)	I-Q40 option 2; respondent participates because they believe we should be able to modify the software we use; G-Q45 option 2	0.737	Not calculated	0.215	Not calculated
	Team members participate because they believe we should be able to modify the software we use; I-Q45 option 2; G-Q50 option 2	0.378	Not calculated	0.347	Not calculated

Group heterogeneity/homogeneity

RQ-C1a: Sociocultural	Geographic location of project members (local-global); I-Q14; G-Q18	0.408	Not calculated	0.000***	Not calculated
RQ-C1b: Interest/ motivational	Paid_or_volunteer; I-Q38; G-Q43	0.013**	Not calculated	0.008***	2.35
	Team motivation derived from motivation index (Homogeneity_motives; I-Q45; G-Q50)	0.2768		0.006***	1.16
RQ-C1c: Asset	Team educational mix	Homogeneity_ education index			

1. Chi-square test with finite population factor. Statistical confidence levels: *** 0.01 (99 percent); ** 0.05 (95 percent); * 0.10 (90 percent).

2. We present odds ratios only when useful. There are two situations where we do not present them: when the result of the chi-squared test is not statistically significant; and when the contingency table involves more than two responses. In both of these circumstances, we note this with the phrase "not calculated."

3. Chi-square test with Rao-Scott second-order correction. Statistical confidence levels: *** 0.01 (99 percent); ** 0.05 (95 percent); * 0.10 (90 percent).

4. In some instances where there were more than two answers, we added categories together to get an appropriate odds and odds ratio. Full calculations are provided in appendix 10.A, available at http://www.umass.edu/opensource/schweik/supplementary.html.

10.3, row H-C1) comparing the answers between success and abandonment in the initiation and growth stages reveal no statistically significant differences. In other words, user-innovators are equally distributed between successful and abandoned projects in both stages.

We then followed this with a second question (I-Q45; G-Q50; for projects with more than one developer), asking the respondent whether a personal need for the software motivates other team members to contribute to the project. Here, we found similar percentages of yes answers, with the slight exception of AI projects. For SI, AG, and SG projects with multiple team members, we discovered 71, 85, and 73 percent of the projects, respectively, have team members who have a personal need for the software. Only AI projects had a slightly lower percentage (21 out of 38 projects or 55 percent). This results in a chi-square test that is significant at the 90 percent level for the AI/SI comparison, showing a higher percentage of user-innovators in the SI category.

Next, to explore the effects of firms or organizations as user-innovators, we asked the respondent whether "the organization [they] work for needed the software." Here, we found lower percentages of yes answers in our responses for each category (AI: 42 out of 170 or 25 percent yes; SI: 109 out of 342 or 32 percent yes; AG: 80 out of 246 or 33 percent yes; and SG: 106 out of 268 or 40 percent yes). The chi-square test for differences between yes answers for both the AI/SI and AG/SG comparisons are statistically significant at the 90 percent level.

We then asked the respondent the same question—whether the organization they worked for needed the software—but for projects that had more than one developer. We found relatively similar yes answer percentages for AI (37 percent, or 13 out of 35), SI (44 percent or 37 out of 85), and AG (42 percent or 13 out of 31). The percentage of yes answers for SG projects, though, was substantially higher at 65 percent (75 out of 115), leading to a chi-square test (0.02) that is significant at the 95 percent level of confidence.

In sum, we find mixed results for this hypothesis. On the one hand, we see that a high percentage of developers (respondents and team members) are users of the software they develop, and user-innovators are found in both successful and abandoned cases for both initiation and growth. From this perspective, our data do not support H-C1. Yet our data about organizations as users appear to lend some support to H-C1—projects where employers as users appear to be associated with higher levels of success in the growth stage.

Financial Motivation

H-C2: OSS commons will be more successful when some of the developers are paid participants or make money through products and/or services that depend on the software.

Initiation: *Not supported*

Growth: *Supported*

First, we asked about financial benefits as a motivation for participating in a project. In both the initiation and growth stage, we find no evidence that individual respondents are more motivated to participate in either successful or abandoned projects because they benefit financially (table 10.3, row H-C2, I-Q40 option 6 and G-Q45 option 6). Nevertheless, with 95 percent confidence we find that according to the respondents' perceptions about other project members, SI projects with more than one developer on the team are almost four times (odds ratio 0.26) as likely to have developers who participate because they benefit financially from the project as AI projects (table 10.3, row H-C2, I-Q45). Responses to the growth stage survey (question G-Q50) also reported proportionally more members participating in SG projects because they benefit financially, but the differences were not statistically significant. If respondents are correct in their assessment of other project members' motivations, then we can say that financial benefit as a motivation is only a factor for success or abandonment in projects having greater than one member, and perhaps only in the initiation stage.

Another question in both the initiation and growth stage surveys directly addressed the issue of paid (versus volunteer) project participation. We asked (I-Q38; G-Q43), "Did [project name] receive financial or material support from a business, nonprofit organization, government agency, or any other source of funding?" Respondents were asked to respond yes or no to each of several options about who paid them (if they were paid): a business, nonprofit, government agency, or university. Using these data for each survey, we developed an aggregate count of all projects that had some paid members (from any type of organization) versus all-volunteer ones. In the initiation stage, the chi-square test shows no difference between success and abandonment in projects that have some paid members as opposed to those where no members are paid (table 10.3, row H-C2, I-Q38). But with a high degree of confidence, we can say that SG projects have about twice the chance (table 10.3, row H-C2, G-Q43; odds ratio 0.46) of having paid participants as AG projects. We also inquired about "whether one or more members made money through the use of the software they were developing" (table 10.3, row H-C2, I-Q38 option 5 and G-Q43 option 5). Once again, in the initiation stage the chi-square test was not statistically significant, but in the growth stage SG projects answering yes had about twice the odds of being successful.

Individual respondents, in summary, do not report financial benefit as a strong motivator for participation in OSS projects in either stage (table 10.3, I-Q40 and G-Q45). On the other hand, we find that having paid developers does correlate with success in the growth stage, but not in the initiation stage. Why would this be? It could be that growth stage projects receive financial support *after* they have become successful, but we have not tested for that. In any case, it is important to remember that only 20 percent of the projects we surveyed have paid personnel so this is not likely to be a major factor driving success in OSS projects in general. We will continue to investigate financing below and in the multivariate analysis found in the next chapter.

Serious Leisure

H-C3: OSS commons will be more successful when the project provides substantial enjoyment for developers (especially volunteers) who participate (the serious leisure hypothesis).

Initiation and growth: *Not supported*

Another possible answer to the questions "Why do you participate in [project name]?" and "Why do other team members participate in [project name]?" was "I (or they) enjoy writing code as a leisure activity." This response was included to test our serious leisure hypothesis.

First, we should say that over 88 percent of both initiation and growth stage developers report that they participate because they enjoy writing code; however, chi-square statistics for these questions reveal no differences in responses between success and abandonment in either stage (table 10.3, row H-C3). Successful and abandoned projects, in other words, had similar distributions in terms of people participating for leisure or not. The question that showed the most difference was the initiation stage survey question for the reasons other team members participate, where AI projects were twice as likely (odds ratio 2.13; chi-square p-value 0.110) to have members who participate for leisure (option 4) as SI projects. Of the 124 projects that responded to this question, 32 out of 39 AI projects reported that their teams participate for leisure compared to 58 out of 85 SI projects that completed this question. This suggests, at a low level of confidence, that projects in the stage prior to first release with teams of volunteer serious leisure participants have lower chances of being successful. Yet we didn't find similar data distributions in the growth stage survey.

Skill Level

H-C4a: OSS commons will be more successful when programmers on the team are highly skilled.

Initiation: *Supported* (respondent skill level; knowledge continuity); *not supported* (respondent educational level; respondent a professional developer; team members are professional developers; team member programming skills)

Growth: *Supported* (respondent's education level—slightly); *not supported* (respondent a professional developer; respondent skill level; team members are professional developers; team member programming skills; knowledge continuity)

We included a variety of questions in our surveys trying to measure various development team skill attributes. For starters, we asked the respondents, "What is your highest education level (graduate degree, currently in graduate school, college degree, currently in college, high school degree, or other)?" In the initiation stage, we find no distributional differences between respondents in AI compared to SI projects, but what is interesting is that 52 percent overall say they have graduate degrees (table I-Q43, online appendix 10.A).

In the growth stage, we found similar patterns, with strikingly high percentages of graduate degrees in both AG and SG projects. While the chi-square p-value (0.081; table 10.3, H-C4a) shows a difference between AG and SG responses at the 90 percent level, the raw data and proportions (not shown) reveal no discernible pattern. SG projects have a slightly higher proportion of graduate degrees, and AG projects have a slightly higher proportion of college degrees. In short, the educational level of the respondent is unimportant in distinguishing between success and abandonment in either stage.

We also included other questions in each survey to help us develop a measure of professional skill on the project. First, we asked the respondent (I-Q41 and G-Q46), "Have you ever made a living as a professional software developer (yes or no)?"

In both surveys, a significant majority of respondents have made a living as a professional developer in both abandoned and successful cases. In the initiation survey, 159 out of 213 AI project respondents and 316 out of 403 SI projects answered yes, so the odds of an AI project developer being a professional are not much lower than those of a SI project developer being a professional. The chi-square test results for this question consequently are not statistically significant (table 10.3, row H-C4a). In the growth stage survey, 262 out of 323 AG respondents and 277 out of 331 SG respondents reported being professional developers, with no statistical difference between the AG and SG answer distributions. Professional developers are seen in high proportions across all projects in the two stages.

Next, to get at a measure of the respondent's programming skill, we asked (I-Q42 and G-Q47), "How would you rate your skill as a software developer in comparison to an average professional software developer (more skilled, the same, less skilled, or don't know)?"

In the initiation stage survey, 86 AI respondents rated themselves as more skilled, 82 rated themselves as the same, and 38 rated themselves as less skilled. This compares to 205 SI respondents saying they were more skilled, 129 saying they were the same, and 62 saying they were less skilled. Thus, with about 94 percent confidence (chi-square p-value 0.064; table 10.3, row H-C4a), we can say that slightly higher self-reported skill levels are associated with SI than AI projects. In the growth survey, the distributions of answers were similar between AG and SG projects, with the majority of respondents placing their skill in mostly the more skilled or the same categories. No statistical differences were discovered. Only 38 out of 313 AG respondents and 41 out of 324 SG respondents said they were less skilled than the average professional software developer.

We then also asked the respondent the same two questions about other team members (in instances where there was more than one person on the project). In the initiation stage survey, we discovered no differences between AI and SI in terms of having professional developers on the team (table 10.3, row H-C4a, I-Q46). Similar results were found in the growth survey (G-Q51). The hypothesis that successful initiation or growth stage projects will have more professional developers associated with them is not supported.

We also asked the respondent to assess the programming skill level of the other team members using the same categories (more skilled, the same, or less skilled [table 10.3, row H-C4a, I-Q47 and G-Q52]). The answer distributions between AI and SI projects as well as AG and SG projects were similar, as their chi-square tests show. Based on the respondent's assessment of other team member's skill abilities, there is no evidence to support the hypothesis that team member programming skill levels are different between abandoned and successful projects in either stage.

Given the importance of writing in online collaboration both between developers and with end users, we asked, "How would you rate your writing skills (i.e., for communicating via email, IRC, forums, or other written communication) (excellent, above average, average, below average, or poor)?" We asked a similar question about the writing skills of the other development team members as well. As the statistics in table 10.3, row H-C4a reveal, the respondent's assessment of their own writing skills or the writing skills of others on the development team do not help to distinguish between successful and abandoned projects in either stage.

Finally, for our last measure of a highly skilled development team, we investigated whether knowledge continuity was a crucial discriminator. We assume here that people who have worked on the project since its inception will be more highly skilled than others because they know the software they are developing. Thus we inquired (in both surveys), "Have you participated in [project name] for the entire time it has been hosted on SourceForge.net?" and "If not, is at least one of the people who started [project name] still a 'member' of the project?" To test these results, we combined the answers from the two questions for each stage. As long as an original member was still on the team, in other words, we treated it as continuity of knowledge.

In the initiation stage, 202 of the 231 AI projects that responded had continuity of knowledge, compared to 422 of the 440 SI projects. The chi-square test for differences is highly significant (table 10.3, row H-C4a). The corresponding odds ratio of

0.30 suggests that AI projects have continuity of developers less than one-third as often as SI projects. These statistics are highly significant and suggest that a knowledge continuum favors success.

In the growth stage, 318 of the 340 AG projects that completed this question had someone on the project from its inception, and 350 of the 369 SG projects responding had maintained this knowledge continuum. The corresponding chi-square test (p-value 0.556) shows no significant difference between the two distributions. It therefore appears that in the initiation stage, if one of the founders of the project doesn't continue to work on it, the project is more likely to become abandoned. In the growth stage, knowledge continuity or lack thereof is not associated with success or abandonment. But to keep things in perspective, this will likely not be a major factor in our multivariate analysis to follow (chapter 11) because 87 percent of AI projects and 94 percent of AG projects have knowledge continuity.

In short, this analysis suggests that for the initiation stage, slightly higher respondent skill levels and maintaining a knowledge continuum appear to help distinguish between success and abandonment. In the growth stage, only one measure—respondent education level—showed some association with success, but just barely. Skill levels do not seem to be important in distinguishing between AG and SG projects.

Opportunities for Learning Skills

H-C4b: OSS commons will be more successful when the project provides opportunities for developers to learn new skills.

Initiation and growth: *Not supported*

Signaling Skills to Others

H-C4c: OSS commons will be more successful when the project provides opportunities for developers to signal their skills to others.

Initiation and growth: *Not supported.*

Contribution to OSS Movement

H-C5: OSS commons will be more successful when it contributes or adds functionality to core OSS technologies related to the open-source movement (the helping the OSS cause hypothesis).

Initiation and growth: *Not supported*

To get at these three hypotheses, we turn back to two questions we summarized earlier: "Why (respondent) do you participate in [project name]?" (I-Q40 and G-Q45) and

"Why do other team members participate in [project name]?" (I-Q45 and G-Q50). We provided various yes-or-no answers to address these hypotheses.

To test the learning hypothesis (H-C4b), we analyzed the yes/no responses associated with the answer, "To learn and improve [my/their] skills." As shown by the chi-square test p-values in table 10.3, row H-C4b, no differences between successful and abandoned projects exist between answers for the individual respondent or team member question, in either stage. Our data (see online appendix 10.A) in general reveal that most respondents participate in part to learn and build skills, regardless of whether the project is classified as abandoned or successful.

To examine the skill-signaling hypothesis (H-C4c), we analyzed the yes/no answers associated with the choice "I [or they] want to show others their programming skills." In the initiation stage survey, 32 percent (51 out of 158) of the AI respondents said yes to this question, while 38 percent (122 out of 321) of the SI respondents agreed to this statement. Statistically, there was no significant difference between the two groups (table 10.3, row H-C4c). Similar responses were reported for growth stage projects. Moreover, results for the team assessment questions produced similar yes/no distributions between AI and SI as well as AG and SG (roughly just under 50 percent yes answers for each). Skill signaling is an important motivator generally for many participants, but there is no evidence that successful projects have more participants motivated by this compared to abandoned projects in either stage.

To investigate the helping the OSS cause hypothesis (H-C5), we analyzed answers associated with the choice "I [they] believe we should be able to modify the software we use." Recall that in chapter 8 we found no support for this hypothesis, in our investigation of various SF variable categories (e.g., operating system, database environment, etc.). Given that we were asking about other motivations that might lead to project success, though, we felt it was worth adding a follow-up question in these surveys. In the initiation stage survey, 72 percent (232 out of 321) of the SI respondents agreed with this statement, and 71 percent (119 out of 168) of the AI respondents also agreed. In the growth stage survey, slightly higher percentages are revealed (81 percent yes for AG projects, and 77 percent yes for SG projects). These results reveal substantial support for the idea that code should be open and available, but there appears to be no association between an allegiance to the openness as a public good philosophy and these projects' success (table 10.3, row H-C5). These findings corroborate our findings in chapter 8.

Group Heterogeneity

We discussed the concepts of group heterogeneity/homogeneity in chapter 4, noting there that some of the research on common property management in environmental commons focused on aspects related to the homogeneous or heterogeneous composition of groups. We also observed that this concept was broad and had many dimensions. Our literature review led to three measurement categories: sociocultural, interest/ motivational, and asset heterogeneity. With this foundation, and given that we had no a priori expectations, we posed the following research questions.

Sociocultural Heterogeneity

RQ-C1a: What, if any, aspects of sociocultural heterogeneity (such as cultural or linguistic heterogeneity) appear to influence whether an open-source commons can succeed or become abandoned?

Because of our concerns about the length of the survey and an adequate response rate, we included only one specific question capturing some aspects of sociocultural heterogeneity of OSS commons. This question investigated the geographic distribution of participants on the assumption that geographic proximity would correlate with cultural and linguistic homogeneity. Specifically we asked (I-Q14 and G-Q18), "Which of the following best describes the geographic location of all project members?" Respondents were asked to choose one of the following answers: all members are very close (e.g., same building); same city; same state, province, or region; same country; multiple countries across a continent (Europe, Africa, Asia, North America, or South America); multiple continents; or I am the only member.

The raw results to this question are quite interesting, and are presented in tables 10.4 and 10.5 (initiation and growth stage surveys, respectively). These tables report the data only for projects that had more than one developer and show that our survey responses cover a wide range of team composition types, from the standpoint of their participants' geographic location. For example, in the initiation survey, about 42 percent of the projects with more than one member have all members in the same building or city, 16 percent are in the same country, and 26 percent are on multiple continents. The remaining 18 percent are in multiple countries. Similar patterns are revealed in the growth stage (table 10.5), with the exception of the larger number of multicontinent SG projects (which we will return to in a moment).

These tables also reveal a limitation in our data. There are no projects that involve participants collaborating within Africa, South America, or Asia. (There could be projects with participants from single countries within those regions, however. These would be listed in the count of projects where participants are all in one country.) It was surprising to us to find no projects in our random survey that involved people working across the South American or Asian continents, given that we have read discussions about emerging OSS collaborations in these regions. It could be that projects from these regions are being hosted on locations other than SF.

Given the variability in our answers to this question about team geographic mix, what do chi-square test for differences show? One must obviously have a group in order to have any level of group heterogeneity. Consequently, to investigate this and

Table 10.4

Counts of initiation stage survey projects with multiple developers by geographic distribution (no one-member projects are listed here)

	Very close (same building)	Same city	Same state, province, or region	Same country	Multiple European countries	Multiple African countries	Multiple Asian countries	Multiple North American countries	Multiple South American countries	Multiple continents	Total
AI	26	15	9	18	3	0	0	3	0	23	97
SI	48	28	11	26	16	0	0	2	0	47	178
Total	74	43	20	44	19	0	0	5	0	70	275

Table 10.5

Counts of growth stage survey projects with multiple developers by geographic distribution (no one-member projects are listed here)

	Very close (same building)	Same city	Same state, province, or region	Same country	Multiple European countries	Multiple African countries	Multiple Asian countries	Multiple North American countries	Multiple South American countries	Multiple continents	Total
AG	22	14	9	11	7	0	0	2	0	20	85
SG	23	16	6	24	17	0	0	5	0	99*	190
Total	45	30	15	35	24	0	0	7	0	119	275

* This is a particularly interesting finding; 52 percent of successful growth projects involve participants from multiple continents.

the other heterogeneity questions below, we eliminated all one-member projects from this analysis.

In the initiation stage survey (table 10.3, row RQ-C1a), the p-value shows there is no significant difference between distributions of AI and SI along geographic (local to global) gradients. We have examples of projects where team members are all geographically colocated and ones that span multiple continents, but there is no apparent difference comparing AI and SI distributions (chi-square p-value 0.408). Yet the chi-square test comparing the distributions between AG and SG for the growth stage is highly significant (99 percent confidence level; table 10.3, row RQ-C1a). A closer look at the data in table 10.5 reveals that 52 percent (99 out of 190 projects) of the SG projects fall under the multicontinental class. We carefully double and triple checked this result in our raw data, because this is such a striking and intriguing finding.

Moreover, in a table similar to table 10.5 that we developed (not shown due to space limitations), we included counts of all the one-member projects in AG and SG. A substantially larger proportion of one-member projects fall in the AG class (257 out of 350 or 73 percent) compared to the SG class (161 out of 370 or 43 percent). We believe that these results provide evidence that the road to project success often involves finding people over the Internet (potentially culturally heterogeneous) who share a similar need, passion, or interest. Although it is possible that the negative effects of heterogeneity are outweighed by the advantages of having additional developers, it does not appear that cultural or linguistic heterogeneity significantly hinders success in either stage of project development.

Interest or Motivational Heterogeneity

RQ-C1b: What, if any, aspects of interest or motivational heterogeneity (such as the paid versus volunteer dichotomy) appear to influence whether an open-source commons can succeed or become abandoned? Can teams with heterogeneous interests operate satisfactorily?

We did not create questions specifically to measure interest or motivational heterogeneity, but two variables we did create potentially provide some hint as to the effect of this type of heterogeneity. First, as described above in regard to H-C2, we created the paid or volunteer variable, which may give some insight into interest heterogeneity. This variable has a value of zero if the project is all volunteer and a value of one if at least one team member is paid to work on the project. Thus for zero values the project is homogeneous. But note that our questions did not ask how many or which developers were paid, so it is possible that some paid projects (having a value of one) have all paid developers and thus are homogeneous rather than heterogeneous. Nevertheless, we think it reasonable to assume that a substantial number of paid projects are heterogeneous.

For the purposes of assessing interest heterogeneity, we took values for the paid or volunteer variable only for projects having greater than one member. The results of logistic regressions (not shown) for the paid or volunteer variable versus our dependent variable (abandonment versus success, hereafter called the response variable) show that the coefficient for paid or volunteer is statistically significant for both the Initiation and Growth stages, and that the odds ratio for success versus abandonment more than doubles for either stage for projects that have paid participants. This result indicates that if interest heterogeneity hinders successful collaboration, the negative effects are likely outweighed by the advantages of having paid participants.

For our second motivational or interest metric, we created the homogeneity motives index that sums only the answers to the question, "Why do other team members participate in [project name]?" (I-Q45 and G-Q50 only, with a maximum of ten options for each survey). This variable measures heterogeneity in projects with more than one developer, with the caveat that we cannot tell whether the motivations attributed by the respondent to others on the team are attributable to a single other member or are distributed between other members. Univariate regressions between the homogeneity motives index and our response variable (also not displayed) reveal no significance for the initiation stage, and for the growth stage, about a 30 percent increase in the odds of success over the range of values for the variable. Thus, to the extent that either of these variables measures motivational heterogeneity, we see no proof that heterogeneity hinders success in either stage.

Unfortunately, we cannot be certain how well either of the two metrics measure interest or motivational heterogeneity, and much better measures could be constructed by surveying all team members rather than only one, as our surveys did. To the degree that our measures do measure these types of heterogeneity, we find no evidence of negative effects on team collaboration.

Asset Heterogeneity

RQ-C1c: What, if any, aspects of asset heterogeneity (such as technical skill, education, or knowledge) appear to influence whether an open-source commons can succeed or become abandoned?

As described in chapter 9, we created a homogeneity education index (I-Q48 and G-Q53) that measures whether projects are educationally heterogeneous or homogeneous. We asked respondents, "Which of the following best describes the mix of educational levels of [the project name's] 'members'?" The possible answers were all have graduate degrees, all have college degrees, all have high school degrees, a mix of graduate and college degrees, a mix of graduate and high school degrees, a mix of college and high school degrees, or a mix of graduate, college, and high school degrees. Projects were deemed homogeneous if the respondent chose one of the first three answers, and heterogeneous if they picked any other answer. We included one-person projects and counted them as homogeneous, for obvious reasons. In this index, heterogeneous projects have a value of zero, and homogeneous projects have a value of one.

For the purposes of this section, we selected projects having more than one developer on the team from the homogeneity education index for both stages and call the new variables team education. We performed logistic regressions using team education as the predictor versus our success/abandonment response variable. For the initiation Stage the regression coefficient (–0.46) is not significant (p-value 0.22), but indicates that projects that are educationally homogeneous only are 63 percent as likely to be SI as projects with educational heterogeneity. For the growth stage, once again the coefficient (–0.05) is not significant (p-value 0.87). To corroborate the regression results, the Pearson's r correlation statistic for the initiation stage is –0.09 and for the growth stage is –0.017, which shows that, if anything, educational heterogeneity slightly favors success.

Why should we see this result rather than the result that heterogeneity hinders success? Once again, we can speculate that educational heterogeneity is correlated with larger team sizes and that the advantages of having a larger team outweigh the negative effects of heterogeneity. In any case, we have no evidence to suggest that any of our three forms of heterogeneity (sociocultural, motivational, or asset heterogeneity) present significant obstacles to successful collaborations in OSS software projects.

Leadership

H-C6a: OSS commons will be more successful when they have one or more leaders who generate excitement and demonstrate leadership through doing.

Initiation and growth: *Supported*

In chapter 4 we discussed the likely importance of leadership in OSS commons. Recall that in chapter 8, we had indications that leadership mattered as evidenced by the importance of the PII. We felt this was strong proof, but that it would be helpful to investigate this concept more deeply through this developer survey. Several questions addressed this notion.

First, in both surveys we asked the respondents (who usually were project administrators), "On average, how many hours per week did you work on [project name] [before or after] its first release? (< 1 hour/week; 2–4 hours/week; 5–7 hours/week; 8–10 hours/week; >10 hours/week)." The chi-square test for the initiation stage is highly significant (table 10.6, row H-C6a). Our response data (online appendix 10.A) show that the administrators of many AI projects (40 percent) work less than an hour on the project, while in contrast, only 11 percent of the administrators of SI projects work more than an hour. In every other category, SI projects work more hours, proportionately, than do AI projects. The average hours worked by respondents in AI projects was 4.15 per week compared to 6.62 hours per week by SI respondents. This provides strong support to the leadership through doing (H-C6a) hypothesis in the initiation stage. Similar statistics and proportional patterns were found in the growth stage survey, except that there were more SG projects that had respondents putting in small numbers of hours per week. But in general, SG projects had leaders working more hours per week than AG projects. The average hours worked per week by respondents in AG projects was 2.1 compared to 4.2 in the SG projects.

Second, in both surveys we asked the question, "During the development period [before or after] the 'first release' of the [project name] software, was there a technical leader who motivated others through their production of code (yes, no, or don't know)?" For the initiation stage, the odds ratio says that AI projects are 74 percent as likely to have a technical leader compared to the SI projects, and the p-value doesn't quite reach the 90 percent confidence level standard. There is thus weak support for the idea that a technical leader is a factor for success in this stage. In the growth stage, however, we discovered that the AG projects are only 25 percent as likely to have a technical leader motivating through the production of code in comparison to SG projects. In other words, the odds of a SG project having a technical leader is four times the odds of an AG project, and the chi-square p-value is highly statistically significant (table 10.6). Technical leadership is associated with SG projects.

H-C6b: OSS commons will be more successful when they have well-articulated and clear goals established by the project leader(s).

Initiation and growth: *Supported*

We also asked in both surveys, "Were there clear goals established for the development of the software [before or after] the project's first release (yes, no, and don't know)?" Table 10.6, row H-C6b presents the chi-square test results.

For the initiation stage, both the p-value and odds ratio show a significant difference between AI and SI projects. In our data (online appendix 10.A), three of every four SI projects answered yes and set goals before the first release, while only three of every five AI projects reported that they set goals before the first release. The corresponding odds ratio of 0.49 suggests that SI projects are twice as likely to have had goals prior to the first release compared to AI projects.

Similar results were found in the Growth stage data. Projects that set goals have nearly three times the odds of being successful. In other words, our survey data show that only one-third of AG projects had established goals compared to nearly two-thirds of the SG projects.

Table 10.6

Contingency table results: Community attributes (refer back to table 4.2)

Concept/hypothesis/research question	Survey variable; survey question number (I: Initiation survey; G: Growth survey)	Initiation stage results		Growth stage results	
		Chi-square p-value[1]	Odds ratio[2]	Chi-square p-value[3]	Odds ratio
Leadership					
H-C6a: Leader(s) demonstrate through doing (initiation and growth: Supported)	Average hours worked by respondent per week; I-Q16; G-Q14	0.000***	Not calculated	0.000***	Not calculated
	Technical leader motivating through code production; I-Q13; G-Q13.	0.101	0.74	0.000***	0.25
H-C6b: Clear goals (Initiation and growth: Supported)	Clear goals established; I-Q18; G-Q7	0.000***	0.49	0.000***	0.36C
Social capital					
H-C7a: Regular face-to-face meetings (Initiation and growth: Not supported)	How often all members meet face-to-face; I-Q50; G-Q55	0.031**	0.50	0.085*	0.41
	How often at least some meet face-to-face; I-Q51; G-Q56	0.628	Not calculated	0.632	Not calculated
H-C7b: Trust between team members exists (Initiation and growth: Not supported)	Trust; I-Q25; G-Q30	0.448	Not calculated	0.160	0.41
RQ-C2: Reciprocity	Specific reciprocity; I-Q26; G-Q32	0.048**	Not calculated	0.135	Not calculated
	General reciprocity; I-Q27; G-Q33	0.042**	Not calculated	0.405	Not calculated
RQ-C3: Geographic proximity	Geographic location of project members (local-global); I-Q14; G-Q18	See table 12.3, RQ-C1a (heterogeneity), and tables 12.4 and 12.5		See table 12.3, RQ-C1a (heterogeneity), and tables 12.4 and 12.5	

Group size

RQ-C4: Group size	See RQ-C4 discussion in chapter 8				

Financing

H-C8: Financing (Initiation: Not supported; Growth: Supported)	Project financing; I-Q38; G-Q43	0.201	0.75	0.000***	0.33
	Project received some kind of support (legal, financial, advice, equipment, or software); I-Q39; G-Q44	0.017**	0.60	0.000***	0.39

Marketing

RQ-C5: Marketing approaches	Advertising; I-Q21; G-Q21	0.007***	0.60	0.000***	0.48
	Web site quality; I-Q35; G-Q39	0.000***	Not calculated	0.000***	Not calculated
	Project plan communication methods; I-Q11a; G-Q9a Options:				
	1. Info on SF	0.399	Not calculated	0.003***	0.39
	2. Info on project Web site	0.226	Not calculated	0.003***	0.45
	3. Developer email lists	0.943	Not calculated	0.005***	0.38
	4. User email lists	0.717	Not calculated	0.005***	0.31
	5. Other communication methods with developers	0.806	Not calculated	0.039**	0.56
	6. Other communication methods with user community	0.895	Not calculated	0.004***	0.42
	7. Plan communicated only through the code documentation/comments	0.291	Not calculated	0.659	Not calculated

1. Chi-square test with finite population factor. Statistical confidence levels: *** 0.01 (99 percent); ** 0.05 (95 percent); * 0.10 (90 percent).
2. We present odds ratios only when useful. There are two situations where we do not present them: when the result of the chi-squared test is not statistically significant; and when the contingency table involves more than two responses. In both of these circumstances, we note this with the phrase "not calculated."
3. Chi-square test with Rao-Scott second-order correction. Statistical confidence levels: *** 0.01 (99 percent); ** 0.05 (95 percent); * 0.10 (90 percent).

Social Capital

In chapter 4, we thoroughly discussed those elements that are thought to make up the general concept of social capital. Notions of social capital were also important factors in our OSGeo case study of successful projects in chapter 6. If a respondent noted that the project had more than one developer, we followed with a number of questions investigating various hypotheses related to the social capital established within that development team.

H-C7a: OSS commons will be more successful when participants hold regular face-to-face meetings.

Initiation and growth: *Not supported* and opposite relationship discovered

To investigate this hypothesis, in both surveys we asked two different questions of projects having more than one developer or member: "Which of the following best describes how often all 'members' of [project name] meet face-to-face?" and "Which of the following best describes how often at least some 'members' of [project name] meet face-to-face?" Both questions provide the same options as answers: never, once a year, once every six months, once a month, once a week, or daily.

In the Initiation stage question where we asked how frequently all members meet face-to-face, we found that 34 percent of the AI projects surveyed meet daily or weekly, while only 15 percent of the SI projects do the same (for the raw contingency table data for this and other statistics presented here, see online appendix 10.A). More specifically, 21 percent of all AI projects that have more than one team member say they meet daily, compared to only 6 percent in the SI cases. The chi-square test's p-value shows that the difference between AI and SI is statistically significant at the 0.95 level of confidence (table 10.6, row H-C7a). This is one of our most surprising results, and is contrary to distributed work and social capital theory (refer back to chapter 4). These results suggest that SI projects tend to meet face-to-face less often than their abandoned counterparts.

In the initiation stage question where we asked how often at least some of the members meet face-to-face, we discovered no statistical difference between AI and SI projects. Yet our totals overall (combining AI and SI counts for each answer) reveal some interesting results. Overall, 29 percent of the projects (AI and SI) report that some members meet daily or once a week, while at the other end of the spectrum, 42 percent of the projects report that some of the team has never met face-to-face.

We found similar statistical comparative results in our growth survey questions, but slightly less extreme. Our data for the all members question show that about 13 percent (8 out of 61) of the AG projects have frequent (either weekly or daily) meetings, compared to only 7 percent (11 out of 169) in the SG projects. Conversely, 37 out of 61 (or 60 percent) of AG projects never have all-team face-to-face meetings, compared to 131 out of 169 or 78 percent of SG projects. The chi-square test is significant at the 90 percent confidence level, revealing slight differences between AG and SG, and again indicating an opposite relationship than we would expect—that face-to-face meetings are more closely associated with abandonment. Finally, similar to our initiation findings, the growth stage question asking about face-to-face meetings for some participants revealed no statistically significant difference between AG and SG projects.

The no statistical difference contingency table findings for questions of at least some members suggests that face-to-face meetings may sometimes help build social capital and at other times may not. In other words, face-to-face meetings don't seem to make much difference between abandonment and success in both stages. Recall that this was one of our findings in the OSGeo case study reported in chapter 6.

The discovery that projects where all members meet face-to-face are associated more with abandoned projects is surprising and puzzling, though, and goes against distributed work and virtual team theory. In that theory, we would expect all team face-to-face meetings to build project social capital and be more associated with successful projects. But our best explanation for this finding relates to the discussion we had earlier in the sociocultural heterogeneity discussion above (RQ-C1a). If sizable numbers of successful projects span multiple countries or even continents (see tables 10.4 and 10.5), then it is more likely that these projects will not have opportunities where all members can meet face-to-face. This is one potential explanation for this curious finding.

H-C7b: OSS commons will be more successful when a level of trust exists between team members.

Initiation and growth: *Not supported* statistically, but slight evidence of support in growth stage results

To investigate this hypothesis we asked in each of the two surveys, "How much or how little trust existed between project 'members' [prior to or after] the first release?" Respondents could choose between one of four options: a lot of trust, some trust, no trust at all, or don't know.

In both surveys, our results show that the majority of projects have established some level of trust between developers. In the initiation stage, only 3 out of 60 AI (5 percent) and 9 out of 126 SI projects (7 percent) report no trust at all. In each class, AI or SI, well over 50 percent of respondents report a lot of trust (online appendix 10.A). The chi-square test also reveals no distributional differences between AI and SI answers. Both AI and SI collaborative projects appear to have established reasonable levels of trust.

Growth stage survey responses for this question also demonstrate that projects have established levels of trust, with 91 percent of the AG responses and 96 percent of the SG responses reporting either some or a lot of trust. But what is different, comparing the initiation and growth responses, is that over half (55 percent) of the AG projects are in the some trust category and not the higher, a lot of trust one. In other words, for the abandoned projects category to the growth survey, proportionally fewer projects report a lot of trust compared to the initiation survey, suggesting that a reduction of trust exists to AG stage projects. The chi-square test comparing answer distributions between AG and SG responses is not statistically significant (p-value 0.16; table 10.6, row H-C7b), but signals a slight difference between the two categories because of this slight downward shift in trust in the AG projects. In short, statistically speaking, the trust hypothesis, H-C7b, is not supported in either survey, although there is some slight evidence for it in the growth stage results.

Let us turn now to an investigation of some of the community attribute research questions where no theoretical hypothesis can be yet stated.

RQ-C2: What kind of reciprocity characterizes successful collaboration in OSS commons? Is it specific (I return favors only to people who have done favors for me) or general (I cooperate fully with anyone within the group)?

In chapter 4 in our discussion about the role of reciprocity as a building block of social capital, we noted that there are two kinds of reciprocity: specific and general. We asked several questions in both surveys to investigate whether these distinguish between success and abandonment of OSS commons.

First, to get at specific reciprocity, we asked, "Do you agree or disagree that [project's] 'members' contribute in some way to the project (documentation, testing, code, etc.) because they know a specific member will also contribute?" The possible answers were strongly agree, agree, neutral, disagree, and strongly disagree. Second, to get at general reciprocity, we inquired, "Do you agree or disagree that [project name's] 'members' contribute to the project because others, in general, will contribute now or at a later time?" The possible answer choices had the same five options.

The chi-square results for these four questions are provided in table 10.6, row RQ-C2. As this table shows, the chi-square test for distributional differences is statistically significant at the 95 percent level for both initiation stage tests, but not for the growth stage questions. A closer look at the response counts in the contingency tables (online appendix 10.A, tables I-Q26, G-Q32, I-Q27, and G-Q33) reveal in each case that roughly half the respondents were neutral to both the specific and general reciprocity questions. For the growth stage, the others answer in about equal proportions in the agree or disagree categories. In other words, in some growth stage projects, specific and/or general reciprocity is a motivation, and in other cases they are not. But most important for our efforts here, these results show that these forms of social capital generation are not something that distinguishes successful from abandoned growth stage projects.

In the initiation stage, however, the story appears slightly different. We find that in the initiation survey specific reciprocity question, 16 percent (21 out of 128 responses) of the SI projects strongly agreed that members contribute because they know someone else specifically will also contribute, compared to 8 percent (5 out of 63 responses) in the AI class. A similar pattern is revealed for the initiation stage general reciprocity question, where only 3 percent (2 out of 60 responses) of AI projects strongly agreed while nearly 10 percent (12 out of 126 responses) of SI projects said they strongly agreed with the idea.

This analysis suggests in short that both the ideas of specific and general reciprocity are more strongly associated with successful projects in the initiation stage, but do not appear to help discriminate between success and abandonment in the growth stage. Crucially, this analysis indicates that having at least one other developer who can be relied on for contributing code (specific reciprocity) might be a factor that helps move initiation projects toward success.

RQ-C3: Does geographic proximity matter in the success or abandonment of OSS commons?

Related to social capital, we assume that projects that are more localized will likely have more frequent face-to-face interaction and hence build social capital—an idea that is supported in some of the virtual team and distributed work literature (see chapter 4). Yet this topic of geographic proximity is closely related to our earlier analysis for H-C7a above (regular face-to-face meetings) as well as the earlier discussion of RQ-C1a—aspects of sociocultural heterogeneity. Recall that in our analysis of sociocultural heterogeneity (see above and table 10.3, row RQ-C1a), the contingency table chi-square p-value (0.408) reveals no statistically significant difference between the distributions of AI and SI responses along geographic (local to global) gradients. On the other hand, also recall that the chi-square test comparing the distributions between AG and SG for the growth stage is highly significant (0.99 level; table 10.3, row RQ-C1a), and that our closer look at the data (table 10.5) discovered that 52 percent (99 out of 190 projects) of the SG projects fall under the multicontinental class.

Based on our question specifically asking projects with multiple members about geographic proximity, then, the answer to this research question appears to be no for both stages. In fact, in the growth stage there appears to be evidence of higher levels of success in geographically distributed (e.g., multicontinental) projects.

Group Size

RQ-C4: What, if any, notable direct relationships exist between group size and project success in OSS? Is there any support for Brooks's law and Olson's theory, Linus's law, or the core team theories?

We covered this question thoroughly in chapter 8, and will revisit it again in the multivariate analysis in chapter 11. Our survey results appear consistent with our earlier findings (e.g., that larger development teams are associated with growth stage success), although most successful growth stage projects are still comprised of small groups (e.g., one to three developers). But when other variables are considered, developer count ranks behind other factors in overall importance.

Financing

H-C8: OSS commons will be more successful when they have financial backing.

Initiation: *Not supported*

Growth: *Supported*

In our conclusion to the OSGeo case study in chapter 6, we noted that most of the projects studied had some kind of financial support. Under H-C2 above and in the section on interest homogeneity, we examined the effect on project success of whether individuals had financial motivations, were paid to work on the project, or made money from the software's use. We look here at whether projects that received cash donations, material donations, or any other form of financial support—in addition to having paid developers or developers who made money from the software—are more often successful. In other words, are projects that have any type of financial support at all more likely to succeed than projects that do not?

To address this hypothesis, we use I-Q38 for the initiation stage and G-Q43 for the growth stage. We described these two questions and their answers in detail under H-C2, but they simply ask whether the project had any type of financial support and provide answers that cover all possible types of financial support. We created a yes/no contingency table from the responses depending on whether the respondent indicated the project had some type of financial support (online appendix 10.A).

For the initiation stage, the chi-square test (p-value 0.201; table 10.6, row H-C8) shows that there is no statistically significant difference between the number of AI and SI projects with respect to having or not having financial support, although with 80 percent confidence the odds of an AI project having financing are only 75 percent as great as those of an SI project having it. In the initiation stage, we asked if the financing had been received before the first release and thus before the project became successful.

For the growth stage, the chi-square test (p-value 0.000; table 10.6, row H-C8) displays a highly significant difference, with the odds of an AG project having financing being only 33 percent of the odds of an SG project. Sixty-five out of 310 AG projects (21 percent) have financing, while 143 out of 322 SG projects (44 percent) have financing. Still, we need to be clear that our question merely asked if the financing had been received after the project's first release, so the project may have received financing before or after it became successful in the growth stage. Although financing seems to be associated with success, only 22 percent of initiation stage projects and 33 percent of growth stage ones have any type of financing. In addition, many projects that have received financing are abandoned, so we do not expect that financing will be a major factor in OSS success in general.

Marketing

RQ-C5: What marketing approaches appear to be most readily used by successful OSS commons? Are different approaches used in successful compared to abandoned projects?

In chapter 4, we briefly discussed marketing strategies in OSS and noted that little scholarly literature on this subject appears to be available. In our survey, we included two questions that addressed this concept directly—one on project advertising, and the second on assessing project Web site quality. We also asked a third question relevant to marketing about how project functionality plans were communicated—a concept that is related to both project marketing and leadership.

But these three concepts are also the same three questions we used above to investigate RQ-T1 (collaborative infrastructure" used). There we found significant differences between successful and abandoned projects in both stages. For one, successful projects in both stages advertise more than abandoned projects, and this is highly statistically significant. Web site quality also tends to be higher in successful projects in both stages, but more important in the growth stage. And all forms of communication for functionality plans were utilized more in SG projects compared to AG projects (this is not true for the initiation stage). For more details, we encourage the reader to return to the discussion about these three marketing-relevant questions under the heading collaborative infrastructure RQ-T1 above.

Understanding OSS Institutions

As we noted in chapter 5, much less work has been done analyzing OSS institutions, and what has been done has mostly focused on large OSS projects like Debian Linux. One of the goals of this study is to get a better understanding of OSS institutions across all project sizes. Because of this lack of understanding, we first presented a number of research questions in table 5.5. The OSGeo study in chapter 6 investigated, in a fairly rich and detailed manner, the institutions found in a set of successful OSS geospatial technologies in much smaller team settings than the Debian situation. We found there that institutions as social norms were more prevalent than formalized (e.g., written) rules, significant variation exists in the institutional systems in place, and many of the operational rules in place are embedded within the collaborative technology used (e.g., version control systems). The programmers using these systems sometimes don't even recognize these as operational rules that govern how work is undertaken.

The OSGeo case is certainly helpful, but it represents only one case (or really a set of cases all falling under the OSGeo nonprofit foundation). In this section, we now are in a position to investigate a larger number of projects quantitatively to address the institutional questions posed in table 5.5. For readability, as in previous sections, we will address each question posed earlier in sequence, and in each case we conducted analysis for the initiation and growth stages. The results below are summarized in tables 10.7–10.14.

RQ-I1: How are OSS projects governed?

Related to this question in chapter 5 we proposed two hypotheses: H-I1 (large team hypothesis) and H-I2 (hybrid team hypothesis).

H-I1 (The Large Team Hypothesis): OSS commons with larger teams will have more formalized and complicated institutional designs compared to ones with smaller teams.

Initiation and growth: *Supported*

To investigate this hypothesis we asked the question, "How were the day-to-day operations of the project managed [prior to or after] the [project name's] first release?" We provided three yes-or-no options:

1. Through unwritten but understood norms of behavior
2. Through controls within the versioning system (e.g., CVS, Subversion, etc.)
3. Through a formal document that outlines how the project is organized and will operate

We then created a six-value rule options (rule_ops) index based on these yes-or-no answers. The scoring for this index is as follows, and gets more formalized as the index value goes from 0 to 6:

0: Very informal rules; set if all three options above are "no"
1: Informal rules; set if only option 1 (unwritten norms) is set to "yes"
2: Informal with codified rules; set if options 1 (norms) and 2 (versioning system) are set to "yes"
3: Codified rules only; set if option 2 (versioning system) is set to "yes," but the others are "no"
4: Informal and formal; set if options 1 (norms) and 3 (formal document) above are "yes"
5: Informal and formal; set if all three options are "yes"
6: Formal; set only if option 3 (formal document) is "yes"

With this index created for each survey, we analyzed these data in two ways. First, we looked at the average number of developers for projects associated with each of the rule options index values above (table 10.7). A review of these data presented in this table shows a general increasing trend with some slight fluctuations for rule options index scores of 3 and 5, where the average developer count goes down slightly for these categories. But the overall trend supports H-I1 for both the initiation and growth surveys. Because of the fluctuations, but more important because we felt conceptually and theoretically that options 2 and 3 (informal with codified rules) as well as options 4 and 5 (informal and formal options) could be considered similar concepts, we also present table 10.8, which combines the results for these groupings. In this table the increasing formalization of rules with larger development teams becomes even more apparent, especially in the growth stage data.

Next, we ran a simple regression to explore this relationship further. Here, our formalized rule option index is the dependent variable and the project developer count is the independent variable. Results for the initiation and growth surveys are presented in table 10.9. For the initiation survey we find a positive coefficient for developer count with significance at the 99 percent level. But the coefficient value is small (0.112), suggesting that we need to have more than eight developers (1/0.112) to shift from one level or category of rule options to another. Residual plot analysis (not shown) reveals that the model fits well for developer counts higher than eight, but not as well for smaller developer count situations. We find similar findings with the growth survey data (table 10.9), where the developer count coefficient (0.077) is positive and highly statistically significant, but the coefficient value (0.077) is even smaller than that found in the initiation survey results. This suggests that we would need an increase of more than thirteen developers to shift to the next category or level of the rule options index. Similar to the initiation survey data, residual plot analysis of the growth survey data (not shown) reveals a relatively good fit for developer counts greater than eleven, but not as good for smaller team sizes.

This analysis, in short, provides clear support for H-I1. In both stages we find evidence that as team size increases, the institutional designs will become more formalized. While tables 10.7 and 10.8 show that teams with average sizes of three (initiation) and four to five (growth) offer evidence of formalization, it is likely that higher levels of institutional formalization will occur more often in "the extreme tail" of OSS projects where development teams are fairly large, as we expected. This is in line with the Debian Linux analysis conducted by O'Mahony and Ferraro (2007) that we described in chapter 5.

H-I2 (The Hybrid Team Hypothesis): All-volunteer OSS commons will have less formalized institutional designs compared to hybrid (e.g., volunteer and paid) ones.

Initiation and growth: *Supported*

Table 10.7

Investigating H-I1: Average number of developers for projects organized by rule options index score

	Rule options index score							
	0: Very informal rules	1: Informal rules	2: Informal with codified rules	3: Codified rules only	4: Informal and formal rules	5: Informal and formal (all three questions yes)	6: Formal rules only	Overall average
Average number of developers: Initiation survey, n = 450	1.31	1.84	2.6	1.83	2.07	1.27	3.05	1.87
Average number of developers: Growth survey, n = 463	1.51	2.31	2.5	2	4.27	2.33	4.62	2.73

Table 10.8

Investigating H-11: Average number of developers for projects organized by rule options index score, combined 2 + 3 and 4 + 5 option results

	Rule options index score					
	0: Very informal rules	1: Informal rules	2 + 3 combined: Informal with codified rules	4 + 5 combined: Informal and formal rules	6: Formal rules only	Overall average
Average number of developers: Initiation survey, $n = 450$	1.31	1.84	2.49	2.01	3.05	1.87
Average number of developers: Growth survey, $n = 463$	1.51	2.31	2.44	4.20	4.62	2.73

Table 10.9

Investigating H-I1: Simple (ordinary least squares) regression of rule options index on project developer count, initiation and growth survey results

	Estimated coefficient	Standard error	T-statistic
Developer count: Initiation survey, n = 450	0.112	0.039	0.005**
Developer count: Growth survey, n = 463	0.077	0.017	0.000***

Statistical significance codes: *** 0.001 (99 percent); ** 0.01 (95 percent); * 0.05 (90 percent).

To investigate this hypothesis, we utilized data from two questions that were included in both surveys. We first needed to develop a measure for each project on whether it was an all-volunteer effort or had some team members who were paid to participate. To determine this, we asked, "In the time [before or after] the first release, did [project name] receive financial or other material support from a business, nonprofit organization, government agency, or any other source of funding?" Respondents answered yes or no to each of the following options:

1. One or more members were paid by a business to work on the project
2. One or more members were paid by a nonprofit to work on the project
3. One or more members were paid by a government agency to work on the project
4. One or more members were paid by a university to work on the project

We then created a paid or volunteer index based on these yes/no responses. If the respondent answered yes to any of the four options, we consider the project to be a hybrid one. If the respondent answered no to all four options, then we consider the project an all-volunteer effort.

To get at the formalized institutional designs component of the hypothesis, we utilized a question that asked about project governance. Specifically, we asked respondents (in both surveys), "Which of the following best describes how [project name] was governed during the period before the first release?" Respondents could choose only one of the following options:

1. No governance: The project had/has only one member so there was no reason to establish rules or procedures for how the project team collaborates
2. Very informal: There are no recognized positions of authority or development-related rules or procedures for how the project team collaborates
3. Informal: There are recognized positions of authority and some informal development-related rules for how the project team collaborates
4. Formal: There are assigned positions of authority and/or some formal (written) development-related rules or procedures on how the project team collaborates

Table 10.10

Contingency table investigating H-I2: The hybrid team hypothesis, initiation survey results

	Very informal	Informal	Formal	Total	Chi-square p-value[1]
All volunteer (0)	77	32	5	114	
Hybrid team (some paid developers) (1)	20	28	7	55	0.001***

1. Chi-square test with finite population factor; statistical confidence levels: *** 0.01 (99 percent); ** 0.05 (95 percent); * 0.10 (90 percent).

Table 10.11

Contingency table investigating H-I2: The hybrid team hypothesis, growth survey results

	Very informal	Informal	Formal	Total	Chi-square p-value[1]
All volunteer (0)	96	45	5	146	
Hybrid team (some paid developers) (1)	33	28	11	72	0.001***

1. Chi-square test with Rao-Scott second-order correction; statistical confidence levels: *** 0.01 (99 percent); ** 0.05 (95 percent); * 0.10 (90 percent).

Given that our interest is collaboration, which requires at least two people, we dropped projects that chose option 1 (only one team member) and utilized only answers from options 2–4. In short, answers to this question created a governance scale from 1 (very informal governance) to 3 (formalized governance).

With the volunteer or hybrid (paid) and formalized institutions/governance measures created, we turned once again to contingency table analysis, looking for differences between successful and abandoned projects (tables 10.10 and 10.11 for, respectively, initiation and growth). The p-value in both cases for the chi-square test is highly significant. A closer look at the counts for each option in each contingency table shows a higher percentage of projects fall in the informal and formal options for hybrid projects, compared to a higher percentage of projects stating very informal in the volunteer cases. In other words, projects with some paid participation (the hybrid case) tend to move more toward institutional designs that establish some recognized positions of authority, and in some cases, assigned positions and more formalized development-related rules. There is strong evidence to support H-I2 in both stages.

RQ-I2: What kinds of rules (e.g., position, boundary, and choice) are commonly found in OSS commons?

Because of the need for brevity to ensure a reasonable response rate—and the fact that in order to address this research question adequately, it would require not a single question but instead a whole series of them—we did not investigate this in our surveys. Much of chapter 6—the OSGeo case study—was devoted to these topics, though.

RQ-I3: Does sponsorship or foundation involvement appear to influence the institutional design of OSS projects?

In this research question we are trying to understand if there is proof that organizations that somehow sponsor a project or overarching nonprofit foundations (like OSGeo in chapter 6) influence the governance structures as well as institutional designs of OSS commons. To investigate this, we utilize two questions that were included in both surveys.

The first question looks at the kinds of organizations that support the project, and the kinds of support they provide. Specifically we ask, "What kind of support did you receive from each of the following during the time [before or after] the first release?" We provided a check-box matrix with five options on the y-axis: nonprofit foundation, other nonprofit, business, government agency, and other organization. On the x-axis we provided six support options: legal, financial, advice, equipment, software, and other. Respondents were encouraged to mark all that apply for their project. If a project had legal support from a nonprofit foundation, for example, that check box would be marked. Using these data, we created a financial and other support index, or f_index for short, that supplies a count of all checked options for each project. The survey data we received for all projects ranged from 0 (no support whatsoever) to 11 (a variety of support types from a variety of organizational types). This index provides a measure of sponsorship that we can use to investigate this question.

To get at the variable we want to explain, the institutional design of the project, we again utilize the project governance measure described above in our discussion of H-I2. Recall governance was an ordinal measure with four options: no governance, very informal, informal, and formal.

The research question above (RQ-I3) is asking whether our financial or other support index has a relationship with our governance variable. Since we were only interested in seeing whether a relationship existed between the two, we decided to treat these variables as continuous, and utilize a simple regression of governance on the financial and other support index. The results for both surveys are presented in table 10.12. Note that the coefficient of the support index is positive and highly statistically significant for both surveys. The positive coefficient suggests that as financial or other support goes up, the governance moves from more limited and highly informal governance to more formalized governance structures.

To investigate how well our support index correlates with project governance, we rounded the predicted value of the simple regression equation that was produced for

Table 10.12

Investigating RQ-I3: Simple (ordinary least squares) regression of governance on financing and other support index, initiation and growth survey results

	Estimated coefficient	Standard error	T-statistic
Support index: Initiation survey, $n = 175$	0.010	0.020	0.000***
Support index: Growth survey, $n = 218$	0.120	0.024	0.000***

Statistical significance codes: *** 0.001 (99 percent); ** 0.01 (95 percent); * 0.05 (90 percent).

each survey (e.g., the equation govern = 1.33858 + 0.12042*support index for the growth stage survey) and then compared our governance prediction to our actual governance data for each project in our surveys. In the initiation survey, we had a correct classification rate of 65 percent (113 out of 175). In the growth survey, we had a correct classification rate of 61 percent. These demonstrate a relatively strong relationship in both stages while at the same time recognizing the limitations of simple regression.

In sum, this analysis finds that there is a positive relationship between financial or other support and governance structures, and suggests that higher levels of support move a project to informal or formalized governance systems. A relationship doesn't imply causation, of course, but theoretically this is the result we had expected.

RQ-I4: Is there an evolutionary pattern to OSS institutions?
H-I3 (The Institutional Evolution Hypothesis): OSS commons will move from informal norms to more formalized rules and governance structures as more developers join the project, or as firms or other organizations become involved.

Initiation and growth: *Not supported* in most cases

The findings reported above—H-I1 and RQ-I3—indicate that the institutional designs will be more formalized in situations where there are larger numbers of developers, or if firms or organizations are involved. The question we are investigating here is whether there is an evolutionary or steplike process that occurs in these projects as they grow or get older, and if so, what are the driving factors.

We included two questions in each survey to expore this institutional evolution idea. First we asked, "Over time, did [project name] move from a more informal project governance system to one that is more formalized?" To clarify what we meant by formalized, refer back to the earlier I-H2 analysis above, with the four answers of no governance to formal. Respondents had the choice of answering yes, no, or don't know.

If they answered yes, we asked a second question: "Did any of the following con-tribute to your shift to a more formalized governance system? (choose only one answer)" The choices were:

1. A need to replace a key project leader
2. A requirement by a nonprofit foundation
3. A requirement by a firm with interests in the project
4. Other (describe)

Our results are provided in table 10.13. The vast majority of our survey responses in both surveys report no institutional evolution. Only 26 out of 591 initiation surveys and 24 out of 630 growth surveys reported institutional evolution. In the surveys that mentioned a specific reason, requirements by firms were the dominant answer in the initiation responses, and the need to replace a leader was the dominant answer in the growth responses.

Based on these responses, our results suggest that the vast majority of OSS projects (at least on SF) experience little or no evolution toward formalized institutions. Thus H-I3 (institutional evolution hypothesis) is rejected.

Do Institutions Matter for Success?

With a better understanding of institutions in SF project settings established, let us now return to the question of factors that appear to discriminate between successful and abandoned projects. In table 5.5, we presented several other institutionally related research questions and hypotheses that we can now address. Again, for the reader's ease, we will restate the research question or hypothesis presented earlier, describe the questions we asked in the surveys, and supply the results. Many of these analyses will use contingency tables as well.

RQ-I5: Does the choice in OSS license effect the success or abandonment of a project? For instance, do GPL-compatible licensed projects outperform GPL-incompatible proj-ects, or vice versa?

The first research question we presented in table 5.5 related to the project's licens-ing component, which can be considered one of the primary constitutional-level institutions (refer back to the IAD framework in chapter 3). In our two surveys, however, we didn't include questions to investigate this issue because we addressed it in chapter 8. Recall that in the classification tree analysis, we found that the general choice of a more restrictive GPL-like license or less restrictive non-GPL license appears to have little relationship with success and abandonment in either stage. Success and abandonment are well distributed across different license types in both stages.[3]

Table 10.13
Investigating RQ-I4 and H-I3: Evolution in OSS institutions

	No evolution	Evolution: To replace leader	Evolution: Required by nonprofit	Evolution: Required by firm	Evolution Reason "other"	No response to second question	Total
Initiation	565	1	2	7	9	7	591
Growth	606	6	2	4	6	6	630

RQ-I6: Are certain governance structures associated with the success or abandonment of OSS commons?

Related to this research question, we proposed two hypotheses, addressed sequentially below.

H-I4 (The Friction Hypothesis): The more formalized institutions get, the more likely the project will be abandoned.

Initiation and growth: *Not supported*

This friction hypothesis tests the assertion described in chapter 5 that more formalized rules and other institutions in OSS serve as a disincentive for programmers to participate. We look at this from a number of different angles based on several questions in our surveys (table 10.14).

First, we utilize the data on formalized governance (explained earlier when we addressed H-I2). This captures concepts related to collective choice and constitutional-level institutions (refer back to chapters 3 and 5). Specifically, we asked respondents of both surveys, "Which of the following best describes how [project name] was governed during the period [before or after] the first release?" Respondents could choose only one of the following options: no governance, very informal, informal, and formal, where these categories are referring to the establishment of positions of authority or rules for how collaboration occurs. (We should remind the reader that a no governance answer related to situations where there was only one developer or member on the project.)

A review of the contingency table 10.14 results for H-I4 (the friction hypothesis) comparing the chi-square p-values (row RQ-I6) reveals no statistically significant differences between success and abandonment in the initiation survey data, but highly statistically significant results in the growth stage responses. The raw contingency table data (see online appendix 10.A, G-Q37) show that AG projects have a high proportion of no governance responses (258 out of 320 total responses) while SG reveals a marked movement toward more governance, although mostly informal (only 15 out of 340 were formal). In addition, only 16 (out of 660 total in the growth survey) noted that they had formal (assigned positions of authority and/or some formal [written] development-related rules or procedures related to collaboration), and 15 of these exist in the SG class.

Our conclusion is that in both stages, formalized governance structures appear to be avoided, and the ones that do exist are associated not with abandonment but rather success. (For more details, see online appendix 10.A, G-Q37.)

Second, in both surveys we investigated the formalization of operational rules and day-to-day practices, getting at operational-level institutions (refer back to chapters 3 and 5). We specifically asked, "During the time period [before or after]

Table 10.14

Contingency table results: Institutional attributes (refer to table 5.5)

Concept/ hypothesis/ research question	Survey concept and question number (I: Initiation survey; G: Growth survey)	Initiation stage results		Growth stage results	
		Chi-square p-value[1]	Odds ratio[2]	Chi-square p-value[3]	Odds ratio
Institutional design and success/abandonment					
RQ-I5: License; GPL/ non-GPL	Not asked. We tested this in chapter 8				
RQ-I6: Governance structures and success	H-I4: The friction hypothesis				
	Formalized governance: I-Q33; G-Q37	0.219	Not calculated	0.000***	Not calculated
	Unwritten norms of behavior: Q-I30 option 3; G-Q34 option 1	0.304	Not calculated	0.011**	0.59
	Operations managed by versioning system: Q-I30 option 2; G-Q34 option 2	0.469	Not calculated	0.000***	0.46
	Formal document on operational rules: Q-I30 option 3; G-Q34 option 3	0.786	Not calculated	0.178	Not calculated
	H-I5: The Debian hypothesis				
	Evolution to a more formalized system: I-Q34; G-Q38	0.108	Not calculated	0.000***	0.15
RQ-I7: Democratic collective choice	Tests H-I6 developers have a say: I-Q31l; G-Q35	0.108	0.61	0.001***	2.05

1. Chi-square test with finite population factor; statistical confidence levels: *** 0.01 (99 percent); ** 0.05 (95 percent); * 0.10 (90 percent).

2. We present odds ratios only when useful. There are two situations where we do not present them: when the result of the chi-squared test is not statistically significant; and when the contingency table involves more than two responses. In both of these circumstances, we note this with the phrase "not calculated."

3. Chi-square test with Rao-Scott second-order correction; statistical confidence levels: *** 0.01 (99 percent); ** 0.05 (95 percent); * 0.10 (90 percent).

the first release, how were the day-to-day operations of the project managed?" Here we provided three options, and the respondent could choose yes or no for each of them:

1. Through unwritten but understood norms of behavior
2. Through controls within the versioning system (e.g., CVS, Subversion, etc.)
3. Through a formal document that outlines how the project is organized and will operate

We developed contingency tables for each of these options and surveys. Table 10.14, row RQ-I6 (under H-I4) provides the results, and like all other analyses, the complete raw survey responses and contingency tables (for I-Q30 and G-Q34) are available in appendix 10.A (online).

The responses for the three options show no significant yes/no distributional differences between successful and abandoned projects in the initiation survey results. In terms of the day-to-day operational management, both abandoned and successful projects tend toward the use of unwritten norms of behavior (option 1) to get work done (appendix 10.A). In each case (AI and SI), about half also rely on controls maintained via the version control system (option 2), and half report that they do not. Much smaller numbers of projects utilize formal documents to manage operations (18 out of 161 AI, and 38 out of 316 SI). In the initiation stage, none of these options help to distinguish success and abandonment.

Nevertheless, the growth stage results reveal a significant difference in operational management. SG projects have higher odds of saying yes to both unwritten norms and using versioning control (table 10.14, row RQ-I6). But like their initiation survey counterparts, in both AG and SG cases, formally written operational rules tend to be avoided (see appendix 10.A, G-Q34).

So what does this tell us about H-I4? In both the initiation and growth surveys, we find that formalized operational systems are the exception rather than the norm. Slightly higher numbers of formalized systems are discovered in successful projects in both stages (see appendix 10.A, I-Q30 and G-Q34), but the differences are not enough to be statistically significant. In short, both successful and abandoned projects strongly tend to avoid formalized operational systems, bolstering the idea of institutions as frictions, yet the hypothesis that formalized systems will fail is not supported in either stage.

H-I5 (The "Debian" Hypothesis): As OSS projects evolve and grow (in terms of developer numbers), formal institutions become a necessary condition in order to avoid abandonment.

Initiation and growth: *Not supported*

To investigate this hypothesis, we return to the question we explored to analyze RQ-I4 above. Recall that we asked, "Over time, did [project name] move from a more informal project governance system to one that is more formalized?" To clarify what we meant by formalized, we referred back to the earlier question with the four answers of no governance to formal. Respondents had the choice of answering yes, no, or don't know. But in this analysis, we provide a contingency table looking at the distributions of yes/no answers as they relate to success and abandonment in the two stages. The chi-square p-values are provided in table 10.14 row RQ-I6, H-I5.

Our initiation stage data show that at the 85 to 90 percent confidence level, we can say that there is a slight difference between AI and SI projects, with SI projects having about twice the chance of moving toward a more formalized governance structure. The raw counts of responses (appendix 10.A, table I-Q34), however, tell us that only about 4 percent of the initiation stage projects (26 out of 591) have had some evolution toward formality.

In the case of the growth stage, our survey data for this question reveal a highly statistically significant difference between AG and SG, with SG projects moving toward formal governance at seven times the rate of AG projects. Like the initiation stage, though, the numbers of projects that have made this evolution from informal to formal governance is quite small, compared to the number of projects reporting (24 out of 630, AG and SG combined). Moreover, the 24 projects that answered this question affirmatively are spread out along the development team size distribution rather than being clustered at the larger team sizes: 6 of the 24 are one-developer projects, 6 are two-developer projects, 7 are between three- and ten-developer projects, and 5 have greater than ten developers on the project.

In short, we have some statistical evidence suggesting that successful projects in both stages more often move toward more formalized governance structures than abandoned projects, but the proportion of successful projects that do this is quite small. Even in projects with greater than ten developers, there are many that report very informal governance structures. It does not appear that "institutions become a necessary condition in order to avoid abandonment" as the size of the development team increases, so H-I5 is not supported in either stage.

RQ-I7: Are OSS projects that exhibit more democratic, collective choice mechanisms more successful than ones appearing more autocratic?

In chapter 5, we proposed one hypothesis related to this research question:

H-I6 (The Aggregation Rule Hypothesis):   OSS commons with aggregation rules where the developers have a say in the design of those rules will be more successful than ones where developers have little or no say.

Initiation: Not supported

Growth: Slight support

To investigate this hypothesis in both surveys, we asked, "Which of the following best describes how major project decisions were made during the period [before or after] the 'first release'?" Respondents were only allowed to choose one of these options:

1. A single, benevolent, or autocratic dictator makes all the major project decisions.
2. A few "members" have more rights and authorities for the project than other "members."
3. All "members" have a voice in the direction of the project, share similar rights and responsibilities, and vote on major project decisions.
4. All "members" must reach agreement/consensus on the direction of the project, and on rights and responsibilities.

Like other analyses, contingency tables and chi-square tests were conducted for the two surveys, and the p-value and odds ratio results are presented in table 10.14, row RQ-I7. Full contingency tables are in our online appendix 10.A (tables I-Q31 and G-Q35).

In the initiation stage, we found a slightly higher proportion of benevolent dictatorships in the SI class compared to the AI class (80 versus 72 percent), and this difference results in a chi-square test that is nearly significant at the 90 percent confidence level.[4] This outcome suggests that benevolent dictatorships may slightly favor success in the initiation stage. Yet in the growth stage, we see the opposite: 84 percent of AG projects report benevolent dictatorships compared to 72 percent in the SG class. We also find a higher proportion reporting option 2 ("a few members have more rights") in SG (17 percent of surveyed projects) compared to the AG class (7 percent). H-I6 thus is rejected in the case of initiation and to some degree supported in the growth stage.

But perhaps the most interesting finding here is the dominance of benevolent dictatorships across the two stages as well as the abandoned and success categories, and that 72 percent of the successful growth projects fall under benevolent dictator forms of decision making. While we see some limited support for the hypothesis in the growth stage, a slight shift to more democratized decision-making models where at least a few developers help make decisions, this finding is still quite different than our theoretically based expectations and what has been empirically shown to be the case in natural resource commons. As we discussed in chapter 5, in natural resource commons settings, Ostrom (1990) and others after her have demonstrated that commons are more successful and sustained when the participants have a say in the direction or management of the commons. In OSS settings, it appears that more of the decision making is placed in people of accepted authority following meritocracy principles. Other participating developers may not have as much of a say, at least when it comes to major project decisions. Moreover, perhaps the most intriguing part of these data is the degree to which benevolent dictator governance structures exist across all categories; benevolent dictator decision-making largely drives abandoned and successful projects in both the initiation and growth stages. What we haven't sufficiently covered here is the role to which the broader end user community helps drive major decision making though dialogue with and encouragement of the developers. The extent to which this happens is still an open question.

Conclusion

In this chapter, we took all the work done in earlier ones, combining it to systematically investigate the hypotheses and research questions related to OSS collaborative success and abandonment presented in chapters 2–5. We have learned much that had not been previously known about OSS projects and the Internet-based collaborations on which they depend. Now we have nearly reached the end of our research endeavor. Only one thing remains to be done. We must put all the noteworthy variables we considered in this and previous chapters together, and see how each stands in importance when compared with all the others. Only then will we have done our best to answer the remaining question:

What factors lead some OSS commons to success and others to abandonment?

We take that final step in chapter 11.

11 Putting It All Together in Multivariate Models of Success and Abandonment

with Meng-Shiou Shieh

This chapter describes the final step in our empirical research, drawing on all the work presented thus far to try to answer our central research question:

What factors lead some OSS commons to success and others to abandonment?

We performed the statistical analysis below during the fifth and final year of our research effort. In this analysis, we put all the variables we have developed into the same metaphoric pot and use well-established statistical techniques to try to make sense of it all.

At this point in our research we were still uncertain about the final outcome. Would we be able to find key factors for OSS success and abandonment, or are OSS projects so diverse and complex as to make that task almost impossible? This chapter begins with a short discussion of the statistical techniques we used to answer that question and then moves directly to the worthwhile results of applying those techniques. Next, we summarize and interpret our findings, examining the initiation stage first, followed by the growth stage analysis. In the end, we had moderate success in finding crucial factors for the initiation stage and excellent success in the growth stage, and tell the story in detail. Readers who are not interested in the details of our statistical analyses may wish to skim parts of this chapter, and instead focus mainly on the sections below that describe our findings for both the initiation and growth stages.

Our Methodology

Our modeling uses the five independent variables (developers, tracker reports, page visits, forum posts, and PII) that we found to be most important in chapter 8, but updated, using 2009 data from the Notre Dame SF repository, to accurately reflect the state of projects at the time of our survey. We also include the thirty-six new independent variables identified in the theoretical work in chapters 2 and 5, and operationalized through our survey questions (for a summary, see chapter 9, table 9.6, or the variable construction document on our Web site).[1] In addition, we utilized the 2009

Notre Dame data to update our dependent variable, using the same methodology described in chapter 7, so that it would accurately reflect the state of project success and abandonment at the time of the survey.

Our surveys contain a substantial amount of missing data (see table 9.6), and since logistic regression requires a complete data set, regression on all variables was not feasible. Therefore as we did in chapter 8, we used classification tree analysis, which can handle missing data, to discover the most critical variables in our model. (For readers unfamiliar with classification tree analysis, please see chapter 8.) To validate the classification tree output, we also performed a stepwise logistic regression that produced similar, although slightly less accurate models than our classification tree analysis. The stepwise regression results are available on our supplementary material Web site, but we do not present them here.[2] We used the OSS *R* to do all our statistical work, and in the spirit of openness—and to encourage further work using our dependent variable—our statistical scripts are also available on this Web site.

We present our classification tree results for both the initiation and growth stage below. Since some researchers frown on the data-mining approach of classification tree analysis, we also provide a logistic regression analysis of the most important variables, and remind readers that all these variables are grounded in theory from the book's early chapters. The logistic analysis is possible because the key variables in the model have much less missing data than the entire data set. For consistency, and because it is easy to understand, we use the logistic regression coefficients of the most important variables to predict whether projects in our data set are successful or abandoned. We then take these predictions and create confusion matrices, correctly classified percentages, and kappa statistics, which are the same statistical tools we use to evaluate the tree results. This technique allows for direct comparison of the classification tree output and corresponding logistic regression output.

Initiation Stage Models

Before presenting the results for the initiation stage, we need to mention a few caveats regarding our data. First, as described in chapter 8, we cannot use the downloads variable for our analysis in the initiation stage because downloads are part of the definition of our initiation stage dependent variable. Second, we noted in chapter 8 that tracker reports and forum posts were not critical variables in the initiation stage, even though they appeared to be among the most significant variables in the classification tree output. This finding results from the fact that tracker reports and forum posts multiply dramatically *after* a project becomes successful in the initiation stage (SI), and therefore these two variables give us little information on what factors *lead* to success in the initiation stage. For this reason, we have eliminated tracker reports and forum posts from our final models for the initiation stage.

An even more important change in the initiation data used for our modeling relates to the PII. The key finding in chapter 8 was that higher PII values before a project's first release were correlated with a project becoming SI. Unfortunately, sometime after 2006—the period when the chapter 8 data were collected—SF began to require that persons registering projects on SF make selections for at least five of the variables that comprise the PII. This means that all newly registered projects on SF have a PII value of at least five, and hence, the PII is no longer as useful for deciding if a project will become successful in the initiation stage.[3] Despite this fact, we have created the PII from May 2009 Notre Dame data and included it in our analysis for completeness. Although this development regarding the PII is disappointing, our chapter 8 finding deduced that elements of leadership and project utility were likely reasons for higher PII values. Fortunately, in part to validate the earlier PII findings, we included leadership and utility questions in our survey, so in effect, the concepts that we think the PII variable captures are still present and thus tested in the initiation stage models presented below.

Finally, we need to mention two additional caveats regarding the hours and community variables in our initiation stage data. As shown in chapter 9, table 9.6, the hours variable is constructed using responses to Q16 and Q17 from the initiation stage survey. Although Q16 asked specifically, "How many hours did you work on [project name] before its 'first release'?" In Q17 we failed to specify "before the first release" when we asked how many hours per week were worked by "other" project members. Due to this oversight, it is possible that responses to Q17 reflect hours worked by additional members *after* the project became SI. Therefore, we have created the variable hours_Q16_only, which includes only Q16 responses, and used it in our initiation stage analysis. Using hours or hours_Q16_only, however, produced nearly identical classification trees, so luckily our oversight had little negative effect. We made a similar error on one of the questions that comprise the community variable (Q28 and Q29). Owing to the omission of the phrase "before the first release" in Q28, we created the variable community_Q29_only from responses to Q29 alone and substituted it for the community variable in the following analysis.

Initiation Stage: Classification Tree Results

We generated the classification tree, shown in figure 11.1, using thirty-seven of the forty-three initiation stage variables. As described above, we eliminated downloads, tracker reports, and forum posts from our analysis, and substituted hours_Q16_only and community_Q29_only for, respectively, the hours and community variables. We also used leadership_without_hours instead of the leadership_with_hours variable.

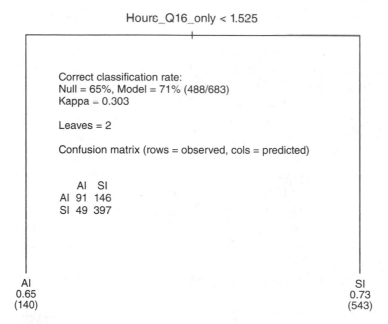

Hours_Q16_only < 1.525

Correct classification rate:
Null = 65%, Model = 71% (488/683)
Kappa = 0.303

Leaves = 2

Confusion matrix (rows = observed, cols = predicted)

    AI SI
AI 91 146
SI 49 397

AI
0.65
(140)

SI
0.73
(543)

Figure 11.1
Initiation stage tree

The tree shown in figure 11.1 is compact and reveals that the most important factor distinguishing success from abandonment in the initiation Stage is the hours that individual survey respondents worked on their respective projects. (Again, for those unfamiliar with the statistics shown within the tree diagram, please refer to the classification tree description in chapter 8.) Using the hours_Q16 variable alone, this model correctly classifies 71 percent of the initiation stage projects with an improvement of 30.3 percent over the expected result for a random classification, as shown by the kappa statistic. We will discuss this result further in the initiation findings section below.

Although the tree above produces a moderately accurate model of OSS success and abandonment, it does not provide much information about the other variables in our model. Table 11.1 depicts additional output from the tree algorithm and provides more detailed information about variables that might have been used as the primary splitting variable in place of hours_Q16_only.

In descending order of importance, table 11.1 shows that the most crucial variables in addition to hours_Q16_only are leadership_without_hours, marketing, continuity, and community_Q29_only. The leadership_without_hours variable is simply the leadership variable (see table 9.6) with hours_Q16_only removed. We separated hours_Q16_only from the leadership variable to more clearly illustrate the significance of

Table 11.1
Relative importance of the major variables in the initiation stage model (2009 survey and Notre Dame data)

Variable name	Improvement in Gini index
Hours_Q16_only	32.75
Leadership_without_hours	16.31
Marketing	11.55
Continuity	8.67
Community_Q29_only	6.80

hours_Q16_only. The improvement in the Gini index in table 11.1 describes how much it would have improved had the corresponding variable been used as the primary splitting variable. The decrease in Gini as we go down the table gives an indication of the relative importance of each variable in the model, but the differences in the index from marketing to the bottom of the table are so small as to make the ordering as well as the variables themselves not important.

As mentioned in the methodology section, we performed a stepwise logistic regression (not shown) that resulted in Hours_Q16_only and continuity being the most significant variables, followed by complexity and leadership_without_hours. With the exception of complexity, which is suspect because 14 percent of its data are missing, the stepwise regression revealed essentially the same variables as being important, despite distortions due to the regression eliminating records with missing data. Although the ordering was different in the stepwise regressions, the fact that hours_Q16_only turned up as most crucial gives us added confidence in the tree results. Because the classification tree process handles missing data better than stepwise logistic regression, we consider the tree results our best information about variable importance for the initiation stage.

Initiation Stage: Logistic Regression Results

Lastly, for those who prefer parametric models, we present a logistic regression model based on the variables shown in table 11.1. None of these variables are highly correlated with one another, so colinearity should not be a problem affecting coefficient values. Table 11.2 depicts the output of the regression model, and we see in the logistic regression output that hours_Q16_only is the variable with the highest significance (7.893, E-10), which agrees with the tree output shown in table 11.1. Continuity is the second most significant variable, but this disagrees with the tree output in table 11.1, which shows leadership_without_hours as the second most important splitting variable. The variation in the results of the two tables and also the stepwise regression

Table 11.2
Logistic regression model based on most important initiation stage variables

Variable	Coefficient	Standard error	Z value	Pr(>|z|)	Significance	Odds ratio[‡]
(Intercept)	−1.6686	0.4102	−4.067	4.75 E−05	***	
Hours_Q16_ only	0.1536	0.2499	6.147	7.893 E−10	***	1.17
Continuity	1.2677	0.3734	3.395	6.86 E−4	***	3.55
Marketing	0.3420	0.1766	1.937	0.053	*	1.41
Leadership_ without_ hours	0.0805	0.0744	1.082	0.279		1.08
Community_ Q29_only	−0.0086	0.0131	−0.654	0.513		0.99

Statistical confidence levels: *** 0.01 (99 percent); ** 0.05 (95 percent); * 0.10 (90 percent).
[‡] For a description of the odds ratio, see chapter 10. In logistic regression, generally the odds ratio changes in the amount shown with every unit increase in the corresponding variable.

Table 11.3
Confusion matrix based on the logistic regression model (rows = observed, columns = predicted), correct classification rate = 74 percent and kappa = 0.304

	AI	SI
AI	65	127
SI	30	372

are probably due to the fact that the regression models eliminated responses with missing data, so we are really comparing slightly different data sets in each case.

Nevertheless, in order to compare the logistic models' goodness of fit to the classification tree model for the initiation stage, table 11.3 shows a confusion matrix constructed by using the coefficients of the table 11.2 variables to predict whether a project is successful or abandoned. Recall that logistic regression gives the probability of the dependent variable (successful or abandoned in this instance) based on the values of the coefficients and variables for each case in the data set. Based on the regression coefficients and value of the variables for each project, we simply labeled the project as successful if the logistic regression's output was greater than or equal to 0.5 (50 percent probability), and labeled the project abandoned if the probability was less than 0.5.

As seen in table 11.3, the correct classification rate for the parametric model (74 percent) is similar to that for the tree model shown in figure 11.1 (71 percent), and the kappa statistics are even closer: 0.304 for the parametric model, and 0.303 for the tree. These results give us confidence that the nonparametric modeling based on classification trees produces similar results to parametric modeling based on logistic regression.

Initiation Stage Findings

Now that we have described our models as well as verified that both the nonparametric and parametric models produce similar results, what can we say about the factors for success and abandonment in the initiation stage?

Initiation Stage Finding 11.1: The number of hours that project members worked on a project before its first release is the most important causal factor for success in this stage.

The classification tree in figure 11.1 shows that when the survey respondent worked less than about 1.5 hours per week on the project, the project was abandoned 65 percent of the time, and when the respondent worked more than 1.5 hours per week, the project was successful 73 percent of the time. Using the sum of the number of hours that the respondent worked and the respondent's estimate of the number of hours worked by other project members (i.e., the hours variable) produced nearly identical results (not shown). The odds ratio column of table 11.2 for hours_Q16_only (1.17) indicates that the odds of success increase by 17 percent for each additional hour worked per week on the project. Our survey data reveal that respondents were putting in more than 10 hours per week for 131 SI projects and 33 AI projects. This information suggests that putting in greater than ten hours per week results in the project having nearly four times the chance of being successful versus abandoned (131/33 = 3.97). Because these hours were put in before the first release, we can make a reasonable (and unsurprising) argument that working more hours causes a project to be successful.

Initiation Stage Finding 11.2: Our survey results verify that leadership is a causal factor for success in the initiation stage.

In chapter 8, the PII was the most important variable for discriminating between successful and abandoned projects in the initiation stage. We deduced that the PII was significant because it represented a measure of leadership and good project management, so we included questions in our survey that we could use to create a leadership index—the leadership_without_hours variable (see table 9.6)—in order to further test this finding. Our survey questions about leadership all asked specifically about the time period "before the first release," so that we could investigate leadership factors that may cause success in this stage. We created the leadership_without_hours index variable from answers to survey questions about having:

- An architectural design for the software
- A plan for software functionality
- Clear goals for the project
- Exemplary code production by the leader
- Good documentation
- A quality Web site
- The leader's ability to mobilize members having different motivations

The improvement in the Gini index for the leadership_without_hours variable (16.31) shown in table 11.1 demonstrates that if the leadership_without_hours was the primary splitting variable in our initiation stage classification tree, it would help discriminate between successful and abandoned projects. The logistic regression result displayed in table 11.2, however, reveals that the leadership_without_hours variable does not have statistical significance in that model. On the other hand, our stepwise logistic regression did include the leadership_without_hours variable with significance at the 90 percent level. Taken together, these three models indicate that leadership_without_hours is a factor for success in this stage, although not a particularly strong one.

In our chapter 8 discussion of the PII, we mentioned that project administrators who were more diligent or committed would be more likely to answer questions about the project attributes. Based on our survey results, it appears that the high PII values reported in that chapter resulted primarily because those who were diligent—and therefore worked more hours on their projects—tended to record the categorical data that comprises the PII, rather than because the PII measures utility or other aspects of leadership. Yet we know that leadership_without_hours is correlated with success from our tree and logistic regression output. Our supplemental contingency table data also show that SI projects have twice the odds of receiving a contribution before the first release, and we can envision that these contributions arise because the project has practiced good leadership. Furthermore, all the elements of the leadership_without_hours variable were asked about the time period before the first release, so we have the temporal element of causality. Thus we have identified three important components of causality: correlation with success, a plausible mechanism linking leadership_without_hours to success, and the fact that leadership preceded success. To the extent it is a key variable, then, we have a strong argument that leadership, defined by the seven concepts above and operationalized using our leadership_without_hours index, is a causal factor for success in the initiation stage.

Initiation Stage Finding 11.3: Marketing, continuity, and community_Q29_only are minor factors for success, and have little power to discriminate between successful and abandoned projects.

The marketing index variable combines three questions from our survey, and measures whether or not a project advertised itself in places other than SF, the respondent's opinion of the quality of the project's Web site, and how many ways the project communicated its plan for the software's functionality. Although this variable appears in our classification tree results, it has a low Gini value, indicating low relative importance. Marketing did not appear in our stepwise regression, and it has minimal significance in our logistic regression. Consequently, we do not see it as an important l factor for success in the initiation stage.

Continuity is a yes or no variable based solely on a question where we asked whether an active member has been with the project since it was first registered on SF. Although continuity has high significance and a high odds ratio in our logistic regression results (table 11.2), our data show that 624 of the entire set of 673 initiation projects (AI and SI classes) that responded to this question indeed had continuity (i.e., an active member on the project since registration). While many more AI than SI projects did *not* have continuity resulting in the high odds ratio (3.55:1), since nearly all projects (both AI and SI) do have continuity, this variable is not a major factor for discriminating between success and abandonment.

Finally, our measure of the community concept—community Q29 only—a question that asked the respondent to give a "best estimate of the number of nonmembers who made nonfinancial contributions," has the lowest Gini value and an odds ratio of nearly one in table 11.2, thus showing that it is even less important than marketing or continuity.

Initiation Stage Finding 11.4: Many variables that we thought might be important factors for initiation stage success are not important, including financing, paid versus volunteer members, need for the software, OSS experience, and professional skill levels.

Although we included thirty-seven variables in our initiation stage classification tree model, at least thirty-two of them were not important factors for distinguishing between success and abandonment in the entire project population represented in our survey results.[4] Recall that we discussed our survey response in chapter 9, and made the case that our response appears to be quite representative of the SF population. To the degree that our survey response is representative, the nonfindings below can be considered to hold true for the SF population. Since space considerations preclude exploring all the nonfindings, we will highlight a few particularly interesting ones.

Financing (the finance variable) in the initiation stage slightly increases the odds of a project being successful, but only 141 out of 632 survey responses (22 percent) indicate that the project had financing before the time of its first release. Because relatively few projects have financing, and because the projects that do have financing are fairly evenly distributed into both the AI and SI categories, financing is not a major factor for determining success or abandonment when all projects are considered.

We can make an identical argument for projects that have at least some paid members versus all-volunteer projects (the paid_or_volunteer variable). Although having paid participants slightly increases the odds of success, only 18 percent of all initiation projects in our survey data set had paid participants before the first release, and the projects that did have paid participants were distributed into both the AI and SI categories. Therefore, the paid_or_volunteer variable is not an important factor helping to explain variation in the entire population of successful or abandoned projects.

We also hypothesized that need for the software might be a significant factor based on ideas about user-driven innovation (von Hippel 2005). The need variable is an index built on four questions we asked about the reasons why the respondent and other members participate in the project. These questions specifically asked whether respondents participate because they use the software for their personal use, or because the organization they work for uses the software they are developing. We sum the number of yes responses to produce a need index that ranges from 0 (all no) to 4 (all yes), with higher values indicating more need for the software. Although the mean value for the need index variable is higher for SI projects (0.79) than AI projects (0.63), with 95 percent confidence, there are a large number of respondents from both AI and SI projects that expressed a need for the software. So while von Hippel's notions are supported, the need variable is not a major factor helping to distinguish success from abandonment in the initiation stage, based on a similar contention as for the finance and paid variables.

Finally, we reasoned that experience with OSS projects and professional skill levels could be important factors, so we asked respondents what year they started participating in OSS and how many projects they had been involved in (the OS_experience variable). We also asked respondents for their assessment of their skills and those of any other project members as compared with an average professional software developer (the professional_skill variable). Both these variables are numerical, and a comparison of the means for AI projects and SI projects for both these variables shows small differences that are not statistically significant in either case. In short, there is no significant difference between OSS experience or professional skill levels for AI or SI projects, and hence these are not crucial factors in this stage.

Growth Stage Models

The results and findings for the growth stage are more complex as well as more explanatory than the findings for the initiation stage. As discussed previously, we have included the conflict variable in the growth stage model for a total of forty-four as opposed to forty-three variables (only thirty-seven were actually used) in the initiation stage (see table 9.6). In addition, we have used the community, hours, and leadership_with_hours variables in the growth model rather than the community_Q29_only, hours_Q16_only, and leadership_no_hours variables that we used in the initiation model. We have utilized these three variables in the growth stage because the reasons for using the three alternative variables in the initiation stage (described above) are not present here. We also consider all our old variables, including downloads, to be valid for the growth stage model.

To summarize, we have used forty-one variables in our growth stage model, or the forty-four total variables shown in table 9.6 minus community_Q29_only, hours_Q16_only, and leadership_no_hours variables that we used only in our initiation stage model. In chapter 9, we explained how our survey responses were skewed disproportionately toward the SG class when compared with the SF population. Therefore, in the growth stage analysis, where necessary, we have weighted the data to correct for this imbalance.

Growth Stage: Classification Tree Results

In the growth stage, as in the initiation one, we used classification trees to identify the most significant variables because classification trees handle missing data better than stepwise logistic regression. Rather than simply creating a single weighted data set for analysis, we decided it would be more robust to take many properly weighted random samples from our responses and then average the results of the variable importance output of the tree algorithm for each sample. By properly weighted, we mean that the proportions of AG and SG projects in each random sample are the same as in the SF population in our 2009 SF data set. The variable importance output for a classification tree, similar to table 11.1, takes the form of improvement in the Gini index. For a detailed description of the variable importance function of the classification tree algorithm, please refer to Brad Compton's white paper "Using Cartware in R."[5]

Each of our properly weighted random samples used 500 responses randomly selected from our total of 720 responses for the growth stage survey. We ran a classification tree analysis on each of 100 random samples. Table 11.4 below shows the mean improvement for each variable in the Gini index for 100 properly weighted random samples consisting of 500 randomly selected survey responses each.

For comparison with the results captured above in table 11.4, our stepwise logistic regression on an unweighted data set containing all 720 responses (not shown) returned downloads, tracker reports, leadership_with_hours, and community, in that order, as the most important variables.

Figure 11.2 illustrates a classification tree made from 1 of our 100 weighted random samples. Since each weighed random sample was a different data set, our 100 random

Table 11.4

Relative importance of the major variables in the growth stage classification tree model

Number	Variable name*	Mean improvement in Gini index for 100 weighted random samples of 500 survey responses each
1	Downloads	77.32
2	Tracker_reports	58.58
3	OS_experience	57.27
4	Leadership_with_hours (leadership_hours) *	55.88
5	Community	55.86
6	Marketing	45.78
7	Forum_posts	39.16
8	Hours	34.33
9	Requirements_index (require_index)*	33.19
10	PII_unconsolidated (pii_uncons)*	31.29
11	Motivation	31.26
12	Developers (dev_count) *	28.28
13	PII_consolidated (pii_cons)*	28.00
14	Need	18.52
15	Utility	14.55
16	Complexity	14.53
17	Professional_skill (prof_skill)*	13.25
18	Homogeneity_motives (homo_motive)*	12.75
19	Leisure	12.69
20	Writing	12.48
21	Financial_index (f_index)*	12.29
22	Modularity	11.99
23	Social_capital (soci_capital)*	10.71
24	Governance (govern)*	8.90
25	Finance	8.75
26	Education	7.83
27	Continuity	7.63
28	Paid_or_volunteer (paid_volunteer)*	7.36
29	Financial_motive (fin_motive)*	5.40
30	Proprietary	5.24

Table 11.4

(continued)

Number	Variable name*	Mean improvement in Gini index for 100 weighted random samples of 500 survey responses each
31	Conflict	5.18
32	Homogeneity_geographic (homo_geog)*	4.54
33	Competition	3.87
34	Operational_level_rules (rule_ops)*	3.86
35	Rule_to _replace_leader (rule_leader)*	3.15
36	Project_decisionmaker (rule_decision)*	2.82
37	Found_member_on_Internet (memb_inet)*	2.65
38	Reciprocity_general (recip_general)*	1.70
39	Homogeneity_education (homo_edu)*	1.52
40	Reciprocity_specific (recip_specific)*	0.51
41	Governance_evolution (gov_evolution)*	0

* The variable names in parentheses are older ones that we have included to allow cross-referencing with documents (including R code) on the book's supplementary material Web site.

samples produced 100 different trees. We selected the tree depicted in figure 11.2 because it reflects the variable importance order shown in table 11.4. The correct classification rate and kappa represent values that consistently appeared for similarly sized trees in our samples.

The model in figure 11.2 predicts growth stage success and abandonment with an impressive 90 percent accuracy along with a 74 percent improvement over a random prediction (see the kappa statistic in figure 11.2). From the confusion matrix, we see that the model misclassified only 7 AG projects as SG and 45 SG projects as AG, for 52 misclassified projects out of 500 in total. The correct classification rate for AG projects is 98 percent (334/341), while the correct classification rate for SG projects is 72 percent (114/159). This model is almost perfect at predicting abandonment, and predicts abandonment considerably better than success.

Examining figure 11.2 a little closer, we see in the first node to the left of the primary split (on downloads) that projects having less than 1,089 downloads have been placed in the AG category with a correct classification rate of 0.9 or 90 percent. This means that 90 percent of the 283 projects in this node (255 projects) are correctly classified as AG projects. We should note, however, that 10 percent or 28 of the projects in this node are SG projects that have been misclassified as AG ones. These misclassified SG projects represent ones that have a small user base, as indicated by having less than 1,089 downloads. From the SG row of the confusion matrix, we see that

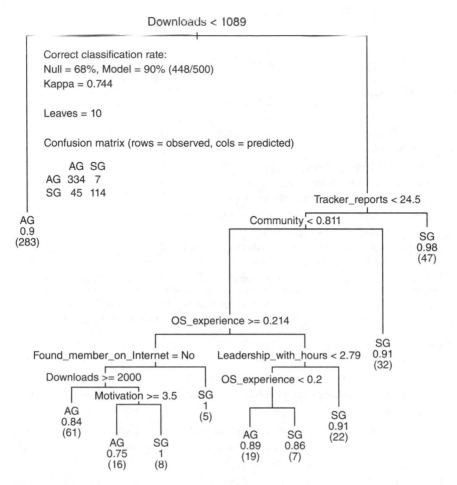

Figure 11.2
A representative growth stage classification tree

there are 114 plus 45, or 159 SG projects, included in this particular sample, so we can estimate that SG projects with a small user base comprise about 18 percent (28/159) of the SG projects in our model.

Growth Stage: Logistic Regression Results
To complete the growth results section, we present a logistic regression model based on a hundred weighted random samples of five hundred responses each. In other words, we used the same sampling strategy we utilized to produce table 11.4 above, but performed logistic regressions (instead of a classification tree analysis) on each of the hundred samples. Recall that logistic regression requires completed data for each

Table 11.5

Logistic regression model using the most important growth stage variables identified through theory and classification tree modeling (mean values for 100 weighted random samples of 500 responses each)

Variable	Coefficient	Standard error	Z value	Pr(>|z|)	Significance	Odds ratio
(Intercept)	2.49 E+00	3.017 E-01	−8.24	5.97 E-12	***	
Leadership_ with_hours	3.48 E-01	8.01 E-02	4.34	1.15 E-03	***	1.4160020
Tracker_ reports	6.05 E-02	1.56 E-02	3.72	2.39 E-03	***	1.0624263
Community	1.498 E+00	4.51 E-01	3.30	2.19 E-02	**	4.4488427
Downloads	6.126 E-05	1.99 E-05	2.87	3.65 E-02	**	1.0000613
OS_ experience	−1.188 E+00	6.74 E-01	1.66	1.99 E-01		0.3049260

Statistical confidence levels: *** .001 (99 percent); ** 0.05 (95 percent); * 0.10 (90 percent).

variable, so we have used only the five most important variables from table 11.4 in order to minimize the amount of missing data. Table 11.5 shows the mean values of the output of the logistic regressions, which eliminated only six responses on average from the analysis due to missing data. The variables are in descending order with the most statistically significant one on top.

Looking at table 11.5, we first notice that the order of the variables is different than the variable importance order shown in table 11.4. This was also true in the initiation stage logistic regression, as expected, since the classification tree analysis is a different statistical technique that uses all the variables in our model as opposed to the logistic regressions in table 11.5, which use only five of the variables. Note that the logistic output for the OS_experience variable is only significant with 80 percent confidence (0.199), while table 11.4 shows it to be the third most important variable. In addition, the negative coefficient indicates that more OS_experience correlates with lower success rates.

The output for the classification tree shown in Figure 11.2, on the other hand, reveals conflicting results regarding the OS_experience variable. As we explained in chapter 8, cases in the classification tree where the expression evaluates as true are always sorted into the left node on all nodes of the tree. Also, the left node always has a higher proportion of abandoned projects, and the right node always has a higher proportion of successful projects on all nodes of the tree. In figure 11.2, the first split for OS_experience (>= 0.214) indicates that having higher OS_experience values (i.e.,

Table 11.6
Confusion matrix based on the growth logistic regression model (rows = observed; columns – predicted), correct classification rate = 82 percent (406/494) and kappa = 0.55

	AI	SI
AI	318	18
SI	70	88

more experience) leads to greater abandonment rates (which agrees with Table 11.5), while the second split for OS_experience (<0.2) indicates that higher OS_experience values lead to greater success rates. This disagreement serves to highlight the differences between the two statistical techniques, and we will discuss it further below.

We created the confusion matrix displayed in table 11.6 by predicting whether projects were successful or abandoned using the coefficients in table 11.5. For a more detailed description of our prediction methodology, see the initiation stage results above. The correct classification rate shown in table 11.6 is 82 percent as compared to 90 percent for the classification tree in figure 11.2, and the kappa is 0.55 as compared to 0.74 for the tree. Although the two models are reasonably close, we believe the classification tree is capable of modeling more complex relationships than the simple log-linear relationship modeled with logistic regression, and thus is capable of producing more accurate results. Nevertheless, for those who prefer parametric models, the logistic output reveals that the most important variables from table 11.4 are statistically significant (with the exception of OS_experience) and create a model that has substantial predictive ability.

Growth Stage Findings

The growth stage classification tree model portrayed in figure 11.2 has an excellent ability to predict whether a project is AG or SG. In the findings and discussion below, we attempt to dissect our growth stage model in order to clarify the most important factors that lead to success or abandonment.

Growth Stage Finding 11.1: The majority of successful growth stage projects have greater than approximately one thousand downloads.

As we noted in chapter 8, it easily could have turned out that a majority of SG projects had a small number of downloads and therefore a small user base. In other words, the majority of SG projects could have been, for example, specialized software (e.g., bioinformatics) of interest to only a small number of academics or other specialized users. But this is not the case. To put it positively, the majority of successful growth stage projects hosted on SF—and quite possibly in the open-source population in general—have a significant number of users. Based on the figure of 1,089 downloads shown in

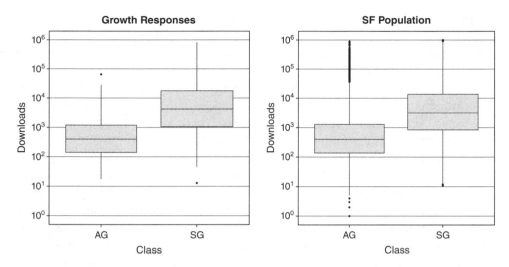

Figure 11.3

The distribution of downloads for growth stage survey responses versus the SF population

figure 11.2, and estimating several downloads (newer versions of the software) per user, we can guess that the majority of successful projects have at least roughly two hundred users.

Figure 11.3 below uses box plots to show the distribution of the number of downloads for our growth stage survey responses versus the number of downloads in the SF population. Looking at figure 11.3, we see that 1,000 downloads (10^3 downloads) defines an important juncture in both charts. In both our survey responses and the SF population in general, approximately three-quarters of abandoned projects (class AG) have fewer than 1,000 downloads, and approximately three-quarters of successful projects (class SG) have greater than 1,000 downloads.

Our finding about downloads also supports the idea the success is associated with the software usefulness to a substantial number of users, as discussed previously in chapter 8. But while it is easy to understand that the number of downloads reflects the software's utility for users, how does this utility translate into a successful OSS software project? Our next finding helps to make this connection.

Growth Stage Finding 11.2: The tracker reports and community variables, taken together, support the idea that contributions and participation by those who are not formal project members are correlated with, and likely a major causal factor in, OSS success.

This finding gets at the heart of what is generally assumed about OSS projects—the involvement of the broader user community. Tracker reports consist of the total number of bug reports, feature requests, patches, and support requests submitted to a project via the collaborative infrastructure provided to each project by SF. The community index variable is a combination of survey questions that get at the time the respondent spent helping users, the number of nonfinancial contributions made by those who are not listed as formal project members, and the number of different kinds of contributions made (software code, documentation, testing, bug reporting, or other). We created the community index variable by scaling each of these three elements from 0 to 1, and then adding them together to create a potential range of values going from 0 to 3. In actuality the maximum value of the community variable in our growth survey responses is 1.84. Because the two variables—tracker reports and community— each measure contributions to the project to some degree, we would expect a correlation. Yet Pearson's r for the correlation between them has a modest value of 0.21.

Table 11.4 shows that the both the tracker reports and community index variable have substantial ability to discriminate between successful and abandoned projects, and table 11.5 indicates that both these variables have statistical significance in a parametric model, so we know that participation in a project by users and other non-members is correlated with success. Our data also reveal that 435 of 673 growth stage respondents (65 percent) report having received a contribution of software code, documentation, software testing, bug reporting, or some other type of contribution from nonmembers of the project, so we can envision that user participation leads directly to improvements in the software, thereby making the software more useful. We thus have a statistical model demonstrating how contributions lead to greater software utility that, in turn, could be part of a virtuous circle that translates greater utility into even more participation, even greater utility, and continuing success.

Unfortunately, in our growth stage survey we did not ask whether tracker reports or the three elements of community happened *before* a project became successful, so our survey did not provide the temporal element that would be an essential part of contending that building community participation causes success. Fortunately, we have the Notre Dame SF data set to investigate causality.

First, in our success/abandonment classification system, many of the projects that are classified as IG are in transition. That is, they just achieved a first release and hence moved out of the initiation stage, but it is too early in their growth stage for us to classify them as a successful (SG) or abandoned (AG) project. Recall that in chapter 8, we took advantage of this information and used the increase in mean developer counts as projects progressed from the IG class to the SG class to assert that developer counts increase, on average, before a project becomes successful, and thus increasing team size is a causal factor for success. Here we make a similar claim for tracker reports and, by association, the community variable.

Table 11.7 lists the mean number of tracker reports by project class for the population of SF projects in our 2009 data set. Referring to the mean number of tracker

Table 11.7

Mean number of tracker reports by project class in the SF population

Project class	Total number of projects in class	Number of projects having tracker reports	Mean number of tracker reports per project
AI	67,126	4,044 (4045)	0.65 (2.63)
II	16,806	409 (410)	0.19 (0.49)
IG	12,052	1,853 (1,854)	3.66 (17.81)
AG	53,450	14,205 (14,209)	2.65 (5.70)
SG	24,899	15,455 (15,455)	52.26 (52.26)
Totals	174,333	35,973	

Note: The numbers in parentheses indicate the population numbers including outliers. We have omitted a small number of outliers in order to give a more accurate representation of the means. We eliminated one outlier in class AI, one outlier in class II, one outlier in class IG, and four outliers in class AG. There are no outliers in the SG class.

reports column, we see that (when corrected for extreme outliers) the II class has a mean of 0.19 tracker reports per project, and the IG class, which a project enters immediately after it has its first release and leaves the II class, has a mean of 3.66.[6] This progression seems to indicate that projects gain traction from increasing participation by members, users, or others during the maximum two-year period that the project can be in the IG class. The AG class has a mean of only 2.65 tracker reports, so the IG projects with higher numbers of tracker reports apparently go on to become SG projects, since the SG class has a much higher mean of 52.26. If this were not so, it seems likely that the AG class would have a mean that was closer to that of the IG class. Since a substantial increase in tracker reports, in many cases, probably suggests an increase in the size of the community associated with the project, we can deduce that an increase in both tracker reports and the community variable—as measures of increasing community activity—occur before a project enters the SG class and are likely important causal factors for success. This is aligned with conventional wisdom on OSS about the key role of the broader user community, but may be one of the first large-scale empirical studies with strong evidence of this phenomenon.

Growth Stage Finding 11.3: Leadership is highly correlated with success in the growth stage and is arguably a major cause for success.

Our leadership_hours index variable for the growth stage differs from the leadership_without_hours index variable we used in the initiation stage because it incorporates the data from the questions where we asked the survey respondent how many hours were worked on average per week, by all formal members of a project after the first release of the project's software. We used leadership_without_hours in the initiation stage so that we could more accurately represent the importance of the hours_Q16_only variable, but this was not necessary in the growth stage. Other than the inclusion of hours, the leadership_hours variable used in the growth stage analysis is consistent with the leadership_without_hours variable used in the initiation stage. It also combines questions, asking whether the project has an architectural design, a functionality plan, clear goals, exemplary code production by the leader, good documentation, a quality Web site, and the ability of the leader to mobilize members having different motivations. Referring to Table 11.4, we see that leadership_hours has more ability to discriminate successful from abandoned projects than the hours variable alone. Since the hours variable has the same values for hours as the leadership_hours variable, the other elements of leadership_hours must contribute significantly to the ability of this variable to discriminate between success and abandonment.

So we have established that elements of leadership—hard work, planning, goals, and good project management, as reflected by documentation and a good Web site— are highly correlated with success in the growth stage. In fact, the odds ratio for leadership_hours shown in table 11.5 indicates that for each 1-point rise in the leadership_hours variable (with the values ranging from 0 to 7.3), the odds of the project being successful rise by approximately 42 percent. To make this odds number more concrete, our data reveal that for projects having a leadership_hours value of 0 to 1, 47 are SG while 130 are AG (odds ratio of 0.36). For projects having a leadership_hours value from 3.8 to 7.32, 133 are SG while only 47 are AG (odds ratio of 2.83). Although we did not formulate our growth stage survey questions to establish causality, we found that leadership_without_hours was a causal factor for success in the initiation stage. Since all successful growth stage projects were at one time successful initiation stage projects, we can infer that leadership is also a causal factor in the growth stage, with the caveat that to some degree, the leadership reported by growth stage respondents may have come after the project became successful in that stage.

Growth Stage Finding 11.4: OSS experience appears to be important, but only in certain circumstances.

The OS_experience index variable consists of two elements: the number of years that the respondent has been involved in OSS, and the number of OSS projects that the respondent has participated in. Individually, we scaled the responses to these questions so they both were in a range between 0 and 1, and then added them together to create the index. The OS_experience variable consequently ranges between 0 and 1.714. Earlier, in discussing logistic regression results for the growth stage, we showed that success rates actually go down as OS_experience increases, while the classification tree modeling results reveal that success rates both go up and down as OS_experience increases.

This apparent contradiction stems in part from the fact that classification trees can model more complex interactions in the data than simple linear relationships. In the logistic regression, the coefficient for OS_experience represents a uniform log-linear relationship with all other variables in the model (i.e., downloads, tracker_reports, leadership_hours, community, and the dependent variable) as they vary across the entire range of their values. In the classification tree model, in its first appearance, the OS_experience variable only becomes important in the subset of the weighted data (138 projects or 27.6 percent of the sample) that has greater than 1,089 downloads, less than 24.5 tracker reports, and a value for the community variable of less than 0.811 (figure 11.2). Thus the classification tree models the more complex relationship that occurs when a project has significant downloads, but has not yet built a strong community (as indicated by a lower number of tracker_reports and a lower value for community).

As a result, in situations where a project has a substantial number of downloads (and therefore utility), but has not been able to establish a strong community, it appears that more experienced OS developers (OS_experience > −0.214) may leave the project, leading to higher rates of abandonment. In the second appearance of OS_experience (<0.2), it may be that some of the less experienced developers who stick with the project may be able to ultimately achieve success if they have good leadership skills (evidenced by leadership_with_hours >2.79) along with OS_experience between 0.2 and 0.214, which is just below the median value for this variable.

Although these explanations make theoretical sense and are quite satisfying, we need to recall that the tree shown in figure 11.2 is only one of many different trees produced by different weighted random samples. We would need to do more statistical work to be confident of the details of the relationship between OS_experience and the rest of the variables. Nonetheless, it seems certain that OS_experience plays a crucial role in success and abandonment in the growth stage, particularly in light of the variable's strength in table 11.4.

Growth Stage Finding 11.5: Many variables that we thought might be important factors for success in the growth stage are not, including financing, professional skill levels, modularity, complexity, found member on the Internet, education, and writing skills.

Although the growth stage classification tree depicted in Figure 11.2 is more complex than the initiation stage tree portrayed in figure 11.1, there remain many variables in our growth model that we theorized might be major factors for success but are not. While as we stated earlier, 22 percent of all initiation stage projects (AI and SI) had financial support, we find that 33 percent of all growth stage projects (AG and SG) have financial support. According to our financing analysis in chapter 10, the chances that an AG project had financing are only one-third the chances that an SG project had financing, so financing is correlated with success (with a p-value of 6.2, E-10). Still, two-thirds of growth stage projects do not have financing, and there are a large number of both successful and abandoned projects in that category. So while financing favors success, it is not a major factor for discriminating between success and abandonment in all growth stage projects.

Another factor we thought might be important for discriminating between success and abandonment in this stage was whether people on the team were professional programmers or not. In our survey results, the vast majority of respondents (82 percent) report that they have made a living as a professional software developer at some time. As in the initiation stage, however, there is no significant difference between the mean values for the AG and SG class for the numerical variable professional_skill, which is an index capturing answers to questions about the team being professional programmers and also an assessment of its skills. In addition, professional_skill ranks seventeenth in importance in table 11.4. While it seems intuitive that programming skill levels should be a key factor for discriminating between AG and SG projects, this does not appear to be the case. Yet we should remember that these are self-reported skill levels by a lead project person only rather than objective assessments.

In chapter 4 we noted that modularity is often mentioned as an important element in OSS projects, because dividing software into modules allows for different programmers to work independently on manageable pieces of the software. Our survey respondents indicated that 82 percent of growth stage projects are designed for modularity, so modularity is an important element of OSS projects. But as we revealed in chapter 10, both AG and SG projects usually design for modularity, so modularity is not a major factor for determining success or abandonment.

Earlier in this book project, when we developed our theoretical expectations on OSS, we hypothesized that it might be easier to produce software that was less complex, so lower complexity might favor success. But our survey responses indicate the opposite. The complexity variable has values ranging from 0 to 4, with a value of 4 being "much more complex." The mean value for AG projects is much lower (1.03) than the mean for SG projects (1.63), with a p-value statistically significant at the 99 percent level. Thus projects that respondents deem more complex are more likely to be successful. This variable, though, is not a major factor in discriminating between successful and abandoned projects, as indicated in table 11.4.

In our survey, we asked respondents if they gained a member who had found the project via the Internet (the found_member_on_Internet variable). We found that ninety-seven SG projects and only thirteen AG projects had gained a member via the Internet. Gaining a member through the Internet favors success, and the difference between SG and AG projects is highly statistically significant (p-value < 0.000). Yet gaining a member via the Internet only applies to projects having greater than one member. Since 58 percent of growth stage projects have only one member, less than half our respondents answered this question. Furthermore, many SG projects have only one member, so the found_member_on_Internet variable is not a major variable in discriminating between success and abandonment in *all* growth stage projects. We did find that the community variable is the key to success in the growth stage, though, because additional members and users contribute to improving the software. Adding a new member is a powerful force for success in the cases where it happens.

Our education index variable is based on the responses to two survey questions about the respondent's educational level, or composition of the development team's educational level if the project had more than one member. According to our survey results, educational levels are high among OS developers; 85 percent have a college or graduate degree, or are currently enrolled in graduate school. On the other hand, educational levels are about the same for AG and SG projects, so education is not an important factor driving success or abandonment.

Finally, we have come across anecdotal evidence that writing skills could be important in OS success (Fogel 2006), so we included questions about this in our survey. We asked respondents to rate their own writing skills along with those of the rest of the development team on a 5-point scale (values 1–5), ranging from 1 equals poor to 5 equals excellent. Since writing is the main method for communicating for OS project members, it seems reasonable to think that good writing skills should favor success. The opposite appears to be the case, however, at least based on these subjective evaluations of writing skills. The mean value for the writing variable is 4.04 for AG projects and 3.80 for SG projects, and the difference is highly statistically significant (p-value 1.77, E-4), so AG respondents report better writing skills than SG respondents. Since educational levels are high for both AG and SG projects, we suspect that most OS developers write reasonably well. In any case, writing skills are not a major factor for discriminating success from abandonment in our growth stage model.

Conclusion

The end of this chapter has nearly brought us to the end of our book, but two enjoyable things remain to be done. First, part III has covered a lot of ground, starting with our qualitative study of OSGeo and then describing our dependent variable, exploration of SF data alone, survey, analysis of our many hypotheses, and in this chapter, quantitative multivariate models of OSS success and abandonment in both stages. However, we still need to summarize and reflect on this substantial body of empirical research, and we have the pleasure of doing so in the following chapter, "Thinking About Part III: A Review of Our Empirical Research."

Second, the purpose of this chapter was to uncover key factors that lead to OSS success, and we did that for both the initiation and growth stages by using various statistical techniques, and then describing our findings. We still need to interpret our findings in the context of the many issues raised earlier. For example, what do our findings say about OSS in general, and can we now articulate design principles for OSS commons? How do our results apply to Internet collaborations involving content other than software, such as documents, music, or videos? Can Internet collaborations help solve global problems? Do evolving OSS institutions say anything about the evolution of our economic institutions as our economies become less industrial and more information oriented? Now that we have research results on which to base our answers, we will take up the satisfying task of exploring these and other questions in the book's conclusion, chapter 13.

12   Thinking about Part III: A Review of Our Empirical Research

We undertook this study because the power of openness in combination with the Internet's global reach excited us. As long ago as 2004, we understood that because of its phenomenal growth and impact, OSS might hold keys to understanding collaboration in the Internet era. Furthermore, studying OSS might help us recognize how these clues could be applied to solve problems in areas other than software. Thanks to a grant from the U.S. National Science Foundation, we were fortunate to be able to study OSS in substantial depth over the last five years.

To begin our study, we identified theoretical factors that might be important for success or abandonment of OSS projects (see part II). Next, we created ways to carefully define and accurately measure success and abandonment in our two stages of OSS project development: initiation and growth. Because of our interest in OSS projects as forms of online collective action—or more specifically, Internet-based collaboration—we wanted to be conservative in our measure(s) so that small projects developed and used by specialized groups of people along with large projects characterized by large numbers of developers and even larger numbers of users would both be identified as successful situations (see figure 3.2). Chapter 7 fully described how we operationalized and validated the success and abandonment measure that we use for the dependent variable in our statistical work. In chapter 8, we examined the SF data that we use for some of our independent variables, and in chapter 9, looked at how we created more independent variables from a survey we conducted, *The Survey on Free/ Libre and Open-Source Success*. There is no need for us to review our variables here, and readers unfamiliar with them can refer to the chapters mentioned above and table 9.6. Rather, in this chapter, we focus on the exciting discoveries we made in part III about OSS and Internet-based collaboration.

We begin with a short reminder of how we defined OSS commons success and abandonment in chapter 7. Next, we review chapter 8's analysis of the data from more than 107,000 OSS projects hosted on SF in 2006, and then highlight the major findings from chapter 10's analysis of the more than 1,400 survey responses we received from SF developers. Some readers may have noticed that some of the variables that had importance in chapter 10, where we systematically analyzed individual survey questions, did not reappear as significant in our models in chapter 11. We explain this curious result below, and summarize the overall statistical modeling results for the initiation and growth stages that are fully presented in chapter 11. All of this leads to a discussion of the OSS commons story that has emerged through our research. This process sets the stage for the final chapter, where we consider our findings in a broader context.

Investigating OSS Success Using SF 2006 Data

Chapter 7 reports our careful, systematic efforts to define a dependent variable that provides a robust measure of OSS commons success and abandonment for our two longitudinal stages. We combined the use and popularity aspects proposed by Crowston, Annabi, and Howison (2003) and Weiss (2005) with project life and death metrics (e.g., Robles-Martinez et al., 2003). These are conservative measures of ongoing collective action, because they define both projects that are developed and used by small, specialized groups of people (e.g., projects in bioinformatics) and projects with a large number of potential users and developers as success situations. Operationally, they utilize SF project data such as life span (calculated as the difference between the project start date and the data collection date), number of releases, first release date, last release date, and number of downloads.

In chapter 8 we used our success/abandonment measure to analyze 2006 SF data, and began to identify an initial model of success and abandonment in OSS commons. In both stages of that early model, initiation (before the first public release of software) and growth (after the first public release), three concepts helped to differentiate between success and abandonment in the SF population of OSS projects:

• A clearly defined vision for the software (H-T1)
• Software utility (H-T3a)
• Elements of leadership (leading by doing and clear goals—H-C6a and H-C6b)

In this chapter, we also described how three of our variables—the PII, downloads, and page visits—led us to those findings, but since we arrived at them partly through a process of deduction, we needed to verify those early findings through later work. In addition, we noted that the 2006 SF analysis alone was an incomplete model since there were many concepts we could not measure using just the 2006 SF data. Most of these missing concepts related to either community or institutional attributes in the IAD framework (chapter 3). This in turn motivated us to do the OSGeo case study in chapter 6 as well as the online survey work presented in chapters 9, 10, and 11. We will discuss the OSGeo case more as we look at our institutional findings below, but next we summarize the discoveries we made in chapter 10 by analyzing our survey questions alone.

Analyzing the *Survey on Free/Libre and Open-Source Success*

Chapter 9 fully describes how we conducted a random-sample survey of SF OSS developers in cooperation with the corporation that owns and manages SF. Although we received relatively low response rates, we gathered a total of over fourteen hundred responses that appear to be quite representative of the SF population. In chapter 10, we analyzed our survey responses alone, using contingency tables, and presented those results in detail. Here we simply summarize the most important and interesting findings from this work.

The Survey Results Support Our Earlier Findings

The analysis of survey responses supported our earlier chapter 8 findings, so we present that part of the analysis first. (Note that in the following discussions, the code in parentheses that follows the concept refers to a specific hypothesis that we first presented in the theoretical chapters found in part II.)

Vision (H-T1)

We asked six separate questions in our initiation and growth stage surveys related to a vision for the software. These questions asked about having goals for the software, plans for software functionality, and plans for software architecture. The answers produced highly statistically significant results supporting the idea that OSS projects that have goals and well-defined plans for the software are more likely to be successful, regardless of the stage.

Utility (H-T3a)

This was the most important finding in chapter 8 for the growth stage, using page visits and downloads as a measure. But in our survey we asked additional questions about functionality and software quality, which are both related to the utility of the product being developed. In chapter 10, we found both functionality and quality differentiated successful growth stage (SG) projects from abandoned growth stage (AG) ones with high statistical significance as well as high odds ratios.

Leadership

In both our initiation and growth stage surveys, we asked two central questions (four questions in total) about leadership. We asked how many hours the respondent worked on the project per week and if there was a technical leader who motivated others on the project. The responses produced statistically significant results that indicated leadership is more often associated with OSS success rather than abandonment. Although our survey asked many other questions related to leadership, there is no need to mention them here, other than to say that our chapter 8 findings about leadership were well supported by our survey results in chapters 10 and 11.

Other Interesting Results Based on Survey Responses Alone

Granularity (H-T2b)

In chapter 8 we had no way to test the task granularity hypothesis (see table 4.1), but in chapter 10 we found highly significant statistical support suggesting that SG projects had higher numbers of fine-scaled tasks in place for potential contributors to undertake compared to AG projects.

Limited Competition (H-T4)

This hypothesis proposes that OSS commons will be more successful when there is limited or no competition. We could not address this hypothesis in chapter 8 because of a lack of data. Our findings in chapter 10 suggest the opposite relationship than expected in the growth stage: SG projects are more frequently found in environments where there is more competition, not less, compared AG projects. Yet the response rate for this question was moderate (73 percent), and the answer counts and distributions in the contingency table data suggest that the factor is minor in its influence.

Collaborative Technologies (RQ-T1)

In chapter 8, we reported that the use of bug tracker and forum technologies were the second most important discriminating variables in SG and AG comparisons, and that these technologies are more widely used in SG projects. The use of these technologies provides evidence of a vibrant community discussing software-related issues. In chapter 10 (table 10.2), we found that other collaborative technologies—external Web sites, developer email lists, and user email lists—used to convey project planning information were more readily utilized in SG compared to AG projects. It thus appears that these tools are essential components for building community (the most crucial factor for growth stage success) and also provide evidence of community participation.

Financial Backing (H-C8a)

We discovered that financial support is more important in the growth stage than in the initiation stage. In initiation, there is weak support for the idea that financial backing helps projects become successful, but in growth, projects that have financial support are much more likely to be successful than those that do not.

Project Complexity (Code Complexity; H-T2d)

Related to this hypothesis, we found the opposite relationship than anticipated. Less complex code is associated with AG projects, and more complex code is associated with SG projects. We think this finding suggests a natural evolutionary factor in SG projects—the more and longer the software is worked on, the more rich and complex the code base will become.

Sociocultural Heterogeneity (RQ-C1a)

Our survey question about the geographic location of team members for the growth stage revealed some *extremely* intriguing results. We assumed projects made up of developers from one town, one state, or one province would be more alike culturally than those that are more geographically distributed. As we reported in chapter 10, we found that of the 275 growth stage projects with more than one developer, 52 percent of the SG projects (99 out of 190 in that class) were multicontinental projects (meaning, actually, North America and Europe for the most part). This indicates that sociocultural heterogeneity is not a barrier to success.

In addition, we discovered in chapter 8's analysis that adding even one more developer to a growth stage project raises the likelihood that the project will be successful, and this is a causal factor. Our interesting multicontinental geographic finding suggests that OSS teams are often connecting to an additional developer via the Internet. As we reported in chapter 11, we also specifically asked respondents about whether they found other team members through the Internet. Ninety-seven SG projects and only thirteen AG projects responded affirmatively, and this difference between AG and SG projects is highly statistically significant.

Here is a key point. These two questions—the geographic location and whether teams found additional members on the Internet—strongly suggest that either SF, Google, or other search engines frequently allow people with similar passions, interests, needs, and capabilities to *find* each other, even though they are located far apart. Our evidence strongly indicates that these search systems are acting as an Internet-based intellectual matchmaker of sorts. We think this is a very important and interesting finding, demonstrating how the Internet is linking people with similar interests across time and place.

Institutional Attributes

In chapter 6, we undertook a qualitative study of OSGeo to better understand OSS communities and institutions, and help inform the development of our survey. OSGeo is a confederation of OSS projects with a nonprofit foundation that supports and shelters the member projects. We found that most of the seven OSGeo projects we studied had managed to build strong communities. In terms of institutions, we saw that despite the institutional complexity of the overarching OSGeo foundation itself, most projects had few, if any, formal rules. Although these projects had variation in their institutional structures, the rules usually took the form of social norms, and many rules were built into and automated by the software versioning system that projects use. The OSGeo study provided the basis for many of our institutional attribute survey questions, and in the following paragraphs, we highlight some key survey results.

Chapter 10 presented evidence that helps to reject the friction hypothesis (H-I4), which states that as institutional systems become more formal, the more likely it is that programmers will abandon the project. In fact, we discovered statistically significant proof supporting the opposite relationship: that there are differences between AG and SG, and it is in the SG class where more formalized governance situations are more often found.

Finally, in chapter 10, there is slight statistical evidence suggesting that SG projects offer more democratic participation to at least some of the developers on major project decisions compared to AG projects. We found that the vast majority of the projects in both classes, however, fall under the benevolent dictator category, and hence the variable is not important in the multivariate analysis in chapter 11.

Unsupported Hypotheses in the Initiation Stage

The list of unsupported hypotheses is much larger than the one reported at the end of chapter 8, because in chapter 10 (via our survey) we have measures for *all* the hypotheses and research questions we presented in chapters 3, 4, and 5 (tables 3.2, 4.1, 4.2, and 5.5). For brevity, we will not repeat each hypothesis or research question posed; we'll just summarize by concept (for details, see chapter 10).

Several concepts do not help to distinguish between success and abandonment in the initiation stage because they are commonly found across all projects in both classes.

Modularity (H-T2a)

A vast majority of AI and SI projects report they are modular in design.

Project Complexity (H-T2c and H-T2d)

Complex projects (as measured by code complexity and previously closed source) are found in both successful and abandoned situations.

Utility (H-T3a)

There are no statistically significant distributional differences in respondent's assessment of the functionality or quality of the product they created in the initiation stage. This is one finding that differs from chapter 8's results, where utility was found to be important based on deductions about the PII variable.

Limited Competition (H-T4)

No statistically significant distributional differences were identified between AI and SI projects. Some projects had significant competition in each class, and some had little competition.

Collaborative Infrastructure (RQ-T1)

We discovered that successful projects (SI) advertised more and had, on average, higher-quality external Web sites.

Developer Motivations (H-C1 through H-C5)

We saw high levels of developers motivated because they are users of the software (H-C1, or the von Hippel hypothesis). User-centered innovation is widespread in both AI and SI projects. In addition, we found no differences between SI and AI along other motivational dimensions, such as paid participation (H-C2), serious leisure (H-C3), learning (H-C4b), skill signaling (H-C4c), or helping the OSS cause (H-C5).

Developer Skill Attributes (H-C4a)

We also investigated education levels, having professional developers on the team, and assessment of writing skills—and found no distributional differences between AI and SI projects across these dimensions.

Trust among Developers (as a Component of Social Capital) (H-C7b)

We found that the vast majority of the two- or higher-developer projects have established either some or a lot of trust. Very few exhibit little trust. Moreover, the distributions along these dimensions are similar in AI and SI contexts.

Heterogeneity/Homogeneity (RQ-C1)

For the initiation stage, we saw no evidence that heterogeneity (sociocultural, motivational, or asset) has negative effects on collaboration.

Institutional Attributes (H-I4 and H-I5)

Neither the friction hypothesis (H-I4, or that more formalized institutional systems will lead to abandonment) nor the Debian hypothesis (H-I5, or the idea that as OSS projects grow in terms of developer team size, formal institutions will become a necessary condition in order to avoid abandonment) was supported in the initiation stage.

Regarding the friction hypothesis, we found that the majority of projects in AI and SI report either no governance or very informal governance. We did investigate this question further, and developed a contingency table (not shown) for projects with two or more developers. The results reveal a more equalized distribution across projects for the answers no governance, very informal (governance, or in other words, social norms), informal, and formal. As expected, a high number of the no governance responses drop out when one-developer projects are removed. But even after this, the distributional differences in this table between AI and SI were not statistically different.

Democratic Collective Choice (RQ-I7)

In this analysis, we discovered slightly higher proportions of benevolent dictator projects in the SI class compared to the AI class, but these results are just under the 90 percent statistically significant standard. We also found that the benevolent dictator governance structure, where this leader makes all major project decisions (as opposed to one that provides some of all developers with some rights, authorities, or voice in the project's direction), dominates both SI and AI projects. This finding, like some others, is accentuated because of the large number of one-developer projects.

Finally, we did not investigate several concepts in chapter 9's initiation stage survey because chapter 8 already provided solid evidence, and/or we were trying to keep the initiation survey as short as possible. These include:

- Granularity (H-T2b): Not asked due to survey brevity needs
- Critical or foundational infrastructure (H-T3b): Not supported in chapter 8
- Preferred technologies (H-T3c): Not supported in chapter 8
- License choice (GPL versus non-GPL) (RQ-I5): Not supported in chapter 8

Now we turn to a similar summary of growth stage findings based on chapter 10.

Unsupported Hypotheses in the Growth Stage

Like in our initiation stage analysis, a number of variables were not important in distinguishing between SG and AG projects. We note which ones they were here, and briefly explain why this is the case.

Modularity (H-T2a)

Like initiation, the overwhelming majority of projects in both AG and SG classes reported that they are modular in design. This is clearly a crucial element in OSS, but not one that distinguishes between success and abandonment.

Project Complexity (Formerly Closed Source; H-T2c)

In chapter 10, we reported that there are no statistically significant differences between AG and SG projects with regard to whether their code was originally closed-source software. This is good news for closed-source software projects that are considering opening up their code.

Critical or Foundational Infrastructure (H-T3b) and Preferred Technologies (H-T3c)

We did not investigate these hypotheses in chapter 10, because the findings were so conclusive in chapter 8 that they are not factors that distinguish between SG and AG.

Developer Motivations (User-Centered Innovation, Paid, Serious Leisure, Learning, Skill Signaling, and Helping the OSS Cause; H-C1 though H-C5)

We were unable to investigate these hypotheses in chapter 8, because there were no SF variables that captured motivational aspects. Yet our survey specifically asked about these motivations, and here we had mixed results.

Regarding von Hippel's hypothesis, we saw similar results to what we found in initiation: user-driven innovation is clearly a motivator in both AG and SG projects, but doesn't help to distinguish between them.

Findings related to the "paid programmer" hypothesis were mixed. On the one hand, we found that individual respondents did not report financial benefit as a strong motivator for participation, but on the other hand, we found that having paid developers on the OSS team did correlate with success in the growth stage.[1]

The serious leisure motivation is plainly a motivation for some of our respondents, but the related question had a relatively low response rate, and thus does not help to distinguish between SG and AG.

We found that a significant majority in both AG and SG report they (and their team members) are participating so that they can learn and improve their skills (chapter 10). Moreover, skill signaling shows up as a motivation for some projects in both classes, but it is not as important a motivation as learning. Neither of these motivations, though, helps distinguish between AG and SG.

Finally, a vast majority of respondents answered favorably to the helping the OSS cause motivation in both AG and SG situations. This variable too does not aid in distinguishing between AG and SG projects.

Developer Skill Attributes (H-C4a)

This was another area that we couldn't investigate in chapter 8 due to lack of adequate data, but in our survey we asked questions about three characteristics: respondent and team education levels; whether the respondent and the team are professional developers; and a self-assessment of respondent and team writing skills. None of these helped to distinguish between SG and AG in our analysis in chapter 10. Education and writing skill levels are generally high across the board in AG and SG projects, and although it seems intuitive that programming skill should help distinguish between SG and AG, our results show that it isn't the case. Still, we need to be cautious with these results for they reflect only the respondent's assessment of the team's skills.

We also found in the initiation stage analysis that knowledge continuity was important in distinguishing between SI and AI. Interestingly, this is not the case in the
growth stage. We saw that a high percentage of respondents in both SG and AG projects had participated the entire time since a project was initiated on SF.

Social Capital (Face-to-Face Meetings, Trust, and Reciprocity; H-C7a, H-C7b, and RQ-C2)
Like other community variables, we had no means to test this in chapter 8, so we
addressed this in our surveys. But like other variables in this section, responses did
not align themselves with the AG and SG classes. A rather large majority of both AG
and SG projects report *never* having times where all members meet face-to-face, and
a sizable proportion in both classes note situations where at least some of their
members either never or only rarely (e.g., once a year) meet face-to-face. Our case
study in chapter 10 also found that face-to-face interactions were not important. This
body of evidence suggests that the significance of face-to-face meetings appears to be
diminished in OSS compared to what is reported in distributed work and virtual team
theory.

Similarly, having trust is about equally distributed in AG and SG projects. And
finally, in a finding different from the initiation stage, the existence of specific or
general reciprocity doesn't seem to differentiate SG from AG projects.

Heterogeneity/Homogeneity (RQ-C1)
We've already looked at the interesting finding related to sociocultural heterogeneity
(that it doesn't get in the way). We also saw no evidence that interest, motivational,
or asset heterogeneity hinders collaborative success.

A Review of Our Final Multivariate Models

At this point in our studies, we had developed our success/abandonment measure for
our dependent variable, and had conducted our survey and analyzed the results on a
stand-alone basis. We also had found ways, using survey data and SF data, to create
measures for all the independent variables that we discovered through our literature
review and thinking, described in part II. Finally, literally after years of work, we were
ready to do a multivariate analysis to discover which factors were important for discriminating between success and abandonment among OSS projects overall. By overall,
we mean factors that are strong enough and apply to a sufficient number of projects
to be common elements for distinguishing success from abandonment when all OSS
projects on SF are considered.

To prepare for our multivariate analysis, we updated our dependent variable and
the most important independent variables from our chapter 8 studies, using 2009 SF
data gathered from the Notre Dame SF repository. We did this work to ensure that all

the data we were using came from the same time period as our survey. Although our final models analyzed only 683 projects in the initiation stage and 720 projects in the growth stage—because those were the numbers of survey responses we received—these data appear to be quite representative of the SF population in 2009, and thus we believe that our findings apply to the entire SF population. Furthermore, we contend that SF was probably the most representative data on the greater OSS population (see chapter 7), so we believe that the statistical analysis we performed in chapter 11, taken together with our other empirical research, is arguably the most comprehensive understanding of OSS to date. We summarize the results of chapter 11's analysis in the following paragraphs (and tables 12.2 and 12.3 below), but first we describe how our multivariate analysis in chapter 11 differs from our analysis of survey responses alone in chapter 10.

Why Our Chapter 10 Findings Differ from Our Chapter 11 Models

Those who have read chapter 11—or those who read the summary of chapter 11 presented below—may ask, Why are some variables that correlate with success or abandonment in chapter 10 not identified as important in the multivariate models in chapter 11?

There are several reasons. First, statistically significant differences between successful and abandoned projects sometimes appear in chapter 10, but they are not influential in the multivariate analysis because the survey question applied to only a small subset of the SF population. This occurs frequently in the community and institutional questions (IAD framework; see chapter 3) that address teams of two or more developers. A significant number of our survey responses are from single-developer projects—446 out of 683 cases (65 percent) in the initiation survey, and 418 out of 720 cases (58 percent) in the growth survey. Therefore, some of the institutional or community level (IAD) questions about collaboration with other developers do not apply in these instances. We identified a statistical difference, in other words, for projects with more than one developer, but there are so many cases where the question does not apply that the relationship gets muted in the multivariate analysis.

Second, sometimes the chi-square test for differences between abandoned and successful projects reveals a significant distributional distinction in chapter 10, and we have a high response rate for that question (e.g., the first issue above does not apply), but the number of projects that answer the question in a particular way is relatively small. In the initiation survey, for example, significant differences exist between AI and SI responses in one of the questions regarding project financing, but only 141 (22 percent) of our 632 responses for that question said they had financing prior to their first release. As a result, the differences between AI and SI responses do not apply to enough projects to be identified as an influential factor in the multivariate analysis, where we look for factors that apply to OSS projects overall.

Table 12.1

Contingency table for downloads in the growth stage survey

	Downloads < 1,000	Downloads > 1,000	Odds
AG	252	98	2.57
SG	89	281	0.32
		Odds ratio	8.10

Lastly, in order for a variable to be identified as important in the multivariate modeling, there not only needs to be statistically significant differences between the answers for success and abandonment cases, but the odds ratio needs to be large as well. For instance, in a two-by-two table, the diagonals in one direction need to be relatively large numbers and the diagonals in the other direction need to be relatively small in order for the variable to be detected in multivariate modeling as a key factor.

Table 12.1 provides an example related the number of downloads, the most important variable in the multivariate growth stage model in chapter 11. In that table, the values along the diagonals are high in one direction (e.g., large numbers of AG projects having downloads less than a thousand as well as large numbers of SG projects having downloads greater than a thousand) and low in the other direction (small numbers of AG projects having downloads greater than a thousand and small numbers of SG projects having downloads less than a thousand). This kind of structure results in high odds ratios. AG projects in this case have 8.1 times the chance of having less than a thousand downloads as SG projects, so downloads has substantial power to distinguish successful from abandoned projects. In these kinds of situations, where there are large and small numbers in opposite diagonals, the variables stand out as more important in the multivariate analysis.

For these reasons, variables identified in chapter 10 as statistically significant sometimes do not appear as important in the multivariate analysis. This is not to say that the chapter 10 findings are unimportant; it just means that the important chapter 10 findings missing from the chapter 11 findings are not major factors when the entire population of SF projects is considered as a whole.

Overall Results for the Initiation Stage

Our initiation stage models, presented in chapter 11, have only moderate ability to distinguish between successful and abandoned projects. The classification tree model correctly classified 488 out of 683 projects (71 percent) with about a 30 percent improvement (kappa 0.30) over a random classification of these projects. The most important variable turned out to be the number of hours worked on the project by the survey respondent (see table 11.1), but the model also showed that other elements of leadership, like having a vision and goals for the project, had the power to distinguish between successful and abandoned projects, thus verifying our chapter 8 and 10 findings.

What we find striking is that chapter 8 and chapter 11 use completely different measures as well as data to capture leadership elements: chapter 8 uses SF project metadata to come to this conclusion, and chapter 11 uses measures of leadership captured by our survey questions. Our multivariate analysis in chapter 11 shows that these elements of project leadership—leading by doing or hard work (finding 11.1) and other elements of leadership (finding 11.2) are key for getting a project to a first public release.

In addition to these crucial factors, we found that marketing the project and having someone on the project since its beginning (see table 9.6, marketing and continuity) both had weak, but statistically significant abilities to distinguish between successful and abandoned projects (table 11.2). We therefore include these two variables as minor factors in table 12.2 below. For convenience, we list the hypotheses supported by our initiation stage multivariate analysis here. OSS commons will be more successful in the initiation stage when:

H-T1: The project had a relatively clearly defined vision and a mechanism to communicate this vision early in the project's life, before getting to the growth stage.
H-C6a: The team has one or more leaders who generate excitement, and demonstrate leadership "through doing."
H-C6b: The project has well-articulated and clear goals established by the project leader(s).

Overall Results for the Growth Stage

Our growth stage multivariate models in chapter 11 have a much better ability to differentiate between successful and abandoned projects than our initiation stage models. The growth stage classification tree model was able to correctly classify 448 out of 500 projects, for an impressive 90 percent correct classification rate. The model improved classification rates over a chance classification by 74 percent (kappa 0.74). The most important variables in the growth stage in descending order are downloads, tracker_reports, OS_experience, leadership_with hours, and community (see tables 9.6 and 11.4). We summarize our findings about these variables below.

Downloads

In chapter 8, we discovered that downloads and page visits were the most important variables for distinguishing successful from abandoned projects in the growth stage. Our chapter 11 analysis included many more variables than our chapter 8 analysis because it included variables derived from our survey results, but downloads remained at the top in terms of importance.

Our theoretical discussion in chapter 4 paid great attention to the role of group size in OSS development. There are two dimensions here: the development team's size and the size of the broader community. The size of the development team was one of our most important findings in chapter 8 for the growth stage. We found evidence that increasing team size is a causal factor for success in the growth stage, even though the average team is still small (two to three developers). Regarding the second dimension, we believe a greater number of downloads indicates that the software has more utility for users, and thus is associated with a larger user community. Therefore, because downloads are associated with success, a larger user community is also associated with success.

Tracker Reports

The tracker reports variable represents the total number of bug reports, feature requests, patches, and support requests for a project, and like downloads, this variable was at the top of the list of key variables in our chapter 8 and chapter 11 analyses. We believe that the number of tracker reports correlates with the existence of a broader end user community. Because a higher number of tracker reports is also associated with success, we have additional evidence that a larger community is associated with success.

OSS Experience

We investigated several dimensions of growth stage skill, such as team levels of education and whether team members were professional developers or not. The dimension of skill that stands out most, however, is the concept of OSS experience (finding 11.4). Our chapter 11 classification tree analysis placed this variable among the most important for determining success versus abandonment, but our logistic regression analysis indicated that this variable was not statistically significant. We believe that this contradiction exists because classification trees can model more complex interactions than logistic regression.

To illustrate this ability to model complex interactions, higher values for experience seem to lead to higher rates of abandonment in some situations and higher rates of success in others, but in almost all cases, OS_experience appears deeper in the trees after the other major variables have exerted their influence. Due to this complexity, more study will be needed to understand the precise effect of this variable. Open-source experience nevertheless stands out in terms of importance in the growth stage.

Leadership (with Hours)

Finding 11.3 reports the same kind of relationships for leadership as we saw in the initiation stage results above. We were able to show that elements of good leadership such as hard work, good planning, goal establishment and articulation, and project management (captured in terms of good documentation and a quality Web presence) are highly correlated with SG projects. Moreover, we found evidence that leadership by a technical person is associated with success. While we are unable to prove leadership as a causal variable for success with the data we had from our growth survey, we were able to demonstrate, with high confidence, causation in our initiation stage analysis. By inference we are confident that elements of leadership are likely causal variables in growth as well.

Community

The community variable measured both the number and range of different types of nonfinancial contributions to projects. Our analysis of the community variable supports the idea that contributions and participation by those who are not formal project members are correlated with, and likely a major causal factor in, OSS growth stage success. When taken together with the downloads and tracker reports variables that almost certainly indicate a larger community, the community variable provides the linchpin for the emergent OSS commons story, because it supplies the direct link between the community's size and improvements to the software. We tell this story in the next section, but first we will simply list the most important hypotheses supported by our chapter 11 analysis. OSS commons will be more successful in the growth stage when:

H-T1: The project had a relatively clearly defined vision and a mechanism to communicate this vision early in the project's life, before getting to the growth stage.[2]
H-T3a: The software produced has higher utility as perceived by the end user community.
H-C4a: The programmers on the team are highly skilled.
H-C6a: The team has one or more leaders who generate excitement, and demonstrate leadership through doing.
H-C6b: The project has well-articulated and clear goals established by the project leader(s).

The Emergent OSS Commons Story

The work we have presented in this book shows that as we expected, the important factors associated with success and abandonment differ between the two longitudinal stages found in OSS projects. Achieving success in the initiation stage—that is, producing a first public release—requires a different set of project attributes than what is needed in time periods after that first release. Chapter 11, which builds on all the work previously done in this book, reveals parsimonious multivariate statistical models of success and abandonment for these two stages that particularly in the growth stage, have fairly strong explanatory power.

In the initiation stage, the most important factors for success originate with the project's designated or de facto leader/developer, who often is the only developer on the project, but nevertheless may be interacting with a community of users. Our data show that those projects with leaders who devote larger numbers of hours to the project are more likely to produce a first release. In addition, putting the elements of our leadership index variable—a plan for architecture and functionality, project goals, good documentation, and a good project Web site—into practice is crucial in the initiation stage, because some projects get contributions from volunteers before the first release, and this in turn helps to lay the foundation for success in the growth stage. We have found evidence that the putting in the hours and leadership variables are not merely correlated with success but also are causes of it in the initiation stage.

In the growth stage, we discovered that although about 15 to 20 percent of the successful projects are of interest only to small audiences (and have few downloads as a result), most successful growth (SG) projects have over a thousand downloads and are of interest to perhaps two hundred users at a minimum. The story seems to be that once a project has its first release (i.e., becomes successful in initiation), then the leadership skills of the project's development team—in addition to the software's utility itself—begin to attract users, and in some cases, at least one additional development team member or other community contributors. Working under (typically) a benevolent dictator type governance structure, existing developers, users, and/or new development team members make contributions that improve the software, which creates a virtuous circle leading to continuing improvements and continuing success. In cases where this virtuous circle does not occur, particularly in ones where the team or individual developer has some prior OSS experience, our data suggest that the developer(s) sees that the project is not achieving what it set out to do and the project is frequently abandoned.[3] In the growth stage, we have found evidence that leadership, gaining developers, and financing are causal factors for success.

To some readers, this story may seem obvious because it is in line with conventional wisdom about the OSS phenomenon. But we remind these readers that our findings are based on a voluminous amount of empirical data covering over 170,000 OSS projects hosted on SF, along with our own survey data of over 1,400 developers. In chapter 7, we emphasized that these projects stored on SF are perhaps the best representation we have of the entire OSS project population (see chapter 7). This is, to our knowledge, the first time that the OSS story has been based on enough empirical evidence to suggest that it applies to the entire OSS phenomenon, as opposed to subsets of the OSS population (e.g., large, high-profile OSS projects). Our findings also remain consistent over a significant time period—nearly the three years from August 2006 to May 2009—indicating that the OSS phenomenon we describe is not only widespread but has constancy over time as well. In addition, having these findings align so well with the conventional wisdom of OSS gives us confidence that the work we have carefully constructed over the last five years has yielded strong, robust results.

We also want to point out that we have uncovered results that are surprising because they either disagree with or shed new light on ideas that many may have assumed to be obvious. For example, some factors like modularity of the software, high levels of trust between project members, developer skill, and high levels of education do not appear to distinguish between success and abandonment. This is not to say that these factors are unimportant but rather that they are common to most OSS projects and therefore do not help distinguish successful from abandoned ones. Furthermore, other often-discussed elements of OSS projects such as the project license, type of software, and programming languages used simply do not seem to be important factors, because both successful and abandoned projects are rather evenly distributed throughout all kinds of licenses, types of software, and different programming languages. We also found strong evidence indicating that collaboration happens across large geographic areas (e.g., continents), and that these teams find collaborators over the Internet who are passionate about the same technical functions to be developed.

Summarizing all our findings is difficult. We throughout this book we have tested over forty theoretically based hypotheses (see tables 3.2, 4.1, 4.2, and 5.5). Readers skimming this chapter are encouraged to review chapter 10, where we analyze these hypotheses one by one. We also present tables 12.2 and 12.3 below, briefly depicting our key findings for the two OSS stages based on the empirical work presented in this book.

Conclusion

We have completed our presentation of the empirical work, and this book is nearly finished. In chapter 1, however, we revealed that our motivations for studying OSS were broad. We wanted to understand OSS and find design guidelines that might help OSS community members create successful projects and avoid abandonment, but we also wanted to understand if the collaboration methods used in OSS could be translated to other types of digital collaborations that might help solve worldwide problems, such as climate change, or food and water scarcity. We also wondered—because of the incredible economic value created by OSS projects—whether emerging OSS institutional structures might foreshadow changes in our economic institutions. Could the power of openness in combination with the Internet foster transformations in the world?

We believe that our empirical studies have made substantial progress toward understanding OSS projects, and in the final chapter, we will present design principles for

Table 12.2
Summary of initiation stage (before first release) findings

Key factors that help to explain success over abandonment	Leadership by doing (working more hours)* Clear vision* Well-articulated goals*
Minor factors	Project marketing Knowledge continuity: Someone on the project since its early days Specific and general reciprocity higher in successful, multideveloper projects
Factors found in both successful and abandoned projects	Modularity Motivations: User-driven innovation and learning dominant; serious leisure and skill signaling less important High levels of social capital between developers Benevolent dictatorships are dominant
Other factors that do not seem to matter much	Task granularity: Establishing fine-scaled tasks The project contributes to critical or foundational infrastructure Preferred technologies (e.g., programming languages, certain databases, etc.) General licensing choice: GPL or non-GPL Complexity (e.g., originally closed source) Utility Competition Collaborative infrastructure (although there is not much variation in our SF data set here) Heterogeneity or homogeneity of developers Formalized institutions or governance structures

* Evidence that the finding is a "cause" of success.

Table 12.3
Summary of growth stage (after first release) findings

Key factors that help to explain success over abandonment	Utility as represented by downloads
	Group size: Slightly larger development teams and outside communities, although development team still can be small (2–3 people)*
	Clear project vision and goals established and articulated*
	Leadership by doing*
	OSS experience seems to stand out in circumstances where the project has not yet built a supportive end user community, but its effect is unclear at this time
	Marketing of the project
Minor factors	Granularity: Projects have small tasks ready for people who only can contribute small bits of time
	Financing is correlated with success*
	Motivations: User-driven innovation; learning and serious leisure are dominant; skill signaling less important; particular motives are not correlated with success, but a greater number of motives is
	More formalized institutions exist in a relatively small number of cases, but these tend to fall in the successful growth class
Factors found in both successful and abandoned projects	Modularity
	High levels of social capital between developers
	Benevolent dictatorships are dominant
	High levels of developer skill: High levels of education
	A majority of professional developers
Other factors that do not seem to matter	Developer skills (education levels, professional experience, and writing skills) do not seem to help discriminate between success and abandonment

* Evidence that the finding is a "cause" of success.

OSS commons and some suggestions for OSS users. We also hold that some of our empirical findings extend beyond OSS, so we discuss some of the theoretical implications of our study for commons theory, collective action theory, and Internet-based collaboration. Finally, we take up the quite speculative but stimulating task of applying some of our findings to hypothetical Internet collaborations in areas other than OSS, with an eye toward solving complex scientific, political, and social problems. The final chapter, "Our Study in Perspective," is, for us, the icing on the cake that took five years to make.

IV Conclusions

13 Our Study in Perspective

Historically, much of the research on OSS has focused on large development team, high-profile projects. These kinds of studies are indeed important and useful, but too much concentration on these unusually large projects may skew our understanding of what is really happening in the OSS phenomenon. In much of this study—with the exception of chapter 6—we have tried to use data sets on OSS that are more closely aligned with the entire population of OSS projects. The great majority of these projects are made up of small developer teams interacting with an external user community. Our primary goal for this study has been to investigate how teams of programmers, large or small, coupled with their associated user communities, are able to maintain collective action and continued productivity. The core research question we have asked is, again, What factors lead some OSS commons to continued success and others to abandonment?

By answering this question, we hoped to better understand not only OSS but also the power of openness and how it might be innovatively applied in the Internet era. We have almost reached the end of our story about our five-year research endeavor, but perhaps the best is yet to come. Here we gather the fruits of our labor— that is, our research results—taking the time to consider what they mean for OSS developers, OSS users, and scholars in various disciplines. We also indulge in some speculation about what our results may mean for Internet collaborations involving digital content other than software, and whether these collaborations might help solve global problems. We end with some ideas about what kind of research might naturally follow.

Some Practical Implications of Our Study

For OSS Developers

In our interactions with OSS developers at conferences and in our interviews, we have been asked numerous times, "Is there practical guidance you can provide to people already involved in or starting up new OSS projects?" and "Can you advise projects on what to do to avoid project abandonment?" To some degree we now think we can.

Here is our initiation (before first release) stage guidance, in order of importance:

1. Put in the hours. Work hard toward creating your first release.
2. Practice leadership by administering your project well, and thinking through and articulating your vision as well as goals for the project. Demonstrate your leadership through the hard work noted just above, and by working toward the vision and goals you have established for the project.
3. Establish a high-quality Web site to showcase and promote your project.
4. Create good documentation for your (potential) user and developer community.
5. Advertise and market your project, and communicate your plans and goals with the hope of getting help from others.
6. Realize that successful projects are found in both GPL-based and non-GPL-compatible situations.
7. Consider, at the project's outset, creating software that has the potential to be useful to a substantial number of users. A larger potential user community will help you later, should you get to the post-first-release growth stage. Most successful growth stage projects (perhaps 80 percent of them in our data set) have substantial numbers of users—we estimate a minimum of two hundred.

And here is our growth (after first release) stage guidance, also in order of importance:

1. Your goal should be to create a virtuous circle where others help to improve the software, thereby attracting more users and other developers, which in turn leads to more improvements in the software, and so on. Focus on building that community through leadership and project administration. Elements that appear to help are many of the same crucial leadership factors identified in the initiation stage: lead through doing—put in the hours and provide technical leadership; maintain architectural and functionality goals and plans; communicate these plans via the project Web site and developer/user email lists or other communication methods; and maintain and keep up to date a high-quality project Web site.
2. Advertise and market your project, so others know about it and you can continue building a broader community. Our data show that successful growth projects are frequently ones where at least one new developer has been added to the team in the growth stage. Moreover, most successful growth stage projects have established a user community that actively interacts with the development team.
3. Make sure you have some small tasks available to do for those who have limited time to contribute.
4. Competition seems to favor success, so welcome it if and when it occurs.

5. Projects with financing have much higher success rates, so consider accepting offers of financing or paid developers.

6. Keep institutions (rules and project governance) as lean and informal as possible, but do not be afraid to move toward more formalization if it appears necessary.

For OSS Consumers

We are often asked what users can do to choose the best or most cost-effective OSS software. Much of this decision has to do with the functionality needed by the user, which only the user can assess by reading project documentation or trying the software. We can make suggestions, however, that may help to choose software that is long-lived and regularly improved over time. The more the characteristics below you find, the more likely the software will endure and improve in the future.

1. The longevity of a project is probably related to the level of community that has been developed, but more analysis of our data is needed to be certain. Nevertheless, consumers should check for the following characteristics:

a. Does the project have at least a thousand downloads?

b. Are users participating via the bug tracker and email lists?

c. Are there goals and plans for future software releases listed on the Web site or in project email archives?

d. Does the development team respond quickly to questions, reflecting that they are working hard on the project?

e. Does the project have a good Web site, user documentation, and developer documentation?

2. A larger development team is a positive sign

3. Formal governance structures are not a necessity for successful projects, but may be a positive sign.

Some Theoretical Implications of Our Study

In addition to our desire to present some practical insight about OSS commons, we also hope to inform theory related to OSS, Internet-based collaboration, and collective action. Here we describe some of the most important theoretical insights we gained through this study.

Motivations for Participating in OSS

Returning to our key element of analysis—the OSS developer we described in chapter 3—our data confirm the commonly understood motivations for OSS participation. Across both successful and abandoned projects, we found user-centered need (von Hippel 2005a) as a common driving motive. Developers frequently need the software for personal use, and quite often the organization they work for needs the software. Some developers participate as serious leisure or to learn, or both. Moreover, many developers in our survey signaled their belief that they should be able to modify the software they use and mentioned their desire to give back to the community. We found, somewhat surprisingly, that the idea of demonstrating programming skill to the broader community and financial benefit appear to be less significant motivations. From a theoretical perspective, the most important finding is that no particular motivation seems to be strongly associated with success or abandonment, but the higher the number of motivations reported for an individual programmer or project, the higher the success rates in both the initiation and growth stages. In other words, having more motivations present is associated with higher success rates.

OSS Commons and Collective Action Theory

This study provides strong statistically based evidence indicating that the combination of Web-based search engines like Google and hosting sites like SF acts as an intellectual matchmaker of sorts. Success in OSS projects is strongly correlated with finding like-minded and interested individuals over the Internet, and then establishing working relationships, often across continents. As David Karpf (2010, 12) puts it, SF could be considered a "power-law hub" for OSS software. These are Internet spaces that, according to Karpf, offer "value to their users in direct proportion to the network effects provided by large crowds of similar users" (12). We believe our evidence in this study offers strong evidence to support one of Karpf's main contentions: "Power law topology facilitates a revised logic of online collective action" (13).

OSS, Face-to-Face Meetings, and Social Capital

We have uncovered proof suggesting that face-to-face meetings—something commonly thought to be significant in building social capital in traditional commons settings and virtual collaboration—is not as important in OSS commons. Although in a majority of cases either little or no face-to-face contact occurred between multiple-member development teams, we found trust—a concept considered extremely important in more traditional environmental commons settings—had been built across nearly all projects. Results from our interviews with OSGeo developers specifically asking about the need for face-to-face interaction indicated it was not as critical as prior theory would suggest, and the survey data we collected after those interviews confirm this conclusion. With the help of communication technologies in the era of the Web, email, IRC, text messaging, and Internet-based telephony, the pillars of social capital can be constructed without direct interaction.

For some readers, this point is contentious. We are not, to be clear, claiming that face-to-face interaction is *no* help in forging social capital. It most certainly is. Meeting someone you have been working with over dinner or a beer and having a laugh or two surely helps make connections as well as establish trust. But our findings illustrate that this kind of interaction is not a necessary condition for establishing elements of social capital in OSS commons, given all the ways we can communicate over the Internet today.

OSS and Group Size

As we noted in part III, in addition to the development team, group size in OSS involves the end user community. People interested in OSS have long been aware of the role of this community, to the point where some refer to OSS projects as "community managed" (see, e.g., the body of work by Siobhan O'Mahony in our references). We found strong evidence to suggest that interaction by and with the broader user community is associated with OSS success. This brings us to a key point: we found this to be the case using two different studies with two entirely different data sets. We uncovered proof of this in chapter 8, where we relied on 2006 SF project data only, and came to this conclusion in chapter 11 as well, where we used a different time slice of SF—2009—coupled with survey data we collected ourselves. Returning to our theoretical discussion on group size, our work provides strong support for Linus's law over the group size theories introduced by Olson or Brooks in the context of digital, online, OSS commons. That is, in OSS commons, having more participants appears to be a positive factor for improving the software and sustaining the collective action.

OSS Institutions

Regarding our secondary goal of studying the institutional structure that underpins OSS projects, we saw that the large majority of OSS projects are governed mainly by informal norms. In our empirical work (see chapter 10), we found strong evidence that formalized systems of governance structures and operational rules are resisted in OSS, and that more informal social norms guide how work is done. We also discovered that many OSS programmers do not tend to think in terms of formalized operational rules, because like access rights to the code base, many of these rules are automatically enforced by the version control system in which the software code is stored.

We did uncover statistical proof that suggests, to some degree, that projects evolve toward more formalized structures as development teams get larger. Yet in many cases, more formalized means that many of the rules that structure or guide collaboration are now simply informal, rather than very informal, or that a few people have a say in major project decisions instead of only one person. We also found that these more formalized systems were frequently associated with successful projects as opposed to abandoned ones, which goes against our expectation that formalized rules (these frictions) might lead projects toward abandonment.

Turning to higher-level project decision making and the governance structures around it (e.g., collective choice), it is clear from our analysis that the benevolent dictator model dominates in OSS. In other words, a designated leader, by default or perhaps selected, makes the bulk of the major project decisions. This finding is not in line with environmental commons governance theory, which suggests that commons are better sustained when group members are involved at key decision junctures (e.g., Ostrom 1990).

What about Open-Content Collaborations and Addressing Global Problems?

In chapter 1, we said that one of our major motivations for undertaking the research presented in this book was to discover whether the principles that keep OSS software developers collaborating could be applied to a broader set of open-content projects. Open-content projects are similar to OSS software projects in that some kind of digital product—like written text, music, photographs, or video—is made available to the public at no monetary cost. Examples include Wikipedia, a free online encyclopedia; YouTube, a site to upload and view video for free; MIT Open Courseware, which makes educational content freely available; Science Commons related projects spearheaded by the Creative Commons organization, which is working to speed the process of scientific research; and countless others that many readers may have encountered.[1] When we started our research, we wondered whether the principles that allow complex software to be produced, often by volunteers, might be applied to open-content projects that could help solve difficult problems facing humanity. Although we have not yet studied open content as rigorously as we have studied OSS software (see below), we believe we have some insight into this question. But first let us imagine a hypothetical open-content collaboration.

Could Open-Content Collaboration Help Save Coral Reefs?

A few years ago we had a conversation with a woman—let's call her Kathy—who was then a public sector manager of a coral reef conservation area in the United States. Kathy described the challenges she and other managers faced because of climate change and other issues like overvisitation by humans that cause damage to coral reefs. The problems, she said, were similar in many parts of the world, but coral reef managers were quite limited in the degree they could collaborate or learn from one another, in part because of the vast geographic distances that separated them. Moreover, Kathy explained, in her eyes there was a significant gap between the research products coming out of academia, and the problems she and other coral reef managers dealt with in the field. In hearing about our research, Kathy wondered if OSS-like collaboration might aid this group of geographically dispersed people—coral reef policy analysts and managers—who faced similar threats and had similar needs.

It is not difficult to envision the creation of an SF-like collaborative platform that could assist Kathy and others like her. In this online commons, academics, policy analysts, and public administrators could share work products, and in some contexts also develop new derivatives from the work done by others in similar contexts. For example, a spreadsheet analyzing cost-benefit calculus done by a coral reef analyst in New Zealand might be modified for a similar location in North America. Or a white paper describing a local solution to a pressing coral reef problem might be of interest to others in similar settings elsewhere in the world. Or perhaps a list created by reef managers in the field outlining the top twenty or thirty key research questions they think are important could be shared. Various postings could be voted on and prioritized by the group. This dynamic list could then inform the research agendas of relevant academics and research scientists.[2] In short, we can imagine an open-content commons that contributes to solving a global environmental problem, such as the degeneration of coral reefs, but does our study of OSS commons help us to understand how to create such a commons?

What Our Study Says about Open-Content Collaborations

To begin, we will summarize the similarities and differences between OSS software and open-content projects.

Similarities

1. Both use the Internet as a communications medium.
2. Both create digital products.
3. Both are Internet-based collective action/commons settings that build virtual communities.
4. Both use innovative licensing under existing copyright law.
5. Volunteers and paid participants could contribute in both settings.
6. The digital products created may be valuable in monetary terms to both users and society.

Differences

1. OSS software developers (in our data) are mostly male (98 percent) software professionals between the ages of twenty-two and thirty-five years old. Open-content participants are likely to be much more heterogeneous.
2. OSS software programs provide an objective measure of the collaborative outcome. In many open-content projects (i.e., policy, education, and music), outcomes may be more difficult to anticipate and evaluate.
3. Open content may require different collaborative tools.

Based on the similarities listed above, we can speculate how our major OSS findings might apply to open-content projects.

Group Size and Open Content

In some instances, open-content collaborations may be similar to OSS in that it isn't as much about the size of the collaborative team as it is about locating someone else on the planet who faces similar user needs as well as shares a passion and similar skills for addressing issues like the coral reef problem above. In other settings, as in OSS software, the size of the community of the open-content project will likely be related to the page visits and downloads of the project's content, which in turn will in be related to the content's utility to users or other community members. It seems reasonable to suspect that many users will be motivated to contribute for a variety of reasons similar to the motivations for contributing to OSS software projects (e.g., user-centric needs or collaborative learning). Contributions therefore are likely to produce the virtuous circle of increased content utility, resulting in a larger community and even more contributions, as in an OSS software setting.

Leadership and Open Content

Because both OSS software and open-content projects use the Internet to build community, the leadership skills that are important in OSS software are likely to be equally so in open-content settings. Success in open content will probably be related to hard work, setting goals, producing good documentation, and having an excellent Web site.

Marketing, Matchmaking, and Open Content

We found that successful OSS software projects often find at least one additional member via the Internet. We see no reason why open-content settings should be any different. In many cases, search engines and the intellectual matchmaking capabilities of power hubs similar to SF may allow an open-content project to find another person in the world with similar interests along with the time to participate. In the environmental example above, this suggests the possible need for an SF-like Web hub to share policy and administer open content (see Schweik et al. 2011).

More Thoughts about Open-Content Collaborations and Solving Global Problems

We currently have potential solutions to many global problems, but social and political barriers prevent them from being implemented. Solving global problems involves changing social, political, and ultimately, economic realities. Here is where the differences between OSS software and open-content collaborations become key.

Heterogeneity, Society, and Conflict

Various OSS surveys (Ghosh et al. 2002; David, Waterman, and Arora 2003; Lakhani and Wolf 2005) have found that OSS software developers are quite homogeneous in terms of sex, age, profession, and language, although the user communities surrounding OSS software projects are probably more diverse. Nevertheless, our findings about OSS software projects reveal none of the negative effects of heterogeneity on project success that might be seen in other instances of collective action, and we ran across little evidence of conflict.[3] Since society in general is much more diverse than OSS software development teams, we fully expect that open-content projects will be more heterogeneous and thus more subject to conflict. As in environmental commons settings, the question will then turn to what systems and procedures are put in place to deal with as well as settle or reduce the conflict.

Governance and Open Content

We found that there was little formal governance in OSS software projects, and that many of the operational rules were built into the version control system in which the software was stored. Some open-content projects, like Wikipedia, use software that stores different versions of content automatically and allows previous versions to be restored. In addition, many content management systems and Web sites allow fine-grained, password-protected access that may in many cases parallel some of the functionality found in version control systems used in OSS software projects. Still, because open-content projects are likely to be more heterogeneous as well as subject to greater levels of disagreement and conflict, we think that open-content projects will probably require more formal governance structures than OSS software projects. This is an empirical question that needs to be investigated with new research.

Politics, Economics, and Outcomes

Judging whether a software program does what it is designed to do is largely an objective matter. The software exists, it can be run on a computer, and its performance can be easily evaluated. Open-content projects are likely to develop digital products whose outcomes are more unpredictable and difficult to evaluate. For example, imagine the outcome of a project to compose a piece of music. Evaluating the music produced is largely based on subjective preferences, and listeners are bound to disagree about its value.

In the case of solving global problems, we can envision that open-content projects might propose economic or social policy changes to address social problems. Yet public policy studies teach us that the outcomes of such proposals are notoriously difficult to predict. Even if the changes were predictable, it is likely that there would be winners and losers. Traditionally, these serious issues are debated and decided in the political arena, and like the political arena, these open-content projects are likely to be contentious and more difficult to manage than OSS software projects.

Furthermore, while it is true that the Internet has been used for political organizing and fund-raising, as demonstrated in the United States by MoveOn.org, TeaParty.us, and the Barack Obama and John McCain presidential campaigns, actual political changes must be carried out in the real world through political rallies, meetings, discussions, and ultimately voting.[4] The same is true for the prospect of open-content projects with a focus on solving world problems. While these projects may produce technical solutions, policy solutions, or simply the sharing of innovative new ideas across political borders (consider the coral reef commons idea above), an open-content project cannot directly change political, social, or economic realities, especially in a short time.

New Possibilities

On a positive note, we did find it possible to build trust via the Internet, and that face-to-face meetings are not always required for online collaborations to be successful. Many potential social impediments to effective collaboration in the real world are not readily apparent via the Internet. People who might find it difficult to collaborate in person, for instance—because of social status, physical appearance, or ethnic or religious differences—may discover that they can effectively collaborate via the Internet. In addition and perhaps more important, the low cost and global reach of the Internet have empowered more people than ever before to participate in a worldwide dialogue, which may generate powerful new ideas and technologies. Perhaps someone, or some group, will find a way to combine innovative, new open content with Internet-based political organizing to powerfully translate solutions to critical problems from the virtual world of the Internet to the material world, where real change is sorely needed.

Study Limitations

While we have done our best to approach this study systematically and carefully, and present results that are robust and accurately interpreted, like any study there are limitations. We have tried to make the argument that the SF data sets (2006 and 2009) were the best available to represent the unknown population of OSS, but we know that SF has limitations too. For example, we found that SF does not represent OSS in Asia or the global South very well (our hunch is that the language used in SF—English—may be an important reason for this). We also noticed some errors in the Flossmole data (i.e., tracker reports), so a more careful analysis of the accuracy of the data is warranted, but we did not have the resources to compare the 2006 Flossmole data to the information held in the Notre Dame repository for the same time period. In addition there is some error rate in our dependent variable, as the replication by Wiggins and Crowston (2010) suggests. We doubt that these errors greatly change our overall results, and in fact this is the conclusion that Wiggins and Crowston reached, yet a statistical analysis of the effect of the error rate on our results would be helpful.

While we tried hard to develop robust and well-designed online survey instruments, our survey is still subject to inherent weaknesses. For example, responses are self-reported, nonobjective data, and in some cases, respondents could have misunderstood the questions. There are surely ways that we could have improved the survey methodology had we had the time or resources. We considered surveying multiple people on projects where there was more than one developer to triangulate answers, for instance, but this was infeasible given our research resources. That said, we think the results speak for themselves and support the idea that the survey was well implemented, given that the results agree so well with many of the theoretical expectations and conventional wisdom on OSS.

In the spirit of the openness we study, we are making available on the Web site accompanying this book all our data and statistical scripts (R format) as well as documents outlining our construction of variables, our survey instruments, the raw contingency tables that informed chapter 10 (appendix 10.A), and the MySQL database we used for chapter 8 (2006 SF data).[5] Our chapter 11 (2009 data) and survey data are subject to legal confidentiality restrictions, so we will make that data available to the extent possible under these constraints. We encourage others to replicate and extend our work.[6]

Some Important Future Research Ideas

There are a number of future research ideas that arise from this work, and yet several are particularly important. Although we have had some experience with open-content projects over the five-year period of our research, we have not been able to undertake a systematic study of these projects following a similar success and abandonment approach. Since studying open content with an eye toward solving global problems was an underlying motivation for our work, we hope to do such a study in the future.

We could also do more with our existing OSS data. Given our interest in developing guidance for the population of OSS (and open-content) projects, we felt it was crucial to study one-developer projects in our research. As we have shown, however, there is evidence that the institutional designs of OSS projects do evolve and change in situations where more complicated collaborations emerge plus as teams grow larger. For this reason and others, we think it would be useful to eliminate one-developer projects from our data set and then perform a similar statistical analysis. If we had had the resources to perform such an analysis, we would have done it. We could also perform many analyses on our existing data that might help answer questions important for business consumers. For example, we could use our project longevity data as a dependent variable and discover if any of our existing independent variables are characteristics that make successful projects more long-lived. In addition, here we have only studied snapshots of projects that are in the initiation or growth stage. We need to capitalize on the historical data that is available for existing projects to analyze their evolution over time more carefully.

These types of questions are key for OSS consumers who are asking questions such as: What indicators help to assess whether a project will be around for the long term? We provided some initial indicators for consumers above in an effort to help answer this question. Hopefully the work we've presented supplies readers with ideas on where to focus the next tier of practitioner-needs research.

In chapter 1, we also mentioned the work of Bowles, Edwards, and Roosevelt (2005), and their idea that as the U.S. economy becomes more information and service oriented (i.e., weightless), economic institutions will likely need to adapt to this new reality. Because of the large economic impact of OSS and its weightless nature, we speculated that the evolution of OSS institutions might foreshadow the changes in economic institutions that Bowles, Edwards, and Roosevelt refer to. In this book, especially in chapter 6, we proposed and then implemented a methodology for doing rigorous comparative studies of evolving OSS institutions. Such a study, given that the institutional structure of most OSS projects is informal, would necessarily concentrate on larger projects with more formal and complex institutional structures. Although we have made a start in this book, we would need to undertake a much broader comparative study of OSS institutions before we could say anything meaningful about their relationship to shifts in economic institutions.

Conclusion

In chapter 1 and throughout this book, we have emphasized the importance of OSS collaboration and its relevance to fields outside computer science. Computer programmers, as we all know, developed much of the Internet. These programmers have had significantly more time to figure out how to collaborate over the Internet, so it is not at all surprising that a major collaborative innovation like OSS would emerge from the computer programming community. This community has been at it much longer than the rest of us, and has much to teach. We attempted to learn from the computer programmer community in this study and inform people interested in applying their collaborative model—this new kind of Internet-based commons—to other collaborative domains.

Finally, we have learned that these relatively new Internet-based commons are different from traditional natural resource commons in particular ways. In this study, we have tried to identify common threads found in the older types of commons to these new commons (OSS software), and shed light on their implications for broader and even newer open-content efforts. At this juncture in human history, these digital commons are still brand-new experiments in human collective action. Hopefully the success stories we have identified here will inspire some readers to keep extending and experimenting with this collaborative paradigm in areas beyond computer software. In ten years, perhaps we will have many new, productive applications of this type of collaboration in areas such as medicine, climate change, public policy analysis, and we hope, other areas that we cannot even imagine.

Notes

Chapter 1

1. At the time of this writing, we found no way of confirming whether this prediction came true.

Chapter 2

1. In relation to nonhierarchical assignments, this is an interesting and important contradiction to what takes place in more traditional commons settings, where governance and institutional design is critical. See, for example, Ostrom 1990; Dietz, Ostrom, and Stern 2003. We will return to this issue in chapter 5.

2. For Limeservice, see https://www.limeservice.com.

3. For an excellent summary of the GPL and related issues, see Deek and McHugh 2007, 250–261.

4. We witnessed this firsthand at the FOSS4Geo conference in Capetown, South Africa, in 2008. The audience displayed an overwhelmingly positive attitude toward Google and its keynote presenter. Some of the open-source projects represented by those in the audience had, in turn, mentored the student developers who were sponsored by the Summer of Code program.

5. For the Government Open Source Conference, see http://goscon.org.

6. Any person who has used computers for a while now can relate to this problem. For example, it would be hard to find a computer with software that could read old WordStar documents stored on $5^1/_4$-inch floppy disks.

7. XML is a computer language for marking or "tagging" text to give it semantic meaning. See, for example, Sánchez-Fernández and Delgado-Kloosh 2002. Secure Sockets Layer is a protocol or standard used to secure Internet data transmissions. See, for example, Thomas 2000.

8. See http://www.berlios.de/about/.

9. For another look at these motivations as well as government open-source policy issues, see Schmidt and Schnitzer 2003.

10. See, respectively, http://www.nten.org, http://www.techsoup.org, http://www.npower.org, http://www.APC.org, http://www.itrainonline.org, and http://www.geekcorps.org.

11. On the Moodle platform, see http://moodle.org. On MIT's Dspace, see http://dspace.mit.edu.

12. See http://drupal.org.

13. Andrew Vernon, personal communication, Amherst, MA, July 15, 2009.

14. See http://www.open-bio.org.

Chapter 3

1. IAD literature (see, e.g., Ostrom, Gardner, and Walker 1994) refers to technological attributes as "physical attributes," but a reviewer of our manuscript noted that the phrase "technological attributes" fits better in OSS contexts (and other online, digital commons). We agree and are grateful to this reviewer for this suggestion.

2. Anthony Wasserman, personal communication, Moffett Field, CA, 2006.

3. This scenario may become more prominent in future years if software firms continue to consider OSS as part of their business strategies.

4. For a more recent study, see David and Shapiro 2008.

5. We use gender-neutral language with the hope that over time, we will continue to see many more female, transgendered, and other programmers joining these and proprietary endeavors.

6. We are grateful to the economist Bill Gibson of the University of Vermont for suggesting we consider this concept.

7. Here we mean the positive sense of a hacker, as used in programmer circles, rather than the interpretation so often misused in the mainstream media: "criminal hacker" or "cracker."

Chapter 4

1. This is indeed the example that these authors provide. It may be that some people out there find accounting packages more technically cool than they do device drivers.

2. For instance, an interesting comparative study from this perspective would be to examine side by side the fairly large number of content management systems now available (see http://open-sourcecms.com).

3. This point is not all that different at a small scale from the arguments that Lawrence Lessig (2006) makes in *Code Version 2.0* regarding the broad-scale issues of code and architecture in Internet technologies as a kind of law.

4. See http://freenode.net.

Chapter 5

1. This section builds on Ostrom (2005), which provides significant theoretical guidance on how to study institutions.

2. Much of what we will now present draws from Ostrom, Gardner, and Walker 1994; Ostrom 2005.

3. For many suggestions for behavior norms in OSS settings, such as how to communicate in general and how to settle conflict, see Fogel 2006.

4. For instance, at the time of this writing, there were over fifty licenses that complied with the OSS definition managed by the OSS Initiative, a nonprofit entity that works to ensure that new licenses meet its definition (see http://www.opensource.org).

5. Assuming that the project was using a version control system, like CVS or Subversion, however, this would not be a significant problem but rather more of an annoyance.

Chapter 6

1. See http://www.osgeo.org/education.

2. See, for example, the FOSS4G conference in 2009; http://2009.foss4g.org/ (accessed August 12, 2011).

3. Tyler Mitchell, personal communication, October 18, 2009.

Chapter 7

1. This chapter is based on material we previously published in *Upgrade: The European Journal for the Informatics Professional*, http://www.upgrade-cepis.org. We are grateful to the *Upgrade* editors for granting us permission to do so.

2. For FLOSSmole, see http://flossmole.org/ (accessed August 11, 2011).

3. For more detail on the procedures, see appendix 7.1, http://www.umass.edu/opensource/schweik/supplementary.html.

4. Recall from chapter 1 that these terms reflect a philosophical difference, where free or libre software captures the viewpoint that software should be a public good, whereas OSS is sometimes considered more open or willing to work with commercial interests. Recall also that in this book, for ease of reading we use the term open source widely to include both philosophies.

5. As OSS developers know, things change rapidly in this area. This point was true when we first wrote this chapter (2006). Other hosting sites like GitHub and Google code, however, have a substantial project and user base as well. Still even today, SF remains a leading player in the OSS hosting arena.

6. These were different interviews then the ones we discussed in chapter 6 with the OSGeo developer community.

7. For nontechnical readers, *spidering* means writing a program that reads pages on these Web sites and extracts the needed data.

8. In later analyses, had we included these projects with external project Web pages, they could have been falsely classified as abandoned even though they were active on other Web locations than SF.

9. Available at http://www.umass.edu/opensource/schweik/supplementary.html.

Chapter 8

1. These may represent some of the noise that exists in SF, such as software placed on the hosting site by a college student doing work on a project for a computer science course.

2. Available at http://www.umass.edu/opensource/schweik/supplementary.html.

3. Available at http://www.gnu.org/licenses/license-list.html (accessed August 12, 2011).

4. For more information, see appendixes 8.2 and 8.3, http://www.umass.edu/opensource/schweik/supplementary.html.

5. Available at http://www.umass.edu/opensource/schweik/supplementary.html.

6. Although there are some projects with large teams. See appendix 8.2, figure 5, http://www.umass.edu/opensource/schweik/supplementary.html.

Chapter 9

1. This process was essentially replicated using 2006 SF data. See Wiggins and Crowston (2010).

2. For copies of the questionnaires, see http://www.umass.edu/opensource/schweik/supplementary.html.

3. Available at http://www.limeservice.com (accessed August 12, 2012).

4. Available at http://www.umass.edu/opensource/schweik/supplementary.html.

5. Available at http://www.umass.edu/opensource/schweik/supplementary.html.

6. Available at http://www.umass.edu/opensource/schweik/supplementary.html.

Chapter 10

1. Available at http://www.umass.edu/opensource/schweik/supplementary.html.

2. In most questions in our online surveys, we dynamically replaced "project" with the name of the project that the respondent was associated with.

3. This statement is based on our analysis of 2006 SF data from the Flossmole project.

4. SI: 307/382 = 80 percent; AI: 138/193 = 72 percent. We aggregated all the responses for options 2–4 and developed a contingency table (not shown, but available in appendix 10.A) comparing all benevolent dictator responses to all other answers. Here we found highly statistically significant (95 percent confidence) chi-square test results showing that SI projects are more often guided by benevolent dictator governance structures.

Chapter 11

1. Available at http://www.umass.edu/opensource/schweik/supplementary.html.

2. Available at http://www.umass.edu/opensource/schweik/supplementary.html.

3. Recall that we argued that SF project data (and data from other OSS hosting systems) could be considered remote sensing platforms for OSS, similar to the Landsat and other satellites that monitor change on the earth. This problem of the data collected over time is not unlike what happens in remote sensing where technological improvements are made when new satellite platforms are launched (e.g., Landsat 1–7).

4. Recall that descriptions of the construction of all the variables, contingency tables, and other statistics detailing responses to questions comprising these variables are available on our book's Web site, http://www.umass.edu/opensource/schweik/supplementary.html.

5. Available at http://www.umass.edu/opensource/schweik/supplementary.html.

6. The p-value for the hypothesis that the mean number of tracker reports for the II and IG classes is equal is 4.1, E-13. For the IG and AG classes, the p-value is 0.04, and for the AG and SG classes the p-value is 2.2, E-16.

Chapter 12

1. Note that we also investigated this concept through questions related to the "financial backing" hypothesis, H-C8a, discussed earlier, which was supported in the growth stage.

2. This hypothesis was specifically written to address the initiation stage, but we decided to investigate it in the growth stage as well.

3. Our data indicate this, but this point is a bit speculative, and thus more research is needed.

Chapter 13

1. Available at, respectively, http://en.wikipedia.org/wiki/Main_Page, http://www.youtube.com/, http://ocw.mit.edu/index.htm, and http://wiki.creativecommons.org/science, all accessed August 12, 2011. We even recently discovered an example of open collaboration that is applied to the design and production of automobiles (LocalMotors 2011).

2. For interested readers, these ideas of open content, public policy, and administration are presented more completely in Schweik, Evans, and Grove 2005; Schweik et al. 2011.

3. We should note that conflict can and does occur in OSS. The extreme example is "project forking," when a developer subteam splits off to create a new and separate derivative of the project that competes with the parent project. In this study, we didn't hear much about this extreme kind of conflict, and consequently didn't devote much attention to it.

4. Available at, respectively, http://front.moveon.org/ and http://theteaparty.net/. Accessed August 12, 2011.

5. Available at http://www.umass.edu/opensource/schweik/supplementary.html.

6. For example, a similar analysis could be done using a different definition or measure of OSS project success.

References

Abdel-Hamid, Tarek K., and Stuart E. Madnick. 1990. The Elusive Silver Lining: How We Fail to Learn from Software Development Failures. *Sloan Management Review* 32 (1): 39–48.

Agrawal, Arun. 2002. Common Resources and Institutional Sustainability. In *The Drama of the Commons*, ed. Elinor Ostrom, Thomas Dietz, Nives Dolšak, Paul C. Stern, Susan Stonich, and Elke U. Weber, 41–86. Washington, D.C.: National Academies Press.

Agrawal, Arun, and Clark Gibson. 1999. Community and Conservation: Beyond Enchantment and Disenchantment. *World Development* 27: 629–649.

Aigrain, Philippe. 2005. Libre Software Policies at the European Level. In *Perspectives on Free and Open Source Software*, ed. Joseph Feller, Brian Fitzgerald, Scott A. Hissam, and Karim R. Lakhani, 447–459. Cambridge, MA: MIT Press.

Apache. 2011. *The Apache Software Foundation.* http://www.apache.org/ (accessed April 6, 2011).

Asklund, Ulf, and Lars Bendix. 2002. A Study of Configuration Management in Open Source Software. *IEE Proceedings. Software* 149 (1): 40–46.

Baker, J. Mark. 1998. The Effect of Community Structure on Social Forestry Outcomes: Insights from Chota Nagpur, India. *Mountain Research and Development* 18 (1): 51–62.

Baland, Jean-Marie, and Jean-Philippe Platteau. 1996. *Halting Degradation of Natural Resources: Is There a Role for Rural Communities?* Oxford: Clarendon Press.

Baldwin, Carliss Y., and Kim B. Clark. 2006. The Architecture of Participation: Does Code Architecture Mitigate Free Riding in the Open Source Development Model? *Management Science* 52 (7): 1116–1127.

Bass, Len, Paul Clements, and Rick Kazman. 2003. *Software Architecture in Practice.* 2nd ed. Boston: Addison-Wesley.

Becker, David. 2003. Proprietary Software—Banned in Boston? *Cnet News*, September 30. http://www.news.com/Proprietary-software-banned-in-Boston/2100-7344_3-5084442.html?tag=st.nl (accessed August 17, 2011).

Benkler, Yochai. 2003. The Political Economy of Commons. *Upgrade: The European Journal for the Informatics Professional* 4 (3): 6–9. http://www.cepis.org/upgrade/files/full-2003-III.pdf (accessed August 16, 2011).

Benkler, Yochai. 2005. Coase's Penguin, or Linux and the Nature of the Firm. In *Code: Collaborative Ownership and the Digital Economy*, ed. Rishab Aiyer Ghosh, 169–206. Cambridge, MA: MIT Press.

Benkler, Yochai. 2006. *The Wealth of Networks: How Social Production Transforms Markets and Freedom*. New Haven, CT: Yale University Press.

Blanchard, Anita, and Tom Horan. 1998. Virtual Communities and Social Capital. *Social Science Computer Review* 16 (3): 293–307.

Boeder, Pieter. 2002. Non-Profits on E: How Non-Profit Organisations Are Using the Internet for Communication, Fundraising, and Community Building. *First Monday* 7 (7). http://firstmonday.org/htbin/cgiwrap/bin/ojs/index.php/fm/article/view/969/890 (accessed March 12, 2008).

Bollier, David. 2008. *Viral Spiral: How the Commoners Built a Digital Republic of Their Own*. New York: New Press.

Bowles, Samuel, Richard Edwards, and Frank Roosevelt. 2005. *Understanding Capitalism: Competition, Command, and Change*. 3rd ed. New York: Oxford University Press.

Boyle, James, ed. 2003a. The Public Domain. Special issue, *Law and Contemporary Problems* 66 (1–2): 1–463. http://www.law.duke.edu/journals/journaltoc?journal=lcp&toc=lcptoc66winterspring2003.htm (accessed August 17, 2011).

Boyle, James. 2003b. The Second Enclosure Movement and the Construction of the Public Domain. *Law and Contemporary Problems* 66 (1–2): 33–74.

Breiman, Leo. 2001. Random Forests. *Machine Learning* 45 (1): 5–32.

Breiman, Leo, Jerome H. Friedman, Richard A. Olshen, and Charles J. Stone. 1984. *Classification and Regression Trees*. New York: Chapman and Hall.

Bromley, Daniel W. 1992. The Commons, Common Property, and Environmental Policy. *Environmental and Resource Economics* 2 (1): 1–17.

Brooks, Frederick P., Jr. (1975) 1995. *The Mythical Man-Month: Essays on Software Engineering. Anniversary Edition*. Reading, MA: Addison-Wesley.

Bryant, Todd. 2006. Social Software in Academia. *EDUCAUSE Quarterly* 29 (2): 61–64. http://www.educause.edu/ir/library/pdf/EQM0627.pdf (accessed May 14, 2008).

Butler, Howard, and Chris Schmidt. 2007. Open Source #5: The Gift Economy Ain't Free. *Geoconnexion.com* 6 (9) 50–51. http://www.geoconnexion.com/uploads/opensource_intv6i9.pdf (accessed May 29, 2008).

Câmara, Gilberto, and Fonseca Frederico. 2007. Information Policies and Open Source Software in Developing Countries. *Journal of the American Society for Information Science and Technology* 12 (4): 255–272.

Campus Computing Project. 2007. The 2007 National Survey of Information Technology in U.S. Higher Education: IT Security and Crisis Management Pose Continuing Challenges. *Campus Computing Project Newsletter* (October). http://www.campuscomputing.net/sites/www.campuscomputing.net/files/2007-CCP_0.pdf (accessed May 14, 2008).

Capiluppi, Andrea, Patricia Lago, and Maurizio Morisio. 2003. Evidences in the Evolution of OS Projects through Changelog Analyses. Paper presented at the International Conference on Software Engineering, Portland, OR, May 3–11.

Chakravarty, Sujoy, Ernan Haruvy, and Fang Wu. 2007. The Link between Incentives and Product Performance in Open Source Development: An Empirical Investigation. *Global Business and Economics Review* 9 (2–3): 151–169.

CiviCRM. 2008. *About CiviCRM.* http://civicrm.org/aboutcivicrm (accessed March 11, 2008).

Coleman, James S. 1988. Social Capital in the Creation of Human Capital. *American Journal of Sociology* 94 (3): S95–S120.

Collins Sussman, Ben, Brian Fitzpatrick, and C. Michael Pilato. 2005. *Version Control with Subversion.* Sebastopol, CA: O'Reilly Media. http://svnbook.red-bean.com (accessed June 23, 2010).

Comino, Stefano, Fabio Maneti, and Maria Laura Parisi. 2007. From Planning to Mature: On the Success of Open Source Projects. *Research Policy* 36:1575–1586.

Commonwealth of Massachusetts. 2004. *Open Standards Policy.* http://www.mass.gov/Aitd/docs/policies_standards/openstandards.pdf (accessed March 4, 2008).

Costa, Dora L., and Matthew E. Kahn. 2003. Engagement and Community Heterogeneity: An Economist's Perspective. *Perspectives on Politics* 1 (1): 103–111.

Courant, Paul N., and Rebecca J. Griffiths. 2006. *Software and Collaboration in Higher Education: A Study of Open Source Software.* Report commissioned by Andrew W. Mellon Foundation and William and Flora Hewlett Foundation. http://www.ithaka.org/ithaka-s-r/strategyold/oss/OOSS_Report_FINAL.pdf (accessed August 19, 2011).

Crowston, Kevin. 2005. Future Research on FLOSS Development. Special issue no. 2, *First Monday* 0(0) (October 3). http://firstmonday.org/htbin/cgiwrap/bin/ojs/index.php/fm/article/view/1465/1380 (accessed August 19, 2011).

Crowston, Kevin, Hala Annabi, and James Howison. 2003. Defining Open Source Project Success. Paper presented at the twenty-fourth International Conference on Information Systems, Seattle, December 14–17.

Crowston, Kevin, Hala Annabi, James Howison, and Chengetai Masango. 2005. Effective Work Practices for FLOSS Development: A Model and Propositions. Paper presented at the thirty-eighth Hawaii International Conference on System Science, Big Island, January 3–6.

Crowston, Kevin, James Howison, and Hala Annabi. 2006. Information Systems Success in Free and Open Source Software Development: Theory and Measures. *Software Process Improvement and Practice* 11 (2): 123–148.

Crowston, Kevin, James Howison, Jengetai Masango, and U. Yeliz Eseryel. 2007. The Role of Face-to-face Meetings in Technology-Supported Self-Organizing Distributed Teams. *IEEE Transactions on Professional Communication* 50 (3): 185–203.

Cutler, D. Richard, Thomas C. Edwards Jr., Karen H. Beard, Adele Cutler, Kyle T. Hess, Jacob Gibson, and Joshua J. Lawler. 2007. Random Forests for Classification in Ecology. *Ecology* 88 (11): 2783–2792.

Czaplewski, Raymond L. 1994. Variance Approximations for Assessments of Classification Accuracy. USDA Forest Service Research paper RM-316. Fort Collins, CO: USDA Forest Service Rocky Mountain Research Station.

Dafermos, George N. 2005. Management and Virtual Decentralized Networks: The Linux Project. *First Monday* Special Issue no. 2. October 3. http://firstmonday.org/htbin/cgiwrap/bin/ojs/index. php/fm/article/view/1481/1396.

Daffara, Carlo. 2007. *Estimating the Number of Active and Stable FLOSS Projects.* http://robertogaloppini.net/2007/08/23/estimating-the-number-of-active-and-stable-floss-projects/ (accessed August 19, 2011).

Dalziel, James. 2003. Open Standards versus Open Source in E-Learning. *Educause Quarterly* 4: 4–7.

David, Paul A., and Francesco Rullani. 2008. Dynamics of Innovation in an "Open Source" Collaboration Environment: Lurking, Laboring, and Launching FLOSS Projects on SourceForge. *Industrial and Corporate Change* 17 (4): 647–710.

David, Paul A., and Joseph S. Shapiro. 2008. Community-Based Production of Open-Source Software: What Do We Know about the Developers Who Participate? *Information Economics and Policy* 20(4): 364–398.

David, Paul A., Andrew Waterman, and Seema Arora. 2003. *FLOSS-US: The Free/Libre/Open Source Software Survey for 2003.* Stanford Institute for Economic Policy Research, Stanford, CA. http://www.stanford.edu/group/floss-us/ (accessed July 13, 2009).

De'ath, Glen, and Katharina E. Fabricius. 2000. Classification and Regression Trees: A Powerful Yet Simple Technique for Ecological Data Analysis. *Ecology* 81 (11): 3178–3192.

Deek, Fadi P., and James A. M. McHugh. 2007. *Open Source Technology and Policy.* New York: Cambridge University Press.

de Laat, Paul. B. 2007. Introduction to a Roundtable on the Governance of Open Source Software: Particular Solutions and General Lessons. *Journal of Management and Governance* 11 (2): 115–117.

Dempsey, Bert J., Debra Weiss, Paul Jones, and Jane Greenberg. 2002. Who Is an Open Source Software Developer? *Communications of the ACM* 45 (2): 67–72.

Denzau, Arthur T., and Douglass C. North. 1994. Shared Mental Models: Ideologies and Institutions. *Kyklos* 47 (1): 3–31.

Dietz, Thomas, Nives Dolšak, Elinor Ostrom, and Paul C. Stern. 2002. The Drama of the Commons. In *The Drama of the Commons*, ed. Elinor Ostrom, Thomas Dietz, Nives Dolšak, Paul C. Stern, Susan Stonich, and Elke U. Weber, 1–36. Washington, D.C.: National Academies Press.

Dietz, Thomas, Elinor Ostrom, and Paul C. Stern. 2003. The Struggle to Govern the Commons. *Science* 302 (5653): 1907–1912.

Dillman, Don A., Jolene D. Smyth, and Leah Melani Christian. 2009. *Internet, Mail, and Mixed-Mode Surveys: The Tailored Design Method*. Hoboken, NJ: Wiley.

Drupal Association. 2009. *About the Drupal Association*. http://association.drupal.org/about (accessed July 19, 2009).

Dube, Line, and Guy Pare. 2001. Global Virtual Teams. *Communications of the ACM* 44 (12): 71–73.

Edwards, Kasper. 2001. Towards a Theory for Understanding the Open Source Software Phenomenon. Department of Manufacturing Engineering, and Production, Technical University of Denmark, Lyngby. http://cdwards.dk/towards.pdf (accessed June 23, 2010).

Elliott, Margaret S., and Walt Scacchi. 2002. Communicating and Mitigating Conflict in Open Source Software Development Projects. Working paper. Institute for Software Research, University of California, Irvine. http://www.ics.uci.edu/~wscacchi/Papers/Open-Source-Research/OSSE3-Elliott.pdf (accessed August 11, 2011).

English, Robert, and Charles M. Schweik. 2007. Identifying Success and Tragedy of FLOSS Commons: A Preliminary Classification of SourceForge.net Projects. *Upgrade: The European Journal for the Informatics Professional* 8 (6): 54–59. http://www.cepis.org/upgrade/files/full-VI-07.pdf (accessed August 20, 2011).

Esteban, Joan, and Debraj Ray. 2001. Collective Action and the Group Size Paradox. *American Political Science Review* 95 (3): 663–672.

Evans, David S., and Bernard J. Reddy. 2003. Government Preferences forPromoting Open-Source Software: A Solution in Search of a Problem. *Michigan Telecommunications and Technology Law Review* (9): 313–394. http://www.mttlr.org/volnine/evans.pdf.

Ewusi-Mensah, Kweku. 1997. Critical Issues in Abandoned Information Systems Development Projects. *Communications of the ACM* 40 (9): 74–80.

Ewusi-Mensah, Kweku. 2003. *Software Development Failures: Anatomy of Abandoned Projects*. Cambridge, MA: MIT Press.

Fischer, Gerhard, Eric Scharff, and Yunwen Ye. 2004. Fostering Social Creativity by Increasing Social Capital. In *Social Capital and Information Technology*, ed. Marleen Huysman and Volker Wulf, 355–400. Cambridge, MA: MIT Press.

Fitzgerald, Brian. 2005. Has Open Source Software a Future? In *Perspectives on Free and Open Source Software*, ed. Joseph Feller, Brian Fitzgerald, Scott A. Hissam, and Karim R. Lakhani, 93–106. Cambridge, MA: MIT Press.

FLOSSMetrics. 2006. *Free/Libre and Open Source Software Metrics.* http://flossmetrics.org/ (accessed February 11, 2008).

FLOSSmole. 2005. http://flossmole.org/ (accessed August 20, 2011).

FLOSSmole. 2006. SourceForge Raw Data, August 1, 2006. http://sourceforge.net/projects/ossmole/files/sfRawData/sfRawData01-Aug-2006/ (accessed August 15, 2011).

Fogel, Karl. 2006. *Producing Open Source Software: How to Run a Successful Free Software Project.* Sebastopol, CA: O'Reilly Media. http://producingoss.com/ (accessed August 12, 2011).

Fogel, Karl, and Moshe Bar. 2003. *Open Source Development with CVS.* Scottsdale, AZ: Paraglyph Press.

Fountain, Jane. 2001. *Building the Virtual State: Information Technology and Institutional Change.* Washington, DC: Brookings Institution Press.

Freedman, David, H. 2007. Mitchell Baker and the Firefox Paradox. *Inc. Magazine.* http://www.inc.com/magazine/20070201/features-firefox.html (accessed August 20, 2011).

FSF (Free Software Foundation). 2008. *Free Software and the GNU Operating System.* http://www.fsf.org/about (accessed April 12, 2011).

FSF (Free Software Foundation). 2009. *What Is Copyleft?* http://www.gnu.org/copyleft/ (accessed November 30, 2009).

Ganz, Joan Safran. 1971. *Rules: A Systematic Study.* The Hague: Mouton.

GBDirect. 2008. *Linux and Open Source Software Support.* http://software-support.gbdirect.co.uk (accessed March 2, 2008).

George, Alexander L., and Andrew Bennett. 2005. *Case Studies and Theory Development in the Social Sciences.* Cambridge, MA: MIT Press.

Ghosh, Rishab Aiyer. 1998. Cooking Pot Markets: An Economic Model for the Trade in Free Goods and Services on the Internet. *First Monday* 3 (3). http://firstmonday.org/htbin/cgiwrap/bin/ojs/index.php/fm/article/view/580/501 (accessed June 23, 2010).

Ghosh, Rishab Aiyer. 2005. Understanding Free Software Developers: Findings from the FLOSS Study. In *Perspectives on Free and Open Source Software,* ed. Joseph Feller, Brian Fitzgerald, Scott A. Hissam, and Karim R. Lakhani, 23–46. Cambridge, MA: MIT Press.

Ghosh, Rishab Aiyer. 2006. *Study on the Economic Impact of Open Source Software on Innovation and the Competitiveness of the Information and Communication Technologies (ICT) Sector in the European Union: Final Report.* A technical report prepared by UNU-MERIT, Netherlands. http://ec.europa.eu/enterprise/sectors/ict/files/2006-11-20-flossimpact_en.pdf (accessed June 23, 2010).

Ghosh, Rishab Aiyer, Ruediger Glott, Bernhard Krieger, and Gregorio Robles. 2002. *Free/Libre and Open Source Software: Survey and Study.* Technical report prepared for the International Institute of Infonomics, University of Maastricht, Netherlands. http://www.flossproject.org/report/FLOSS_Final4.pdf (accessed August 15, 2011).

Gibson, Cristina B., and Susan G. Cohen. 2003. *Virtual Teams That Work: Creating Conditions for Virtual Team Effectiveness*. San Francisco: Jossey-Bass.

Godin, Seth. 2000. *Unleashing the Ideavirus: How to Turn Your Ideas into Marketing Epidemics*. London: Simon and Schuster.

Goldman, Ron, and Richard P. Gabriel. 2005. *Innovation Happens Elsewhere: Open Source as a Business Strategy*. San Francisco: Morgan Kaufman Publishers.

Gonzalez-Barahona, Jesús M., Gregorio Robles, Miguel Ortuño-Pérez, Luis Rodero-Merino, José Centeno-Gonzalez, Vicente Matellán-Olivera, Eva Castro-Barbero, and Pedro de-las-Heras-Quirós. 2005. Analyzing the Anatomy of GNU/Linux Distributions: Methodology and Case Studies (Red Hat and Debian). In *Free/Open Source Software Development*, ed. Stefan Koch, 27–58. Hershey, PA: Idea Group Publishing.

Google. 2011. *Google Summer of Code*. http://code.google.com/soc/ (accessed April 6, 2011).

Haas, Peter. 1992. Introduction: Epistemic Communities and International Policy Coordination. *International Organization* 46 (1): 1–35.

Hamel, Michael P., and Charles M. Schweik. 2009. Open Source Collaboration: Two Cases in the U.S. Public Sector. *First Monday* 14 (1). http://firstmonday.org/htbin/cgiwrap/bin/ojs/index.php/fm/article/view/2313/2065 (accessed June 22, 2010).

Hahn, Robert William, ed. 2002. *Government Policy toward Open Source Software*. Washington, DC: Brookings Institution Press.

Hardin, Garrett. 1968. The Tragedy of the Commons. *Science* 162 (3859): 1243–1248.

Hars, Alexander, and Shaosong Ou. 2002. Working for Free? Motivations for Participating in Open-Source Projects. *International Journal of Electronic Commerce* 6 (3): 25–39.

Healy, Kieran, and Alan Schussman. 2003. The Ecology of Open-Source Software Development. Working paper. University if Arizona. http://www.kieranhealy.org/files/drafts/oss-activity.pdf (accessed August 12, 2011).

Heckman, Robert, Kevin Crowston, and Nora Misiolek. 2007. A Structurational Perspective on Leadership in Virtual Teams. In *Virtuality and Virtualization: Proceedings of the International Federation of Information Processing Working Groups 8.2 on Information Systems and Organizations and 9.5 on Virtuality and Society,* July 29–31, 2007, Portland, Oregon, ed. Kevin Crowston, Sandra Sieber and Eleanor Wynn 151–168. New York: Springer.

Helm, Sabrina. 2000. Viral Marketing: Establishing Customer Relationships by "Word-of-Mouse." *Electronic Markets* 10 (3): 158–161.

Hertel, Guido, Sven Niedner, and Stefanie Herrmann. 2003. Motivation of Software Developers in Open Source Projects: An Internet-Based Survey of Contributors to the Linux Kernel. *Research Policy* 32 (7): 1159–1177.

Hess, Charlotte. 2007. *The Comprehensive Bibliography of the Commons*. Digital Library of the Commons, Indiana University. http://dlc.dlib.indiana.edu/cpr/index.php (accessed May 11, 2008).

Hess, Charlotte, and Elinor Ostrom. 2003. Ideas, Artifacts, and Facilities: Information as a Common-Pool Resource. *Law and Contemporary Problems* 66 (1–2): 111–145.

Hess, Charlotte, and Elinor Ostrom, eds. 2007. *Understanding Knowledge as a Commons: From Theory to Practice.* Cambridge, MA: MIT Press.

Himanen, Pekka. 2001. *The Hacker Ethic and the Spirit of the Information Age.* New York: Random House.

Hinds, Pamela J., and Suzanne P. Weisband. 2003. Knowledge Sharing and Shared Understanding in Virtual Teams. In *Virtual Teams That Work: Creating Conditions for Virtual Team Effectiveness,* ed. Cristina B. Gibson and Susan G. Cohen, 21–36. San Francisco: Jossey-Bass.

Hissam, Scott A., Charles B. Weinstock, Daniel Plaksoh, and Jayatirtha Asundi. 2001. *Perspectives on Open Source Software.* Technical report prepared for the Software Engineering Institute Joint Program at Carnegie Mellon University. http://repository.cmu.edu/sei/648/ (accessed January 10, 2007).

Hoffer, Jeffey A., Joey F. George, and Joseph S. Valacich. 2001. *Modern Systems Analysis and Design.* 3rd ed. Upper Saddle River, NJ: Prentice Hall.

Holck, Jesper, and Niels Jørgensen. 2005. Do Not Check in on Red: Control Meets Anarchy in Two Open Source Projects. In *Free/Open Source Software Development,* ed. Stefan Koch, 1–26. Hershey, PA: Idea Group Publishing.

Hosmer, David W., and Stanley Lemeshow. 2000. *Applied Logistic Regression.* 2nd ed. New York: Wiley.

Howison, James, Megan Conklin, and Kevin Crowston. 2006. FLOSSmole: A Collaborative Repository for FLOSS Research Data and Analyses. *International Journal of Information Technology and Web Engineering* 1 (3): 17–26.

Howison, James, and Kevin Crowston. 2004. The Perils and Pitfalls of Mining SourceForge. Paper presented at the Workshop on Mining Software Repositories at the International Conference on Software Engineering, Edinburgh, May 23–28.

Hyatt, Josh. 2006. MySQL: Workers in 25 Countries with No HQ. CNNMoney.com, June 1. http://money.cnn.com/2006/05/31/magazines/fortune/mysql_greatteams_fortune/ (accessed June 22, 2010).

Institute for Software Research. 2008. URL: http://www.isr.uci.edu/research-open-source.html.

Isaac, R. Mark, and James M. Walker. 1988. Group Size Effects in Public Goods Provision: The Voluntary Contribution Mechanism. *Quarterly Journal of Economics* 103 (1): 179–199.

Isaac, R. Mark, James M. Walker, and Arlington W. Williams. 1994. Group Size and the Voluntary Provision of Public Goods: Experimental Evidence Utilizing Large Groups. *Journal of Public Economics* 54 (1): 1–36.

Ives, Blake, and Margrethe H. Olson. 1984. User Involvement and MIS Success: A Review of Research. *Management Science* 30 (5): 586–603.

Jacobs, Jane. 1992. *The Death and Life of Great American Cities*. New York: Random House.

Johns, Adrian. 2001. The Birth of Scientific Reading. *Nature* 409 (6818): 287.

Johnson, Justin Pappas. 2002. Open Source Software: Private Provision of a Public Good. *Journal of Economics and Management Strategy* 11 (4): 637–662.

Johnson, Justin Pappas. 2006. Collaboration, Peer Review, and Open Source Software. *Information Economics and Policy* 18 (4): 477–497.

Johnson, Ronald N., and Gary D. Libecap. 1982. Contracting Problems and Regulation: The Case of the Fishery. *American Economic Review* 72 (5): 1005–1022.

Jones, Paul. 2000. *Brooks' Law and Open Source: The More the Merrier?* IBM publication. http://pascal.case.unibz.it/retrieve/3816/merrier.pdf (accessed June 22, 2010).

Jørgensen, Niels. 2007. Developer Autonomy in the FreeBSD Open Source Project. *Journal of Management and Governance* 11: 119–128.

Judge, Peter. 2008. Gartner: Open Source Will Quietly Take Over. Zdnet.com, April 4. http://www.zdnet.co.uk/news/it-strategy/2008/04/04/gartner-open-source-will-quietly-take-over-39379900/ (accessed June 22, 2010).

Karpf, David. 2010. What Can Wikipedia Tell Us about Open Source Politics? In *Proceedings of JITP 2010: The Politics of Open Source*, ed. Stuart W. Shulman and Charles M. Schweik, 2–30. http://scholarworks.umass.edu/jitpc2010/1/ Amherst, MA: University of Massachusetts (accessed August 10, 2010).

Katzenbach, Jon R., and Douglas K. Smith. 1993. The Discipline of Teams. *Harvard Business Review* 71 (2): 111–120.

Kelly, Seamas, and Matthew Jones. 2001. Groupware and the Social Infrastructure of Communication. *Communications of the ACM* 44 (12): 77–79.

Kelty, Christopher. 2005. Free science. In *Perspectives on Free and Open Source Software*, ed. Joseph Feller, Brian Fitzgerald, Scott A. Hissam, and Karim R. Lakhani, 415–430. Cambridge, MA: The MIT Press.

King, Gary, Robert O. Keohane, and Sidney Verba. 1994. *Designing Social Inquiry: Scientific Inference in Qualitative Research*. Princeton, NJ: Princeton University Press.

Kiser, Larry L., and Elinor Ostrom. 1982. The Three Worlds of Action: A Metatheoretical Synthesis of Institutional Approaches. In *Strategies of Political Inquiry*, ed. Elinor Ostrom, 179–222. Beverly Hills, CA: Sage Publications.

Keohane, Robert O. 1986. Reciprocity in International Relations. *International Organization* 40 (1): 1–27.

Kogut, Bruce, and Anca Metiu. 2001. Open Source Software Development and Distributed Innovation. *Oxford Review of Economic Policy* 17 (2): 248–264.

Kotonya, Gerald, and Ian Sommerville. 1998. *Requirements Engineering: Processes and Techniques*. West Sussex, UK: Wiley.

Kranich, Nancy. 2004. *The Information Commons: A Public Policy Report*. Free Expression Policy Project, Brennan Center for Justice, New York University School of Law. http://www.fepproject. org/policyreports/InformationCommons.pdf (accessed May 11, 2008).

Krishnamurthy, Sandeep. 2002. Cave or Community? An Empirical Examination of 100 Mature Open Source Projects. *First Monday* 7 (6). http://firstmonday.org/htbin/cgiwrap/bin/ojs/index. php/fm/article/view/960/881 (accessed August 21, 2011).

Krishamurthy, Sandeep. 2005. An Analysis of Open Source Business Models. In *Perspectives on Free and Open Source Software*, ed. Joseph Feller, Brian Fitzgerald, Scott A. Hissam, and Karim R. Lakhani, 279–296. Cambridge, MA: MIT Press.

Kronick, David A. 1990. Peer Review in Eighteenth-Century Scientific Journalism. *Journal of the American Medical Association* 263 (10): 1321–1322.

Lakhani, Karim R., and Eric von Hippel. 2003. How Open Source Software Works: "Free" User-to-User Assistance. *Research Policy* 32 (6): 923–943.

Lakhani, Karim R., and Robert G. Wolf. 2005. Why Hackers Do What They Do: Understanding Motivation and Effort in Free/Open Source Software Projects. In *Perspectives on Free and Open Source Software*, ed. Joseph Feller, Brian Fitzgerald, Scott A. Hissam, and Karim R. Lakhani, 3–22. Cambridge, MA: MIT Press.

Lerner, Josh, and Jean Tirole. 2000. *The Simple Economics of Open Source*. Working paper series, no. 7600. Cambridge, MA: National Bureau of Economic Research. http://www.nber.org/papers/ w7600 (accessed August 21, 2011).

Lerner, Josh, and Jean Tirole. 2002. Some Simple Economics of Open Source. *Journal of Industrial Economics* 50 (2): 197–234.

Lerner, Josh, and Jean Tirole. 2005. The Economics of Technology Sharing: Open Source and Beyond. *Journal of Economic Perspectives* 19 (2): 99–120.

Lessig, Lawrence. 2006. *Code Version 2.0*. New York: Basic Books.

Lewis, James. 2010. *Government Open Source Policies (Version 7)*. http://csis.org/files/publica-tion/100416_Open_Source_Policies.pdf (accessed April 6, 2011).

Linux Foundation. 2011. *About Us*. www.linuxfoundation.org/en/About (accessed August 20, 2011).

LocalMotors. 2011. *How It Works*. http://www.local-motors.com/howItWorks.php (accessed April 8, 2011).

Lohr, Steve. 2007. Group Formed to Support Linux as Rival to Windows. *New York Times*, January 22, technology sec. http://www.nytimes.com/2007/01/22/technology/22linux.html (accessed August 21, 2011).

Lynn, Laurence E., Jr., Carolyn J. Heinrich, and Carolyn J. Hill. 2002. *Improving Governance: A New Logic for Empirical Research*. Washington, DC: Georgetown University Press.

Madey, Gregory. 2010. *SourceForge.net Research Data*. http://www.nd.edu/~oss/Data/data.html (accessed August 21, 2011).

Madey, Gregory, Vincent Freeh, and Renee Tynan. 2002. Agent-Based Modeling of Open-Source using Swarm. In Eighth Americas Conference on Information Systems, 1806–1813. Dallas. http://aisel.aisnet.org/amcis2002/201/ (accessed August 21, 2011).

Manley, Monty R. 2000. *Managing Projects the Open Source Way*. http://www.welchco.com/02/14/01/60/00/10/3101.HTM (accessed May 12, 2004).

March, James G., and Herbert A. Simon. 1958. *Organizations*. New York: Wiley.

Markus, M. Lynne. 2007. The Governance of Free/Open Source Software Projects: Monolithic, Multidimensional, or Configurational? *Journal of Management and Governance*. 11 (2): 151–163.

Margolis, Jane, and Allan Fisher. 2002. *Unlocking the Clubhouse: Women in Computing*. Cambridge, MA: MIT Press.

Marwell, Gerald, and Pamela Oliver. 1993. *The Critical Mass in Collective Action: A Micro-Social Theory*. Cambridge: Cambridge University Press.

Maxwell, Elliot. 2006. Open Standards, Open Source, and Open Innovation: Harnessing the Benefits of Openness. *Innovations: Technology, Governance, Globalization* 1 (3): 119–176.

Maznevski, Martha L., and Katherine M. Chudoba. 2000. Bridging Space over Time: Global Virtual Team Dynamics and Effectiveness. *Organization Science* 11 (5): 473–492.

McKean, Margaret, and Elinor Ostrom. 1995. Common Property Regimes in the Forest: Just a Relic from the Past? *Unasylva* 46 (180): 3–15. http://www.fao.org/docrep/v3960e/v3960e00.htm (accessed May 13, 2008).

McQuillan, Dan. 2003. Open Source is on the Map. http//www.icthukknowledgebase.org.uk/opensourceonthemap.

Mitasova, Helena, and Markus Neteler. 2004. GRASS as Open Source Free Software GIS: Accomplishments and Perspectives. *Transactions in GIS* 8 (2): 145–154.

Mitchell, Tyler. 2009. OSGeo's Open Source Mapping Stack. Paper presented at the Military Open Source Software (Mil-OSS) Working Group, Atlanta, August 12–13. http://svn.osgeo.org/osgeo/community/presentations/20090812-MILOSS-Atlanta/tmitchell_osgeo.pdf (accessed November 2, 2009).

Mockus, Audris, Roy T. Fielding, and James D. Herbsleb. 2002. Two Case Studies of Open Source Software Development: Apache and Mozilla. *ACM Transactions on Software Engineering and Methodology* 11 (3): 309–346.

Molinas, Jose R. 1998. The Impact of Inequality, Gender, External Assistance, and Social Capital on Local-Level Collective Action. *World Development* 26 (3): 413–431.

Mueller, Dennis C. 1986. Rational Egoism versus Adaptive Egoism as Fundamental Postulate for a Descriptive Theory of Human Behavior. *Public Choice* 51(1): 3–23.

Muffatto, Moreno. 2006. *Open Source: A Multidisciplinary Approach*. London: Imperial College Press.

Nardi, Bonnie A., and Steve Whittaker. 2002. The Place of Face-to-face Communication in Distributed Work. In *Distributed Work*, ed. Pamela J. Hinds and Sara Kiesler, 83–112. Cambridge, MA: MIT Press.

Narduzzo, Alessandro, and Alessandro Rossi. 2003. Open/Free Software as a Complex Modular System. Paper presented at the Italian Association for Informatics and Automatic Calculation Annual Conference, Trento, Italy, September 15–17.

Narduzzo, Alessandro, and Alessandro Rossi. 2005. The Role of Modularity in Free/Open Source Software Development. In *Free/Open Source Software Development*, ed. Stefan Koch, 84–102. Hershey, PA: Idea Group Publishing.

National Academy of Sciences and Institute of Medicine. 2008. *Science, Evolution, and Creationism*. Washington, DC: National Academies Press.

Nee, Victor, and Paul Ingram. 1998. Embeddedness and Beyond: Institutions, Exchange, and Social Structure. In *The New Institutionalism in Sociology*, ed. Mary C. Brinton and Victor Nee, 19–45. New York: Russell Sage Foundation.

Netcraft. 2011. *August 2010 Web Server Survey*. http://news.netcraft.com/archives/2010/08/11/august-2010-web-server-survey-4.html (accessed January 9, 2011).

Neus, Andreas. 2001. Managing Information Quality in Virtual Communities of Practice. In *Proceedings of the 6th International Conference on Information Quality*, ed. Elizabeth Pierce and Raïssa Katz-Haas. Cambridge, MA: MIT Sloan School of Management. http://pascal.case.unibz.it/retrieve/3266/neus.pdf (accessed August 12, 2011).

North, Douglass C. 1990. *Institutions, Institutional Change, and Economic Performance*. Cambridge: Cambridge University Press.

NOSI (Nonprofit Open Source Initiative). 2008a. *About NOSI*. http://www.nosi.net/about (accessed March 11, 2008).

NOSI (Nonprofit Open Source Initiative). 2008b. *Nonprofit Use of FOSS Survey Report 2008*. http://www.nosi.net/system/files/NOSISurveyReport08.pdf (accessed March 11, 2008).

NOSI (Nonprofit Open Source Initiative). 2008c. *NOSI's Survey of FOSS Use in the Nonprofit Sector*. http://www.nosi.net/projects/survey (accessed March 11, 2008).

NTEN (Nonprofit Technology Network). 2008. http://www.nten.org/ (accessed March 12, 2008).

OGC (Open Geospatial Consortium). 2008. *OGC History*. http://www.opengeospatial.org/ogc/history (accessed October 10, 2008).

Olson, Gary M., and Judith S. Olson. 1997. Making Sense of the Findings: Common Vocabulary Leads to the Synthesis Necessary for Theory Building. In *Video-Mediated Communication*, ed. Kathleen E. Finn, Abigail J. Sellen, and Sylvia B. Wilbur, 157–172. Hillsdale, NJ: Lawrence Erlbaum Associates.

Olson, Mancur. 1965. *The Logic of Collective Action: Public Goods and the Theory of Groups*. Cambridge, MA: Harvard University Press.

O'Mahony, Siobhan. 2003. Guarding the Commons: How Community Managed Software Projects Protect their Work. *Research Policy* 32 (7): 1179–1198.

O'Mahony, Siobhan. 2005. Nonprofit Foundations and Their Role in Community-Firm Software Collaboration. In *Perspectives on Free and Open Source Software*, ed. Joseph Feller, Brian Fitzgerald, Scott A. Hissam, and Karim R. Lakhani, 393–413. Cambridge, MA: MIT Press.

O'Mahony, Siobhan. 2007. The Governance of Open Source Initiatives: What Does It Mean to Be Community Managed? *Journal of Management and Governance* 11 (2): 139–150.

O'Mahony, Siobhan, and Fabrizio Ferraro. 2007. The Emergence of Governance in an Open Source Community. *Academy of Management Journal* 50 (5): 1079–1106.

O'Neil, Mathieu. 2009. *Cyberchiefs: Autonomy and Authority in Online Tribes*. New York: Pluto Press.

Open Directory Project. 2011. *Open Source: Project Hosting*. http://www.dmoz.org/Computers/ Open_Source/Project_Hosting (accessed February, 17, 2011).

Open Source. 2005. Now It's an Ecosystem. Special report, *Business Week*, October 3. http://www. businessweek.com/print/technology/content/oct2005/tc2005103_0519_tc_218.htm?chan=tc (accessed March 30, 2010).

Oram, Andrew. 2011. Promoting Open Source Software in Government: The Challenges of Motivation and Follow-Through. *Journal of Information Technology and Politics* 8 (3).

O'Reilly, Tim. 1999. Lessons from Open-Source Software Development. *Communications of the ACM* 42 (4): 33–37.

O'Reilly, Tim. 2004. The Open Source Paradigm Shift. Article based on presentation at the Warburg Pincus Technology, Media, and Telecommunications annual conference, May 2003. http://www.oreillynet.com/pub/a/oreilly/tim/articles/paradigmshift_0504.html (accessed October 12, 2009).

O'Reilly, Tim. 2010. Opening the Door to Innovation. http://radar.oreilly.com/2010/08/opening-doors-government-innovation.html (accessed August 21, 2011).

OSGeo. 2008. *The Open Source Geospatial Foundation*. Accessed March 13, 2008, http://www.osgeo .org.

OSGeo. 2009a. *Foundation Officers and Board of Directors*. http://www.osgeo.org/content/foundation/board_and_officers.html (accessed August 7, 2009).

OSGeo. 2009b. *Membership Rules*. http://www.osgeo.org/membership (accessed October 8, 2009).

OSGeo. 2009c. *OSGeo Mission Statement*. http://www.osgeo.org/content/foundation/about.html (accessed March 10, 2009).

OSGeo. 2011. *Open Source Geospatial Foundation Created to Strengthen Collaborative Development of Open Geospatial Technologies*. http://www.osgeo.org/content/news/news_archive/open_source_geospatial_foundation_initial_press_release.html (accessed April 12, 2011).

OSI (Open Source Initiative). 2008. *About the Open Source Initiative*. http://www.opensource.org/about (accessed March 12, 2008).

OSSI (Open Source Software Institute). 2008. *Open Source Software Institute*. http://www.oss-institute.org (accessed March 13, 2008).

Ostrom, Elinor. 1990. *Governing the Commons: The Evolution of Institutions for Collective Action*. Cambridge: Cambridge University Press.

Ostrom, Elinor. 1992. *Crafting Institutions for Self-Governing Irrigation Systems*. San Francisco: ICS Press.

Ostrom, Elinor. 1998. A Behavioral Approach to the Rational Choice Theory of Collection Action. *American Political Science Review* 92 (1): 1–22.

Ostrom, Elinor. 1999. Institutional Rational Choice: An Assessment of the Institutional Analysis and Development Framework. In *Theories of the Policy Process*, ed. Paul Sabatier, 21–64. Boulder, CO: Westview Press.

Ostrom, Elinor. 2005. *Understanding Institutional Diversity*. Princeton, NJ: Princeton University Press.

Ostrom, Elinor. 2008. Developing a Method for Analyzing Institutional Change. In *Alternative Institutional Structures: Evolution and Impact*, ed. Sandra S. Batie and Nicholas Mercuro, 48–76. Oxford: Routledge.

Ostrom, Elinor, and Toh-Kyeong Ahn. 2001. A Social Science Perspective on Social Capital: Social Capital and Collective Action. Paper presented at the European Research Conference on Social Capital: Interdisciplinary Perspectives, Exeter, UK, September 15–20.

Ostrom, Elinor, Joanna Burger, Christopher B. Field, Richard B. Norgaard, and David Policansky. 1999. Revisiting the Commons: Local Lessons, Global Challenges. *Science* 284 (5412): 278–282.

Ostrom, Elinor, Roy Gardner, and James Walker. 1994. *Rules, Games, and Common-Pool Resources*. Ann Arbor: University of Michigan Press.

Pan, Guohua, and Curtis J. Bonk. 2007. The Emergence of Open-Source Software in North America. *International Review of Research in Open and Distance Learning* 8 (3): 1–17. http://www.irrodl.org/index.php/irrodl/article/view/496/950 (accessed August 21, 2011).

Pecorino, Paul. 1999. The Effect of Group Size on Public Good Provision in a Repeated Game Setting. *Journal of Public Economics* 72 (1): 121–134.

Peizer, Jonathan. 2003. Realizing the Potential of Open Source in the Nonprofit Sector. Open Society Institute. http://www.soros.org/initiatives/information/articles_publications/articles/realizing_20030903 (accessed March 10, 2008).

Perens, Bruce. 2005. The Emerging Economic Paradigm of Open Source. Special issue, *First Monday* 2 (October 3). http://firstmonday.org/htbin/cgiwrap/bin/ojs/index.php/fm/article/view/1470/1385 (accessed April 15, 2008).

PloneGov. *Welcome to the PloneGov Initiative.* http://www.plonegov.org/ (accessed March 9, 2008).

Portes, Alejandro, and Julia Sensenbrenner. 1998. Embeddedness and Immigration: Notes on the Social Determinants of Economic Action. In *The New Institutionalism in Sociology*, ed. Mary C. Brinton and Victor Nee, 127–150. New York: Russell Sage Foundation.

Poteete, Amy R., and Elinor Ostrom. 2004. Heterogeneity, Group Size, and Collective Action: The Role of Institutions in Forest Management. *Development and Change* 35 (3): 435–461.

Pretty, Jules. 2003. Social Capital and the Collective Management of Resources. *Science* 302 (5652): 1912–1914.

Putnam, Robert D. 1993. *Making Democracy Work: Civic Traditions in Modern Italy.* Princeton, NJ: Princeton University Press.

Putnam, Robert D. 2000. *Bowling Alone: The Collapse and Revival of American Community.* New York: Simon and Schuster.

Putnam, Robert D. 2007. E Pluribus Unum: Diversity and Community in the Twenty-First Century. The 2006 Johan Skytte Prize Lecture. *Scandinavian Political Studies* 30 (2): 137–174.

Rainey, Hal G. 2003. *Understanding and Managing Public Organizations.* 3rd ed. Hoboken, NJ: Wiley.

Ramsey, Paul. 2007. The State of Open Source GIS. Paper presented at the Free and Open Source Software for Geospatial Conference, Victoria, Canada, September 24–27. http://2007.foss4g.org/presentations/view.php?abstract_id=136 (accessed August 21, 2011).

Raymond, Eric S. 2001. *The Cathedral and the Bazaar: Musings on Linux and Open Source by an Accidental Revolutionary.* Sebastopol, CA: O'Reilly.

Raymond, Eric S. 2004. *Terminology Wars: A Web Content Analysis.* http://catb.org/~esr/writings/terminology/ (accessed February 7, 2008).

Richardson, Matthew, and Pedro Domingos. 2002. Mining Knowledge-Sharing Sites for Viral Marketing. Presented at the eighth ACM Special Interest Group on Knowledge Discovery and Data Mining Conference, Edmonton, Canada, July 23–26.

Riehle, Dirk. 2007. The Economic Motivation of Open Source Software: Stakeholder Perspectives. *IEEE Computer* 40 (4): 25–32.

Rischard, Jean-François. 2001. High Noon: We Need New Approaches to Global Problem-Solving, Fast. *Journal of International Economic Law* 4 (3): 507–525.

Rittel, Horst, and Melvin Webber. 1973. Dilemmas in a General Theory of Planning. *Policy Sciences* 4 (2): 155–169.

Robles, Geogorio, Hendrik, Schneider, Ingo Tretkowski, and Niels Weber. 2001. Who is Doing It? A Research on Libre Software Developers. http://widi.berlios.de/paper/study.html.

Robles-Martínez, Gregorio, Jesús M. González-Barahona, José Centeno-González, Vicente Matellán-Olivera, and Luis Rodero-Merino. 2003. *Studying the Evolution of Libre Software Projects Using Publicly Available Data.* Portland, OR: ICSE International Conference on Software Engineering. May 3–11.

Rosen, Lawrence. 2004. *Open Source Licensing: Software Freedom and Intellectual Property Law.* Upper Saddle River, NJ: Prentice Hall.

Rusovan, Srdjan, Mark Lawford, and David Lorge Parnas. 2005. Open Source Software Development: Future or Fad? In *Perspectives on Free and Open Source Software,* ed. Joseph Feller, Brian Fitzgerald, Scott A. Hissam, and Karim R. Lakhani, 107–121. Cambridge, MA: MIT Press.

Sánchez-Fernández, Luis, and Carlos Delgado-Kloosh. 2002. XML, Panoramic of a Revolution. *Upgrade: The European Journal for the Informatics Professional* 3 (4): 3–5. http://www.cepis.org/upgrade/files/full-2002-IV.pdf (accessed August 21, 2011).

Sandler, Todd. 2004. *Global Collective Action.* Cambridge: Cambridge University Press.

Scacchi, Walt. 2002. Understanding the Requirements for Developing Open Source Software Systems. *IEE Proceedings. Software* 149 (1): 24–39.

Scacchi, Walt. 2003. Faster, Better, Cheaper: Open-Source Practices May Help Improve Software Engineering. National Science Foundation press release, December 3. http://www.nsf.gov/od/lpa/news/03/pr03132.htm (accessed June 26, 2008).

Shilling, Melissa. 2000. Toward a General Modular Systems Theory and its Application to Interfirm Product Modularity. *Academy of Management Review* 35 (2): 312–334.

Schlager, Edella. 1999. A Comparison of Frameworks, Theories, and Models of Policy Processes. In *Theories of the Policy Process,* ed. Paul Sabatier, 293–320. Boulder, CO: Westview Press.

Schmidt, Klaus M., and Monika Schnitzer. 2003. *Public Subsidies for Open Source? Some Economic Policy Issues of the Software Market.* CEPR discussion paper no. 3793. London: Centre for Economic Policy Research. http://www.cepr.org/pubs/new-dps/dplist.asp?dpno=3793 (accessed August 21, 2011).

Schweik, Charles M. 1998. The Spatial and Temporal Analysis of Forest Resources and Institutions. PhD diss., Indiana University. CIPEC dissertation series, no. 2. Bloomington: Center for the Study of Institutions, Population, and Environmental Change, Indiana University.

Schweik, Charles M. 1999. Optimal Foraging, Institutions, and Forest Change: A Case from Nepal. *Environmental Monitoring and Assessment* 62 (3): 231–260.

Schweik, Charles M. 2005. An Institutional Analysis Approach to Studying Libre Software "Commons." *Upgrade: The European Journal for the Informatics Professional* 6 (3): 17–27. http://www.cepis.org/upgrade/files/full-2005-III.pdf (accessed August 21, 2011).

Schweik, Charles M., Keshav Adhikari, and Kali Nidhi Pandit. 1997. Land-Cover Change and Forest Institutions: A Comparison of Two Sub-Basins in the Southern Siwalik Hills of Nepal. *Mountain Research and Development* 17 (2): 99–116.

Schweik, Charles M., and Robert C. English. 2007. Tragedy of the FOSS Commons? Investigating the Institutional Designs of Free/libre and Open Source Software Projects. *First Monday* 12 (2). http://firstmonday.org/htbin/cgiwrap/bin/ojs/index.php/fm/article/view/1619/1534 (accessed June 18, 2010).

Schweik, Charles M., Robert C. English, Meelis Kitsing, and Sandra Haire. 2008. Brooks' versus Linus' Law: An Empirical Test of Open Source Projects. Paper presented at the ninth International Digital Government Research Conference, Montreal, May 18–21.

Schweik, Charles M., Tom P. Evans, and J. Morgan Grove. 2005. Open Source and Open Content: A Framework for Global Collaboration in Social-Ecological Research. *Ecology and Society* 10 (1): 33. http://www.ecologyandsociety.org/vol10/iss1/art33/ (accessed August 21, 2011).

Schweik, Charles M., Ines Mergel, Jodi R. Sandfort, and Yong Zhao. 2011. Toward Public Administration Scholarship. *Journal of Public Administration: Research and Theory* 21: i175–i198.

Schweik, Charles M., and Andrei Semenov. 2003. The Institutional Design of Open Source Programming: Implications for Addressing Complex Public Policy and Management Problems. *First Monday* 8 (1). http://firstmonday.org/htbin/cgiwrap/bin/ojs/index.php/fm/article/view/1019/2426 (accessed June 18, 2010).

Serrano, Nicolas, and Ismael Ciordia. 2005. Bugzilla, ITracker, and Other Bug Trackers. *IEEE Software* 22 (2): 11–13.

Shah, Rajiv, Jay Kesan, and Andrew Kennis. 2007. Lessons for Open Standard Policies: A Case Study of the Massachusetts Experience. Paper presented at the first International Conference on Theory and Practice of Electronic Governance, Macao, China, December 10–13.

Shah, Sonali, Patrick Wagstrom, and James Herbsleb. 2008. Value Creation and Cooperative Resource Exchange through Open Technology Platforms. Paper presented at the Alfred Sloan Foundation Industry Studies Annual Conference, Boston, May 1–2.

Simon, Herbert A. 1955. A Behavioral Model of Rational Choice. *Quarterly Journal of Economics* 69 (1): 99–118.

Simon, Kimberly D. 2005. The Value of Open Standards and Open-Source Software in Government Environments. *IBM Systems Journal* 44 (2): 227–238.

Singleton, Sara. 1998. *Constructing Cooperation: The Evolution of Institutions of Comanagement.* Ann Arbor: University of Michigan Press.

Sliwa, Carol. 2006. Massachusetts OpenDocument Plans Questioned by Disabled. *Computerworld* (May): 9. http://www.computerworld.com.au/article/156547/massachusetts_opendocument_plans_questioned_by_disabled?fp=16&fpid=0 (accessed March 5, 2008).

Smith, Mark K. 2007. Robert Putnam, Social Capital, and Civic Community. *Encyclopaedia of Informal Education.* http://www.infed.org/thinkers/putnam.htm (accessed May 29, 2008).

SourceForge. 2011. *About.* http://sourceforge.net/about (accessed April 13, 2010).

Spaeth, Sebastian, Matthias Stuermer, Stefan Haefliger, and Georg von Krogh. 2007. Sampling in Open Source Software Development: The Case for Using the Debian GNU/Linux Distribution. Paper presented at the fortieth Annual Hawaii International Conference on System Sciences, Big Island, January 3–6.

SPI (Software in the Public Interest). 2008. *SPI Projects.* http://www.spi-inc.org/projects (accessed March 12, 2008).

Spier, Ray. 2002. The History of the Peer-review Process. *Trends in Biotechnology* 20 (8): 357–358.

Stallman, Richard M. 1999. The GNU Operating System and the Free Software Movement. In *Open Sources: Voices from the Open Source Revolution,* ed. Chris DiBona, Sam Ockman, and Mark Stone, 53–70. Sebastopol, CA: O'Reilly Media.

St. Laurent, Andrew M. 2004. *Understanding Open Source and Free Software Licensing.* Cambridge, MA: O'Reilly Publishing.

Stallman, Richard M. 2002. *Free Software, Free Society: Selected Essays of Richard M. Stallman.* Boston: Free Software Foundation.

Standish Group International. 1994. *The Chaos Report.* http://www.dwaynewhitten.com/info621/chaos1994.pdf (accessed June 17, 2009).

Stebbins, Robert A. 2001. Serious Leisure. *Society* 38 (4): 53–57.

Stewart, Katherine J., and Anthony P. Ammeter. 2002. An Exploratory Study of Factors Influencing the Level of Vitality and Popularity of Open Source Projects. Paper presented at the twenty-third International Computer and Information Systems Conference, Barcelona, December 15–18.

Tait, Peter, and Iris Vessey. 1988. The Effect of User Involvement on System Success: A Contingency Approach. *Management Information Systems Quarterly* 12 (1): 91–108.

Thomas, Stephen A. 2000. *SSL and TLS Essentials: Securing the Web.* New York: Wiley.

Tversky, Amos, and Daniel Kahneman. 1990. Rational Choice and the Framing of Decisions. In *The Limits of Rationality*, ed. K. Schweers Cook and M. Levi, 60–89. Chicago: University of Chicago Press.

Tyran, Kristi Lewis, Craig K. Tyran, and Morgan Shepherd. 2003. Exploring Emerging Leadership in Virtual Teams. In *Virtual Teams That Work: Creating Conditions for Virtual Team Effectiveness*, ed. Cristina B. Gibson and Susan G. Cohen, 183–195. San Francisco: Jossey-Bass.

Ullmann-Margalit, Edna. 1977. *The Emergence of Norms*. Oxford: Clarendon Press.

U.S. National Science Foundation Office of Cyberinfrastructure. 2007. *Software Development for Cyberinfrastructure*. Program solicitation. http://www.nsf.gov/pubs/2007/nsf07503/nsf07503.htm (accessed May 14, 2008).

Van Antwerp, Matthew, and Greg Madey. 2008. Advances in the SourceForge Research Data Archive. Paper presented at the fourth International Conference on Open Source Systems, Milan, September 7–10. http://www.nd.edu/~oss/Papers/srda_final.pdf (accessed August 21, 2011).

van Laerhoven, Frank, and Elinor Ostrom. 2007. Traditions and Trends in the Study of the Commons. *International Journal of the Commons* 1 (1): 3–28.

Varughese, George, and Elinor Ostrom. 2001. The Contested Role of Heterogeneity in Collective Action. Some Evidence from Community Forestry in Nepal. *World Development* 29 (5): 747–765.

von Hippel, Eric. 2005a. *Democratizing Innovation*. Cambridge, MA: MIT Press. http://web.mit.edu/evhippel/www/democ1.htm (accessed August 21, 2011).

von Hippel, Eric. 2005b. Open Source Software Projects as User Innovation Networks. In *Perspectives on Free and Open Source Software*, ed. Joseph Feller, Brian Fitzgerald, Scott A. Hissam, and Karim R. Lakhani, 267–278. Cambridge, MA: MIT Press.

von Hippel, Eric, and Georg von Krogh. 2003. Open Source Software and the "Private-Collective" Innovation Model: Issues for Organization Science. *Organization Science* 14 (2): 209–223.

Wade, Robert. 1994. *Village Republics: Economic Conditions for Collective Action in South India*. San Francisco: ICS Press.

Waters, Donald J. 2006. Preserving the Knowledge Commons. In *Understanding Knowledge as a Commons: From Theory to Practice*, ed. Elinor Ostrom and Charlotte Hess, 145–168. Cambridge, MA: MIT Press.

Wayner, Peter. 1999. Germany Awards Grant for Encryption. *New York Times*, November 19, technology sec. http://www.nytimes.com/library/tech/99/11/cyber/articles/19encrypt.html (accessed August 21, 2011).

Weber, Steven. 2004. *The Success of Open Source*. Cambridge, MA: Harvard University Press.

Weinstock, Charles B., and Scott A. Hissam. 2005. Making Lightning Strike Twice. In *Perspectives on Free and Open Source Software*, ed. Joseph Feller, Brian Fitzgerald, Scott A. Hissam, and Karim R. Lakhani, 143–159. Cambridge, MA: MIT Press.

Weiss, Dawid. 2005. Measuring Success of Open Source Projects Using Web Search Engines. Paper presented at the First International Conference on Open Source Systems, Genova, July 11–15.

West, Joel, and Siobhan O'Mahony. 2005. Contrasting Community Building in Sponsored and Community Founded Open Source Projects. Paper presented at the thirty-eighth Hawaii International Conference on System Sciences, Big Island, January 3–6.

White House, The. 2009. *The Open Government Initiative*. http://www.whitehouse.gov/OPEN/ (accessed October 12, 2009).

Wiggins, Andrea, and Kevin Crowston. 2010. Reclassifying Success and Tragedy in FLOSS Projects. In *Proceedings of the Sixth International Conference on Open Source Software*. Notre Dame, IN., ed. Pär Ågerfalk, Cornelia Boldyreff, Jesus González-Barahona, Greg Madey, and John Noll, 294–313. Berlin: Springer.

Ye, Yunwen, Kumiyo Nakakoji, Yasuhiro Yamamoto, and Kouichi Kishida. 2005. The Co-Evolution of Systems and Communities in Free and Open Source Software Development. In *Free/Open Source Software Development*, ed. Stefan Koch, 59–82. Hershey, PA: Idea Group Publishing.

Zigurs, Ilze. 2003. Leadership in Virtual Teams: Oxymoron or Opportunity? *Organizational Dynamics* 31 (4):339–351.

Ziman, John M. 1969. Information, Communication, Knowledge. *Nature* 224 (5217): 318–324.

Index